James Allanson Picton

City of Liverpool

Municipal archives and records, from A. D. 1700 to the passing of the municipal

reform act, 1835

James Allanson Picton

City of Liverpool
Municipal archives and records, from A. D. 1700 to the passing of the municipal reform act, 1835

ISBN/EAN: 9783337295745

Printed in Europe, USA, Canada, Australia, Japan

Cover: Foto ©ninafisch / pixelio.de

More available books at **www.hansebooks.com**

LIVERPOOL
MUNICIPAL RECORDS.

City of Liverpool.

MUNICIPAL
ARCHIVES AND RECORDS,

FROM A.D. 1700 TO THE PASSING OF THE

MUNICIPAL REFORM ACT, 1835.

EXTRACTED AND ANNOTATED BY

SIR JAMES A. PICTON, F.S.A.,

AUTHOR OF "MEMORIALS OF LIVERPOOL," ETC.

Published with the sanction of the City Council.

LIVERPOOL:
GILBERT G. WALMSLEY, 50, LORD STREET.
1886.

TO HER MOST GRACIOUS MAJESTY,

VICTORIA, QUEEN OF ENGLAND,

THIS VOLUME OF

RECORDS OF THE ANCIENT AND LOYAL CITY OF LIVERPOOL

IS, BY HER ROYAL PERMISSION,

MOST RESPECTFULLY DEDICATED,

IN MEMORY OF HER AUSPICIOUS VISIT TO THE CITY

IN MAY, 1886, BY

THE COMPILER.

PREFACE.

The present Volume is a continuation of the previous one, published in 1883.

The former Volume brought down the Records to the end of the seventeenth century, at which period the town and port had commenced that career of marvellous progress which has distinguished them ever since.

The documents here presented, though not quite so quaint as the preceding ones, are very copious, and throw a flood of light on the commerce, the navigation, the retail trade, the manufactures, the municipal government, the social habits and daily life, of a busy, active, progressive community, self-governing, and little interfered with by the central authorities.

The Corporation had a very marked character. The Burgesses, qualified by birth or servitude, constituted a large proportion of the inhabitants, and down to a late period in the last century, offered a determined hostility to the settlement of strangers amongst them. The Common

Council, owing to circumstances stated in the previous Volume, had, in defiance of the Charters, usurped the power of filling up vacancies in their own body, and, though often attacked, maintained their position. Within the precincts of the Borough they possessed considerable powers and privileges. They levied dues on all merchandize passing through the port. They farmed under the Crown, during a long period, the Customs duties, and in the 17th century they became by purchase lords of the manor. A large portion of the land belonged to them, which has been a considerable source of income to the present time. They possessed the ecclesiastical patronage, appointing the Rectors and other clergy, and even the churchwardens and church functionaries. The Borough had from time immemorial, under the grant of *sac* and *soc*, possessed courts of its own, both civil and criminal, and the Burgesses were prohibited under heavy penalties from carrying their causes to other courts. The Recorder was appointed by the Council, and their exclusive jurisdiction was on several occasions admitted by the higher courts.

This rigid adherence to privilege, and these claims of rights, became as time advanced somewhat relaxed, but much remained unchanged down to the date of the Municipal Reform Act. A distinctive character was thus given to the community, which is vividly reflected in the pages of the Records.

The mode of treatment in bringing these documents under the public eye required much consideration. To have printed them in chronological order would have been the simplest task, but in that case the interest arising from following out a particular subject or illustration would have been lost in the necessity for picking it out in detached portions spread over a long period. On the other hand, to have taken a special subject and pursued it through the hundreds of years comprised in the Records would have destroyed the connection, and the relations which the various contemporary events had with each other, and have prevented any general view.

I have adopted a middle course. I have divided the Records in each volume into four periods or chapters, and grouped together the events and documents in each, conceiving that by this method, a series of synoptical views is presented, which will repay perusal to those who feel interested in the subject.

I have brought the record down to the Municipal Reform Act of 1835. With that enactment, just and necessary as it was, the picturesque aspect of our civic institutions came to an end. The independence which they enjoyed became subordinated in great measure to the central authority, and the quaint traditions of ages were merged in the modern system of utilitarianism. Still, the history of the past may not be without its bearing on the present and future, and if the spirit of our old Corporations can be maintained, freed from the abuses to which they were liable, the story of our old Records will not have been learned in vain.

In conclusion, I have to express my obligations to the Finance and Estate Committee of the City Council, for their courtesy in granting me free and unrestricted access to their Records, Charters and other Muniments, and for their valuable aid in the transcription of documents, thus considerably lightening the burden of a task which, though agreeable and interesting, was necessarily from the nature of the case somewhat onerous.

J. A. P.

SANDYKNOWE,
    WAVERTREE.

CONTENTS.

	Page
CHAPTER I.—From 1702 to 1727 ...	1
Municipal Government	3
Corporate Estate and Revenues ...	30
Trade and Commerce... ...	47
Streets and Buildings... ...	57
Ecclesiastical	66
National Affairs	77
Manners and Customs ...	80
CHAPTER II.—From 1727 to 1760.	
Municipal Affairs	86
Corporate Estate and Revenues	132
Trade and Commerce... ...	141
Streets and Buildings... ...	152
Ecclesiastical	163
CHAPTER III.—From 1760 to 1800.	
Municipal Affairs	175
Corporate Estate and Revenues ...	221
Trade and Commerce...	236
Streets and Buildings...	254
Ecclesiastical Affairs	276
CHAPTER IV.—From 1800 to 1835.	
Public and National Affairs...	286
Municipal Affairs	306
Corporate Estate and Revenues	338
Trade and Commerce... ...	347
Streets and Buildings... ...	363
Ecclesiastical Affairs	386

CHAPTER FIRST.

REIGNS OF QUEEN ANNE AND GEORGE I.
1702—1727.

THE beginning of the 18th century was the commencement 1700. of that tide of commercial progress in Liverpool which has continued to flow on ever since. Down to the period of the Civil Wars it can scarcely be said that the town had made any progress at all. The population was stationary, and in the Progress. reign of Elizabeth it had actually diminished. The commerce was of a very restricted kind, and so hampered by imposts, exclusions, and difficulties, that it almost seemed as if the object of the townsmen had been rather to drive business Stagnation. away than to attract it to the port. Shippers, with import cargoes, were required in the first place, if the authorities so determined, to offer their goods to the Corporation at a price to be agreed upon; the cargo was then divided amongst the burgesses as a syndicate or joint stock company. If this was not thought expedient, the importer was allowed to sell his goods on a payment to the Corporate funds, in addition to the ordinary town dues. Under this system commerce could not but be exceedingly limited; yet in the 16th century there were a few merchants, Robert Corbett, Anthony Early Merchants. Sekerston and others, who carried on business with success, and steadily resisted the attempts of Chester to treat the Mersey as a mere creek ancillary to their own port.

New Era. With the reign of Charles II. there commenced a change for the better; the manufactures of Lancashire were assuming an important position, and Liverpool was found the most convenient place of export. In addition to this, attracted by the incipient progress, capitalists from London and elsewhere were induced to settle in the place. Sugar from the West Indies, and Tobacco from Virginia became articles of import; sugar refineries were erected, and land began to be in demand.

Johnson, Cleveland, &c. Amongst the new race of merchants during the last quarter of the 17th century, were the Johnsons, the Clevelands, the Claytons, and a few years afterwards the Earles, the Rathbones, the Cunliffes, the Gildarts and others, who were all strangers in the town, but identified themselves with its progress and enterprise. A number of these realised fortunes, and retired to found families in the ranks of the landed gentry. A few names still remain which have stood prominent amongst us in the mercantile world for nearly two centuries.

I have adopted, in the present volume, the same arrangement as in the previous one, viz., the division into periods or chapters; chronologically grouping together within each period the documents relating to special subjects.

Chapters. The First Chapter relates to the reigns of Queen Anne and George I., 1702—1727.

The Second Chapter, the reign of George II., 1727—1760.

The Third Chapter, from the accession of George III., 1760—1800.

The Fourth Chapter, from 1800 to the passing of the Municipal Reform Act, 1835.

FIRST PERIOD 1702—1727.
MUNICIPAL GOVERNMENT.

The early part of this period was signalised by serious disputes respecting the meaning and application of the terms of the charter of 1695. *1700.*

The history of the successive charters granted to the borough has been given in previous volumes.[1] *Charters.*

It may suffice here to state that in the charter of Charles I. (1626), no provision was made for the election of a Common Council. A Council however was elected, and from a mere temporary arrangement had grown up into a self-elected body, usurping the entire management of the Corporate affairs, leaving only to the burgesses the annual choice of the Mayor. In 1677, by a surreptitious and underhand procedure, a charter was procured from Charles II., in which a Council of sixty members was appointed, with power to elect their successors. This was set aside by the charter of William III. (1695), which enacted that a Council of "forty and one honest and discreet men" should be appointed, but the manner of their appointment was left so vague as to give rise to serious misunderstandings, it being maintained by one party that the power of filling up vacancies and electing officers rested with the Council, and by the other that the power belonged to the burgesses in Common Hall assembled. *Council.*

In 1710 Mr. Thos. Robinson was elected by the burgesses on St. Luke's Day to fill the office of Sub-bailiff, but on his refusal Mr. James Halsall was elected by the Council to fill the vacancy. He also refused to serve, and gave for reason "that if every officer that is regularly elected on St. Luke's *Bailiffs.*

---

[1] See "Memorials" and "Records," passim.

Day be excused, then all officers may be chosen by the Council and not by the majority of the freemen; so that this office in such circumstances cannot legally be forced upon him." The Council however decided that they had power by the charter to elect, and followed up their decision by fining the recusant member ten pounds.

Council Proceedings. The proceedings in the Council at this period were anything but harmonious, being mixed up with party national politics on the one hand, and the local disputes about the charter on the other.

Election. 1710. In October, 1710, a general election took place, attended with considerable tumult. Out of a population of little more than 8,000, nearly 1,000 Burgesses recorded their votes. Sir Thos. Johnson and Mr. Jno. Cleveland were elected by a narrow majority. After the election, a pamphlet was published in a very bitter tone, making serious charges against the authorities. The authorship of this pamphlet was traced to the Revd. Henry Richmond, one of the recently appointed Rectors.

1711. 1711. April 4th. The Council adopted a Resolution as follows :—

Disputes about Charters. "Whereas it hath been this day propounded and made appear in Councill, that some attempts have been lately made and is now carrying on, to destroy the present constitution of this Corporation, and to vacate and sett aside the present charter by the management of Mr. Henry Richmond, one of the Rectors of this town, who was presented to that benefice by the Mayor, Aldermen, Bayliffs and Comon Councill of this Burrough, acting under and by force and vertue of the same charter, in order to overturn the method of electing a Mayor and other officers, and thereby take from the Freemen some of their most antient priviledges, and establish it in the Comon Councill, a form contrary to the antient usage of the Corporation ever since it was so created, as appears by the eldest records thereof, which are from and ever since the year 1552, save that on some unhappy difference which happened in or about the Twenty ninth year of King Charles the Second's reign touching the election of a Burgess to serve in Parliament.

"A new charter was then obtained by a few persons without the knowledge and consent of the greatest part of the Burgesses and Freemen, and without the surrender of the former charter then in being, and that on the coming in of King James II. that last charter was also changed, tending to the manifest prejudice and destruction of the Constitution, and so continued till the year 1695, when the present charter was obtained, which restores and confirms the said former charter that was not surrendered, made by King Charles I., with some other privileges by and under which this town hath been governed ever since and greatly increased in their riches and trade more than ever was known before.

"It is therefore ordered and enacted by this assembly, that the present charter and Constitution and the ancient priviledges, . . . be defended and supported at the publick charge of this Corporation, and that all Suites or Process brought against the Mayor Bayliffs and Burgesses, or against any particular member of this Corporation whereby to bring the same in question be immediately communicated to this assembly, and be likewise defended, and the persons sued therein indemnified at the said publick charge, and that Sir Thomas Johnson, Jasper Maudit, Esqr and Ald^n Richard Norris have power to employ solicitors and others learned in the law to take all needful measures to defend the same, and that all charges expended therein shall be disbursed and paid by and out of the publick rents, revenues, and stock of this Burrough and Corporation, &c., &c., and that all publick treats and works doe cease untill these unhappy differences be finally ended and determined." Disputes about Charters.

(Signed by 17 Councillors.)

On May 20th, 1711, the following entry occurs:—   1711.

"The Corporation being greatly divided into partys of High Church and Low, and a petition preferr'd to her Maj^{tie} in the names of the Mayor, Aldermen, and Burgesses for a '*Scire facias*' to try the vallidity of the present charter, alledging that the charter granted by K Chas the 2nd was never surrendered, nor the present charter accepted, which was referred to the Attorney and Sollicitor Generall, and notice given to hear all parties; many Affidavits of the most ancient freemen have been prepared by the directions of Mr. Thomas Bootle, a young student in the Temple, proving that the charter of K Chas the 2nd was surreptitiously obtained, and that the present charter was fully accepted by the whole town, and that the very persons that now petition against it have all along acted under it, petitioned for and taken leases from the acting Corporate body,—and the ancient usage and manner of electing of Mayors, Bayliffes, &c., by the freemen in gen'all are now sent upp and Ald^n Richard Norris hath examined the Records, and takes upp sev^l extracts thereof for our defence therein." *Scire facias*.

1711. Oct. 5. It is ordered and enacted,

Defence of Charters.

"That a Deed be duly executed and passed under the Corporation Seal to convey over the Town's Customs to Sr Thomas Johnson, Mr. Maudit, and Mr. Norris, to enable them to defend the present charter and constitution till the present contest be finally closed, &c."

Dispute in Council.

The Council were by no means of one mind on this matter. On the 20th February following (1712) we read:—

"It being propounded that the keys of the town's chest be now brought and the chest opened and inspected, sitting this Councill; whether the Comon Seale and the charters and other the evidences of this Corpⁿ are secure therein, since broke open, and Mr. Mayor, Mr. Tyrer, Mr. Benn, and sev^{ll} others being for deferring it till to-morrow, and tho' a majority of the Councill are for opening it now, yet Mr. Mayor still refusing to consent thereto. It is thereupon propounded that the chest be now opened and that five new locks be affix'd on the said chest; and order'd so to be, and that the same shall not be open'd hereafter without the consent and order of the Councill, and that the keys be kept by Mr. Maudit, Mr. Norris, Mr. Moorcroft, Mr. Kelsall, and Mr. Kendrick."

1712.

1712, July 2nd.

Scire facias.

"Mr. Mayor having communicated to the Comon Councill that he, the Baylives and Town Clerk have been served with a '*Scire facias*' issued out of and returnable in the Chancery of England in the Petty Bag Office or Latin side, to shew cause why the present charter or Letters Pattent granted to the Mayor, &c. of this Burrough and Corporation by his late Maj^{tie} K William ought not to be repealed. It is ordered that a warrant of attorney under the Corporation Seale be made and granted to Sir Thomas Johnson, Jasper Maudit, and Richard Norris, Esqrs., or to such attorney or clerk as they shall think fit to employ . . . . . to

Defence.

enter appearance and make such defence as they shall be advised by Councill, &c."

1712, July 14th.

Richmond. Certiorari.

"The Revd Henry Richmond brought a *certiorari* to remove the Presentment against him last October Sessions to the Assizes at Lancaster; but he, not having delivered the *certiorari* to the Town Clerk to make a return thereto, he lost the benefitt of the Writt, and now Moved by Councill at this Sessions to quash the said Presentm^t being in English and should have been in Latin, and for that and other reasons now shewn, the Court orders it to be quashed and destroyed."

1712, August 6th.

"It being communicated to the Councill that another '*Scire facias*' returnable in this County hath been served for repealing the present charter, It is ordered that the like Warrant of Attorney given under the Comon Seale ordered the last Councill day, be given for the '*Scire facias*' returnable to the Chancey of England. <small>Warrant of Attorney.</small>

This dispute was allowed to subside for a time, but was revived some years afterwards, as will appear in due course.

The new charter of 1695 required a revision of the oaths of the Mayor and the other officials. The following is the revised oath of the Mayor:— <small>Oaths.</small>

THE OATH OF THE MAIOR OF LIVERPOOLE. <small>Oath of Mayor.</small>

"You shall depose to be a true Leige Man unto the Queen's Majesty, our Soveraign Lady, and no treason do or know, to be done unto her Majesty; But that with all speed you shall give knowledg to her Majest^s Privie Councell; and also you shall execute the office of Maior of this her Majest^s Town of Liverpoole untill the next Election day. And to ye utmost of y^r power and knowledg, you shall execute or cause ye Queen's Majest^s laws to be executed with true and indifferent justice, without favour, need or dread, fear or affection. And also, all Acts and Statutes made by ye Queen's Highnesse and her most noble Progenitors, Kings and Queens of this realm and their honrb^l councell^{rs} you shall execute or cause to be executed within this town, franchises, and liberties thereof, to ye best of your power and knowledg. And furthermore, all liberties of this town, and franchises thereto appertaining, you shall mentaine to your power. And also you shall see that all inferiour officers of this town do their duty in their offices; and such as do offend, punish accordingly. And furthermore, you shall not of yourself make any new Act or order within this town and liberties of ye same, unless you have the assent and consent of such as have been Maiors of this town, with the consent of ye most antient Burgesses thereof. And also that all other thing and things that do appertaine unto ye office of a Maior of this Corporation and Liberty, you shall minister or cause to be putt in due execucon to ye best of y^r knowledg. So help you God."

The oaths of the other officials are to the same purport *mutatis mutandis*. They comprised the Recorder, Town Clerk, Councillors, Merchant Appraisers, Stewards, Registrar <small>Other Oaths.</small>

of Tanned Leather, Mossreeves, Scavengers, Hayward, Alefounders, &c.

<small>Mayor's allowance.</small> It had been customary from an early period to make an allowance to the Mayor to sustain the dignity of his office. This sometimes consisted of the prizage of wines, and sometimes of an appropriation of the freemen's fines on admission. In 1712 an alteration was made, which is thus recorded :—

1712, Oct. 8.

<small>Freemen's Fines.</small> "Whereas the debts of this Corporation by reason of our unhappy differences daily encrease and are become so very great; it is highly reasonable that all such of the revenues thereof as are apply'd otherwise than towards dischargeing the same, and the necessary affairs of the Corporation, should be so apply'd for the future that the persons bound or concerned in the same may in some reasonable time be discharg'd from such their obligations, and that in particular the profits of the Grant to the Mayor, Bayl^s and Burgesses of this Corporation of the Prizage of all wines imported into this county which in time of peace is hop'd will be considerable, and which by order of this Councill of the 7th March 1708 was order'd to be taken and received bye the Mayor for the time being without rendring any account for the same, as also two of the best fines of freemen by an order of Council of the 17th September 1707. And it being propounded to this Councill that the ancient allowance to the Mayor towards defraying his extraordinary expenses being thentofore only the second best fine of the freemen that should be made in his year: It is thought convenient so to be hereafter and order'd accordingly untill these differences be ended, and that the future Mayor and Baylives doe take notice of and comply with this order, and account for them accordingly."

<small>1714.</small> In 1714 this was repealed by the following minute :—
Oct. 22nd.

<small>Prizage.</small> "The order made the 8th October 1712 for applying the Prizage with respect to the late Mayor is now order'd to be repealed, and that the Prizage and the two best freemen's fines be allowed to him for his good service, as was allowed before the making of the order."

The connection of the house of Stanley with the town of Liverpool has always been of the most friendly character.

MUNICIPAL GOVERNMENT.

During the 17th century the chair of the Chief Magistrate was filled nine times either by an Earl of Derby or by a member of his family. In 1707 we find the following record:—
Oct. 1st.

1707.

"The R^t Hono^{rble} James, Earle of Derby, paying a vissitt to the Corpora- Earl of tion in his way to Halnaker in Sussex from Lathom, on this 1st day of Derby. October, Mr Mayor and the Aldermen and Comon Councell waiting on him, gave his Lord^{pp} an entertainm^t in the Exchange; and it being propos'd to elect his Lord^{pp} Mayor for the year ensueing, a Councell was directed by Mr Mayor to be summoned for their assembling att eight o'clock the next morning, in order to elect his L^{dpp} one of the Comon Councell and thereby to capacitate him to be elected Mayor. Att which assembly held the second day of October 1707, the R^t Hono^{rble} James, Earle of Derby, Lord Stanley and Strange &c., Chancellor of the Dutchy and County Pallatine of Lancaster, Lord Livetenn^t and *Custos Rotulorum* of the said county, Chamberlain of the County Pallatine of Chester, one of her Maj^{ties} most Honble Privy Councell, was, in full Councell, *nemine contradicente* elected one of the Comon Councell of this Burrough. And the Bay^{lls} being appointed to waite on his Lord^{pp} att his lodgeing and acquaint him thereof, his L^{d}pp very kindly came into the Comon Hall, and honour'd the Corporation with his acceptance thereof."

1707, Nov. 1st.

"The Rt. Honor^{ble} the Earl of Derby being elected Mayor, the Ald^{r}men Lord Derby and Councell signify'd the same to his Lord^{pp} by a general letter to which Mayor. his Lord^{pp} return'd this kind answer, directed to the Aldermen and Bayliffs of the Corporation of Liverpoole, dated ye 1st November, 1707, from London; his Lord^{pp} being come upp thither from Halnaker in order to be sworn by spe^{all} commission:—

"Gentlemen, I cannot but acknowledge myself very much oblidg'd to Letter. you for your kind letter, and the favo^r you are pleased to doe me in choosing me so unanimously Mayor. I wish I had it in my power to make any returne, but you may be assur'd that I shall always make it my endeavour to shew myselfe a faithfull member of your Corporation. I am extremely concern'd business so falls out; so that I am oblidg'd to be out of the country; that I cannot so behave myself to you as I would heartily have wished; I should have sent this sooner, but that I had a mind att the same time to give you an acc^t how matters went as to my takeing the oath, which, though I have not yet done, I shall, I believe, very soon. But if I could not have done it here, I should have mad a journey to your town to have done it in forme there, for I was resolv'd since you had been

B

so kind to choose me Mayor, no neglect of mine should have hinder'd me from shewing how sencesible I was of your favo', who really am
"Gentlemen,
"Your most hearty and
"very affectionate frend,
"DERBY."

Sworn in London.

"Whereupon My Lord not comeing down, advice of Councell was had and taken how he might be sworn Mayor att London, which att first seeme'd very difficult, not any Writ of Dedim⁸ haveing been granted by the Lord Chancellor out of the High Court of Chancery for that purpose except where by the charter there is a method provided for swearing by Dedim⁸. However, according to S' Edw⁴ Northey's opinion, in case My Lord did not or could not quallify himselfe (which he must have a reasonable time to doe) the Corporation, notwithstanding St. Luke's Day is lapsed, upon petition might have a Writt, impowering the Corporation to choose another person, without any p'judice to the Corporation. But upon further advice had from S' Thomas Parker and others, a President (precedent) was found, which was, 'A writt made out by the direction of the Queen in Councell upon a petition to her impowering sev'all persons in the Writt named to swear the person elected Mayor, into that office, and in the Writt the charter of that town is recited, whereby it appeares they are to choose upon a p'ticular day, and the Mayor is to be sworn before his predecessor as in our case; which was att Penzance, about which there have been great contests to try the validity of it, but it was always adjudg'd good.'

Dedimus Commission.

"Which method being pursued in our case upon a petition to the Queen and Councell, the Lord Chancellor of Great Brittain by the advice of the Solicitor Gen'all, pursuant to the order from her Maj⁽ᵗⁱᵉ⁾ in Councell, granted a '*Dedimus*' to Edw⁴ Lloyd Esq. (who is Secretary to the Earl of Derby, Chancellor of the Dutchy) as Chancellor, and to Mr. Richard Worthington, the said Earle's Gentleman, and Francis Peters of the City of London, Gent. impowering them to give the oath of a Mayor and other oathes to the said Earle, which accordingly was done on the thirteenth day of November instant at London, and the Earle then executed a deputation to Richard Norris, Esq. and Sylvester Moorcroft, Gent. which was immediatly sent down and is in these words, viz' :

Issue of Writ.

"To all Christian People to whom this present writeing indented shall come, I, the Right Honourable James Stanley Earle of Derby, Chancello' of the Dutchy and County Pallatine of Lancaster, Lord Lieutenant of the same County, Chamberlain of Chester, Lord of Mann and the Isles, &c., one of Her Maj⁽ᵗⁱᵉˢ⁾ most hon⁽ᵇˡᵉ⁾ Privy Councell, and Mayor of the Burrough and Corporation of Liverpoole in the County of Lancaster, aforesaid send Greeting.

"Whereas I, the said Earle, canot in person attend the duty of my said

office of Mayor of the said burrough and Corporation. Know ye therefore, that I, the said Earle, for divers good causes and considerations me hereunto moveing, have assigned, made, ordained and constituted Richard Norris Esq and Sylvester Moorcroft Gent, and each of them jointly and severally Deputy and Deputys of the said office of Mayor and Deputy Mayor of the said burrough, to hold, exercise, and execute, the said office, with all fees, profitts and perquisites thereunto belonging, . . . during the pleasure of me the said Earle, in as large and ample manner as I the said Earle might, could, or ought to do it, personally present. Given under my hand and seale this thirteenth day of November Anno Regni Reginæ Anne Mag^{æ} Brittan &c Sexto ; Anno que Dom 1707.
"DERBY."

The Corporation in thus honouring the grandee of the neighbourhood were not unmindful of their own interests, as the following entry will show.

1708, Feby. 10th.   1708.

"The R^t Hono^{ble} James Earl of Derby being Chancellor of the Dutchy, did this month of February, out of his great favour and respect to this Corporation, and its honour and advancement, not only freely give his own right as Chancellour to the prizage of all wines imported into this country, but also interceded to, and obtain'd from her Maj^{tie} a patent or lease for the same to the Mayor, Bayl^s and Burgesses of Liverpoole, for the term of thirty one years, which pattent is in the great chest, and entered on this record."   Grant of Prizage.

"Also on application to the said Earle, he readily p'sented to her Maj^{tie} the peticōn of the Mayor, Bayl^s and Burgesses for another Markett Day and obtain'd the same. In order whereunto a commission issued forth of the Dutchy called an '*Ad quod Dampnum*' which is also entred.   Additional Market Day.

"Both which were brought down by Ralph Peters, Town Clerk from London and a letter of thanks return'd to the said Earle, and to p'serve the said favours of the said Earle in memory, the new Markett to be settled in the late castle is named—'DERBY SQUARE.'"   Derby Square.

The name of Lord Derby will appear again in the next chapter under circumstances not quite so harmonious.

The honorary freedom of the borough was frequently conferred on the public men of the day. Within the limits of the present chapter this compliment was paid to the Earl of Strangford, Sir Robert Walpole, Sir John Blair, Sir George Warburton, Sir Wm. Read, two sons of Secretary Braithwaite, Mr. Legh of Lyme, and others.   Honorary Freemen.

Amongst the enterprising local magnates of this period none played a more distinguished part than Sir Thomas Johnson, who was Mayor in 1695, and represented the borough in Parliament from 1701 to 1722. The constitution of the parish as separate from Walton, the erection of St. Peter's and St. George's churches, the construction of the original dock, the grant of the castle, and the establishment of the market in Derby Square, were principally owing to his activity and influence. His knighthood is thus recorded:—

Sir Thos. Johnson.

"James, Earl of Derby Mayor.

"1708. April 14. Mem^{dm} That Thomas Johnson Esq, one of the Representatives in Parliam^t for this Corporation waiteing on the Earle of Derby, p'sent Mayor; upon presenting an address to her Majesty from the Corporation, had the honor of Knighthood conferr'd on him by her Majesty the 20th day of March $A\bar{n}o$ Dom 1707/8.

Johnson knighted.

"VIVAT REGINA!"

Johnson, with all his enterprise and public spirit, was never a wealthy man, and was frequently in difficulties. After his last election, in 1722, his pecuniary qualification (£300 per annum) was called in question by Mr. Thos. Bootle, the unsuccessful candidate, and by Aldermen Norris and Moorcroft, who had been his friends and associates. The records contain a statement of this, with the affidavit which he took, stating that he had property of the required amount situated in various places in the county.

Objections to Johnson.

Not long after this occurs the following entry:—

"Mem, The second day of February 1723 the Honble Langham Booth^1 was elected Representative in Parliam^t for this Burrough in the room of Sr Thos Johnson, who hath accepted of a place under the Governm^t," being that of Collector of Customs in Virginia.

Resignation of Johnson.

Booth elected.

Mr. Thos. Heywood, in the comments on the Norris Papers, so graphically descriptive of Liverpool at that period, laments that "Johnson, who was always poor, lies probably

---

^{1} Langham Booth was brother to the first Earl of Warrington, and Groom of the Chambers to Frederick, Prince of Wales, father of George III.

in some obscure corner of Virginia." This, however is not borne out by the records.

The office appears to have been much in the nature of a sinecure, since Johnson's name continues to be entered as present at the meetings of the Council. On St. Luke's Day, Oct. 18, 1728, it appears for the last time, with a subsequent insertion in the margin—"*Mort.*"

The only remaining record of him in the town which he did so much to serve, is the name of the street, Sir Thomas's Buildings, which was formed and built by him.

In the former volume an account is furnished from the Records of a very unseemly controversy between the Corporation and the Town Clerk, Dobson, in the year 1637. In 1707 an imbroglio on a smaller scale occurred with Mr. Jno. Sandiford who was appointed Town Clerk in 1701.

Dispute with Sandiford.

Under date July 11th, 1707, it is recorded:—

" Att a Councell &c
" Whereas Mr. Mayor hath this day deliver'd into Councell a list of a number of high omissions and irregular transactions committed by John Sandiford Town Clarke of this Corporation, in relation to the Records and other matter relateing to his said office, whereupon this Councell hath unanimously voted to suspend ye said John Sandiford from his office of Town Clarke untill Wednesday ye Twentie third of this instant, when he is to appear before this Councell and answer the said charge this day given him."

On the 23rd of the same month it was

"Voted by a greate Majority y^t Mr John Sandiford is not capable of discharging the office of a Town Clarke."
"Order'd that the 20th day of this instant Augt is apointed for ye electing a Town Clerke by vote."

"1707 Aug. 20th Att an Assembly &c Sylvester Moorcroft Mayor
"This day being appointed for the electing of a Town Clerk; it is therefore order'd that whosoever is chosen shall, before he be establish'd, give security to pay to the use of this Corporation one Hundred guineas within three months after the death of Mr. John Sandiford (if he so long live). And also shall pay to the said John Sandiford Fourty Pounds ⅌ Annum dureing his life at four quarterly payments; and that he shall quitt

Election of Town Clerk.

CHAP. I, A.D. 1702—1727.

all practice as an attorney, except what particularly belongs to or has been done by the former Town Clerks of this Corporation, nor shall he receive any other fees than what have formerly been pay'd except by order of the Mayor and Councell.

Ralph Peters elected.
"Mr. Ralph Peters is this day chosen Town Clerk, and one of the Councell (conforming to the above order) *Quamdiu se bene gesserit; eod die jurat* in Council."

Annuity to Sandiford.
"1707 Dec. 3rd Ord^d That Mr John Sandiford late Town Clerk have security under the Corporation Seale for his fourty pounds ℔ ann. granted by former order, and that Ralph Peters p'sent Townclerk give security at the same time to the Corporation according to former order."

"It is afterwards declar'd in Councell April ye 14th 1708 that the said fourty pounds ℔ ann. is to be clear of all taxes."

Retirement of Recorder.
1709, Aug. 19th. The Recorder (Mr. Jno. Entwisle) tendered the resignation of his office. He was elected about the time of the Restoration, and through the successive periods of trouble and commotion had faithfully served the interests of the town. The Record runs as follows :—

1709.
"John Seacome Esq Mayor.

"Att a spe'all Councell held this 19th of August *Anno Dñi* 1709.

Entwisle.
"This assembly having this day received a letter (a copy whereof is underwritten) from John Entwisle Esq Recorder of this Burrough, whereby he desires to be discharg'd by reason of the infirmity of his age; they doe pursuant thereto remove and discharge him from the office of Recorder, and also from being of the Comon Councell of this Burrough and his attendance therein."

"A copy of the letter directed to the Worpf^ll John Seacome Esq, the Mayor, Aldermen and the rest of the Comon Councill of the Burrough and Corporation of Liverpoole.

"Gentlemen

Letter.
"I have served your Corporation as Recorder upwards of forty years faithfully to the best of my skill and knowledge. I am now near eighty-four years old, and find that the infirmities of my age render me less capable of dispatching business than formerly. As my real desire of the prosperity and welfare of your Corporation hath made it a pleasure to to me to serve you hitherto, the same reason now makes me desirous to be discharg'd of that trust, since I cannot pay the attendance necessary in order to a due execution of it, and I heartily wish you may fix upon a successor that may second my sincere endeavours for yor prosperity. If you pitch upon one of my family it will be a great satisfaction to me, and

I hope my concern for yo' welfare may go allong with the office to him from "Gentlemen
"Omskirke "Yo' old faithfull and humble serv'
"y⁰ 17ᵗʰ of Aug' 1709." "JOHN ENTWISLE.

"And then the Councell proceeding to an eleccon of a Recorder of this Burrough, they doe unanimously elect and choose Bertie Entwisle of Wigan Comon Councell man of this burrough in the room of John Entwisle Esq late Recorder and also Recorder of this Burrough, '*Quamdiu se bene gesserit*,' and order that he shall have and receive the due and accustom'd fee and stypend for the said office of Recorder."

Election of Recorder.

The connection of the family of Bootle, now represented by the Earl of Lathom, with the town of Liverpool, is interesting as set forth in the Records at this period.

Thomas Bootle, a native of Liverpool, who was a counsel learned in the law, is introduced as follows:—

Thomas Bootle.

"1713, Aug. 5. Thomas Bootle, of the Inner Temple, Esq., admitted free gratis,"

and was immediately promoted to the Common Council.

In 1722 he stood as Tory Candidate for the representation of the borough against Cleveland and Johnson (Whigs), when the numbers stood:—

1722.

Election.

Cleveland	882
Johnson	758
Bootle	393

Mr. Bootle petitioned against the return of Johnson, on the ground of his want of a qualification, which led to the proceedings mentioned above,⁽¹⁾ which, however failed. On the resignation of Johnson, in 1723, Bootle was passed over and Mr. Langham Booth returned.

In 1726 he was elected Mayor, and when a new Parliament was summoned, in August, 1727, on the accession of George II., he again offered himself as a candidate. Being, as Mayor, the returning officer, it was necessary that he should

Mayor resigns.

⁽¹⁾ *Vide supra*, p. 12.

resign his office. To this, however, there was considerable opposition.

The Records state as follows :—

"1727 August. Mem^{dm} That our present Mayor Thomas Bootle Esq being desirous to surrender his office of Mayor, comunicated the same at a gen'all meeting of the principall Burgesses and Freemen, and a day was appointed for a Common Hall to be held whereof all the Freemen that were in town to have notice, and accordingly a sumons in print was serv'd or left at the house of ev'y freeman giveing them notice that the first day of August was appointed.

"Aug 1st Att a Comon Hall or Gen'all Assembly of the Mayor Baylives and Burgesses of the burrough and Corporation of Liverpool, held this first day of August $A\overline{n}o$ Dni $Georgii$ $Secund$, &c in the Comon Hall of and in this Burrough, pursuant to publick notice and sumons, deliv'd to every freeman or left at the house of ev'y such as happen'd to be out within this town and the liberties thereof, and publick notice given in writeing, and by the Bellman as usuall, Mr Mayor propos'd to surrender his office of Mayor for the remainder of his Mayoralty, being till the eighteenth day of October next. Whereupon sev'all Burgesses oppos'd the acceptance of his surrender, and join'd in a Poll of all the freemen against the acceptance of such surrender, which he executed in publick court, and is as follows :—

Opposition.

"Whereas I Thomas Bootle of the Inner Temple, London Esq was on the eighteenth day of October last past elected Mayor of the Burrough of Liverpool to serve in that office for the space of one year then next ensuing, and was duely sworn and admitted into the said office.

Resignation.

"Now know all men by these presents, that I the said Thomas Bootle, for divers good causes and considerations me hereunto moveing, do by these presents resign and surrender into the hands of the Baylives and Burgesses . . . the said office of Mayor,—together with all liberties, priviledges, rights, powers and franchises thereto belonging, and do depart from the said office and all exercise of the same and from henceforth do quitt the same, and do now disclaim all right and title to the said office of Mayor, &c.

"In witness whereof I have hereunto sett my hand and seale this first day of August *Anno primo R^i Georgii Secundi* &c (1727.)

T. BOOTLE."

1727, Aug. 1st.

Poll taken.

"The surrender of Thomas Bootle Eq &c—being openly read in publick court after he had executed the same, a Poll was begun for and against the acceptance of such surrender, and the names of all the Burgesses and freemen that were pleas'd to give their vote therein, amounting in the whole to nine hundred and eighty six were taken down in a Poll book.

And after the Poll was ended upon casting up the books it appeár'd that there was a great majority for accepting of the said surrender, vizt:

"For accepting it 545
"Against it 441

"104 Majority.

"And thereupon an instrument of the acceptance of such surrender . . . was then sign'd by John Martindale and Robert Whitfield, the p'sent Baylives of the said Burrough and also by sev'all Burgesses in open court, and the seale affix'd thereto, and the said Thomas Bootle deliv'd up his staffe, and the Court adjourned."

Here follows the instrument of acceptance, signed by 32 Councillors and Burgesses. *Resignation accepted.*

"Whereupon the staff being delivered by the said Thomas Bootle to the Baylives, they agreed to proceed to the election of a Mayor for the remaining part of the year of Mayoralty."

"Aug. 5. George Tyrer Esq was thereupon elected Mayor for the ensuing twelve weeks to St Luke's day."

"A contest then took place for the Mayoralty when Mr John Hughes was elected. A scrutiny was demanded, which was refused."

Mr. Bootle was returned to Parliament without opposition. He sat for the borough until the general election of January, 1735, when he was ousted by Mr. Richard Gildart, and was subsequently elected for Midhurst. He was appointed Chancellor to Frederick, Prince of Wales, and Attorney General for the County Palatine of Durham. In 1745 he was knighted. In 1724 he purchased the Lathom estates which had passed by marriage from the Stanleys to Lord Ashburnham, where he took down the ancient hall and erected the present mansion in its place. Bootle's niece and heiress married Mr. Rd. Wilbraham, of Rode Hall, Cheshire, whose descendants have been ennobled, first under the title of Baron Skelmersdale, and subsequently as Earl of Lathom. *Bootle returned.* *Earl of Lathom.*

The Town Clerk was not the only officer who incurred the displeasure of the Council.

Mr. Sylvester Moorcroft, an Alderman, a leading man in

Corporate affairs, was elected Mayor in 1706, it was said much against his will. When the old Custom House, which stood at the bottom of Water street, was removed on the construction of the Old Dock in 1709, Mr. Moorcroft erected a new Custom House at the East end of the Dock, which answered its purpose for nearly a century and a half. In 1716 he was elected Treasurer to the Corporation at a salary of £50 per annum.

Moorcroft, Treasurer.

In 1720 some dissatisfaction arose which led to the following record:—

1720, Oct. 13th.

"Whereas it is made appear to this Councill that Ald^n Sylv^r Moorcroft Town's Treasurer, who since the last Councill held, hath not only comitted a very great misdemeanour in carrying the books of orders of this Councill upon some ill designe to disclose, publish, or destroy, some of the orders therein, which might tend to the manifest prejudice of this Burrough and Corporation; but also voluntarily and obstinately refus'd to attend in Councill when duly sumon'd; by means whereof the Corporation affaires have been very much delay'd, and the publick business retarded. This Councill have thought fitt to remove and doe remove and discharge the said Ald^n Moorcroft from being Treasurer, and doe elect Mr Peter Hall, Treasurer in his stead, to hold upon the same terms, and giveing like good security as Mr Moorcroft, by the order of the Council of 31st August 1716, was order'd to doe."

Dismissed.

Hall appointed.

This no doubt arose out of the controversy at that time going forward respecting the constitution and authority of the Council.

Mr. Hall's appointment cannot have been quite satisfactory, for we read on the 20th March following (1721):—

"Then elected Mr Henry Trafford Treasurer, for the benefit of Mr Peter Hall, who is att present under some misfortunes, he giveing security imediately to lay his accounts monthly before the Councill, and to have twenty five Pounds ⅌ ann^m sallary."

Dismissed.

We get occasionally interesting glimpses into the mode of conducting the business of the Council.

"1716, Nov. 7. Order'd that the former order of Councill enjoining ev'y Councill man to wear a cloak when he appears and sitts in Councill, be and is hereby reviv'd and made a standing order and law." *Councillors' Cloaks.*

The Mayor, when he appeared in public, was attended by Halberdiers.

"1713, Oct. 23. Order'd that the Halberdiers have new Coates &c as usuall, the three yeares now expireing." *Halberdiers.*

"1721, Sept. 6. Order'd that the two Halbert bearers that attend every Sunday at the Hall door, dureing Mr Mayor's being there, shall have an allowance of sixpence every Sunday between them."

The attendance of Councillors was rigidly enforced.

"1715, Sept. 16. It is order'd that ev'y Councill man that does not attend at two o'clock on the first Wensday in ev'y month being Council day according to custom (unless sufficient cause be shew'd for his absence) or within half an hour after two o'clock in the afternoon peremptorily, shall forfeit and pay six shillings and eight pence, imediately after, without any further order or fine to be sett on him by this Councill, and that the Baylives of this Burrough demand and receive the same, and upon failure of payment of such forfeiture they are hereby empowered imediately to levy such forfeiture according to the custom of this Burrough, on the goods and chattels of the offender. *Fines for Non-attendance.*

"The like order and fine for non-attendance when the Councill is regularly sumon'd.

"And it is now declar'd that both these orders remain standing orders for the future."

In case of continued absence the offending member was expelled, thus:—

"1707, Aug. 20. Mem^{dm} What order to be made to discharge the absent Councell men. Order'd that the Town Clerk write to Mr John Hughes, if he will attend or desire to be remov'd out of ye Councell."

The Bailiffs put in a claim for reimbursement. 1721, Nov. 1: The newly-elected Bailiffs, Messrs. Goodwin and Taylor

"Willingly accept the office, but humbly hope the Corporation will consider their expences therein. This Councell therefore takeing into consideracon that they have already serv'd that office once, doe order that the town's treasurer doe pay so much of the necessary expences which they shall be put unto in the discharge of their office, as the Mayor shall allow and order for the present year." *Bailiffs' Claim.*

Again,

"1722, Aug. 1. Bryan Blundell Esq Mayor.

"Whereas there are sev'all bills for publick entertainments had by order of the late Mayor, wch were usually paid by the Mayor and Baylives, are left unpaid by the late Mayor, being his share to have paid, and that he being deceased insolvent, the Bayl^s humbly hope they shall not be charged therewith, and praying relief; And this Councill takeing the same into consideration, and that it would be a great hard^{pp} on the late Bayl^s to pay the same, it being expended for the publick service of the Corp^n. It is now order'd that the said arrear be paid by the treasurer out of the publick mon^s of the Corp^n, and allow'd him in his accounts. And that for the future, the forty pounds allow'd to the Worp^{ll} the Mayor for the time being towards the expenses, instead of two of the best freemen's fines, shall not be paid or allow'd by the treasurer till the Mayoralty be ended, and the publick entertainments discharged."

Mayor's allowance.

Freedom of debate was upheld in the Council, as the following resolution testifies:

Debates in Council.

"1710, July 5. Resolved that it is the undoubted right of ev^y comon Councell man of this burrough att ev'y Assembly, to move what he shall think fitt for the benefitt of the Corporation, and if insisted on, the same to be then decided and determined by the majority of the persons present att all and ev'y such Assembly."

The Council meetings were not always harmonious in the olden time any more than in the modern. In 1714 disputes ran high respecting the appointment of one of the Rectors, and also respecting the appropriation of the revenues of the dock.

Disputes.

Town's Chest.

"1714, June 4. It being propounded that the Comon Seale canott be come att by reason Mr Maudit (treasurer) who was entrusted with one of the keys of the town's chest wherein the same is lodg'd, refuses to deliver the same, p'tending he hath deliv'ed it over to Alderman Geo. Tyrer, who refus'd to attend with it this day to seale some leases; It is order'd that the Serjeant att Mace goe to Mr Maudit and demand the said key.

"And the Serj^t went accordingly and returned. Did not get the key, he telling him the same. It is therefore order'd that in case the said key be not deliv^d to Mr Mayor this night, that Mr Mayor be requested to order the lock whereof he had the key to be knocked off, and a new one plac'd on in the p'sence of the others that have the other keys, and such new key putt into the hands of Mr Robt Low."

MUNICIPAL GOVERNMENT.

Jealous as the Corporation were as to their rights and privileges, they had occasionally to give way to the claims to exemption from the burgesses of other towns, who relied on special charters from the Crown.

A peremptory mandamus of this kind was issued by the Lord Mayor of London, in 1706, as follows:— *Mandamus.*

"1706, Sept. 11. To all to whom these p'sents shall come o ye same shall see, hear, or read; Sir Thomas Rawlinson, Knight, Lord Mayor of ye city of London, and ye aldermen of ye same City send greeting.

"Know yee, that amongst other ye liberties, free customs and priviledges by ye Charters of ye late King Henry ye second, and Henry ye third and other Kings of England to ye Citizens of ye City afores^d granted; And by ye authority of divers Parliam^{ts} ratifyed, approv'd, and confirmed, it appeareth that all ye Citizens of London and all their goods are and ought to be, quit and free from all Toll, Passage, Lastage, Piccage, Pontage, Pavage and Murage, through ye whole realme of England, and ye ports of ye sea; And through ye whole dominions of ye same as well on this side as beyond ye seas, and through ye ports of ye sea, as well on this side as beyond the seas; and that if any man shall take any toll or customs of ye Citizens of London, the Citizens of London may take of ye burrough or town (where any toll or other customs shall be taken) as much as ye said Citizens have given for toll, and are thereby damnified; And that if any man within ye realm of England, or in any ye dominions of ye said Kings on this side or beyond ye seas, or in any ye ports of ye sea on this side or beyond ye seas, shall take any toll or other customs of ye Citizens of London, the Sheriffs of ye said City of London for defaulte of justice in that behalfe, their goods may take at London; and also that ye said Citizens throughout ye whole realme and dominions afores^d, freely and without any lett of ye said Kings or any of their officers or ministers, as well by sea as by land, concerning their goods and merchandizes, in any place or port, may traffick and do their businesse as to them shall seem good, quitt of all custome, toll and payage: And also may abide in any place within ye said realm for doing their businesse as in time past they have accustomed to do. And further it is forbidden upon forfeiture, that none should presume from henceforth to molest or otherwise to disquiett or vex ye said Citizens contrary to ye liberties to them as aforesaid granted. *Claim of London to exemption.*

"Wherefore wee pray and friendly intreate you on behalfe of William Sawrey, who is a freeman of this City and of the Company of Salters of ye same City; that you will not in anywise molest him in his person, nor in his goods, nor (in as much as in you is) suffer ye same to be done by others. And that if you have taken anything from ye said William Sawrey, *Claim of London established.*

his Attorney, Factor, Assignee, or any of them you make restitution unto him his attorney, factor, or assignee, or some of them, without delay according to justice; least wee for want of justice on y' part to be p'formed, should be urged to inflict the penaltyes of y° Charters afores^d on you or some of you, or to prosecute some other hard course against you, which wee hope you will in y' wisdom prevent.

"In Witnesse whereof, wee the said Lord Mayor and Aldermen of y° said City of London, y° Seale of y° office of Mayoralty of y° said City to these p'sents have caused to be affixed. Dated at London, y° eleaventh day of September *Anno Domini* 1706 and in y° fifth year of y° raigne of our Soveraigne Lady, Anne, Queen of England &c."

<small>Bristol, Wexford, Waterford.</small>
The same exemptions were claimed and allowed to citizens of Bristol, Wexford, and Waterford, as appears from documents entered in the records about this period.

The marriage with a freeman's daughter gave partial exemption, as by the following entry:—

"1714, Mar. 9. It is order'd, that Owin Branagan who hath married a freeman's daughter, have liberty to trade within the town during the pleasure of this Councill, paying tenn shillings ₱ Quarter, but so as not to p'judice the town's duties, or other the priviledges and franchises of this Corp°."

<small>Poor Palatines.</small>
This exclusiveness was rather peremptorily interfered with in 1709, by an immigration of foreigners. During the wars then waging on the Continent, in which the English forces under Marlborough were so distinguished, no district suffered more heavily than the country bordering on the Rhine, called the Palatinate. In time of defeat they were plundered by the enemy, and in time of victory by their friends; there seemed to be no end to the march of destructive armies passing and repassing the river. Harassed and dispirited by these continued calamities, they came to a resolution to remove and seek their fortune in a strange land. A large number found their way to England between 1706 and 1709, principally with a view of getting over to America, for which, however, no provision was made. They met with a very cold welcome, from the idea that the influx of so many artizans

would tend to lower the rate of wages. A detachment found their way to the banks of the Mersey, respecting whom the following entries occur.

"1709, Sept. 16. John Seacome Mayor.
"Att a speciall councell &c
"The letters from Sir Alexander Cairnes of the city of London of the 8th and 12th curr' to Mr Mayor signifying his haveing sent one hundred and thirty persons of the poor Pallatines and a list of their names, number of children and trades and imployments. This assembly doth concurr therewith, and doe enact and order that their names be entred upon record, and that they and ev'y of them be receiv'd as settled inhabitants of and in this burrough. And that in consideracōn of five pounds ⅌ head pay'd down with them, they and ev'y of them and their issue shall be permitted to exercise their respective trades and imploymⁿ within this burrough and Corporacōn without disturbance in any wise." *Reception of Palatines.*

Some objections appear to have been made against this action of the Corporation—almost the sole instance of such liberality during their whole history—which led to the following entry:—

"It being declared in this assembly that sev'all persons have discoursed in and about this burrough and Corporacōn, that the Comōn Councell of this burrough have not power to receive persons as inhabitants of and in the same without consent of the parish. *1709. Objections of Parish.*
" It is Resolv'd, That it is the undoubted right of the Comōn Councell of this burrough and Corporacōn to admit and permit any persons whatever to inhabitt and exercise any trade within this burrough and Corporacōn, without consulting or haveing the consent of the Parish in any wise."

The subject came up again in the following month.

"1709, Octr. 5. It is order'd,
" That for the better imployment and settlem' of the Pallatines lately receiv'd into this burrough, and of the poor of this burrough, a Comittee be and is now appointed and establish'd, viz'—
" The Mayor for the time being, the Aldermen and the Baylives for the time being, the senior and the junior Aldⁿ or two of them att least being present, shall have power to make such orders for the imploym' and disposall of the Pallatines and poor, and setling and manageing of a workhouse, or setling them or any of them in any other imployment or manufactuke as they shall think will be for their better maintenance and *Disposal of Palatines.*

Committee appointed.

way of liveing. And that the Corporation haveing receiv'd six hundred and fifty pounds with the Pallatines, the same or such part thereof as the said Comittee or any five (whereof two of the Justices of the Peace vizt, the Mayor, the junior or senior Alderman or two of them to be two) shall think most meet and shall order and direct, shall be laid out in renting a house, houses, or other buildings, and buying in of such stock or stocks as the said Comittee or any five shall direct and appoint; And that the Bayl^s for the time being haveing the said moneys, shall upon all occasions answer and obey all such orders as the said Comittee shall make and direct, &c."

As nothing further is recorded concerning the poor Palatines, it is to be presumed that they became merged in the general population. It is possible that some of the names we meet with half a century afterwards, such as Beeckman, Fewller, Bertyn, Isatt, Rumbold, &c., may have been derived from this source.

Names of Palatines.

It was handed down traditionally that some of the houses in Derby Square were the handiwork of the Palatines, and that workshops were built for them by Sir Thos. Johnson, in Sir Thomas's Buildings.

Supply of Water.

The supply of the town with water formed at this period, and long after, a very anxious subject of inquiry. Originally, the natural springs at the outcrop of the sandstone strata furnished an ample supply from shallow wells, but as the town increased these were no longer sufficient, and the wells were liable to pollution.

With the increase of the town, after the Restoration, the attention of the Council was drawn to the subject, and in 1695 an agreement was entered into with Messrs. Green, Tuttell, and Barrey, by which facilities were given them for bringing water into the town at reasonable rates. The source from which the water was to come [1] was from the springs at Bootle. Nothing, however, was done for some years.

[1] See Vol. I of *Selections from the Records*, p. 320.

1705, Sept. 5th. Mr. John Seacome petitions to supply the town with water on reasonable terms, and if he does not perfect and complete the waterworks in two years he will be obliged to surrender his lease. The source not stated. *1705. Water Supply.*

Messrs. Green & Co. failed to carry out their undertaking, and ten years elapsed without anything being done.

1705, Oct. 24th. Proposals were made by Mr. Simon Edmunds, on behalf of Sir Cleave Moore, Bart., of Bank Hall, offering to supply the town with water from the copious springs at Bootle. On Nov. 7th a document was sent in a more complete form, as under:—

"Proposals humbly made by Simon Edmunds of Liverpoole in y" County of Lancaster Gentlemⁿ in the name and on behalfe of Sr Cleave More of Banckhall, in ye s^d County Knt and Baronette.

"To ye Worp^l ye Mayor, Baylives and Burgesses of ye ancient Burrough of Liverpoole in ye County afores^d for convaying fresh water to supply ye s^d town, pursuant to a peticōn formerly p'sented on ye same acco^t.

"Imp^s That ye s^d Sr Cleave More shall have free liberty to convay to ye s^d town ye river and springs of Bootle through ye wast lands, comons, highwayes, streets, lanes and other avenues, leading to or within ye s^d town, for and during ye tearme of one hundred yeares, and in such manner and upon ye same condicōns as such liberties of convaying of water had been formerly contracted for betweene the Mayor, Baylives and Burgesses of ye s^d burrough, and John Green, Thomas Tuttell and Richard Barrey. *Proposals of Moore.*

"That in regard ye contract formerly made with ye s^d Green, Tuttell and Barrey may be deem'd and judg'd to be and remaine still valid and in force, notwithstanding they have neglected to p'forme any one of ye articles condicōns and agreem^{ts} on their parts for upwards of tenne yeares, and to ye great inconvenience of ye s^d towne. *Green and Tuttell.*

"Therefore it is humbly proposed, That ye Mayor Baylives and Burgesses should concur, agree, consent and endeavour, with ye s^d Sr Cleave More in any legal act or acts whereby ye s^d contract or grant may be declar'd and made voyd; hee ye s^d Sr Cleave More being at all ye charg of obtaining such declaration, or making voyd ye s^d contract, and that till ye obtaining such declaration ye s^d Sr Cleave More shall not require of ye s^d Mayor Baylives and Burgesses any further or other assurance thereof.

"That ye s^d Mayor Baylives and Burgesses be pleased to appoint what time they think reasonable to p'forme and accomplish ye s^d undertaking, and that yᵉ sᵈ Sʳ Cleave More shall give good and sufficient assurance for yᵉ timely and due p'formance of yᵉ same.

Lease to Moore.

"It is this day order'd in Councell (pursuant to yᵉ above peticon) that Sʳ Cleave More shall have a lease for yᵉ Waterworks formerly sett to Messrs Green, Tuttle and Berrey for one hundred yeares, hee yᵉ sᵈ Sʳ Cleave More defending this Corporacon at his own charg from ye sᵈ Green, Tuttle and Barrey, and bringing in and delivering up yᵉ sᵈ lease to yᵉ Corporacon; which intended Waterworks yᵉ sᵈ Sʳ Cleave More shall p'fect, compleat and finish in three yeares time from this day. And shall pay fifetie shillings ⅌ ann during yᵉ tearme, yᵉ rent to commence from this day; and yᵉ first yeare's rent to be pay'd to ye Corporacon next Mich'lmas, and shall give security to yᵉ Corporacon to p'fect and effect yᵉ sᵈ Waterworks for a g'nl supply (on reasonable tearmes) of yᵉ inhabitants of yᵉ sᵈ Corporacon in three yeares' time; otherwise yᵉ lease to be vacant, and that councell learned in yᵉ law shall be consulted in yᵉ making of yᵉ sᵈ lease, according to yᵉ intent and meaning of this order."

Green and Tuttell.

Messrs. Green, Tuttell & Barrey were not so easily disposed of as was imagined, and it was found necessary to apply to Parliament.

1706.

"1706, Feb. 7. Sylvester Moorcroft Mayor.

"Whereas yᵉ Corporacon in yᵉ year 1695 did contract undʳ articl with Jno Green, Thomˢ Tuttell, and Richᵈ Barrey of yᵉ city of London &c., for yᵉ supplying of this toun with water, and yᵉ Port with good and wholesome fresh water, as by yᵉ said contract may more fully appear. And yᵉ sᵈ persons never did anything pursuant to yᵉ sᵈ contract in order to effect yᵉ sᵈ worke, nor pay'd any rent reserv'd to yᵉ Corporacon. And there is no likelihood that yᵉ sᵈ persons will ever go on and finish their p'tended undertaking. And yᵉ sᵈ toun and Port lye undʳ great inconveniencies for want of so good and usefull a worke were willing to encourage any person mindfull to und'take yᵉ same.

"And whereas yᵉ Councell did on yᵉ 24ᵗʰ day of Octobʳ 1705 receive proposals from Sʳ Cleave More, by his agent, Simon Edmunds, Gentˡ for yᵉ supplying of yᵉ sᵈ toun with good and wholesome fresh water (hee having springs convenient for that end); And did then agree to yᵉ sᵈ proposals, undʳ certain condicons and limitacons as ⅌ yᵉ sᵈ order of Councell dated as aforesᵈ may more at larg' appear. Now yᵉ sᵈ Sʳ Cleave More having sent down a peticon to yᵉ Comons of Engl' to be sign'd by yᵉ Mayor, Aldermⁿ &c in order to make voyd yᵉ aforesᵈ contract with Green, Tuttell and Barrey and to enable him to furnish yᵉ toun with fresh water, this *Resolutions about Water.* Councell doth not think fitt to sign the same, but do agree to sign a peticon of their own, on behalfe of themselves and yᵉ rest of yᵉ Corporacon in order to obtain yᵉ aforesᵈ end, and to enable them to close with yᵉ sᵈ

Sʳ Cleave More. And do also impour yᵉ prᵗ Mayor and Baylives to contract under articles with yᵉ sᵈ Sʳ Cleave More, according to yᵉ agreemᵗˢ restrictions & limitacons in yᵉ aforesᵈ order of Councell of yᵉ 24ᵗʰ of 8ᵇʳ 1705 contained."

Another three years elapsed without anything being done, but in 1709 a further movement was made.

"1709, Dec. 8. John Earle Mayor. Moore's Lease.
"Order'd, That Mr Mayor and Baylˢ be impower'd to admitt Sʳ Cleave Moor, Barrᵗ to take a lease from the Corporation for lib'ty and conveniency within their bounderys to make waterworks and bring fresh water from Bootle, prejudiceing no person's private right; under such proper covenᵗˢ as Councill shall advise, to be approv'd of by this Assembly, for 99 yeares, paying tenn pounds ⅌ ann rent, he finishing it in 3 yeares now next, else the Corporation not to be bound by such lease; Sʳ Cleave being oblig'd to sett aside the former lease to Barry, Tuthill and Green, by Act of Parliamᵗ or otherwise as can be best obtained."

In the succeeding Session an Act was passed (8 Anne, cap. 25) "For enabling the Corporation to make a grant to Sir Cleave More, to bring water into Liverpool from Bootle Springs." Act obtained.

Still nothing was done, probably from lack of capital to carry out the works.

After the lapse of another eight years, the energetic Thomas Steers, the engineer for the dock just constructed, along with Alderman Seacome, came to the rescue.

"1717, Octr. 10. Foster Cunliffe Mayor 1717.
"Alderman Seacome and Mr. Steers petitioning for liberty to bring fresh water to the town and to have a lease on such terms as will encourage them to perfect it. Seacome and Steers's plan.
"It is order'd that they give proposalls in writeing next Councill day."

Another twelve months elapsed, when we find the following:—

"1718, Octr. 8. Richard Kelsall Mayor. 1718.
"Order'd That Sʳ Cleave More and Mr Seacome and Mr Steers have liberty to bring water to town upon such terms and condicons as the Councill shall think fitt."

Plan abandoned.

All this parade, for five and twenty years, of propositions, agreements, leases, and applications to Parliament ended in nothing. Sir Cleave Moore sold his Bootle estate, which was purchased by the Earl of Derby.

The closing notice is as follows :—

"1720, Oct. 13. Thomas Fillingham Mayor.

"The order made the eighth day of December 1709 to admit Sr Cleave More to take a lease for liberty to make Waterworks and bring fresh water from Bootle to the town for 99 years, which he undertook to finish in three years, but hath not yet done it, is now vacated, and declar'd void to all intents and purposes."

So the matter rested during the greater part of the century. Its revival will be seen in a future chapter.

Water from Moss Lake.

It may be incidentally mentioned that in 1720 an independent scheme was carried out for supplying the town with water from the Moss Lake on the high land to the east, and a reservoir was constructed in London Road. In 1742, during heavy rain, the reservoir burst, and the rush of water did considerable damage. The scheme was then abandoned and never revived.

The Corporation was always jealous of interference with its jurisdiction, and pugnacious in defence of the independence of the local courts. Thus we read :—

"1709, Jan. 10. John Earle Mayor.

Local Courts.
"Whereas it is propounded to this assembly that the proceedings of and in the Mayor and Bayl^s Court of this burrough in certain causes brought there—and the condemnation and sale of certain goods by them arrested and sold by process out of the said court, are now threaten'd to be call'd in question. It is order'd that in case the same be disputed att law, the charge of justifying and of defending of the proceedings of the s^d court only, shall be borne by the Corporation ; the Town Clerk haveing the managem^t thereof."

Wards.

The division of the town into wards, under the Municipal Reform Act of 1835 was not the first arrangement of the kind.

In 1667, the town was divided, for administrative purposes, into five wards.

During the period now under review we read:—

"1721, Nov. 1. Bryan Blundell Mayor.

"Whereas att the last Grand Portmoot Court held in and for this Burrough it was represented to the court by the Grand Inquest, That by the great enlargemᵗ and increase of this town and the inhabitants thereof—for the better governmᵗ of this Burrough and more effectuall putting the laws in execution especially against immorality and prophaneness, there should be six assistant constables yearly elected. *Constables.*

"It is now order'd and enacted that six proper and fit persons, freemen, and inhabitants of this burrough, be for ever hereafter elected, appointed, and chosen yearly, to be Depᵗʸ Constables, Headboroughs, or assistants to the sub-Baylives and to be obliged to take an oath for the due performance of their office.

"This Councell therefore have and doe proceed to elect such fitt persons and doe appoint that the town be divided into four Wards or Districts and that two including the sub-Baylives be appointed to each ward as follows *Wards.*

      "East Ward or Dale Street District
      "West Ward or Water Street Do
      "South Ward or Castle Street Do
      "Dock Ward—Pool Lane &c Do"

CORPORATE ESTATE AND REVENUES.

The landed estate of the Corporation consisted of an original grant from the Earls of Lancaster of the turbary including the Moss Lake; of various parcels which from time immemorial had belonged to the town; but principally of the Great Heath, which extended from the Pool stream eastward to the present Crown Street, which had been ceded by Lord Molyneux, under the agreement of 1672.

Building Land. The plots of land for building were, in the first instance, leased for three lives only, but as the demand greatly increased with the development of the town after the Restoration, in 1707 the leases were extended to three lives and 21 years.

The disposal of the land became an important and increasing source of revenue.

In addition to the landed estate, there were the following sources of income :—

Sources of Income. The Freemen's fines on admission. This impost was very irregularly and arbitrarily levied; seemingly at the caprice of the leading members of the Council. It amounted to a considerable sum yearly. There were the rents of property in possession, the fines upon new leases and renewals, the market tolls, the town's dues.

The last item was originally a local tax upon the goods of strangers, or foreigners as they were called, the Burgesses and Freemen being exempt; this exemption extending to the citizens of London, Bristol, Waterford and Wexford.

In 1651, immediately after the Civil War, the receipts from all sources amounted to £273 6s. 8d.

CORPORATE ESTATE AND REVENUES.

In 1704 the revenue was £831, derived as follows:—   1704.

Freemen's Fines................	£208	14	2
Rents..................................	104	11	5
Market Tolls	80	5	8
Town Dues	255	2	7
Sundries	9	3	4
Fines from Leases	173	0	0
	£830	17	2

Revenue.

In 1707 the income had increased to £1177 14s.

The records during this period indicate in a very interesting manner the demand for land and the steady extension of the town beyond the pool, which had been for ages the boundary of the town eastward. <small>Demand for Land.</small>

There has always been a tradition that coal existed under the town. In 1698 the Council voted the sum of £10 for experimental boring.

Some bold speculators had an idea that not only coal, but lead ore might be found in the locality. The following entries relate to these propositions:— <small>Search for Coal.</small>

"1717, Mar. 7. Foster Cunliffe Mayor
"Order'd that Aldⁿ Gildart have liberty to boar for coales, within the Corporation lands, and in case any be found, he to pay six pence ₱ work to the Corporation as the Lords part." <small>Grant.</small>

"1723, Aug. 7. Edward Ratchdale Mayor
"Mr Gildart haveing liberty to boar for and gett coales, desires the like liberty to boar for and gett lead oar and other oar (if any) within the liberties of this town. It is order'd that he have a lease of both under such limitations as not any person's private right may be p'judiced thereby, and Mr Recorder to be consulted thereon—paying a tenth part of the oar that shall be gott and 2ˢ 6ᵈ ₱ ann. rent till oar is gott." <small>Lead Ore.</small>

"1723, Nov. 6. The Lease to Aldⁿ Gildart as settled by Mr Recorder for liberty to gett coale, lead oar, and other oar being now read, is approved of and order'd to pass under the Corporation Seale. <small>Lease of Coal.</small>

It need not be said that the attempt to find either of these minerals proved abortive. In the case of the lead ore, better knowledge would have shown the futility of the attempt. In reference to coal, the question is still in doubt, not as to the existence of the coal measures, but as to the practicability of reaching them.

There were other minerals of a much humbler character, which the Corporation were able to turn to account. The clay and the sandstone afforded excellent materials for building and for other purposes.

Bricks. Bricks began to be made on the common or Great Heath in 1615, and several notices occur subsequently of leases and grants for the purpose.

In 1619 the lessee was bound to sell bricks to the Burgesses at 8s. ℔ m̄, giving 1120 to the thousand. In 1685 the price had fallen to 5s. 6d. ℔ m̄, the lessee paying a royalty of 4d. ℔ m̄.

"1716, Mar. 7. Order'd, that Mr Hughes have liberty to gett clay or marle within his field for makeing sugar moulds or potts, and other kind of muggs, paying 2ˢ 6ᵈ ℔ ann."

Stone Quarries. In regard to stone, the Corporation was in possession of two quarries which for many years supplied the wants of the
The Mount. town; one on the eminence called "The Mount," the site of St. James's Cemetery; the other consisting of a rocky
Brown-Low. hill called the "Brown-Low" (anciently Brune-lagh), now the site of University College. They were both worked from time immemorial, until exhausted.

"1705, Dec. 5. The Quarry upon yᵉ Comōn order'd to be lett, and a Bill to be fixt on yᵉ Exchange in order thereunto."

The quarry was accordingly let to one Edward Litherland, of Netherton, for a term of seven years, at a rent of £11 10s. ℔ ann.; but the quarry being intended for the general supply of building stone to the inhabitants, provision was made by a long list of prices of the various articles required, at which the lessee was bound to supply the Burgesses. A few specimens may be given :—

> "Pairpoint Ashlers 11 to 14ins square and 2ft long 3ᵈ ⅌ ashler 30ˢ ⅌ hund. Prices of Stone.
> "Broaken Stone Work with Windows, Corners and Jamms and Tables 7½ᵈ ⅌ yd.
> "Corner stones for Brickwork 2ᵈ ⅌ stone
> "Pound Worke and other rough worke 4¼ᵈ ⅌ yard
> "For 2 Beckett Stones for an arch over a cellar or yᵉ like 2ˢ 6ᵈ
> "For Broad Coping Stones for covering a wall 3ᵈ ⅌ foot
> "For Columbs for a Pillar 10ᵈ ⅌ yᵈ yᵉ Pillar to be measured round about
> "For Grave Stones 2ˢ 6ᵈ ⅌ stone"
> &c., &c.

At the time of the rebellion of 1715, it appears that the town was to a certain extent temporarily fortified, for under date of 1718, May 14th, we read :—

> "It is order'd that the Town Clerk goe to London, to sollicite the obtaining of the charge of the fortifications att the time of the late rebellion; and that the Corpⁿ bear the charge of his journey, and that what moneys shall be obtained, the same shall be apply'd towards the building of the new church." Fortifications

At the commencement of the 18th century the ancient castle was in the possession of the Corporation, on an annual tenancy from the crown.⁽¹⁾

In 1704 a lease was obtained, of which, as it is a very important document, I present the leading features. Lease of Castle.

> "This Indenture made the fifth day of March in yᵉ third year of yᵉ Raign of our Soveraign Lady Anne by yᵉ grace of God Queen &c. and in the year of our Lord 1704, Betweene our said soveraign . . of yᵉ one part and yᵉ Mayor, Bayliffes, and Burgesses of ye town of Liverpoole . . of yᵉ other part.
> "Whereas yᵉ office of yᵉ Constable of yᵉ Castle of Liverpoole within yᵉ County Palᵉ of Lancaster was by Letters Patent under yᵉ seal of yᵉ Duchy and yᵉ sᵈ County Palᵉ bearing date yᵉ tenth day of July in yᵉ twenty seaventh year of yᵉ Reigne of yᵉ late Queen Elizabeth (amongst other

---
⁽¹⁾ See the previous vol. pp. 292-315.

things) granted and confirm'd by y⁰ said Queen unto Richard Molyneux Esq,
therein named. To hold unto him y⁰ said Richard Molyneux and the Heirs
Lease of Castle. male of his body, and for default of such issue to y⁰ Heirs male of y⁰ body
of Sr Richard Molyneux . . with such wages and fees as are therein
expressed.

" And whereas y⁰ greatest part of y⁰ s^d castle is demolished, and y⁰ rest
Ruinous state. thereof is now ruinous and decayed and of no benefit and advantage to y⁰
Queen's Majestie; and y⁰ Mayor, Baylives, and Burgesses of y⁰ s^d Towne
of Liverpoole have by their humble peticon . . besought her s^d Majestie
for a lease of y⁰ scite and soile thereof for y⁰ purposes and during the term
of years hereinafter mentioned. Now this Indenture witnesseth. That y⁰
s^d now Queen's most excellent Majestie y⁰ better to enable y⁰ s^d Mayor,
Provision for Rectors. Bayliffes and Burgesses to maintain and provide for the Rectors of the
Parish Church of Leverpoole and y⁰ Parochiall Chappell within y⁰ s^d Town,
and their successors according to y⁰ intent of an Act of Parliam^t made in
y⁰ tenth year of y⁰ Raign of his late majesty King William y⁰ third, entitled
an act to enable y⁰ towne of Liverpoole in y⁰ County Paletine of Lancaster
Church. to build a church and endow y⁰ same, and for making y⁰ s^d town and liberties
thereof a Parish of itself distinct from Walton, and for and in consideracon
of y⁰ rent and covenants hereinafter and contained on y⁰ part and behalf of
y⁰ s^d Mayor, Bayliffes, and Burgesses to be payd done and performed, and
of y⁰ charges the said Mayor, Bayliffes, and Burgesses are to be at in
building on y⁰ lands hereinafter mentioned and for divers other good causes
and consideracons her said Majesty hereunto especially moving and by and
with y⁰ advice of her Chancellor and Councell of her s^d Duchy of Lancaster,
Hath given, granted, demised and to farm lett unto y⁰ s^d Mayor, Bayliffes,
and Burgesses all that y⁰ scite of her s^d Majest^e late castle there call'd or
known by y⁰ name of y⁰ Castle of Leverpoole, or by what other name y⁰
same heretofore was or now is called or known, together with y⁰ ditch
thereof, and y⁰ soile of y⁰ s^d late Castle and Castle Ditch and all buildings,
inclosures, and improvements thereon or any part thereof made with their
Area of Land. appurten^s, containing in the whole six Thousand two Hundred, seaventy
and three square yards, amounting to two Roods of land and eighteene
Perches of Ground according to y⁰ measure there used, and y⁰ same being
butted and bounded round about, and on the outside of y⁰ s^d Castle
Ditch as followeth (that is to say) on y⁰ north west part or side thereof,
from y⁰ Castle Gate abutting upon and being bounded by the Backside of
a certain street in Leverpoole comonly called the Castle Hill for y⁰ space
of forty eight yards and three quarters of a yard, being y⁰ lands and houses
Boundaries of Castle. of y⁰ Mayor, Bayliffes, and Burgesses of Liverpoole afores^d; and on y⁰ west
part or side thereof, abutting upon and being bounded by y⁰ Backside of
another street there, called Preeson's Row for y⁰ space of seaventy two
yards and an half; being y⁰ lands and houses of y⁰ Mayor, Bayliffes and
Burgesses, and on y⁰ south side or part of y⁰ s^d Castle and ditch abutting

upon and being bounded by yᵉ Backside of a certain other street there, commonly called yᵉ Back of yᵉ Castle, being yᵉ lands and houses of yᵉ sᵈ Mayor, Bayliffes and Burgesses, for yᵉ spac of Eighty and one yards, and on yᵉ East side or part of yᵉ sᵈ Castle and ditch abutting upon and being bounded by yᵉ Backside of a certain other street there, commonly call'd yᵉ street leading to yᵉ Poole Lane for yᵉ space of seaventy sixe yards, being a publick street way, and also abutting upon and being bounded by a part of a certain other street there, upon the Castle Hill leading to Harrington Street for yᵉ space of one and thirty yards and an half on yᵉ North East part up to yᵉ sᵈ Castle Gate, yᵉ same being in yᵉ whole of yᵉ yearly value of Twelve Pounds beyond Reprises, as by a survey thereof made and returned into her said Majestˢ Court of Duchy Chamber and there remaining amongst yᵉ Records of yᵉ sᵈ Duchy.

"To have and to hold yᵉ said scite and yᵉ soil of yᵉ sᵈ late Castle of Leverpoole and other yᵉ p'miss's with yᵉ appurtenᶜ unto yᵉ sᵈ Mayor, Bayliffs, and Burgesses of yᵉ sᵈ Town of Leverpoole and their successors from yᵉ date hereof for and during yᵉ full and whole tearme of fifty yeares Term. now next ensueing, and fully to be compleat and ended, they yᵉ sᵈ Mayor, Bayliffes and Burgesses Yielding and paying into yᵉ hands of yᵉ Receiver Genˡ of yᵉ sᵈ Dutchy of Lancaster for yᵉ use of her sᵈ Majesty her heirs or successors yᵉ yearly rent of six Pounds thirteen shillings and four pence Quit Rent. of lawfull money of England at yᵉ feaste dayes of St John yᵉ Baptist and our Lord Christ in every year by even and equal portions. . .

"And the sᵈ Queen's most excellent Majesty for and on yᵉ consideracons aforesᵈ and by the advice and consent of her Chancellor and Councell, hath given and granted unto the said Mayor &c. free lycence, full power Power to and absolute authority from time to time to demolish yᵉ remaining ruins of Demolish. yᵉ sᵈ late Castle or so much thereof as they shall think fitt and to levell and fill up yᵉ walls and ditches of yᵉ same, and to improve yᵉ sᵈ scite and soil thereof by building thereon, or by such other wayes as to them shall seem meet, and to convert towards such buildings or other improvemˢ the materials of yᵉ sᵈ late Castle without rendering any account to her Majesty for yᵉ same; yᵉ sᵈ demised p'missˢ and yᵉ buildings and other improvemˢ so by them to be made, to be set apart and appropriated towards providing yᵉ maintenance of yᵉ Rectors of yᵉ said new Church and Parochial Chappel within yᵉ sᵈ town of Liverpoole and their successors, according to yᵉ intent of yᵉ sᵈ recited Act, and to be applied to no other use or uses whatsoever to yᵉ p'judice thereof.

"And yᵉ sᵈ Queen's Majesty doth hereby direct and appoint William Lord Viscount Molyneux, now Constable of yᵉ sᵈ Castle by virtue of yᵉ sᵈ Constable. recited Letters Patent of yᵉ sᵈ late Queen Elizabeth, to take notice of this first demise and grant, and to give obedience thereunto and in all things conforme himselfe accordingly."

Then follow covenants to keep in repair the buildings so to be erected, Covenants.

and quietly to yield up possession at the end of the term. Should any proceedings be taken to dispute the Queen's title to the premises, the Mayor, Bayliffes, and Burgesses to defend the same at their own costs and charges.

"And y⁰ s⁴ Mayor &c. do further for themselves and their successors covenant with y⁰ s⁴ Queen's Majesty, that during the continuance of the lease they will apply the rents and profits towards making up the annual sum of Two Hundred Pounds charged upon the Town and Parish of Liverpoole by y⁰ s⁴ Act of Parlem¹ for y⁰ maintenance of and providing for the Rectors &c.

Grant to Rectors.

"And y⁰ s⁴ Mayor &c. further covenant that they will with what convenient speed the same may be done, build, erect and make, and keep in repair some convenient place or building within or upon y⁰ scite of y⁰ s⁴ late castle, or appropriate and sett apart one or more rooms in such other buildings as shall be by them erected, to contain and keep the arms, ammunition and other military stores for the publick use and service of y⁰ militia of y⁰ s⁴ County Palatine of Lancaster.

Armoury.

"Covenants for quiet possession on due fulfilment of conditions.

"Memorand" That on y⁰ first day of June 1705, the original lease, whereof y⁰ precedent is a true copy, was putt into y⁰ iron chest by Wm Hurst Esq pr'st Mayor Jasper Maudit Esq Alderman, Thomas Sweeting, and Mr Peter Hall, one of y⁰ p'sent Bayliffes of Liverpoole, the said lease being lately return'd from London, it being there enrolled."

Copy of Lease.

This lease, efficient as it seems, was but the commencement of a long course of litigation.

Tenants in Castle.

There were a considerable number of tenants claiming vested interests and refusing to be disturbed. A list is given, bearing date March 12th, 1706, from which it appears that there were 22 holdings, paying rents amounting to £21 2s. 3d., and eight tenancies with no rent attached.

"1706, May 8. Mr Ralph Peters (Town clerk) petitions for an order of Councell to save him and others harmlesse w⁰ relacōn to his acting in y⁰ turning out y⁰ inhabitants of y⁰ Castle, and for defraying y⁰ charg thereof, they moving now in y⁰ Queen's Bench therein.

"And that in case any Writts be brought by y⁰ Lord Molyneux or Mr Farrington against any person in respect to y⁰ title of y⁰ Castle, that some persons may be order'd to be Bail therein and be saved harmlesse and that y⁰ same be p'ceeded in as Councell shall advise at y⁰ town's charge. Agreed unto, and that a Rule be drawn against y⁰ next councell day."

"1706, June 5. Y⁰ Hon⁰¹⁰ Lord Viscount Molyneux having spoak to Mr Mayor twice to have a meeting about the Castle.

CORPORATE ESTATE AND REVENUES. 37

"Mem—to speak about y⁰ Castle and meeting Lord Molyneux. The Councell requests Mr Mayor to take such of y⁰ Aldermⁿ with him as hee thinks fitt to discourse wth my Lord Molyneux about y⁰ Castle, and consent to be determined with wh^t Mr Mayor and y⁰ s^d Ald^n concludes on, relating to y⁰ same." *Dispute with Lord Molyneux.*

"1706, Sept. 4. Mem. it's concluded by Mr Mayor, Ald^n and Councell That my Ld Molyneux is to be mett on Monday next at two of y⁰ clock in y⁰ afternoone at y⁰ Alehouse next Derby Chappell by y⁰ persons following viz Mr Mayor, Wm Clayton Esq, Thos Johnson Esq, Ald^n Tho. Tyrer, Ald^n Cuthbert Sharples, Ald^n John Cleveland, and Mr. Jno Seacome to attend them." *Meeting.*

Lord Molyneux, as hereditary Constable of the Castle, claimed an interest in the rents and profits.

1706. Pursuant to the order of May 8th, the Town Clerk took measures to eject the occupants of the Castle, and obtained orders from the magistrates to that effect. The result is told in the following report :—

"1706, Octr. 29. The case of y⁰ Corporacon of Liverpoole relating to Her Majest's Grant of Castle.

"Upon y⁰ Grant several tenants of and in the Castle have attorn'd to y⁰ Corporacon. But some who are poor and likely to become chargable stand out, and y⁰ Lord Molyneux (or Mr Farrington, who claims under him) p'tend a right, and encourage those tenants to pay y⁰ rent to them, or one of them. *Ejecting Tenants.*

"That y⁰ said persons (being poor) the Corporacon removed them to the several places of their settlement as by law they ought.

"That those persons since made affidavit against y⁰ Justices of Peace who sign'd y⁰ orders for removall, Ralph Peters, y⁰ Overseers of y⁰ Poor, y⁰ Constables, and severall others, and moved in the Queen's Bench to have indictm^ts of Riott against them.

"But on setting forth y⁰ whole matter, the Rule they had obtain'd for Indictm^ts (unlesse cause shewn) was sett aside.

"But y⁰ Court order'd y⁰ s^d poor persons to be restored to their possession wch accordingly was done. *Tenants restored.*

"Note—y⁰ orders (as are alledg'd) are defective, for y^t in y⁰ adjudging part of y⁰ order y⁰ Justices of y⁰ Peace have not adjudg'd y⁰ persons to be poor, tho' in y⁰ former part it is said that it appears to them that y⁰ s^d persons are poor &c. But y⁰ Court of Queen's Bench did on y⁰ hearing declare, it ought to be in y⁰ adjudging part.

"That y⁰ Lord Molyneux did in Septemb^r or Octob last desire a *Conference.*

conference, and (as understood) desir'd time to consider of y⁰ proposals made him in behalfe of y⁰ Corporacon.

"That in November, (y⁰ beginning of Mich'm' tearme last) Writts were issued ag' Mr Webster, Ralph Peters, and several others, at the suit of Porter, Green and Lucas, but that not any declarations therein are filed; tho' it's believed it is for breaking and entring into their houses or roomes to remove them, and (as presumed) is prosecuted by y⁰ Lord Molyneux or his order.

Certioraries. "That *certioraries* are brought to remove y⁰ orders made for removall of these poor persons; and they expect to sett y⁰ orders aside next tearme in y⁰ Queen's Bench.

"That it is advisable y⁰ Corporacon take some methods to enforce y⁰ possession of y⁰ Castl' and establish y⁰ title thereof by law. In order to which Councell advise,

"That in case y⁰ s⁰ Porter, Green and Lucas declare for breaking and entring into their houses, the title may be brought in question on these actions. But since they have not (as yet) fyled any declaracons and y⁰ time for serving ejectm'ᵗˢ being now at hand, in order to bring y⁰ matter on next Assizes, y⁰ declaration is now before Councell to be setled.

"It is therefore pray'd y⁰ direction of Mr Mayor Ald'ⁿ Baylives and Comon Councell what proceedings shall be made therein, and that y⁰ persons sued may be saved harmlesse, and their charges reimbursed.

"Which shall be duly and punctually observ'd by

"Y'ʳ obed' serv'

"y⁰ 8 Januar, 1706." "Ra: Peters.

Ejection. "It is order'd in Councell, That y⁰ persons sued shall be indemnified, and that proper methods may be taken about ejection &c."

"1706, Mar. 25. Sylvester Moorcroft Mayor.

Negociations "This Councell doth order. That if any proposals be made by y⁰ Lord Molyneux for an accomodation or agreem' about y⁰ Castle, that Mr Mayor, Ald'ⁿ Cuthbert Sharples, Rich'ᵈ Norris Esq, Alderman John Cockshutte, Ald'ᵐ Jno Clieveland, Mr Thos Coore and Mr Jno Seacome have powr to compromise y⁰ matter with y⁰ Lord Molyneux, and what they shall do y⁰ Councell do unanimously consent unto."

Orders. "1707, June 4. It is order'd at this assembly that Mr Mayor and such of the Councell as shall think fitt to appeare—meet in the Comon Hall of this Burrough every Wednesday at five o'clock in y⁰ afternoon to determine and settle matters relateing to y⁰ castle and its improvem' Whose orders and agreem'ˢ to be effectuall and vallid except made by a lesse number than seven att the least of the Councell."

1707. A long statement of the circumstances was now prepared, of which the following is an abstract:—

CORPORATE ESTATE AND REVENUES. 39

"The Corporation haveing obtain'd a Grant or lease of the old Castle from her Maj[tie] for fifty yeares under the yearly rent of six pounds thirteen shillings and four pence dated ye 5th day of March 1704—did on the 16th of the same month by warrant of attorney, deputé Ralph Peters to make an entry therein, which accordingly was done the 17th of the same month, and most of the tenants attorned and became tenants to the Corporation, —but about 5 or 6 poor families claimed under the Lord Molyneux's title and would not attorn; for the Lord Molyneux and his ancestors (haveing for many yeares been constables of the said Castle by a grant thereof from the crowne) claymed not only the said office, but the soile thereof and all the buildings thereon, and enjoy'd the same except when the crown had occasion for it, and in King Charles the 2[ads] time had orders or Warr[ts] for the immediate slighting the said castle and demolishing so farr the outworks thereof, as thereby to render it untenable for the future, and to take the stones, timber and materialls to his own use and accordingly some of the walls were pull'd down. . . But not many of the Outwalls being pull'd down, in King William's time, the L[d] Macclesfield being then L[d] Livetenn[t] of the County Pallatine of Lancaster, had a grant of the Castle and buildings or the Constableshipp, and took possession thereof, and sett, lett, and held them to his own use ag[t] the Lord Molyneux. But immediately after his death, which was about November A͞no D͞n͞i 1701, the present Lord Molyneux made an entry into the Castle, and made a grant thereof to William Farrington Esq for life, and then sev[r]all tenn[ts] or most of them all, became tenn[ts.] to Mr Farrington; but L[d] Molyneux rec[d] the rentes. [*Statement of Proceedings.*]

"The Castle being esteem'd a privileged place, severall persons of divers trades gott into it and follow'd their trades there to the great p'judice of the Burghers and freemen of the Corporation. And when any of them became poor or chargeable, they were usually remov'd into or charg'd upon the parish of Walton (whereof Liverpoole formerly was part). But in the year 1700, Liverpoole becomeing a parish of it selfe, distinct from Walton by Act of Parliam[t] (tho' the Lord Molyneux did all that in him lay to hinder the same, the Corporation paying him a valluable consideration for his interest as Patron) the Corporation then conceiving that the inhabitants of the castle (if poor) would be chargeable to their parish did att their Quarter Sessions p'sent the inhabitants of the castle who were likely to become chargeable as inmates, and seva'll times sumoned them before the Justices of Peace and acquainted them they were so p'sented. [*Difficulties.*]

"And perticularly one Green, Edward and William Porter, Lucas, Balshaw, and one Pilsbury and their families and order'd them to depart; but they obstinately refuseing, the Justices, upon the Overseers of the poor's compl[t] as the law directs, made orders for removall of them to the respective places of their last legall settlem[t], upon notice of which Pilsbury remov'd but the rest still refus'd, so that on the 16th day of April 1706 the Overseers executing the orders made by the Justices remov'd some [*Resistance.*]

Proceedings. peaceably, but Green being absconded, his wife, as also Lucas and Edwd Porter lock'd themselves upp in their respective rooms, and would not suffer the Overseers to remove them, but on the contrary threaten'd the officers, upon which the Overseers applied to the Mayor and Jasper Maudit Esq for assistance, and they with Wm Clayton and Thos Johnson Esqrs and sev'all others went allong to the Castle to see the peace kept; then the orders were sev'ally read att their respective doors and demand made that they would open the doors and suffer themselves to be remov'd; but they then refused and their doors were broke down and the said sev'all families remov'd and new locks putt on.

" Whereupon the Lord Viscount Molyneux, to be vexatious (for tho' the names of these poor persons were used, yet all the trouble was created and carried on att his charge, who had all allong been very troublesome to the Corporation by incourageing poor persons and papists to come into the Castle and exercise their trades there, tho' not free of the Corporation nor had any settlem^t therein) caus'd a Motion to be made in the Queen's Bench and obtain'd rules of that court ag^t Mr Mayor, the Justices and others that were in the castle at the time of removeing those poor persons . . . to show cause why informations should not be exhibited

Riot. against them for a riott, they haveing suggested to the Court that the said removall of these poor persons was only to get possession (which indeed was thereby intended) tho' the Corporation was ready and willing that the Tytle might be settled by a tryall at law; whereupon severall affidavits were made setting forth the true matter of fact, and on reading them and on the motion of Sr Edward Northy, his Maj^{ties} Attorney Gen'all who was of Councell for the Corporation, the said rule was discharged and another was made that they should be restor'd to their possession which accordingly was offer'd to them. But notwithstanding that rule some of them being remov'd to Manchester, that town contested the settlem^t of them there, and the Corporation on the tryall made good the orders and had the same confirm'd at the Gen'all Quarter Sessions for this County held at Ormskirke.

Actions of Trespass. " Soon after, Green, Lucas and Porter brought actions of trespass against Mr Mayor, the Overseers of the Poor and several others concern'd, which comeing on to be tryed att Lancaster Assizes in Augt 1707, appear'd to be vexatious. A proposall was made in court that all those actions of trespass should cease and each side bear their own costs, which was made a rule of Court.

" The Corporation to putt an end to these troubles and disputes having brought actions of ejectment . . Copys of all the grants and tytle the Lord Molyneux claim'd by, being upon search by Ralph Peters, then att London found; it may not be improper to record the same, that if any more disputes should hereafter happen relateing thereto, the like trouble and charge may be prevented."

Here follows a voluminous record of all the documents *Documents.*
relating to the Castle from the time of Edward III. down to
the recent lease from Queen Anne, which had been referred
by the Privy Council, on petition, to the law officers of the
Crown, with the following result :—

" 1. That notwithstanding the hereditary Constableship granted to the
ancestors of Lord Molyneux, the site and soil of the Castle were beyond *Results.*
all question her Majesty's inheritance, reserving to Lord Molyneux the
annual payment of £6 13s. 4d. as the wages of his office.

" 2. That the proposed lease to the Corporation would be a benefit to
the Crown and an advantage to the Corporation.

" The Corporation thereupon were permitted to enter peaceably into
possession."

" 1708. James Earl of Derby Mayor.

"Jany. 7. Order'd that Mr John Seacome have the Castle Street Tower *Tower.*
of the old Castle, where the gates were, paying £26 18 according to the
valuation."

" 1709, Jany. 6. John Seacome Mayor.

" Order'd that Mr Mayor have power to compound with Edwd and
Willm Porter, now prisoners att Lancaster for costs of suite in the late *Costs of Suit.*
actions of ejectment, wherein they became defendants for some part of the
late castle within this Corporations and for the mesne profitts of their
respective parts from the time of the entry made thereinto by the Corporation on the Queen's grant untill the verdict obtain'd ag^t them; it being
made appeare that they are poor and in a starveing condicon.

" It is also order'd that Mr Mayor with the assistance and advice of
some of the Councell not less than four, have power to pull down, alter, *Taking down*
and make such additionall improvem^{ts} in and about the late Castle as shall *Castle.*
be thought convenient; and to sett and lett the same for the most profitt
and advantage. The charge whereof to be deducted and allowed out of
the growing rents of the said Castle and appurtenances."

1709, July 4th. The Lord Lieutenant (James, Earl of
Derby), by his warrant, empowered the Deputy Lieutenant

" to enter into some room or rooms within Liverpool Castle where the
County Arms are (the keys being lost or mislayd) and to take an inventory
thereof, and deliver the arms, amunicion &c therein to the worpp^{ll} Mr *Arms and*
Mayor and Comon Councill of this burrough or such persons as they shall *Ammunition.*
appoint who is to be answerable for the same.

" It is thereupon Order'd by this assembly, that Ralph Peters the town
clerk be empowered to give a receipt for the same, and that this Corpora-

tion do henceforth undertake the safe keeping thereof during such time as the Governm^t please.

"Which warrant being brought by Mr Richd Edge of Middlehilton Gent; Sr Thomas Johnson, Richd Norris and Jon^a Blackburn Esqrs proceeded thereon and deliver'd the arms accordingly."

"1718. Richard Kelsall Mayor.

Round Tower.

"It is order'd that the tenants in the Round Tower in the late Castle have notice to remove, and that the Ground be levell'd with all convenient speed, the Councill being of opinion that it will be proper to erect the church there."

This is the final record, with which the history of the Castle terminates, after an existence of five hundred years.

Market.

The Corporation having obtained a lease of the Castle and its precincts, immediate steps were taken to establish a market on a portion of the site left open, and called Derby Square. The original market was held at the High Cross, and partially at the White Cross, the intersection of Tithebarn and Oldhall Streets.

1709.

The site of the market could not be removed without a patent from the Crown, which was obtained in 1709, the reception of which is thus recorded :—

"1709, June 2. John Seacome Mayor

Patent for Market.

"The Pattent for the new Markett being obtain'd this month, the same being brought down by Warrington Coachman [1] to Warrington, was fetch'd thence by Mr Baylife Wainwright and Ra. Peters, and accompany'd into town by Mr Mayor and a great number of the Ald^n and Gent^n of the town, the streets being lyn'd by the Honble Leivetenn^t Gen'all Gorge's regim^t of soldiers, who then lay att Liverpoole waiting for a wind to embark for Ireland the 16th day of June 1709 ; and being read in the Comon Hall is lodg'd in the Town's Chest."

The market was established, but for some years was conducted in rather an irregular way.

The next record is as follows :—

1723.

"1723, Nov 6. John Scarisbrick Mayor.

"Whereas an order hath been drawn up for settling the New Markett

---

[1] At this time the London Coach only came as far as Warrington, the road from thence to Liverpool being impassable for carriages until 1760.

in Derby square, and for removing the retailers of Grocerys and Hardware and all their stalls out of that Markett, and for restraining the hucksters from buying and selling again in the same Markett, and has been perus'd by Mr Recorder and hath now been read and is approv'd. It is therefore order'd by this Councill that only butter, cheese, pottatoes, fowles, eggs, bacon and other sorts of victualls (except butchers' meat) shall be retail'd in that Markett, and that Mr Mayor be requested to grant his warrant to the Baylives to see that this order be obey'd and perform'd." Market. Regulations.

The butchers, here prohibited from selling meat in the market, had their shambles in High Street, on a site now occupied by the north wing of the Town Hall. Shambles.

"1723, Mar. 4. It being represented that an improvem' may be made att the upper end of the shambles by erecting and makeing seventeen shops for shoemakers, and Mr. Bayliffe Shaw proposeing to build them and find all for sixty Pounds, he is now order'd to doe them with all convenient speed."

"1724, June 3. Mr Thos Moss petitioning that there may not be any shops built so near as to hurt his windows or darken the lights of his house in the shambles, which were agreed to on the granting the liberty of a passage thro' the Woolpack into Water Street. The same is referred to Mr Mayor and Baylives[a]" Shops.

In 1715 a dispute arose respecting the tolls on fish and potatoes sold in the market. 1715. Fish and Potatoes.

Under a lease of 1678, the Tarleton family held the fish yards and market at the foot of Chapel Street, with power to levy tolls on all fish and potatoes or other roots there sold. This the lessees interpreted as giving a right to tolls on fish and potatoes sold elsewhere. The proceedings are recorded as follows :—

"1715, May 4. Richard Gildart Mayor.

"A dispute having arose whether Mr Tarleton is intituled by virtue of the present lease to the tolls of fish and potatoes brought to other places in the town and there utter'd and sold, or only of all fish and potatoes sold Tolls of Fish.

---

[a] In Chadwick's map of 1724 the Shambles are shown, and in Eyes's map of 1725 the passage in question is added.
The Shambles were removed about 1803, and transferred to Cable Street and South Castle Street, where they remained until about 1865.

att the fish house. The same is referr'd to Mr Mayor, Ald^n Coore and Ald^n Norris, to treat and settle the same with such persons as Mr Tarleton will nominate, and report their proceed^s next Councill day."

The dispute went on for several years, and we find the following entry:—

"1719, Octr. 7. Josia Poole Mayor.

Fish House. "Order'd That a lease be granted to Mr Edwd Tarleton of the fish house and the tolls of all roots brought thither, for two lives, to one life and 21 yeares in being, but as there has been a dispute whether the toll of roots brought to any other part of the town was intended by the present lease to be granted, and under which he claims the toll of all roots brought to any other Markett in town, therefore the toll of roots sold att the Fish *Restrictions.* house Markett is only order'd to be now granted, and the toll of any other place is not hereafter to be granted on any terms whatever, and if Mr Tarleton will accept of such new lease and surrenders the present lease, it is order'd that he have these two lives added gratis."

Ingates and Outgates. Another source of income was derived from the ingates and outgates, which were a sort of octroi levied on all carts with articles of food and provender passing in and out of the town. From these dues, Formby, Altcar, Prescot, and some other villages were exempt by prescriptive right.

In 1701 the dues were leased at £14 ₱ ann. In 1708 they were raised to £20.

In 1709, Octr. 5th, Nicholas Longworth petitions to have the Ingates and Outgates for £25 ₱ an.

"It is order'd to be sett the 13th instant to the highest bidder, and accordingly it was sett to him for £25 ₱ an. he paying halfe a yeare's rent aforehand."

"1710, Sept. 6. Nich^s Longworth peticons that he may have the ingates and outgates another year. It is a very hard rent, and sev^r'all tolls justly due to the Corporation have been withheld from him by sev'all persons.

"But will pay the same rent if ye Councell will not please to order an abatem^t"

"1714, Apl. 7. A complaint being made that the Collector of the Ingates and Outgates takes two pence from ev'y forreigner's cart bringing in freemen's goods, which they haveing also inspected into, doe find justly due.

Toll on Hides "It is therefore order'd, That the same be insisted on, and also the small toll for ev'y hide sold here.

CORPORATE ESTATE AND REVENUES. 45

"The said Collector complaining that Mr. Tarleton insists upon and takes toll for all potatoes brought to other places in town as well as at the Markett att the Fish house, it is now order'd — Potatoes.

"That the order made 17th Aprill 1700 be reviv'd."

The Corporation, in maintaining their dues and monopolies, were subject to continual attacks from all quarters.

"1708, Jany. 7. James Earl of Derby Mayor.

"Some persons who have farmed Hilbree (island) alledging themselves to be citizens of London, and as such exempt from Town's dutys; and the cheife of them being att Hillbree and not in the City of London, so that he is not a Citizen. It is therefore order'd, that Mr. Bryan Dawney doe take the Town's Duty of all rock salt goeing to Hillbree and insist thereof, and he be sav'd harmless therein by the Corporation." — Claims of Exemption.

Here is a reminiscence of the plague, which desolated the town several times in the 16th and 17th centuries. — Plague.

"1707, Augt. 5. Ja. Brookes Mason, petitions y' he may have some reasonable satisfaction for ye loss of ye herbage in Sickman's Lane by reason of ye new Well, for he has formerly sett it for 10^s and 12^s ℔ ann. and this last year he lost ye whole p'fitts of it, and he is still lay'd and tax'd for it.

"Order y^t James Brookes be not taxed for Sickman's Lane for ye future."

There are several records of moneys given and bequeathed to the Corporation for charitable purposes, which seem to have been forgotten and become obsolete. — Bequests.

"1706, July 16. Will. Webster Mayor.

"Memo^r Mr James Scarisbrick has one hundred Pounds by him wch hee is willing to let ye Corporacōn have, paying him intrest during his life, and hee be oblig'd to give ye same to ye Corporacōn (for ye use of ye poor) after his decease; ye Councell accepts of ye same according to ye proposal, and ye Corporacōn is to allow five ℔ cent for ye money during his own life. — Scarisbrick.

This is confirmed on the 4th Sept., with the proviso that the fund shall be disposed of by the Mayor and the Rectors.

"1706, Sept. 4. The Rev^d Mr Robt Styth and ye Rev^d Mr Henry Richmond desires y^t ye fiftie pounds left by ye late Madam Richmond for repairing ye Almshouses (ye late Doctor Richmond her husband left) may be putt into ye Corporacōn's hands, ye Corporacōn (in this Councell) have determin'd to take it into their hands at five ℔ cent." — Richmond.

"1717, May 15. Old Capt. Tarleton haveing left by Will the sume of Fifty Pounds, the interest whereof is directed to be distributed to and — Tarleton.

amongst poor sailors' widows, in Liverpool three fourth parts, and one fourth part to the poor of Walton, and that the sume being now putt into the Corporation Stock. It is order'd that a deed be pass'd under the Corporation Seale to the Rector of Walton for the time being and his successor for the paym' thereof accordingly."

Down to the time of the construction of the Old Dock, in 1709-15, the money transactions of the Corporation were conducted in a very primitive fashion. The money was deposited in a town's chest, with five locks, held by the Mayor and other officials. Money was occasionally taken up at interest and repaid, but there were no banking facilities nearer than London.

Town Chest.

"1709, Decr. 8. John Earle Mayor.

Grant to Dock.

"Five hundred Pounds is order'd to be given towards making the Dock in such manner as shall hereafter be order'd by this assembly out of the Corporacon stock or to be taken upp for that purpose."

Money was borrowed by giving a bond under seal.

After the completion of the Dock, the amount of indebtedness having grown to a large sum, a better system of finance was adopted.

"1720, June 3. Thos Fillingham Mayor.

Loan.

"Mr Mayor having now Comunicated to this Councell that a gentleman in London will lend the Corporation twelve thousand pounds att interest on certain condicons, haveing security under the Corporacon Seale by way of Mortgage of all the Corporation lands, Town Customs, Rents on Leases, Shambles, and all other rents (except the Castle) and also of the fund on tunage ariseing by and out of the Dock Duties. It is order'd that Mr Mayor be requested to doe what is proper and needful therein for obtaining the said sume, takeing advice and care that the covenants be proper and in the manner and method of repaying the same as the profits and incomes yearly arise, &c. A copy of the Charters &c to be sent by the town clerk."

TRADE AND COMMERCE.

The most important event relating to trade and commerce during this period was the construction of the first dock, now Dock. a thing of the past, long ago filled up and the site covered with public buildings; but in its day the cradle of the commerce of the port, and the commencement of the largest system of floating docks in the world.

As the commerce of Liverpool went on increasing in the early years of the 18th century, the accommodation in the Harbour. old harbour or pool became altogether insufficient; ships had to be exposed in the open roadstead, at great risk and inconvenience. In 1701 a stringent set of rules was framed for the regulation of the vessels entering.

Further steps were soon taken.

"1708, Novr. 3. Jno Seacome Mayor.

"Order'd that Sr Thomas Johnson and Richard Norris Esq, the representatives in Parliam^t for this Corporation (being now goeing to Parliam^t) be desir'd and impower'd to treat with and agree for a proper person to come to this town, and view the ground, and draw a plan of the intended Dock."

"1709, Mar. 7. Jno Seacome Mayor.

"One Henry Huss of Derby in Derbishire who comes to survey the Huss Survey. place where to make a dock with Mr Sorocold and draw a plan and estimate of the charge thereof, is admitted free of this Corporacon gratis. But this is not to be a President.

The plan recommended by this gentleman appears to have been that of opening out and deepening the stream which fed the pool, and forming a canal for shipping along what is now Canal. Paradise Street.

"1709, April 13. Wm Bibby petitioning for a lease of the Ground Lease of allong the intended canal between Cable Street end and Thomas Street Land.

end. It is order'd that the same be viewed and that Mr Mayor be requested to take allong with him such of the Councell as he shall think fitt and make report thereof to this assembly next Councell day."

This plan however was not carried out.
We next read :—

Site for Dock. "1709, Octr. 5. It being propounded in Councell that pursuant to an order of this assembly of the third day of November last, a person was agreed with by Sr Thomas Johnson and Richd Norris Esq, who hath view'd the ground wherein is intended the makeing a convenient Dock for the safety of shipps and that a Plan thereof being made, it is conceiv'd that about the sume of six thousand pounds will make and perfect a convenient dock; and that a dock, being highly necessary for the safety of all shipps as well belonging to this Port as to others tradeing to and from the same; It is Order'd and enacted by this assembly that the ground as now sett out or to be sett out be, and is hereby granted and sett apart for a convenient dock for ever. And that the said Sr Thomas Johnson and Richd Norris Esq be requested and are hereby impower'd to obtain (this Petition for ensueing session of Parliam^t) such an Act of Parliam^t for the raising of a sufficient fund for the same, and the makeing and perfecting a convenient dock by such meanes and methods and with such clauses powers and limitations as shall be pray'd directed and agreed on by the merch^ts and owners of this Corporation at a gen'all meeting to be called and had hereafter for that purpose."

Opposition. An Act of Parliament was accordingly obtained, not, however, without opposition. Their old opponents, the cheesemongers of London, who maintained a line of trading vessels to London, which took in their cargoes on the Cheshire side of the Mersey, objected to paying dues for a dock which they could not use. The opposition, however, was unavailing. The Act (8 Anne, chap. 12) authorised the construction, and constituted the Mayor, Bailiffs, and Council the Trustees, with power to borrow £6,000, and to levy dock dues on all ships entering the harbour.

The next stage is indicated by the following record :—

"1710, May 17. John Earle Esqr Mayor.
Proceedings "Att a special Council held this 17th May 1710. The Act of Parliam^t in Council. obtain'd the last sessions of Parliam^t by the managem^t of Sr Thomas

TRADE AND COMMERCE. 49

Johnson and Rd Norris Esq' pursuant of the fifth day of October last, now brought and read for the makeing a Wett Dock or Bason, for the preservation not only of Merch' shipps but also of her Maj'^{ties} Shipps of Warr, being this day taken into consideration, and the Worpp^ll the Mayor Alderm^n Bayl' and Comon Councill being therein nominated, appointed and made Trustees for the ordering and makeing such Dock or Bason. It is resolved *Nemine Contradicente* by the May^r Ald^n, Bayl' and Comon Councill in Councill assembled—That they will proceed to the makeing of the said Dock or Bason in and upon the ground (part of the town's waste) formerly granted in the said Act mencon'd, and as now sett out by Mr Thomas Steers of the City of London, who is brought down on purpose and has Thos. Steers. survey'd and stak'd out the same nearer to the sea than sett out before. And it is order'd and enacted that the said parcel of ground be and remain to such use for ever and to no other use or purpose whatsoever. And that the thanks of this assembly be and is hereby given to Sr Thomas Johnson and Richd Norris Esq for their good service therein.

"And also Order'd that the orders touching the Dock be kept in a book for that purpose by Ralph Peters, Town clerk who is hereby appointed and Peters, Town made clerk therein." Clerk.

"1710, July 5. Further Acts and orders of the same Assembly before the Worp^ll John Earle Esq' Mayor, Francis Goodrick and Henry Taylor Gen. Bayl'.

"Whereas this Corporation hath by their Order of Councill of the eighth day of Decemb^r last, Order'd that any sume or sumes of money not exceeding five hundred pounds be given towards the intended Dock and other works, and that the buoying out of Formby Channell is highly necessary, but the same interfareing with the power of Trinity House, it was not contain'd or granted in the Act of Parliam^t for makeing a dock, so that the charge thereof is not provided for by the said Act.

"It is now order'd that as much as shall be found necessary for the buoying out that Channell shall be had out of that sume so order'd, and Buoying that the same be layd as the managers for the Dock shall from time to Channel. time direct and order."

The name of Thomas Steers is first mentioned in this Steers. record. There is no doubt that to him is due the idea of the floating dock, with lock gates, instead of the canal previously proposed. He settled in Liverpool, where he had a long and prosperous career.

In addition to being the engineer for the Dock, he was appointed Harbour Master. He was also the architect for the erection of St. George's Church. He became a member

G

of the Council, and in 1739 was elected Mayor. He built for himself a handsome stone-fronted mansion in Hanover Street, which in later years became the Branch Bank of England.

Dock opened. The Dock was opened for the admission of vessels on the 31st August, 1715, but was not fully completed at the time.

"1716, Jan. 25. Foster Cunliffe, Mayor.
"Order'd that the Act of Parliam^t for prolonging the time granted by the present Act of Parliam^t for makeing the Dock be prepar'd, and that the Town clerk consult our Members of Parliam^t therein and take such advice of Councill as shall be thought useful."

Second Act. This resulted in the second Dock Act (3rd George I., ch. 1), by which an additional sum of £4,000 was authorised to be raised towards the completion, and the proceeds of the sales of land around the Dock to be similarly applied.

"1717, May 15. Order'd that Mr. Mayor have power to contract with *Landmarks.* Mr Mollinex of Mossborough for ground to build the Landmarks on at Formby for direction of ships comeing into Formby Channell."

1717. "1717, Octr. 10. . . . Then elected Mr Thomas Steers Master of *Dock Master.* attendants or Dock Master, to take care of the Dock and the cleansing of it when and as occasion shall require, and shall be agreed with him hereafter; and of the buoys and Land Marks that are or shall be plac'd and made for direction of ships into the Harbour upon such terms as shall be agreed with him.

"Mem. Mr. Steers's sallary as Dock Master is agreed to be £20 $\wp$ ann from y^e Corporation, and £30 $\wp$ ann from the Dock—£50.

Braddock, Assistant. ". . . Then elected Mr Wm Braddock assistant to Mr Steers, and to perform the office of Water Bayliffe. Mr Braddock's sallary £10 $\wp$ ann from y^e Corp^n and all the Water Bayliffe's perquisitts."

The Dock was very soon found too small for the requirements.

"1718, Decr. 10. Josia Poole Mayor.
Addition to Dock. "Order'd that Mr Steers draw a plan of the intended addition to the Dock Southwards and lay it before the Councill with his opinion thereon, and discourse with Mr Thomas Hurst and the other proprietors of grounds there about it and if any alteration happen in the lives in the leases to Mr Hurst, the Councill will consider it and view and plan the ground eastwards, and consider whether will be most comodious and report his opinion thereon next Councill day.

"Order'd that Mr Mayor be desir'd to request our members of Parliam¹ to forward the petition before the Treasury for making the Dock a place of dispatch and to extend the limitts of our Port thereto." _{Extension of Port.}

The affairs of the Corporation relating to the Dock at this time did not run altogether smoothly. There were, as usual, discontented persons who criticised their proceedings very keenly, and it appears, from the documents, very unfairly. The following entry refers to this :— _{Disputes.}

"1719, Decr. 2. Order'd that Ald⁴ Squire and Mr Isaac Green be desir'd to goe to London to attend and assist in the sollicitation for an Act of Parliam¹ for makeing the river Weaver navigable in concert with our members of Parliam¹ att the charge of the Corporation, and to obtain the charge of fortifying the town in the late rebellion now before the Treasury and Mr Mayor to write to our members thereon." _{River Weaver.}

"1720, Aug. 3. It is propounded that it is highly necessary that a draught or chart be taken of the entrance into this river thro' Formby Channell, and of all the banks that lye off, and of the bearing of the buoys from the Land Marks. _{Chart of Channel.}

"Whereas great complaints are made that the cawsey on the North side of the Dock is so low that the tyde overflows it into the adjacent cellars to the great damage of the tenⁿᵗˢ. It is now Order'd that the same be speedily rais'd att the charge of the Trustees of the Dock and that the watercourse and channell att the bottom of Pool Lane which is a great anoyance to the wharfe and Dock be alter'd and turn'd down the street called King Street or George Street into the comon shore." _{Overflow of Dock.}

"1720, Octr. 13. Thomas Fillingham Mayor.

"Whereas a most unjust insinuation and groundless protest is privately dispers'd and handed about to and amongst the Burgesses and Freemen of this burrough, as if all the Comon Councill (except a few of them) call'd and represented therein by the style of a Sett of men, have sold the Dock to themselves and all the strand, in manifest breach of their trust ; And Whereas the Worpp¹ the Mayor, Sʳ Thomas Johnson, Ald⁴ George Tyrer and others of this Council att a meeting had on Friday night the seventh instant, did offer and propose that in case any other person or persons would within three months propose a better Scheme or method of paying off the debts contracted on account of makeing the Dock, or give more for the publick benefitt of the Corporation than had been offer'd by the undertakers the 16ᵗʰ day of August last, the order made that day, to be sett aside if this Councill thought fitt, and that none might be impos'd on therein nor any person concern'd misrepresented—Publick notice hath been given that ev'y person that is minded to give more or make any other _{Council Proceedings.}

proposalls may have liberty so to doe. This Councill doth entirely agree thereto, and give six months time to receive any new proposall."

The Water Bailiff's office proved more lucrative than was expected, which led to a revision of the appointment of Mr. Thos. Steers as Dock Master.

Dock Master and Water Bailiff.

" 1724, Aug. 12. John Scarisbrick Mayor.
" It being propounded that Mr Thos Steers doe take upon him both the place of Dock master and Water Bayliff (except executing of warrants and attending upon Mr Mayor which he is to find a Dep^y to doe and perform) from the tenth day of October next, and that Mr Steers to have all the perquisitts and fees belonging to the office of Water Bayliffe, but no sallary for either place from the Corporation, and to pay thereout to Mr Wm Braddock in consideration of his resigning the office of Water Bayliffe which he now holds, the yearly sume of twenty five pounds quarterly by equal porcons, and to allow his dep^y the benefitt of the fees for executeing all warrants, and on admissions of freemen and what further they shall agree on.

" It is now order'd that Mr Steers be appointed accordingly Dock Master and Water Bayliffe from the tenth day of October next on the terms and condicons above mention'd.

Ship Building.

The improvement of the harbour led to the development of ship building, of which there are incidental notices.

" 1724, Octr. 16. Capt Nicholas Webb who hath built a large ship at this town by recomendacon of our representative in Parliam^t Thomas Bootle Esq, and laid out considerable sumes of money and haveing agreed to take some lead upon freight from Wales, which he runs the risque of hither by boat rather than take his ship to fetch it or load from thence, and now haveing the honour to be a freeman of this burrough, prays that he may be excus'd the town's custom for such lead; and this Councill takeing into consideration the said p'mises, doe hereby order that the town's custom must be paid, but the town's treasurer is now order'd to return the same to Captn Webb again."

Blowing up Rocks.

" 1724. It being represented to this Councill that a proposall is made to blow up two great stones that lye just att the edge of the Channell into Bowmaris, (where many of our ships are frequently putt into) over against Penmon within Priestholme island, which are dangerous to vessells putting in there, and have by strikeing upon one of them been oversett; the greater of which stones is called Maen Wen Penmon, and are adry only on spring tydes, if this Corp^n will contribute some gunpowder;

"It is now order'd that the Treasurer doe send thirty pounds weight of gunpowder, and seven pounds in cash for the purpose aforesaid, and be allowed the whole in his accounts."

The export of salt, brought down from Cheshire, formed an important part of the export trade. The following notice relates thereto:— *Salt.*

"1706, Feby. 7. Sylvester Moorcroft Mayor.
"Whereas the Merchants in town have suffer'd or are likely to suffer considerably on acc^t of Salt not holding out in Ireland &c to what it takes in on this side; Mr Ralph Peters is sent up to London to sollicite ye s^d affair, in order to get some deficiencies amended of ye s^d Act. It is Order'd in Councill, that the Corporacon do allow twenty pounds out of its comon stock towards ye s^d charg; ye salt trade being so very beneficial to ye Corporacon, and y^t ye money be lodged in ye hands of Wm Clayton Esq and Thomas Johnson Esq their representatives in Parliam^t." *Salt to Ireland.*

The restrictions and penalties on non-freemen attempting to trade were continued with increased rigour.

Thus we find:—

"1710, Octr. 30. George Tyrer Mayor.
"The persons hereafter nam'd are p'sented for exercising their respective trades following within this Corporation not being free:— *Restrictions on Trade*

Wm Cragg	Joyner	Thos Fawcett	Clockmaker
Geo Anderton	Weaver	Thurstan Fogg	Dyer
Jon^n Herford	Do	M Bernard	Upholsterer
Saml Bateman	Do	Thos Turner	Translator
Hen. Holt	Do	Josh Wimsley	Do"
Dorothy Euston	Do		

The number of weavers mentioned is rather remarkable, since it implies that there must have been a considerable number of Freemen weavers, to whom these outsiders caused umbrage. *Weavers.*

The idea that persons could not be allowed to translate a document without being a Freeman, is somewhat grotesque.

"1712, July 2. James Townsend Mayor.
"Att a Councill &c.
"It is order'd that the Town clerk doe prosecute all persons that

CHAP. I, A.D. 1702—1727.

Prosecuting Non-Freemen inhabitt and keep shops within this town and exercise trades within the same not being free, in such manner as the Recorder shall advise and direct, and to comence and prosecute actions att law against such persons in the name of the Mayor, Baylives and Burgesses of this burrough, at the charge of this Corporation.

Children of Freemen. "And it is declar'd that the children of all such freemen as doe not inhabit within this town ought not to be admitted to follow and exercise any trade within the town upon a seperate stock, distinct or seperate from their father's stock.

"Order'd That all persons who live in town and follow any trade or business within this burrough and use the faculty of freemen not being free, shall be oblig'd to pay Quarteridge, otherwise to be prosecuted for such offence as by law they may."

"1724, Nov. 4. John Goodwin Mayor.

"Mr Daniel Birchall Jun. haveing laid before this Councill a petition setting forth that Mr John Hopkins a bookseller who is a forreigner is likely to come to this town without haveing any lycense or leave so to doe and publickly retails all sorts of books, paper &c in great quantities upon the week day, encouraged by Mr Peter Whitfield, a freeman of this town, and uses the faculty of a freeman, which is a manifest breach of the priviledges of the freemen, a great p'judice to the petitioner and an open violation of the ancient constitution of this burrough, and praying relief therein.

Bookseller prosecuted. "It is order'd that the said Mr Hopkins be stopp'd from going on in retailing, and prosecuted for the offence already comitted att the charge of the Corporation; and that Mr Whitfield be sumon'd to answer the p'mises."

"1724, Decr. 9. Mr Peter Whitfield appearing and giving a long answer *ore tenus* too long to be remembr'd,

Whitfield reprimanded. "It is order'd that he give his answer in writing in a week's time to Mr Mayor."

There is no further entry relating to this matter.

"1709, Jany. 10. Presentment by the Grand Jury.

Oysters. "That according to custom and usage of this Corporation no persons bringing oysters or any fish to this Corporation to retail the same there on the usual days, shall sell the same by wholesale to any persons that usually sell the same again in any other markett, or that buy to sell again in any other markett till after 12 o'clock on ev'y Markett Day, on forfeiture of the fish."

"1707, Sept. 17. Sylvester Moorcroft Mayor.

Apprentices. "It is order'd, That all indentures of Apprentice are to be enrolled according to former order, and the same to be sett up in publick on the

TRADE AND COMMERCE.

Exchange that every one may have notice, for which 12ᵈ to be paid for ev'y enrollmᵗ.

Pipe making was at this period a considerable branch of industry in Liverpool, but required protection, according to the following extract:— *Pipe-making.*

"1706, July 16. James Atherton and David Grason Edwᵈ Lyons and others, Pipemakers in Liverpoole do peticon yᵗ whereas sev¹ country Pipe-makers come into town, and do not only sell their pipes to yᵉ Grocers in town, by wholesale, but go from alehouse to alehouse and sell their pipes by retail, to alehouses or other inhabitants, to yᵉ destruction of yʳ petitionᵉ and their familys, who pay'd for their freedome, and are at great charg to support themselves and familyes and are contributors to leyes and taxes lay'd on them as inhabitants therein, to order some relief therein."

The endorsement is "*nihil factum.*"

"1715, July 6. Richard Gildart Mayor.
" It is order'd that the owners of the Pott house att Lord Street end shall pay tenn shillings quarterly for liberty of carrying on their bussiness of makeing and selling earthenware att that Pott house, they not being free of this town; but not to be excus'd from paying town's dues for what they shall import." *Potters.*

Notices are found of the erection of glass houses and flour mills, and of the extension of sugar refining. *Glass Houses*

"1718, May 14. Richard Kelsall Mayor
" Order'd That the Leather Hall be fix'd in the cellar under the great tower (of the Castle) in Derby Square, and the taners be oblig'd to bring, to lay and sell their leather there, and that Widow Grace attend it, she thereupon maintaining herself and family. The taners to pay a reasonable rent to the Corpⁿ." *Leather Hall.*

The following throws some light on the perquisites of the Water Bailiff, to which allusion has already been made.

"1714, April 7. Thomas Coore Mayor
" This Councell haveing requested Mr Mayor and sev'all of the Councill to inspect into the right of the Water Bayliffe who demands and takes one bushell for ev'y hundred bushells of corne imported or brought into this Port, tho' not sold here but often carry'd upp to Warrington, and they, haveing inspected the ancient records and inquir'd into the nature of such *Water Bailiff.*

rights; doe find that the Water Bayliffe is oblig'd to attend all ships bringing in Corn into this Port, and to keep a measure or bushell to measure the same with, on delivering it out, either here or att Warrington being within this Port, but the usuall way hath been for the Water Bayliffe to take half for such as is deliv'd at Warrington, and then he does not measure it out, otherwise he is to measure it out, or find a proper measure and person to attend and measure it out.

"This Councell doth agree that the said right is justly due, and that he insist on and take the same."

STREETS AND BUILDINGS.

The founders of Liverpool seem to have been singularly blind to any provision for the extension and improvement of the town. No idea appears to have entered their minds of any commerce beyond the petty retail trade carried on for many ages on the most contracted and short-sighted principles. The original streets were a congeries of ill-built alleys, not more than seven or eight yards wide. The main streets have had to be expanded and reconstructed in modern times, at an enormous expense, but some of the bye streets still remaining, such as Hackins Hey, Princes Street, Temple Lane, may give an idea of what the general aspect of the town was in the olden time.

Down to the end of the 17th century, little alteration had taken place in the aspect of the town; but about that period the nascent commerce had forced the slumbering Corporation into some progressive action.

One of the first indications of this is found in a minute:—

"1697, Feby. 9. James Benn Mayor.

"Whereas there is a proposal made by Sr Cleave Moor to be admitted to have an opening to two streets from a field at ye North side of ye town, comonly call'd Parlour Hey, and something that may be for his convenience on ye Sea Bank, and to exchang a vacant peece of ground near Jugler Street, betweene ye house of Mr Robt Carter and Mr Georg Gryffith, or some other peece of ground that belongs to Sr Cleave Moor. [Union Street.]

"The Councell doth consent that Mr Mai^r be requested to take to his assistance Ald^m Wm Preeson Ald^m Thomas Johnson Senr & Ald^m Thomas Johnson Junr ye p'sent Baylives, Town clerke, Mr William Travers & Mr Tho. Sweeting, or ye major part of them to conferre with & conclude a contract with Sr Cleave Moor to ye best advantage they can for ye intr'st of ye Corporation."

The two streets here mentioned were Union Street, so named a few years afterwards, on the union of England with Scotland, and Rosemary Lane, now Fazakerley Street. Lord Street had been laid out by Lord Molyneux, about thirty years previously.[1]

Survey.
"1697, Feby. 9. It is also order'd in Councell that a new Survey be made of ye whole town and that the persons here nominated take ye trouble upon them to survey the same and make a returne ag^t next Councell."

Omitting the names of the Councillors so appointed, the list of the streets was as follows, divided into eight groups :—

Streets.
"1 Water Street, Chappel Yard & Coven Garden
" 2 Castle Street, Phenwick Street & Phenwick Alley
" 3 Chapel Street, Lancelot's Hey & Oldhall Street
" 4 Jugler Street, Moorfields & Tyth Barn Street
" 5 Moor Street, Preeson's Row & back o' th' Castle
" 6 Dale Street, Hackins Hey & St Jno Street
" 7 Lord Street, Castle Hey, Cook Street, Poole Lane and Atherton Street
" 8 Red Crosse Street, St James Street and Waterside."

Great Heath.
The next proceeding was the allotment of the Common or Great Heath, which extended eastward from the brook, following the line of the present Whitechapel and Paradise Street. This was still virgin ground, ceded to the Corporation by Lord Molyneux, by the agreement of 1672.

The quantity was about 20 acres, exclusive of the Moss Lake, and was thus allotted :—

The Common
"1697, Feby. 16. At a Survey upon ye comon is return'd this day for—
" Ald^m William Preeson on back of ye Quarry Hill[a] about 4 acres at £5 ⅌ acre.
" James Benn Esq pr^t Mai^r of Liverpoole and Mr Wm Braddock about 5 acres, £5.
" Mr Peter Atherton about 4 acres on ye other side Mosse Lake £4.

[1] See Vol. I., p. 275, &c.
[a] Now the site of University College.

STREETS AND BUILDINGS.

> "Mr William Porter about 3 acres on ye east side Richd Kisshaw's £5.
> "Peter Rainford, a small peece of ground at ye east end of Rich. Culcheths £5 ⅌ acre.
> "Mr Rainford to be at ye charge of removing Culcheth's yate, else not to have ye ground.
> "James Kemp, a small peece near Ald^{rm} Johnson's & Mr Willis's, close by a stone hole 'twixt two wayes over ag'st Mr Pluckington's and Roger Jones £5.
> "Christopher Brees, above ye stone hole, a small peece next Ald^{rm} Johnson's £5."

From this date the Common became gradually laid out and built on, the records being full of the sales and transactions. *Sales.* A few of the most noteworthy may be alluded to.

The Townsend Windmill, at the summit of Shaw's Brow (now William Brown Street), was long a conspicuous object.

> "1704, Mar. 7. William Hurst Mayor.
> "Jno Scofield peticons that ye Councell would be pleas'd to give him p'mission to build near ye Townsend Mill, where hee has already fey'd and ring'd ye seller and enclosed a garden, to a considerable charg. But if they think that place prejuditial, then to appoint him some other place to build on, and give him some allowance for his charg. Referr'd to Mr May^r to appoint him a place—at 6^d ⅌ yd."

> "1707, Nov. 24. James, Earl of Derby Mayor.
> "Mem^{dm} That the new building, lately built in a new street (Key St) *Chapel.* which leads northwards from Moorfields is recorded for a Meeting place for an Assembly of Protestants dissenting from the church of England for the exercise of their religious worp'p in pursuance of an Act of Parliam^t entituled an Act for exempting their Maj'ties Protestant subjects dissenting from the church of England from the penaltys of certain laws, according to the tenor and purport of the said Acts."

This edifice was, about 1790, converted into St. Matthew's Church, and was removed about 1851 for the construction of the Lancashire and Yorkshire Railway.

The following entry is curious, as showing that on the very eve of converting the pool into a dock, public opinion was not prepared for it.

> "1708, May 5. Att an Assembly &c.
> "It being humbly represented to this Assembly that there is an absolute

Bridge over Pool. necessity for the convenience of the Corporation tenn^{ts} over the poole, that a bridge be made over the pool from Pool Lane end or thereabouts lineable with the new intended street over the pool. And Mr Dep^{ty} Mayor with others of this Assembly haveing view'd the same, and consulted Workmen therein, who return that the same may be built for Six Pounds.

"It is order'd that such a bridge be built at the charge of the Corporation."

"1709, May 2. John Seacome Mayor.

Quakers' Meeting House. "Mem^{dm} That the building or house on the east side of Hackins Hey formerly Mr Preeson's Backwards now in possession of Robt Haydock is recorded for a meeting place for an assembly of Protestants dissenting from the Church of England, called Quakers, pursuant to 1^t Wm & Mar."

"1710, Apl. 17. John Earle Mayor.

Daniel Fabius. "Mem^{dm} The House att the bottom of James Street wherein Danl Fabyus lives is recorded for a meeting place for Protestant Dissenters."

This congregation removed in 1722 to Byrom Street, to a chapel afterwards converted into St. Stephen's Church.

Castle. The lease of the ancient castle was granted to the Corporation in 1704, but owing to disputes with Lord Molyneux, some years elapsed before the site could be appropriated. Houses began to be built on the south side.

"1709, Decr. 8. Order'd, That Mr Mayor have power to open a Watercourse or take such proper methods as he shall think fitt to carry off the water off the backsides of the tenn^{ts} on the south side of the Castle called Derby Square.

Derby Square. "Order'd that Mr Mayor with the assistance of some of the Council not less than four, have power to finish the new buildings and alterations in and about the Castle now call'd Derby Square and make such additionall improvem^{ts} there as he and they shall think most convenient, and to sett and lett the same for the most profitt and advantage, the charge whereof to be deducted and allow'd out of the growing rents of the said Castle and appurtenances."

Gaol. At this time the Castle was used as the common gaol.

"1710, May 4. John Earle Mayor.

Market. "The Mayor p'pounded that it might be advantagious to build some addition to the prison towards the entrance into the New Markett. It is order'd, that the same be view'd and an estimate made thereof, what charge the same may cost and amount to. And that Mr Mayor be requested & empower'd to treat with Nehemias Gildoes or Widow

STREETS AND BUILDINGS.

Whitfield for purchaseing and making an opening out of the New Markett into Poole Lane."

"1710, Octr. 30. George Tyrer Mayor.

"Certain petitioners humbly presume that the Castle Ditch being fill'd Castle Ditch. upp, is very p'judiciall to all those houses att the back of the Castle, by turning all the water out of the New Markett upon them, and think they ought to be releiv'd by the Corporation by carrying off the said water as may be thought convenient with what speed may be; sev'all of the houses being scarce tenantable."

"1725, Apl. 7. John Goodwin Mayor.

"Order'd that Ald^n Seacome, Mr Steers and Mr James Shaw be desir'd Plan of to draw a plan of the grounds in the late Castle and report their opinion Castle. how the same may be improv'd to Mr Mayor as soon as may be; who is desir'd to take as many of the Council as he shall think fitt, and view the same, and report all their opinions therein next Council day.

"That such part of the buildings and ground of the late Castle as the Sale of Land. Council shall think fitt to lett out shall be putt into small lots by the gent^n appointed to view it of six yards in a lott, and publick notice be given that the same are to be leas'd to the highest bidder for 3 lives and 21 yeares, paying twelve pence ⅌ yard rent to the front."

"1725, Apl. 15. It is now order'd that the houses over the piazzas in Sales by Derby Square be lotted and leas'd out to the highest bidder, and that Auction. Mr Mayor and Bayl^s be desired to attend at the Comon Hall on Munday the third of May next by two o'clock in the afternoon, att which time it is appointed to putt them up, and continue till all be contracted for, and that in the mean time the sev'all lotts be drawn out with their dimensions and publish'd.

"That the purchaser pay a guinea down to the treas'rer and give notes for paym^t of the remainder of the fine as follows, vizt one fourth in tenn days and halfe of the rest in three months, and the other halfe in three months after."

The site of the Castle was originally much higher than the surrounding land, the descent being very rapid towards James Street.

"1726, Feby. 1. Thomas Bootle Mayor.

"Ordrd That the Wood staires lately built by James Kenyon in the Kenyon's passage out of Derby Square into Preeson's Row be imediately pull'd Steps. down, being p'sented by the Grand Jury to be an encroachment, and the officers doing it to be indemnify'd by the Corp^n.

"That the Castle Wall att the top of Lord Street be imediately pull'd Castle Wall. down, and the ground clear'd for the contractors to build, and the treasurer pay one halfe and Edwd Litherland the other half of clearing the rubbish off it."

The following entry is noticeable :—

"1707, Octr. 17. Sylvester Moorcroft Mayor.

Town's Wall. "It is order'd that Mr Clayton have liberty to build upon the Town's Wall, giving a deed acknowledgeing the same to be the Town's Wall, the Corporation to have liberty to lay in and upon his building there gratis."

We have no record of any town walls, excepting the fortifications thrown up previous to the siege in 1644, to some relics of which this may refer.

Tyrer's Mill. "1719, Sept. 8. Order'd that Mr Thos Tyrer who proposes to erect a wind mill have a lease of a small piece of ground att the south corner of Mr Houston's field on the north side of the highway leading to Prescott for 3 lives and 21 yeares, he building a Mill thereon and paying two shillings and sixpence ⅌ ann. rent from Mich^{us} next ; to be sett out so as not to p'judice the highway."

Gallows Mills. This and another mill adjoining were called the Gallows Mills, from a tradition that after the rebellion, in 1715, some of the rebels were here executed. There was, however, another Gallows Field, of an earlier date, extending eastward from the Pool stream along the north side of the present William Brown Street, which is referred to as early as 1551. The following entry relates to this :—

"1712, Feby 4. Edward Tarleton Mayor.

Lease to Crane. "Mr John Crane petitioning to add one life to two in being of two acres and one third of an acre near the Gallows. It is order'd that he have a lease as petition'd for, paying seven pounds fine, and for a term of twenty one years more twenty eight pounds."

After the construction of the Old Dock, the stream which fed the old Pool was arched over, and the line of Paradise Street and Whitechapel formed. This was at first called Shoreditch.

"1717, May 25. Mr Wm Shaw of Preston having petitioned for all the waste ground from the North side of Atherton Street to the South side of

STREETS AND BUILDINGS. 63

Thomas Street and extending to the street call'd Shoreditch to build on and improve. It is Order'd that the same be granted to him &c." — Shoreditch.

"1717, Feby. 10. Richd Kelsall Mayor.

"Order'd That a Comittee be appointed by Mr Mayor to consider of p'per methods to be taken to obtain a power to land goods in & out of ye dock & to build a Custom house there & to desire our Members of Parliam^t to assist therein." — Custom House.

"1720, March 20. Joseph Clitherall petitioning for a lease of the late Old School in the Old Church Yard, and proposeing to improve it by turning it into a dwelling house. It is order'd accordingly for 3 lives and 21 yeares, paying twenty five Pounds fine and five Shill^s ⅌ ann. rent." — Old School House.

"1724, Aug. 12. It is order'd that twelve yards of ground be granted and sett out att the east end of the Almshouses att Dale Street end, for the Exec^{rs} of Mr James Scasbrick to build more Almshouses upon, pursuant to his last will." — Almshouses.

The pavements were in a very unsatisfactory condition.

"1719, Octr. 7. Josia Poole Mayor.

"It being represented that Old Hall Street is ill pav'd and impassable, — Pavements.

"It is order'd that the Corporation allow eight pounds towards amending the same upon condicon that the person who shall undertake to doe it shall doe it effectually or repay the said 8th."

"1725, Nov. 5. William Marsden, Mayor.

"This Councill, takeing into consideration that the road between this town and Prescott hath been almost impassable, and that the inhabitants of this town have suffer'd much for want of getting their coales home dureing the sumer season, thro' the great rains that have happen'd in these parts, and that it would be highly necessary to gett an Act of Parliam^t for the repairing that road, so that it may be passable at all times of the year, and for erecting a turnpike thereon; It is now Order'd that a petition to the Parliam^t for that purpose be prepar'd." — Prescot Road.

"1726, Jany. 31. The Councill takeing into their further consideration the great charge of bringing coales and merchandizes to this town and port in bad weather, and especially in the winter season and att all times when the weather happens to be wett and unseasonable as it hath happen'd the last sumer, and that the roads to the coalpitts and particularly in Prescott canot be sufficiently repair'd by the statute work as it will be passable att such times without the help and assistance of a toll.

"It is now order'd and agreed that application be made to the Parliam^t to obtain an Act for that purpose, and that the Treasurer doe advance one half of the charge." — Act of Parliament.

Several attempts had been made in the 17th century to

enforce the cleansing and scavenging of the streets, but without success, the officers appointed reporting

Scavenging.

"That they cañot p'vaile with the inhabitants for clenseing of ye streets, but are abused and much afronted in the execucon of their office."

The subject was resumed in 1719, and the following means adopted:—

"1719, Octr. 24. Thomas Fillingham Mayor.

"Ald^n Gildart and Mr Saml Dove proposeing to provide proper carts and carriages and therewith to take away all the muck and dirt in the streets and passages of this town twice eve'y week vizt ev'y Munday and Thursday; It is now order'd that they have liberty att their own charge to make a convenient hole with an iron grate over it att every street end to be approv'd of by Mr Mayor, and have power to take away all the Muck and dirt whatever which they shall find in the publick streets and passages, and in case of failure to forfeit five shillings $\mathbb{P}$ week.

"And to be granted to them for the term of eleven years and a contract thereof entred into imediately."

"1720, Mar. 20. Henry Taylor Mayor.

Highways.

"Mr Ald^n Coore and Mr Ald^n Gildart offering their service to inspect the managem^t of the Supervisors of the highways, who are thought to expend and lay out very extravagantly in repairing the highways &c.

"It is order'd that the Supervisors shall not take upon them to doe anything in the highways without the order of these gent^s."

"1721, Octr. 23. Bryan Blundell Mayor.

"The Grand Portmoot Order

Bellman.

"That the Bellman give publick notice ev'y Saturday night for ev'y person to clean their streets on pain of iii^s iiij^d."

Chadwick's Map.

"1725, Octr. 6. James Chadwick haveing been imploy'd to measure and make a map of the town and the Liberties thereof, It is ordered that he have Six pounds towards it."

This is the first map made from actual survey, the small map, dated 1650, being a compilation. It is very useful in the identification of the alignment of the streets, but furnishes no details of the buildings.

Lighting Streets.

The lighting of the streets was a cause of considerable anxiety. In 1653 the town was content with two lanthorns and two candles burning every night, in the dark moon, at the High Cross and the White Cross.

In 1675 and 1679, all taverns, inns, and alehouses were required to hang out lanthorns and light candles at their doors from the 1st November to the 2nd February.

"1718, Decr. 10. Josia Poole Mayor.

"It being represented that Lamps are much wanted within this town, and Mr James Halsall proposeing to attend and keep them in order and light them ev'y night for tenn shillings a peice ◉ ann. It is Order'd that fourty five Lamps be imediately prepar'd and that the Corporation pay and allow Mr Halsall tenn pounds towards the charge of makeing them and he to repair them afterwards at his own charge; and that what charge shall be expended in placeing them and putting them up shall be consider'd of by the Councill. And that the sub Bayl^s shall collect in person the moneys for Watch and Ward as Mr Mayor and the Just^s of peace shall settle, direct and appoint, and have four Constables to assist them."

Lamps ordered.

ECCLESIASTICAL.

St. Peter's Church.

After the passing of the Act for constituting the Parish of Liverpool, in 1699, no time was lost in the erection of a second church—St. Peter's, which was commenced in 1700 and completed in 1704. The Rev. Robt. Atherton and the Rev. Robert Styth were appointed the first joint Rectors. In 1706, on the death of Mr. Atherton, Henry Richmond, a member of an old Liverpool family, was appointed.

No long period elapsed before serious differences, both ecclesiastical and municipal, arose between him and the Council, as the following documents will show :—

"1711, Octr. 19. James Townsend Mayor.
"At a Portmoot &c.

Complaints against Rector.

"The Grand Jury, takeing into consideration that the Rev'end Mr Henry Richmond, one of the Rectors, hath been absent from his Parish and flock a long time, and therefore neglected his duty, made the following presentm^t—

"We being also to inquire as well for our Sovereign Lady the Queen, as for the burgesses of this burrough, haveing seriously as we ought consider'd her Maj^{ties} gracious Proclamation for the encouragem^t of piety and virtue, and for preventing and punishing vice, prophaneness and immorality read this day unto us, and that notwithstanding her Maj^{ties} most religious care therein there hath been great neglect within this burrough by the not discountenancing and duly punishing vice, prophaneness and imorality, and putting the wholesome laws in execution against them as by the said proclamation is enjoyned, and being deeply sensible of the great increase of all maner of vyce and debauchery, amongst us, and well weighing what to us may seem the cause thereof. We doe humbly lay the same before the magistracy of this town, with our sincere and hearty desires and offers to join and unite in all proper measures for the effectuall remedying and preventyng thereof for the future.

"And first, we think the unhappy divisions amongst us to be one principall cause thereof.

"2ndly another cause thereof we are sorry (but canot in justice forbear) to assign, which is the unaccountable behaviour of the Rev⁴ Mr Hen. Richmond, one of our Rectors, who haveing seemed to renounce or exchange his most holy profession, for four months, or betwixt the last of January and begining of June last past did abandon his flock, and for much longer time hath so farr forgott himself to be the guide of the contending parties who by his Christian offices might have influ'nced and disposed both sides to an acomodation, instead of which he hath rather chose to set himself at the head of the contention, incourag'd the tumults, been the mover and persuader of the most violent councells and measures, and by his rage to the people of one side, and complyance with the other, hath made his publick instruction when attended, unedifying and unprofitable; but what we particularly charge upon him in breach and contempt of the said proclamation is, that within this year last past, and not to goe farther back than her Maj^{ties} most gracious pardon; since that time he hath not once read the said proclamation in his church or parochiall chapell⁽¹⁾ or caused the same to be read or taken any notice thereof, so as to make a discourse suitable thereto as by the said proclamation is enjoin'd.

Disputes with Rector.

"And lastly are the severall scandalous and villanous libells, sett forth or publish'd within this town, especially one entituled "A true and impartiall account of the election of the representatives in Parliam^t for the Corporation and burrough of Liverpool in the County Pallatine of Lancaster, October the 16th, 1710."

"Also another without any tytle page, wherein pa. the 6th the Comon Councell are called "A corrupt Majority," and page the 14th "A packt Councell," which said libell was publish'd by the abovesaid Rector, and that both the said libells, which are false in fact have not only reflected on the Comon Councell of this burrough, but of the town in generall, and rais'd and stirred up so many heats and dissentions as in all appearance tend to distract and destroy all manner of Christian Society to the high displeasure of God and all good men."

The reverend Rector was not disposed to submit to this imputation, and took legal proceedings, which are thus referred to :—

"1712, July 14. Nota. That the Rev^rend Henry Richmond brought a *certiorari* to remove the Presentm^t against him last October Sessions to the last Assizes att Lancaster. But he, not haveing deliver'd the *certiorari* to the Town clerk to make a return thereto, he lost the benefit of the Writ and now mov'd by Councell at the sessions to quash the said Presentm^t,

Certiorari.

---

(1) This refers to the Treason Act of 1709, before the Royal assent to which a proclamation was issued, pardoning all treasons previously committed.

being in English and should have been in Latin, and for that and other reasons now shewn, the Court orders it to be quash'd and destroy'd."

The Council had therefore to succumb.

Two years afterwards another cause of difference arose.

"1714, April 21. Thomas Coore Mayor.

Easter Dues.
"It being represented to this Councill that one Mr Orme as curate to or imploy'd by Mr Richmond one of our Rectors, has taken upon him to collect and receive from the parishioners of this Parish, Easter Dues, which this Councell are of opinion are not due or payable to the Rectors of this Parish, and that the paym^t of £200 ⅌ ann. to the Rectors £55 ⅌ ann. to Mr Richmond of Walton and £6 10 to Mr Marsden is in lieu and in full of all tythes, oblations and obventions whatever intended by the Act of Parliam^t for makeing this town of Liverpool a Parish distinct from Walton, and that the inhabitants of this Parish are thereby discharg'd from all dues whatsoever. It is now order'd that Mr Orme be order'd and requir'd to cease collecting any more, and give an account of what mon^s he has so collected and receiv'd."

"1714, Sept. 27. The Councill, takeing into consideration that Mr Hen. Richmond and Mr Wm Orme had impos'd upon and collected from the inhabitants sev'all sums of money on pretence of Easter Dues, and that Mr Richmond had taken upon him to nominate and appoint one William Grimbleston to be clerk of St Peter's in the room of Richd Sims, deceased, contrary to the ancient custom and power reserv'd to the Corporation, and also hath misbehaved himself in relation to his duty towards his parishoners.

"It is therefore order'd that such proper methods be taken by the Worpp^{ll} the Mayor for the time being as Councill shall advise, to establish and ascertain the right of the Corporation therein and restore the peace and quiet of the inhabitants."

In 1714, on the decease of the Rev. Robert Styth, the co-rector with Mr. Richmond, a dispute arose as to the election of his successor to the mediety.

Election of Rector.
"1714, June 4. Whereas it is made appear to this Councill that a seperate and private presentation of another person to be Rector hath been made and clandestinely (contrary to the form settled and establish'd in the first election of a Rector) sign'd by a few persons claiming a right thereto, and thereby to divest the Corporation, if possible of the right of election, or the majority of electors from makeing a presentation.

"It is hereby declar'd that as it was agreed by the Ald^n to be made the 19th day of May last, and that ev'y one of the electors had due notice thereof, such seperate, private and clandestin proceeding can only tend to heighten our divisions and p'judice the Corporation, and that Mr Thos Bell being elected and presented in a publick manner by a great majority, this Councill doth not only confirm the same, but order that the said presentation shall be maintain'd and effectually supported att the publick charge of the Corporation in such maner as shall be needfull, requesting Mr Mayor's especiall care therein."

The right of the Council to present was sustained, and all succeeding appointments were made by the Council down to the Municipal Reform Act. Rights of Council.

The bad feeling between the Council and Rector Richmond was continually manifesting itself.

"1715, June 1. Richard Gildart Mayor.
"The Rev'end Mr Richmond p'tending to the right of electing a clerk of St Peter's church in the room of Richd Sims dec^d and the Town Clerk by direction of the Mayor haveing entred a caveat to stop his p'tended choice. It is order'd that the charge thereof and of maintaining the right of the Corporation in electing the Parish Clerks according to ancient custom and as reserv'd by the Act for makeing this town a parish be paid by the Corporation." Caveat.

Mr. Richmond died in 1721, and the Rev. Thomas Baldwin was peaceably appointed in his place. Baldwin appointed.

After the lease of the castle was obtained from the Crown, no long time was allowed to elapse before steps were taken to erect a church on the site.

"1715, Mar. 17. Order'd—That proper methods be taken by Mr Mayor to signify the intencon of this Corp^n to build a church on the ground and soile of the late Castle to our representatives in Parliam^t in order to obtain an Act of Parliam^t for the same and to consult Mr Richmond thereupon." St. George's Church.

The Act was obtained in the following session. Nearly two years elapsed before any further steps were taken.

"1717, Jany. 15. Richard Kelsall Mayor.
"This Councill takeing into consideration the necessity for haveing a new church.

"It is now order'd that Mr Mayor be desir'd takeing the assistance of the Aldermen and Comon Councill to view and consider of a proper place where to place and build the new intended church in the most comodious

Castle.

part of the late Castle, on Wednesday next att two o'clock in the afternoon, and that speedy care be taken to apply for the disbursem^{ts} and charge the Corporation hath lately been att in fortifying the town against the rebells, which when obtain'd is order'd to be laid out in building the church."

Tenants ejected.

"1717, Feby. 8. It is order'd that the tenants in the round tower in the late Castle have notice to remove and that the ground be levell'd with all convenient speed, the Councill being of opinion that it will be proper to erect the church there."

The matter remained stagnant for some years.

St. George's Church.

"1724, July 1. Mr Mayor propounding that it was necessary to begin upon building a new church according to the Act of Parliament for granting the inheritance of the late Castle; It is order'd that the Councill be desired to view and consider of a proper place where to sett it and that Plans be drawn and proposalls and estimates of the charge be received."

"1725, Apl. 15. John Goodwin Mayor.

"An Estimate and sev^{ll} plans of a New Church to be erected in the late Castle upon the ground where the old large square stone Tower and the stone buildings adjoining to the same Northward now stand, being now laid before this Councill by Mr Tho Steers and Mr James Shaw,

"And this Councill haveing taken the same into consideration, and being very desirous to promote so pious a work wch is now much wanted, and with all possible speed to erect a convenient church, with a proper spire steeple, doe agree that a new church be there built and a spire steeple att the West side or end and an alcove for a chancell on the east side or end; and in order to perfect the same

Committee.

"It is now order'd that a Committee be appointed, to agree with workmen and contract for building the same, and a Comittee is now appointed vizt Mr Mayor and Bayl^s and all the Aldermen, Mr Tho Steers and Mr James Shaw or any five of them, who are to meet ev'y Munday and Thursday att four o'clock in the afternoon in the Exchange and publick notice be given thereof."

"1725, Nov. 5. William Marsden Mayor.

"It being propounded to this Councill that a proper Modell of the New intended Church sho'd be settled, ascertain'd and fix'd upon. It is now

Model.

order'd that the Walls thereof shall be plain without pillars or pillasters, and the windows after the same forme as in Mr Shaw's Modell, and the whole to be consider'd further of, by the Comittee now appointed who are

"The Worp^ll the Mayor for the time being

"The Aldermen, the two Baylives and Mr Steers and ev'y other of the Councill that please to attend."

"1726, Nov. 2. Thomas Bootle Mayor.

"Mr Sephton haveing drawn some draughts or models of a Church, It is order'd that the Comittee settle his demands, and that the Treasurer doe pay him not exceeding tenn guineas.

"That the Comittee consider of vaulting the Church.   St. George's

"The Comittee appointed for building the New Church representing to Church. this Councill, that they have agreed with Mr Thos Steers and Mr Edwd Steers, Litherland for building the walls and part of the steeple; this Councill Architect. doth approve thereof, and order that a contract be entred into, and a bond for performance, and that they begin imediatly.

"That the old Castle wall att the top of Lord Street be imediatly pull'd Castle Wall. down and the ground clear'd for the contractors to begin."

The church was completed in the next reign.

In the Act of 1699, for constituting Liverpool a parish, provision was made for building houses for the Rectors on a portion of the castle land. This was superseded in consequence of the different appropriation of the site, and the following arrangement was substituted :—

"1718, Sept. 17. Richard Kelsall Mayor.

"Whereas it is now propounded that an Agreem^t was made some yeares agoe, between the Corporation and the Parish that as houses for the Houses for Rectors had not then been built and provided, pursuant to the Act of Rectors. Parliam^t for makeing this town a Parish, and the provission made in the lease towards makeing good their deficiencies; that the Corporation should advance and pay the sume of three hundred pounds towards building such houses, and the parish to be att the charge of the remainder of the building and finishing those houses.

"This Councill doth agree thereto upon condicon that the claim of the Rectors of, in, or to the Castle, shall be discharg'd for ever therefrom.

"But it being further propounded that the said sume of three hundred pounds sho^d be laid out in building an addicon to the Old Church wherein Additions to addiconall seats may be built and sett for a yearly rent, and for the doing Old Church. whereof an order of Vestry was made and agreed to by the Parish in May last, and that the Rectors sho^d have the profitts of those addiconall seats in lieu of houses and other condicons in the said Order menconed. It is now assented to and order'd that such addition be built and perfected att the charge of the Corporation, haveing a faculty from the Consistory Court first for the same, for the purposes in the said last order of Vestry mencon'd, and that the Comon Councill and the Rectors for the time being, have power to sett the said additionall seats, upon the condicons in the said order of Vestry mencon'd and contain'd and not otherwise."

CHAP. I, A.D. 1702—1727.

This scheme was carried out. The order of the Consistory Court was granted on the 1st December, 1718.

The next entry reads as follows:—

"1719, Feby. 4. Josia Poole Mayor.

Precedence in Church.
"Order for regulating the seats of the Ald^n, Bayl^s, Bayl^s Peers and Comon Councill in both churches and of all the seats in the body of both churches, pursuant to the Lycense or Comission from the Consistory Court att Chester the 1st December last to the Worpp^{ll} the Mayor, Bayl^s & Comon Councill, Rectors and Churchwardens for the time being or any six of them; and that the Sexton att each church take care to keep and p'serve the ancient seats of the Ald^n, Bayl^s, Bayl^s Peers & Comon Councill, till Mr Mayor & ye Rector or Minister officiating come to church and to see y^t housekeepers be preferr'd and accommodated with the other seats before servants and such as doe not pay the church rates."

This question of precedence was considered very important.

"1715, July 6. It was Order'd that some proper persons be appointed by Mr Mayor, who is desir'd to recommend the same to the Church-wardens; to attend ev'y Sunday and take care that no person do goe in or be admitted into the seats of the Ald^n and Bayliv^s and Bayliv^s Peers, in both churches before Mr Mayor comes to church att the church he goes to, and before the Minister comes to the other church Mr Mayor does not come to."

The possession of a pew or seat in church was considered a very valuable privilege.

"1698, Nov. 2. Thomas Sweeting Mayor.

Seats in Church.
"Mr Edwd Tarleton peticons for a seat to ye eastward of Mr Poole's in ye North-east gallery... Respited till next Councill day."

"1698, Decr. 7. Mr Edwd Tarleton peticons for a seat in the Northern Gallery, and Mr Green, Randle Galloway and Widow Lyon all peticon for ye same, It appears to ye generallity of ye Councill that ye right of ye seat was in Thomas Watts and devolv'd by him in his lifetime (and since by his widow and son) on Mr Edward Tarleton to whom the town gives a title at ye rate of seven Pounds."

Disturbances occasionally took place.

1699, Aug. 8th. An information is laid before the Mayor by the Rector and one of the Aldermen who depose:—

Disturbances in Church.
"That one Thomas Rudd (as hee calls himself) hath frequently disturbed ye congregation of Liverpoole in time of divine service; one time bawling

about yᵉ church and making a great noise, to yᵉ hindrance of devotion, another time coming into the church in a disorderly irreverend manner and this day particularly he came into yᵉ church and in time of divine service, did speak thre severall tymes and onc said 'howe can yᵉ sing to yᵉ praise and glory of God? how can yᵉ be yᵉ people of God, or sheep of his pasture?' or words to this effect."

The Town Council, by what authority does not appear, took upon themselves the entire management of the affairs of the Parish. They appointed the Rectors and Curates, the Churchwardens, the Sexton, and subordinate officers. They dictated the appropriation of the seats and the rules of precedence. They paid the necessary expenses, and provided the communion plate. *Appointments.*

"1698, Octr. 5. James Benn Mayor.

"The Councell orders, that a peece of Plate be made for yᵉ use of yᵉ Church, to yᵉ Val. of about twelve pounds, and Mr Shields be directed (as to yᵉ fashion) by yᵉ pr't Minister." *Plate for Church.*

"1704, Sept. 6. It is order'd in Councell, that Richᵈ Simms shall be Clerke and Sexton of yᵉ New Church call'd St Peter's from this day, and receive yᵉ fees thereof, but no sallery."

"1704, Octr. 4. Richard Simms, clerke of St. Peter's Church, peticōns for a sallery. The Councell order him to be payd three pounds next Christmas, but no part of yᵉ contributions; and from Christmas 4ᵗʰ ₽ ann. and half yᵉ contributions for that time.

"The sexton further complains—that his wive's son pulls at yᵉ organ, and yᵉ clerke of yᵉ Old Church receives the money."

Frequent mention is made in the Records of the Free Grammar School, for which a small endowment was reserved at the confiscation of the Church Property. *Free Grammar School.*

"1704, May 3. Mr Jno Clayton schoolemʳ and Mr Joseph Cooper, Usher, peticōn yᵗ yᵉ money due on debent' from yᵉ Queen, being 5ᵗʰ odd money neat (ex don' Eliz R'ne) to be added to their sallery."

"1711, Apl. 4. On the representation of the Rev'end Mr Styth, and Mr John Clayton's peticōn to this Assembly. It is order'd and declared that Mr Clayton take upon him the managemᵗ of the whole free school and have the whole sallery; he procureing a suitable usher under him, whom he to have power to remove and displace as shall see needfull and also to pay such usher reasonable wages. The right of electing Schoolmasters

Ancient Schoolroom.

still reserv'd and continued to this assembly as formerly and usuall this order above notwithstanding."

Down to the year 1721 the Grammar School was held in an ancient building in St. Nicholas's Churchyard, originally the Chapel of St. Mary, described by Blome, in 1673, as "a great piece of antiquity." In this year we read as follows :—

"1721, Nov. 1. Bryan Blundell Mayor.

"Whereas by order of Councill of the 21st day of June last past, Mr Mayor was requested to vissitt the free school of this burrough, late in the Old Church yard, but by reason of its scituation on the sea shore was manifestly inconvenient, and a great hindrance to the schollars im‑ *School Lane.* proveing; and is now remov'd and fix'd in School Lane in the building which was heretofore erected for a Charity School, and which being alter'd and enlarg'd att the charge of the Corporation is now made fitt for a school intended for a free Grammar School, instead of the old school, which the Corp^n hath since converted and made into a dwelling-house and apply'd the moneys ariseing therefrom towards the charge of altering and enlargeing such new school.

"And whereas upon such vissitation, it appears and is now represented, that a great number of little children are admitted and taught in the said school that ought not to be admitted into a Gramar School, being under the accidence, and do only learn to spell and read English, which takes up a great part of the Master and usher's time, is a very great impedim^t to the Gramar Schollars and contrary to the originall institution and method of a free Gramar school.

Freemen's Children.

"It is now therefore order'd. That the said school shall hereafter remain and be a free Gramar School to all the freemen's children of this burrough that have before they be admitted there learn'd to or above the accidence, but not any before to be admitted of any kind whatsoever, and that none shall be admitted but such as have a certificate from the Worpp^n the Mayor for the time being. It is also order'd, that the Master *Fees.* shall have liberty to take and receive all gratuities whatsoever such as entrance money, cockpeny, fire money, and quarteridge from such free-men's children as are of abillity and please to give it to the Master for his diligence and care.

"Order'd that the Corp^n doe continue and pay the usuall sallary, and seven pounds ⅌ ann. rent for the school to the Governors of the Charity for ever."

This requires some explanation, a there is an apparent

confusion between the Free Grammar School and the Charity School—afterwards called the Blue Coat Hospital.

In 1708, Captain Bryan Blundell, in conjunction with the Rev. Robt. Styth, one of the Rectors, established a day school for fifty boys; and a subscription was entered into for the erection of a building. A piece of ground in School Lane was granted by the Council for the purpose, 15 yards front and 37 yards in depth.

"1709, Jany. 13. John Earle Mayor.

"At a meeting of the Worpll the Mayor, severall of the Aldermen, Bayliffs and Burgesses and Contributers to the charity school, it is agreed that the Rectors of the new church and the parochial chapell for the time being and also Sr Thomas Johnson, Knight, Richard Norris Esq, William Clayton Esq, Jasper Maudit Esq, Thomas Willis Esq and Alderman John Cleiveland shall be the first trustees for manageing and takeing care of the said charity schoole, and of the money contributed to and for the same, and that the Reverend Robert Styth, one of the Rectors shall be Treasurer thereof and Aldn Wm Hurst coadjuter." Blue Coat School.

Then they elected Wm. Grimbalston master during pleasure.

The Charity School prospered, and in 1718 a new building was erected, and the institution took the name of the Blue Coat Hospital.

The following entry relates the circumstances:—

"1722, Feby. 14. Bryan Blundell Mayor.

"It being now propounded in Councill that whereas upon the representation of the late Rev'end Mr Styth in Decr. 1708 a certain piece of ground part of the Wast of and belonging to the Mayor Bayfs and Burgesses of Liverpool was, by order of Councill of the 6th day of January 1709 sett out att or near the south east corner of St Peter's Churchyard for a charity school to be built thereon, and which hath since been there erected for teaching and instructing poor children in, and that other parts and parcells of the said Wast have been since sett out and added thereto for the same use, and a new school and conveniences for children to lodge in already made, and other Buildgs are propos'd to be added thereto for the benefitt of such school, and that the p'sent Mayor hath purchas'd the present term and intrest of and in a small cottage adjoining on the south-west side for the use of the school and is wanted to be added thereto. It is now order'd that all the said Wast grounds and that cottage shall be legally convey'd by deed to remain for ever for the use, benefitt and advantage of the said school and to and for no other use w'soever."

The old schoolroom, being thus at liberty, was altered, enlarged, and appropriated for the Free Grammar School, as above.

NATIONAL AFFAIRS.

There was, during this period, little interference in Liverpool with national affairs.

There were alternations in the politics of the members sent to Parliament, but the Whigs for the most part prevailed. Liverpool was ardently attached to the house of Hanover, and displayed its loyalty conspicuously on the occasion of both rebellions. Members.

On the breaking out of the War of the Succession, in 1702, the following communication was received from the Government:—

"Whitehall 2ⁿᵈ May 1702.

"To Mr May' of Liv'poole
    "S'

"A Warr being ready to break out betweene these kingdoms & France & Spain, a declaration whereof will speedily be publish'd, I do by her Majest⁵ comand give you this early notice of it by an expresse and desire you to impart yᵉ same forthwith to yᵉ Masters and Comanders of ships that are in yᵉ harbour of Liverpoole & thereabouts & to warn them to take care of themselves & avoid falling into yᵉ hands of yᵉ French and Spanish Privateers, of wᶜʰ wee are inform'd great numbʳˢ are already putt to sea. Letter to Mayor.

"I am &c.
"C. HODGES."

In 1713 peace was proclaimed. The entry is as follows:—

"March 13. A spe'all Councill was call'd just before the proclamation of the peace with Spain and then ord'ᵈ that the charge of a treat on that occasion to be had this day be allowed & born by the Corporation not exceeding £15." Proclamation of Peace.

A depôt of arms existed in the castle, which was removed by warrant in 1709.⁽¹⁾

<small>(¹) *Vide supra*, p. 41.</small>

In consequence of the symptoms of disloyalty which culminated in the rebellion of 1715, the following resolution was passed :—

Abjuration Oath.

"1712, Mar. 4. Edwd Tarleton Mayor.
"Order'd that ev'y person petitioning to be free of this burrough shall take the abjuration oath before the oath of a freeman, and that all those already voted shall come in within a month now next."

On Sunday, the 1st August, 1714, Queen Anne died. The post bringing the news did not arrive until the Friday following. The following entries relate thereto :—

"1714, Aug. 6. Thomas Coore Mayor.

King George proclaimed.

"On Friday the sixth day of August an account was brought by post that Queen Anne departed this life on Sunday before, being the first day of this instant August and that day King George was proclaim'd with loud acclamations and the generall joy of the people, by the Worpp^ll the Mayor, Aldermen, Baylives, and Comon Councill in gowns."

"Sept. 17. Order'd, That the publick rejoicing on the King's arrivall be referr'd to the directions and managem^t of Mr Mayor.

Address to the King.

"That an address be speedily prepar'd and sent to be presented to his Majesty by our most noble Lord the Earl of Derby."

"1714, Octr. 6. Order'd that the Corporation Seale be fix'd to the Address to his Maj^{ties}."

When the rebellion broke out in 1715, prompt measures were taken to put the town in a state of defence. We have no record of the nature of the defences constructed.

That they were costly appears from the following entry :—

Town's Defences.

"1715, Decr. 7. Order'd, that Mr Mayor be desir'd to take upp moneys att intrest to defray the expence of the late fortifications made for the defence of the town, and to preserve and secure it and the port from falling into the hands of the rebels, who haveing rais'd a most unnatural rebellion in Scotland in favour of the Pretender against our most gracious and most undoubted liege lord and soveraign King George, and the happy establishm^t and settlem^t of the Crown in the illustrious House of Hannover, and to have overturn'd our Governm^t both in Church and State, and brought in amongst us Popery and arbitrary power. March'd from thence as farr as Preston, where by the intrepidity of his Maj^{ties} forces under Generall Wills, they were totally defeated, and many of them taken prisoners."

"1716, Jany. 2. Portmoot, but no Grand Jury sworn by reason that the Assizes or Comission for trying the Rebells was then open'd and held here."

Baron Montague, Baron Bury, and Mr. Justice Eyre were the Judges who held the assize. Thirty-four persons were condemned to death, of whom four were executed in Liverpool, on a site in London Road, near two windmills, which thence acquired the name of the " Gallows Mills." *Trial of Rebels.*

The recent loyalty of the Corporation had been costly, and an attempt was made to obtain a reimbursement of the expenditure.

"1717, Jan. 15. Richard Kelsall Mayor.
"Order'd that speedy care be taken to apply for the disbursem^s and charge the Corporation hath lately been att in fortifying the town against the Rebells, which when obtained, is order'd to be laid out in building the church." *Cost of Fortifications*

"1718, May 14. It is order'd that the Town clerk goe to London to sollicite the obtaining the charge of the fortifications all the time of the late Rebellion, and that the Corporation bear the charge of his journey, and the what moneys shall be obtained shall be apply'd towards the building of the new intended church."

It is to be presumed that this application was successful, for the only other record upon the subject is the following :—

"1719, Feby. 26. Order'd, that the charge of solliciting the Governm^t for the moneys laid out about the late fortifications be advanc'd by the towns treasurer, and allow'd him in his accounts."

"1727, June 18. Thomas Bootle Mayor.
"On Sunday the eighteenth day of June $A\bar{n}o$ $D\bar{n}i$, one thousand seven hundred and twenty seven we had the suddain and unexpected account of the decease of our late most gracious sovreigne King George on the Sunday morning before att Osnabrugg in his travell to Hannover.

"On Tuesday the twentieth day of June 1727, our most gracious sovereign King George the Second was proclaim'd in most solemn manner by the Worp^l Foster Cunliff Esqr Depty Mayor, the Ald^n Baylives and Bayl^e peers in their gowns, and by a generall acclamation of the whole town." *Proclamation of George II.*

MANNERS AND CUSTOMS.

The manners and customs of society during the period embraced in the present chapter do not materially differ from those preceding. There was a coarseness of feeling and a separation of classes which modern society has endeavoured to ameliorate and bridge over, with some degree of success.

The old question of "inmates" still continued to vex the souls of the Burgesses.

The original Act of 31 Elizabeth, Cap. 7, enacted that

Inmates.

"From and after the feast of All Saints next ensuing there shall not be any *inmate* or more families or households than one, dwelling or inhabiting in any one cottage made or erected; upon pain that every owner or occupier, placing or willingly suffering any such inmate or other family than one, shall forfeit and lose to the Lord of the Leet within which such cottage shall be, the sum of ten shillings of lawful money of England for every month that any such inmate or other family than one shall dwell or inhabit in any one cottage as aforesaid; And that every Lord of Leet shall have full power and authority to enquire and to take presentment by the oath of Jurors, of every offence in this behalf."

Although this enactment preceded by 12 years the 43rd Elizabeth, the celebrated Poor Law Act, yet there can be no doubt its main object was to prevent poor persons from becoming burdensome in any particular locality. In fact it was an absolute prohibition against keeping lodgers, and was impossible to be carried out in its entirety. The Liverpool records are full of Grand Jury presentments, and of fines inflicted, but the custom continued, and practically became a tax levied on lodgers.

Many of the inmates were persons of loose life, *e.g.*

Prosecutions. "1708, July 12. Presented

"James Blevin and Ann his wife for entertaining lewd women in their house.

"Jane Justice and the said Ann Blevin for encouragers and maintainers of bawdry.

"Margaret Justice, Daughter of the said Jane Justice for incontinency."

The offenders were dealt with rather severely. The above parties, being brought before the Court, and not finding sureties for their good behaviour, were committed and sentenced as follows :—

"That Marg^t Justice be whipt the next day att 2 o'clock in the afternoon att a cart's arse, and Ann Blevin and Jane Justice be carryed in the cart att the same time from the Exchange to Jane Justice's house in Dale Street." *Punishment.*

The custom of presentments against inmates in time became somewhat onerous, and there are several indications of its gradual discontinuance. The following is the last entry on the subject :—

"1711, July 9. The Portmoot Court.

"Many persons are presented as Inmates who upon being sumon'd before the Justices of peace appear not to be, save some few who are order'd to depart, and therefore omitt incerting their names, which would take upp a great space in the records, and be of no maner of use, and have entred them in an Estreat Book." *Presentments*

The ducking stool was still an active institution. *Ducking Stool.*

"1712, Octr. 27. Edwd Tarlton Mayor.
"Order'd that a Ducking Stool be erected at the Flashes."
"1714, Octr. 25. That the Ducking Stool be remov'd to the Flashes or some other convenient place."

If severity of punishment could have deterred from vice, the community should have been most virtuous.

"1712, Jany. 12. It being made appear to the Grand Inquest upon examination of Robt Cowdock of Walton and Jane Meyetye of Woodside that they have been guilty of an infamous offence of lewdness together, to the great dishonour of Almighty God, the ill example of others and in contempt of the laws against imorallity and prophaneness; They doe present them for such offence. *Punishment for Lewdness.*

"The Court thereupon order'd them to be carted on Wednesday next between the hours of twelve and two from Lukenars to and round the Exchange, and that Cowdock be afterwards whipp'd to Dale Street end."

Servants to Plantations.

In the early part of the 18th century labour was in great demand in the plantations in Virginia and the Carolinas. The African trade for negroes had scarcely commenced, and a system of apprenticeship was established, whereby labourers of both sexes were engaged in England and carried to America for terms of years. It is to be feared that, to a great extent, it was little better than kidnapping, and after a few years it was discontinued. During its continuance, a large number were shipped from Liverpool. It is not quite clear what part the Corporation of Liverpool took in the matter, but the records contain a very large number of entries of the persons so shipped.

The following is a specimen :—

"Feby., 1705. To Mr John Lancaster.

	Age.	Years to serve.
"Elizb Stanley of Leverpoole spinst"	26	7
"Mary Winstanley Upholland in yᵉ Co. Lancaster	17	5
"Eliz Yeoman Anglesey in Wales	20	5
"Alice Crompton Freckleton in Lanc.	25	5
"Eliz Fauster Samsberry in Lanc.	21	5
"Mary Greenhalgh Chorley in Lanc.	15	5
"Ann Greenhalgh Chorley in Lanc.	20	5
"Ellen Bradshaw Upholland in Lanc.	14	7
"Anna Linacre Leverpoole in Lanc.	30	4
"Ellen Seed Sawick in Lanc.	26	5
"Jane Vexon Houghton in Lanc.	16	5
"Sarah Reed Wrexham in Wales	20	5
"John McGee Scotland	15	5

1707, Oct. 7th. A curious question of jurisdiction arose between the coroners for the borough and the county, which is thus described :—

Coroners' Disputes.

"Memᵈ That on the 7ᵗʰ day of October 1707 Aldⁿ William Webster Coron' of this Corporation view'd the body of one Patrick Cannon, a saylor, who was drowned in February last out of a boat belonging to the True Love, Mr Thomas Hughes Comander, which oversett in the river in a very high sea, att which time the said Hughes was wonderfully saved by swiming on an oar till another boat came and took him upp. The said

Cannon was cast upp upon the shore towards Garston, but taken upp thence floating and brought down to town in a boat, of which notice was given to the County Coroner; but if within port and brought floating, the Coroner of this Corporation ought to view."

The laws against usury were strictly enforced.

Usury Laws.
"1708, Mar. 20. Peter Alexander, a shoemaker being indicted att the Sessions upon the statute of Usury for takeing greater interest from one Thomas Anderton on a bond given by said Anderton to Alexander for paym^t of £5, than by law is allow'd . . . Pleaded not guilty to the Indictment but the Court ordering him to find sureties to p'secute his Traverse with effect, and he not finding any was comitted.

"Afterwards ye 15th of Aprill instant he withdrew his plea, and Henry Langdale gave security with him to abide such order therein as Richd Norris Esq, Deputy Mayor should make; who order'd him to pay £10 and costs, and afterwards he deliv''d upp the said bond to Anderton, accordingly in discharge of the prosecutor's part."

There are many entries to the following effect :—

Curfew.
"1703, Octr. 25. Wee order William Ashton to ring Corfue Bell at four of ye clock in ye morning and eight of ye clock at night throughout ye year on penalty of five Pounds."

"1704, Jany, 10. Wee pr^t Wm Ashton sexton for breach of an order, in not ringing Curfew Bell at four of ye clock in ye morning, and eight at night.

Lighting.
"We order all Publick Houses to sett forth their lights from sixe of ye clock till nine of ye clock at night on Penalty of three shillings and four pence for each default."

The sports of the period are frequently alluded to.

Horse Races.
"1705, Nov. 7. It is order'd in Councell that to encourage a horse race to be run at ye Waterside, tenne guineas be referr'd to Mr May^r for one year, but not to exceed tenne guineas."

Bull-baiting.
During the early part of the 18th century bull-baiting was a very favourite pastime, partaken of by gentle and simple alike. In order to encourage it, a bye-law was framed that no bull should be slaughtered without being first baited, under a penalty.

"1713, Octr. 26. Order'd That complaints being made that Bulls are kill'd before baited. That ev'y person **exposeing** such bull to sale shall forfeit 6ˢ 8ᵈ for ev'y such offence."

The practice of archery continued much longer than is generally supposed. Entries are found in 1710 and 1711.

Shooting Butts.
"Order'd, That the Shooting Butts be made up by the first of May next, according to custom on penalty of xxˢ."

The Waits, which had been a popular institution during many ages, seem at this period to have got into discredit.

Waits.
"1717, Decr. 4. Att a Councill &c.
"The Waits, petitioning that as they have had no allowance for some yeares past, they may have some compensation for the arreares, and an order for so much certain for the time to come as the Councill please.
"It is Order'd that they have five guineas for the arrears and fourty shillings ℔ ann for the future, if they attend on publick days better than they have done."

1717, March 10th. There is an interesting notice of an old veteran of the Civil Wars.

"It being represented to this Councill that Coll Robert Broadneux is in extream want, it is now Order'd
"That the Town's Treasurer doe lend him weekly the sume of seven shillings and sixpence till further order."

It was probably to spare the feelings of the venerable patriarch that the dole was administered as a loan, since the prospect of repayment must have referred to a draft on the Bank of Faith.

Colonel Broadneux.
Col. Broadneux was born in 1617. He served in the Civil War; was Captain of Horse and Gentleman of the Bedchamber to Oliver Cromwell; and subsequently Lieut.-Col. under William III. At the age of 83, being attacked by a sickness which he apprehended would terminate fatally, he caused his coffin to be made, and slept nightly in it to the day of his decease, 26 years afterwards. It is not known

whether he was a native, but his latter years were spent in Liverpool. He died January 27th, 1727, aged 109 years, having retained his faculties to the last, and was interred in St. Nicholas's churchyard, where his tombstone was visible, recording the above particulars, until worn out by age and passing footsteps.

CHAPTER SECOND.

REIGN OF GEORGE II; 1727—1760.

MUNICIPAL AFFAIRS.

This period was a very stirring and animated one in the progress of the resuscitated borough.

Progress. Mercantile affairs were prosperous, new channels for commercial enterprise were opening out, capital was flowing into the town; and, in spite of the senseless opposition to the introduction of "foreigners," population was rapidly increasing.

St. George's Church. 1728, Nov. 6th. A Committee was appointed for carrying on the New Church (St. George's) and for general purposes, and it was

Coronation. "Order'd That the said Committee (inter alia) sign orders to pay the expence of their Maj^{ties} Coronation day, and likewise to direct the paym^t of the sev'all sumes expended in the prosecutions or other disputes had and carry'd on in defence of the rights and libertyes of the town, occasioned *Bootle's surrender.* by the unprecedented surrender of Thos Bootle Esq, Mr Tyrers refusall of a scrutiny and Mr Hughes's takeing upon him the office of Mayor.

"A motion was then made for entring a protest against the above order relating to Mr Bootle's surrender, Mr Tyrers refusall &c., and also for entring another protest against the order for allowing the expenses in the treasurer's accounts, but the same were both rejected."

The Council proceedings about this time appear to have *Disorder.* fallen into considerable disorder as will be seen from the following record:—

"1729, Mar. 5. Bryan Blundell Esq Mayor.
"Att the Councill held this day
"Whereas by the constitution of this Corporation no business of moment relating thereto can be order'd transacted or done, save only by, or under

the direction of, the Comon Council assembled, and that no Council or assembly can be held without the Mayor and one bayliffe. And whereas Council by an order of Council of the first day of May 1679 it was order'd that the Meetings. first Wednesday in every month sho'd thenceforth be a Council day and duly observ'd; and altho' the same hath since been constantly observ'd and put in practice except in case of sickness or other very extraordinary accidents, untill the time of Mr Bootle's Mayoralty in the year 1726, who Bootle's first declined to hold Councills by himself or deputy as usuall, and after- Mayoralty. wards wilfully and obstinately refused or neglected the same, and made a breach of the said order and then in an unprecedented manner took upon him to surrender and vacate his office of May' and notwithstanding his oath, left the Corporation void of a head or Mayor to act or administer justice, which put the same and the burgesses and inhabitants thereof in the utmost confusion and hath been the source and spring of many great inconveniences, law suits and extraordinary expences, to support the rights of the Corporation ever since, and that by his example and advice, Mr Geo Tyrer, who pretended to act as Mayor after him for remainder of Tyrer Mayor. that year and also Mr John Hughes the year following, did neither of them Hughes. think fitt to pay any regard at all to the said order or other subsequent orders to that purpose or to the repeated sollicitations and request of a majority of the Comon Council, who often desired that a Council might be held in order to elect peace officers, and to carry on and do the publick business of the Corporation for the benefitt and advantage thereof, but on the contrary like enemies to the Corporation, have all out of sinister views regardless to such sollicitations, contemn'd the said order and perversely refused to assemble or meet in Councill, so that none hath been since held Refusals. (save only upon the sixth day of November last) to the great detriment of No Councils. the said Corporation, and the sinking and diminution of the revenues and incomes thereof; inasmuch as without Councils no peace officers were or could be elected, no leases could be renewed, no fines raised noe freemen made, nor any money on that or other accounts as usuall charg'd, impos'd or collected, nor any other important affaires howsoever necessary or ever so much for the good of the Corporation be transacted; which not only put full stop to the carrying on the building and finishing the new church, the cleansing of the dock and other publick works but also to many other necessary matters relateing to the said Corporation, which for want of frequent Councills have been alltogether slighted, hinder'd and obstructed. For remedy whereof and in some measure to supply the defect of Councills, Detriment. but principally to prevent the ill consequences which the majority of this Councill foresaw might in all probabillity attend and greatly affect the body politick in the unjustifiable measures and procedure of such male- contents and designing persons. The said majority of this Council therefore thought it exceeding proper and absolutely necessary not only for the safety of the said Corporation, but as much as possible to prevent

Committee appointed.

the ruin, and the constitution of it for being entirely subverted, to appoint a Comittee of seven of the Aldermen of their said body to meet in 'the Comon hall every Thursday in the afternoon or oftner as occasion sho'd require, to transact such of the Corporation affairs for the good and benefit of it as might probably fall within their care, and any five of them to examine and sign all bills and notes for any thing justly due from the said Corporation and all charges for workmen's wages done at the new church and other publick works and such other demands as might appear to them to be reasonable or justly due and owing, and to transmitt such bills or notes so by them signed to the Treasurer to be paid or to undertake for the paym^t thereof to avoid the expence of law suits for the same: all which the said Comittee observ'd and acted accordingly;

"And this Council being fully appris'd thereof, doe hereby approve of, ratifie and confirm the same and all that the said Comittee have done in pursuance of their directions and the trust reposed in them: And whereas upon the sixth day of November last it being found necessary that a Comittee might still act in manner aforesaid, it was ordained and directed that the same Comittee of seven Aldermen together with the p'sent Mayor should still subsist and act, but no proper or full directions being given to

Payment of Bills.

the Treasurer for paym^t of such notes, bills &c he hath scrupled and refus'd to discharge the same, so that the building of the said new church and other publick works are still at a stand and can't be carried on without the further order and direction of this Councill.

"Wherefore it is hereby order'd that all bills &c which have been allow'd and signed by either of the said Comittees be with all convenient speed paid and discharg'd by the said Treasurer . . . and the said

Instructions to Treasurer.

Treasurer is further to take notice that from henceforth no other sumes or paym^{ts} not so allowed shall on any colour or under any pretence be by him paid to any person or persons, notwithstanding any former order of Council to the contrary. And to avoid all future objections or disputes

Prizage.

concerning the prizage of wine belonging to the said Corp^n which sometimes has by order of Council been given to the Mayor for the time being, and at other times reassumed and recall'd as occasion sho'd happen, and

Payment to Mayor.

also concerning the sume of fourty pounds, which hath for some time past been paid to the Mayor for the time being after he had fully serv'd that office for one year: Now it is hereby order'd and declar'd that all future allowances be and is hereby withdrawn, stay'd and forborn, and that the aforesaid Comittee shall from time to time compound and agree for the said prizage of wine with the importers thereof, and that the Treasurer do collect and receive the said composition and apply the same and the said sume of fourty pounds towards the discharge of the debts of the said Corp^n until such time as the Comon Council in Council assembled shall think fitt otherwise to dispose thereof or appropriate the same to any other use or purpose."

The disputes at this time arose indirectly out of the Disputes. relation of the Council to the burgesses at large. The early charters made no mention of the Council at all, the government being vested in the burgesses in Common Hall assembled. The Council was first appointed in 1580 by the burgesses as a Committee, which gradually arrogated to itself the governing power, and by filling up its own vacancies became self-elected. In the charter of 1626 the Charters. Council was first recognised, but no provision was made for its constitution or election. In the subsequent charter of 1695, the Council was directed to be elected in the same manner as had been done previous to the annulled charter of Charles II. This left the question entirely vague, and was the cause of great dissatisfaction and complaint. Several of the Mayors declined to recognise the authority of the Council and appealed directly to the burgesses. Mr. John Hughes, Hughes Mayor, 1728-9, refused to summon the Council, and in Mayor. conjunction with the Bailiffs and some of the burgesses proceeded to grant leases independently. This led to the manifesto above inserted, claiming the supreme right of the Council to manage the affairs of the Corporation and cutting off the usual allowance from the recalcitrant Mayor.

Under the same date it was enacted that no leases or Leases. other documents should be executed under the Common Seal unless they had been examined and confirmed by the Committee appointed by the Council.

1729, Aug. 8th. Bryan Blundell, Mayor.

Articles were exhibited against Mr. Jno. Hughes, the late Articles Mayor, for his misbehaviour and neglect of duty during his Hughes. against Mayoralty in not duly summoning the Councils, and in acting independently of their jurisdiction.

The question was adjourned, but unfortunately the result is not entered on the record.

M

Mandamus.

About the same time the Council were served with a mandamus on behalf of one Thomas Vernon, who had applied to be entered on the Burgess roll and was refused. The writ, which is in Latin, states that from time immemorial the ancient and laudable custom had existed in Liverpool that the son of a freeman, born in Liverpool, on attaining the age of twenty-one was entitled to be sworn and enrolled as a freeman; that Vernon had so established his claim, and the Council were ordered to admit him to the privileges and franchises on pain of penalties for contempt.

Admission of Freemen.

A practice had been growing up, which was subsequently carried to a great extent, of admitting a large number of freemen on the eve of a Parliamentary election. Probably both political parties were equally in fault. In order to check this the following regulation was passed:—

"1729, Sept. 3. Bryan Blundell Mayor.

"Whereas many and great inconveniences, disputes and confusions have arisen by the irregular entries of the petitions and admissions of persons to their freedom within this Corporation and thereby swell'd the records to an unnecessary bulk.

Claims to Freedom.

"It is now order'd by this Council that all persons for the future who have any right to their freedom by birth or servitude, shall first apply to the Committee appointed for the purpose."

They were to attend personally at stated times, to be published by advertisement, and their cases were to be reported to the Council.

The record proceeds:—

Dispute in Council.

"The above order was read in full Councill and thereupon Mr Mayor withdrew out of Councill, and Mr Hughes, Mr Cunliffe and Mr Tyrer went with him, but the question was putt before he went away, for the passing the said order without any adjournment of the Councill."

Public opinion appears to have been considerably excited. 1729, Oct. 24th, we read:—

Libels published.

"Whereas a base and scandalous paper hath been putt up and was found upon the publick Exchange, and was taken off on the 15th day of this instant; which being now read is declar'd by this Councill to be a high reflection on the body of the Comon Councill of this burrough, a scandalous libell and unjust charge upon them; and it is now order'd that inquiry be made after the author and publisher thereof, and that publick notice be given that a reward of tenn guin^s shall be paid by Mr Hen. Trafford to such person as will effectually discover the author and publisher of that paper or either of them."

"1729, Nov. 5. Order'd that in case the worpp^n the Mayor for the time being, or in his absence his dep'ty shall and doe refuse to swear any of the persons aforenam'd free upon their tendring themselves to him to take upp their respective freedoms; that then the sen^r Alderman with one or two more Aldermen and one of the Bayl^s att the least, may and they are hereby impower'd to administer the oath of a freeman of this burrough with the oaths to the Governm^t to any such of the persons before voted, free gratis. *Conduct of Mayor.*

"Mem^{dm} That upon the motion of Ald^n Gildart for voting the aforenam'd p'sons to be free, gratis, and two or three of them being read, Mr Mayor without moveing to adjourn this Councill withdrew out of Councill abruptly, arbitrarily, and illegally, with Ald^n Tyrer, Ald^n Poole, Ald^n Hughes and Mr Bayliffe Whitfield." *Withdrawal of Mayor.*

"1730, Feby. 6. Geo. Tyrer Mayor. It is now declar'd by this Councill that the sev'll persons whose names are entred before as voted free, gratis, begining with the R^t Honble the Lord Viscount Malpas and ending with the name of John Lobsey of Lincoln, and the above sev'all orders ther under being entred after the late Mayor withdrew out of Councill the 5th day of November 1729, are void to all intents and purposes, and that they nor any of them are thereby voted free, nor have any claim of right to their freedom by the said entry of the s^d 5 November 1729, and that the said orders thereunder are absolutely void and of none effect. *Freemen rejected.*

"Order'd That some eminent Councillor at Law be appointed as standing Councill for the Corp^n to advise with on the Corp^n affairs as they shall have occasion, and have a sallary of 20 Guin^s ⅌ ann. to be paid by the Trea'rer dureing the pleasure of this Councill. *Standing Counsel.*

"Order'd That not any member of this Councill when assembled shall leave the same without consent of the Councill and till they be adjourned.

"Then Mr. Gildart mov'd that the Hall door sho'd be lock'd, and it was order'd by the Council to be lock'd, and he lock'd it accordingly. Then mov'd that these persons following might be admitted free, whereupon Mr Mayor withdrew off the bench, but their names were read before he left the room." *Locking door.*

"1731, Oct. 18. Richard Gildart Mayor.

"Order'd that Ald^n Josia Poole, Ald^n Wm Squire, Ald^n Thos Bootle and Mr Chas Pole, who are remov'd out of town and doe not inhabitt within this burrough or the liberties thereof and have neglected their duty of attending in Councill be sumoned. *Censure on Councillors.*

CHAP. II, A.D. 1727—1760.

Summonses were accordingly served as directed.

Poole expelled.
"1731, Decr. 13. Mr Josia Poole by vote of the Councill was removed and discharged from his office as Councillor."

"1732, Nov. 9. Thos. Brereton Mayor.

Lord Willoughby.
"Mr Mayor acquainting the Councill that the Right Honble Hugh Lord Willoughby of Parham is in town, it is order'd that he be complemented with his freedom, and that the Bayl^r and town clerk do wait on his Ld^{pp} and desire his acceptance thereof."

"1733, Feby. 12. Mr Mayor proposeing, That the Corporation sho'd contribute towards the releif of such poor unfortunate persons as are willing to go and settle at Georgia, and the account of the designs of the Trustees for establishing the colony of Georgia in America being now read,

Emigration to Georgia.
"It is resolv'd and order'd, that the Treasurer do pay the sume of fifty Pounds to the trustees appointed by his Maj^{ties} charter towards provideing for such persons as are or shall be sent to settle there in the name of and as a benefaction from the Corporation of Liverpool and be allowed the same in his accounts."

River Dee.
1733, Sept. 24th. An Act was passed in the previous session of Parliament "to recover and preserve the navigation of the river Dee," which was unsuccessfully opposed by the Corporation of Liverpool. The following resolution explains the circumstances :—

Opposition to Bill.
Hoyle Lake.
"Whereas it was thought necessary to preferr a petition the last sessions of Parliam^t on behalf of this Corporation against the Act to recover and preserve the navigation of the river Dee, as being apprehended would tend to the p'judice of this port, and more especially to destroy Hoyl Lake, and that Mr Arthur Hamilton, and Mr Robt Dixon who were then in London on account of the merch^{ts} and tradesmen of this town to oppose the collecting of the duties on tobacco and wine by way of Excise, did in conjunction with Sr Roger Mostyn (to whom most of the lands on the shore of the road or harbour at Parkgate belongs) imploy a sollicitor to manage the same, and that his bill of the charge therein which is now produc'd amounts to £240 15s. od, one half whereof is to be paid by this Corporation and the other half hath been or is to be paid by Sr Roger Mostyn ; it is now Order'd that the treasurer do immediately pay to Mr Hamilton and Mr Dixon fifty Pounds in part thereof to be remitted to the said sollicitor, and in the meantime that Mr Hamilton do write to Sr Roger Mostyn to know how much he hath paid towards the said charge, and whether he does not intend to have the bill taxed or examin'd by some proper officer; it being looked upon as a very extravagant charge."

It may be mentioned that the operation of this Act has had very disastrous results. By diverting the current of the river and enclosing large tracts in the upper reaches, thereby impairing the scouring power of the ebb current, the estuary has become silted up to such an extent as almost to destroy the navigation. The Hoyle Lake, referred to above, is now dry at low water.   *Disastrous results.*

Party spirit, both municipal and political, ran very high at this time. The election for Mayor, on St. Luke's Day, 1733, was very disorderly. It is thus described in the records :—   *Party spirit.*

"1733, Oct. 18. Thomas Brereton Mayor.

"Att an Election Court held according to Charter &c. Read the Act for the more effectuall preventing bribery and corruption.   *Disorder.*

"A Poll being demanded, the same was begun and continued for severall hours, but the people becomeing so tumultuous, and complaint made to Mr Mayor that the Freemen were insulted and abus'd in comeing to give their votes, he order'd the court and poll to be adjourned till tomorrow morning at eight o'clock which was accordingly adjourn'd, and the other party acquiesc'd therein; there having been a great majority then poll'd for Mr Pole.

"Att the same Election Court, this nineteenth day of October, the poll was entred upon again, and continued till all the freemen that thought fitt to appear had given their votes; and the majority being for Mr Wm Pole Gent⁸, he was declar'd by publick proclamation to be duly elected Mayor of this burrough and Corporation for the year ensueing, and the said Wm Pole took the oath of Mayor, and according to ancient usage nominated John Brooks Gent to be Mayor's Bayliffe for the year ensueing.   *Pole Mayor.*

"And a poll being afterwards demanded for the Baylives, the Court gave for answer that as the Mayor's Bayliffe was sworn they could not grant a poll for both; but if they would poll for the town's Bayliffe the Mayor declared they might proceed and he would stay to take it, and recommended Owin Pritchard Gent. to be Town's Bayliffe; but they demanding of Mr Mayor to adjourn the Court, and the town clerk having taken a poll for said Mr Pritchard from sev'all persons, the Court was adjourn'd till next morning.   *Bailiffs.*

Court adjourned.

"On the twentieth day of October Mr Mayor and Baylives came into court, and declared that as there was not any provission in the Act of Parliam¹ for p'venting inconveniences ariseing for want of elections of Mayors being made on the days appointed by charter or usage for making elections, after the day next after the expiration of the day of   *Mayor elected.*

election by charter, he apprehended they could not make any election this day, but that the election made last night must stand, and afterwards Mr Pritchard haveing the majority on the Poll last night was proclaim'd and took the oath of Bayliffe accordingly."

The opposition party were not satisfied with this result, and applied to the King's Bench for a writ of *Quo Warranto*, relative to which is the following record :—

"1733, Nov. 7. William Pole, Mayor.

Quo Warranto

"It being now represented to this Councill that Mr Mayor and Bayliffs have been lately serv'd with a Rule from the King's Bench to shew cause why an information in the nature of a *Quo Warranto* sho'd not be exhibited against them to shew by what authority they claim to be Mayor and Bayliffs of this town; and that as the Poll after the adjornm' was fairly and regularly carried on, and that Mr Pole had indisputably a great majority of legal votes, and was accordingly duly elected and sworn into the office of Mayor. This Councill is of opinion and do now order that they be indemnify'd by the Corporation and sav'd harmless from all expence that they shall be putt unto in defending themselves against the said prosecution in the King's Bench, and that Mr Richard Aldersey Rec^r of the town's customs do immediately pay to Mr Ald^n Brereton thirty guineas towards carrying on their defence on the said Rules, and be allow'd the same in his accounts, and not to be accountable to the Treasurer for the same."

Defence.

The manufacture of Freemen for political purposes, on the eve of an election, began about this time, and as will be seen hereafter, was subsequently carried on to a shameless extent. The following entry refers to this :—

Admission of Freemen.

"1733, Dec. 5. It being now represented to this Councill that a List hath been lately printed and dispersed about, of the names of persons that have been voted and admitted free of this Corp^n since the 18th day of October 1731, wherein are severall suggestions as if many of them were admitted as haveing a right, but had not; and that it is highly necessary to print a true list of all those that have been so admitted, to the end that the falseness of such former list may be fully laid open, and that the great care of this Councill therein made publick. It is now therefore order'd that a perfect list be printed distinguishing therein the respective rights of such as have been so admitted—those admitted on fines, and such as have been complimented with their freedom."

It has always been the custom to pay to the Mayor a

salary or allowance for the expenses of his office. In 1707 this was fixed to consist

"Of the two best fines which shall be pay'd by any two freemen admitted in such Mayor's time."

"1733, Decr. 5. It being now represented in Council that Mr Mayor have the same allowances as were made to the late Mayor. It is Order'd that Mr Mayor be allow'd the prizage of all wines imported into this County dureing his Mayoralty, and also the sume of fourty pounds in lieu of the two best freemen's fines, and that the treasurer do pay the same accordingly." *Mayor's allowance.*

The above minute was varied as follows :—

"1734, Sept. 30. Wm Pole Mayor.
"It is Order'd, that the Treasurer shall have and receive the prizage of all wines and apply the moneys ariseing thereby in such manner as shall from time to time be order'd by the Councill; and that the Treasurer retain in his hands the fourty Pounds that have usually allow'd to the Mayor in lieu of the fines, till the Councill think fitt to order the same to be paid." *Prizage.*

Disputes and wrangling still went forward in the Council.

"1726. On the 10th August Mr Robt Whitfield was elected a Common Council Man and took the prescribed oath."

He appears to have been implicated in the disputes about the admission of Freemen, and to have absented himself from the Council meetings. On the 2nd January, 1734, he was summoned to attend, but neglected to do so. After being twice further summoned, he was served with a peremptory order to appear on the 6th February, to show cause why he should not be removed and discharged from his office. He did so attend, but not showing sufficient cause he was, by vote of the Council, removed and discharged. *Whitfield expelled.*

He then applied to the King's Bench for a mandamus, March 20th, 1734. The cause was sent down to Lancaster to be tried, and an order was given by the Council to produce the charters and books of the Corporation, and to the treasurer to pay £50 on account of expenses.

1734, July 4th. A further order is given to the Customs' Receiver to pay any money in his hands towards the expenses of the suit.

Funds.

"1734, Sept. 30. It being represented to the Comon Councill that there is a great necessity to take up the sume of five hundred pounds to discharge the great expence that the Mayor and Bayliffs have been lately putt unto in makeing their defence to the informations brought and prosecuted against them in his Majesties Court of King's Bench, and that at present there is not any moneys in the hands of the Receiver of the town's customs to answer the same. It is now order'd that the said sume of £500 be taken up at interest under the Corporation Seale, and that it be repaid out of the town's customs as soon as the same can be rais'd by and out of the town's customs."

Lord Derby Mayor.

1734, Octr. 18th. The Right Hon. James, the 10th Earl of Derby, was duly elected Mayor for the second time, having previously filled the office in 1707-8. In the disputes which were now agitating the Corporation he took the popular side, and with the concurrence of the two Bailiffs, he called a Common Hall of the burgesses, at which by-laws were made.

1735, Feby. 1st. The Earl of Derby died; his deputy, Bryan Blundell, succeeding him.

Blundell

"Feby. 4th. At a meeting of the Council, Mr. Deputy Blundell declared he was for restoreing Mr Whitfield, and afterwards moved to have the order read for displaceing him from being one of the Comon Council; but Mr Aldⁿ Pole insisted that the Minitts and orders of the last Council should be first read, and a dispute ariseing, Mr Tyrer delivered in a paper containing Mr Whitfield's reasons against his being remov'd, and desired it might be read, and declared he would not stay to do any other business but only that for which the Councill were call'd together, which was to make a return to the Mandamus issued forth of his Majesties Court of King's Bench for restoreing said Robert Whitfield to the office of one of the Comon Council of this town, or to restore said Robert Whitfield to his place.

Dispute.

Whitfield.

"Then Aldⁿ Cunliffe declared he was for restoreing Robert Whitfield, and delivered it in writing subscribed by himself.

"Then Mr Tyrer delivered in the like, and afterwards Mr Dep^{ty} Mayor delivered in the like.

"Then Mr Kelsall moved, That two persons that were at the door might be called in to be witnesses to his delivery to the Deputy Mayor and Bayliffs a return to the said mandamus, which was signed by the majority of the Comon Council present, and as those two persons came into the hall, Mr Tyrer the Bayliffe withdrew and went away, Mr Kelsall delivering it. The same was then read." _{Return to Mandamus.}

This return recapitulates the circumstances stated above, and proceeds to assert:—

"That the Mayor Bayliffs and Comon Council or the major part of them had time out of mind used for any reasonable cause, to displace any one of the Comon Council as often as occasion required and that for the causes aforesaid the said Robert Whitfield was displaced, and we cannot restore him."

1736, Sept. 23rd. ' Foster Cunliffe, Mayor.

The legality of the proceedings of the Earl of Derby when Mayor, in conjunction with the Bailiffs in calling a Common Hall of the Burgesses, was called in question, and the following protest entered on the minutes. It would appear that from the 4th Feby., 1735, no Council meeting had been called. _{Legality questioned.}

"Whereas since the holding of the last Comon Council to witt in or about the month of July 1735 in the Mayoralty of the Right Honourable James Earle of Derby, the then Mayor and Bayliffs did take upon them in an arbitrary and illegal manner to sumon and hold a meeting or assembly at which were present the said Mayor and Bailiffs and a small number of the burgesses of this Corporation, which meeting they thought fit to call a Comon Hall, and then and there pretended to make certain orders or By-laws relateing to the government of this Corporation, contrary to the charters and immemorial usage thereof, which arbitrary proceedings this Court taking into consideration. _{Protest.}

"It is hereby declared that the said meeting or assembly and the Orders or By-laws pretended to be made thereat, and all proceedings of the said pretended Comon Hall, were and are illegal and contrary to the known and immemorial usages, customs, privileges and the very constitution of this burrough, and are hereby declared to be absolutely null and void to all intents and purposes whatsoever. _{Common Hall invalid.}

"And it is hereby further ordered; That all Orders, By-laws and proceedings whatsoever had or made or pretended by the said pretended assembly or meeting called the Comon Hall, which may or have been entred in any of the books or records of this Corporation, be, by the town clerk now produced and forthwith expunged and cancelled.

98   CHAP. II, A.D. 1727—1760.

Action against Aldersey.

"And whereas by order of the said pretended Comon Hall an action of debt was sometime since brought in his Majesties Court of Exchequer at Westminster in the name of the Mayor, Bailiffs and Burgesses of the town of Liverpool against Richard Aldersey for the sume of one thousand pounds upon bond conditioned for his accounting and paying the moneys received by him as Receiver of the town's customs or revenues of the said town, in which action judgment hath been obtained against the said Richard Aldersey;

Proceedings stayed.

"And whereas the said Richard Aldersey is by orders of Comon Council to pay the moneys in his hands in manner in such orders mentioned. Now it is hereby ordered that all proceedings in the said action or upon the said judgment be and the same are hereby stayed till further order of the Comon Councill, and Mr Daniel Dandy the Attorney in the said Court of Excheq' for the said plaintiffs is hereby required and directed to stay proceedings accordingly and that the Common Seal of this Corporation be affixed to this order and sent to the said Mr Daniel Dandy. Wherefore, we, the Mayor, Bailiffs and Burgesses of the town of Liverpool have hereunto affixed our Comon Seal this 23rd day of September 1736.

By-Laws.

"The Town Clerk being now call'd upon to produce the above mentioned orders or by-laws, declares he hath not them in his custody, nor hath he entred them in any book or record in his custody belonging to the Corporation.

"And whereas the said assembly or Meeting pretended to be a Comon Hall was sumoned and held by George Tyrer and John Hughes, Gentlemen the then Bailiffs as well as by the said Earl of Derby, the then Mayor of this Corporation ; We the Mayor, Bailiffs and Burgesses of this burrough now in Comon Councill assembled, looking on the said pretended meeting or assembly as illegal and wholly subversive of the very constitution of this burrough, and that the same was sumoned and held by the said Mr Tyrer and Mr Hughes the then Bailiffs, in which we apprehend they acted manifestly in breach of the trust in them reposed as Councilmen of this burrough, and for the said high offence they be and are hereby dismissed to all intents and purposes from their respective office of Councilmen of this burrough.

Dismissal of Councillors.

"And it is hereby ordered and directed that the Comon Seal of this burrough be affixed to this order, and that the town clerk do serve the said Mr Tyrer and Mr Hughes therewith, and that Mr Mayor, Mr Brereton Mr Gildart Mr Moorecroft and Mr Kelsall or any three of them be appointed to affix the Comon Seal to the said orders."

"These be rare words! a brave world!" It is probable that had the Earl of Derby lived to carry out his plan of reform, or rather the return to the primitive constitution, the

Council would have had to succumb, but his untimely death before anything had been accomplished, threw all into confusion, and the Council resumed their self-asserted domination without opposition. They were not disposed to give any quarter. *Resumption of Council.*

"1736, Nov. 3. Richard Gildart Mayor.

"Aldⁿ George Tyrer and Aldⁿ John Hughes, now attending, pursuant to the liberty given last Council day refus'd to give any answer in writing, but own'd that they were p'sent at the holding of the Comon Hall, as charg'd against them, and only said they were illegally dismiss'd from their respective offices of Comon Councilmen. Therefore this Council doth now confirm the former order made the 23rd day of September last past for dismissing them from their respective offices of Comon Councilmen of this burrough and Corporation." *Dismissal confirmed.*

The Counsel learned in the law, who had been their adviser, came in for a share in their indignation.

"It being now made appear to this Councill, that John Ratcliffe Esq who was appointed standing Council to this Corpⁿ the 6th Feby 1730, did refuse to attend Aldⁿ William Pole, late Mayor on the 18th day of October 1734, when sent for on the adjornm^t of the Poll that night to advise the Mayor therein. *Censure of Ratcliffe.*

"It is now order'd that the sallary order'd on the 6th of February to be paid him shall be paid by the treasurer to the said 18th October 1734 and no more and to cease from that time."

During Lord Derby's short term of office a large number of freemen had been admitted whilst the Common Council was in abeyance. The following protest was recorded by the restored Council.

"1736, Novr. 19. An order made 21st November 1646 That no person should be admitted free of this Corporation without the consent and assent of the Mayor Aldⁿ and Comon Council being now read, and it being now represented that one hundred and twelve persons were admitted free of this Corporation in the last mayoralty of the late Earl of Derby, by his deputy without the assent of the Comon Council. This Council are of opinion that the admitting any person or persons free of this Corporation without the assent and consent of the Mayor Aldⁿ and Comon Council was an arbitrary, illegall, and partial act in the Deputy Mayor and contrary to the usage of this Corpⁿ and the said order made in 1646, and tends to *Freemen illegally admitted.*

weaken the rights and franchises of such persons who have right to freedom by birth or service, and do declare and enact that not any person whatsoever shall be hereafter admitted free of this Corpn without the assent and order of the Comon Council of this Corporation in Council assembled.

Notwithstanding this protest it does not appear that any steps were taken to disfranchise the freemen so alleged to have been irregularly admitted.

These controversies were expensive, but money was never an object with the Corporation of Liverpool in defending their own position.

Payment to Watson.

"1736, Nov. 3. It being now represented that there is a considerable sume due to Mr Hugh Watson Sollicitor for the Corporation in the late contests. It is now Order'd that the treasurer do remit him the sume of two hundred pounds and to be allow'd the same in his accounts."

Mr. Hughes was kept out of the Council for four years.

"1740, Octr. 24. Henry Trafford Mayor.

"It being now represented to this Council that Aldn John Hughes who was dismissed from his office and place of Comon Councilman the 23rd day of September 1736 for misbehaviour the year before as Bailiff to the late Earl of Derby, then Mayor; being very sensible of his fault hath been to wait upon the Worppll Mr Mayor and acknowledged the same and given full assurance of his future good behaviour.

Hughes restored.

"It is now order'd and enacted, that the said Aldn John Hughes be restored to his office and place of Comon Councilman, and established to be one of the Comon Council of this burrough as fully and effectually to all intents and purposes as he had or might have held and enjoyed before such dismission."

This ebullition subsided for a time, but in 1750 it broke out again with increased violence.

Petition to Parliament.

In that year the Council presented a petition to Parliament, setting forth certain difficulties in the administration of the law, for want of additional justices, the necessity for a deputy recorder, and for a grant of the waste shore. Under cover of these applications, they petitioned that the usurped powers of the Council might be legalised. They recite as follows :—

"That a Charter was granted by King William the third in 1695 which ordained 'That for the future to preserve the peace, tranquillity and good government of the town of Liverpool and its inhabitants there shall or may be for ever, the officers and ministers following, viz Forty one good and discreet burgesses, who shall be called the Common-Council of the said Vill,' omitting to give them the least power in express words, tho' it was the manifest, if not the sole intent of this Charter to give forty one the power in the first recited clause of King Charles's Charter, in order to prevent the populous meetings of the burgesses upon every trifling occasion, as the town was so extremely encreased since that time; and therefore from that time to this, such Common Council's actings have been acquiesced in, to the great advantage and satisfaction of the whole town. But it may hereafter cause disputes unless the said Charter is explained for this purpose by adding the clause of King Charles's Charter, or in such manner as your Majesty in your great wisdom shall think fit." *Recital of Charters.*

This petition, in the first instance, was not made public, but as some objection was taken, the Council published it with an explanation in which they say :—

"The reason why this application was not made public at the time it was in agitation was, that they could not, consistent with their duty as guardians and trustees of the public estate, discover it to your enemies and opponents; by whom we mean those foreigners who were invading your rights by following their trades in town, and others who were attempting and threatening to take part of the public estates from you. And we repeat it again that for those and only those good and just ends was the following petition preferred." *Explanation.*

This brought another combatant into the field, in the person of Mr. Joseph Clegg, a Common Councilman, and Mayor in 1748. He issued a pamphlet, in which he strongly animadverted on the conduct of the Council, who he alleged, suppressed the charters, and published false statements in order to maintain their usurped power. For this pamphlet he was prosecuted, at the instigation of the Council, by one Galley, and the cause was entered to be tried at Lancaster, in 1752. For the purpose of the prosecution, several of the *Clegg's Pamphlet.* *Prosecution.*

Councillors were temporarily disfranchised by the Council, and subsequently re-admitted.

In the meantime the petition had been presented and referred to Sir Dudley Ryder, Attorney General, and Mr. (afterwards Lord) Mansfield, Solicitor General.

Report on Petition. They reported against confirming the assumed powers of the Council, but in favour of additional justices of the peace and other minor matters, and a charter was granted accordingly.

Compromise. This opened the way for a compromise between the contending parties. An arbitration was entered into and an entry made that the award be ratified and confirmed, and that such confirmation be passed under the Common Seal. Unfortunately the terms of the award are not given.

A list is given of 35 Burgesses who had been disfranchised in order to enable them to give evidence, and afterwards restored.

Fees. The fees to counsel are entered as 25 guineas to the senior and 20 guineas to the junior. .

Prosecution for Libels. "1753, Octr. 3. It is ordered, that the Author, Printer and publisher of a most infamous and scandalous paper lately printed at Liverpoole, purporting to be an address to the freemen of Liverpoole, dated Sept. 20, 1753 and highly reflecting on and most malitiously defaming the characters, reputation integrity and actions of the Common Council of this borough and Corporation be prosecuted; and which said paper is signed Freeman, be prosecuted at law with effect, and that this order be made publick."

Sadler's Confession. "1753, Novr. 7. Mr John Sadler the printer, having now before this Council confessed and owned himself to be the printer of the most infamous paper signed FREEMAN as also who were the author and publishers thereof. It is Ordered that the prosecution lately ordered to be commenced against him be stopt, on account of his open and candid confession, and on his signing his submission to the Council, which is now ordered to be published in the Newspapers."

Mandamus. The controversy with Mr. Clegg did not end here. Five years after these transactions, the Council, on the 1st Feby., 1758, removed him from his office as Alderman and discharged him from the Council. He immediately applied to the Court of King's Bench for a mandamus to compel his restoration. The return to this writ is given in full in the records in very lengthy form. The substance is as follows :—

It first recapitulates the history of the Municipality, especially referring to the charter of Charles I. as explained by the subsequent charter of William III., under which the Council lay claim to be the governing body, and stating that these claims have always been acknowledged, and

> "That from time whereof the memory of man is not to the contrary the Mayor, Bailiffs and Common Council . . have of right removed and been accustomed to remove for any reasonable and lawful cause any of the Common Council, and that the persons so removed have accordingly been and continued absolutely and effectually discharged."

Answer.

The document then sets forth the valuable property and revenues belonging to the Corporation, and the important trust confided to those who have the management of them. It then proceeds :—

> "That before the removal of the said Joseph Clegg he sought his trade or living by buying and selling and was adjudged Bankrupt under a commission dated July 7, 1756, and that he had not obtained a certificate of discharge, and that he is therefore unfit for the place and office of one of the Common Council, so being an office of great trust and power with respect to the management, receipt, controul, and application of the issues, rents, and profitts of the estates, revenues, &c. That at the time of his discharge twenty six of the Council were present, and Mr Clegg being also present had nothing to allege why he should not be removed and discharged, and he accordingly was so discharged."

Clegg discredited.

This line of defence did not succeed. The writ of mandamus was issued on the 31st January, 1759, peremptorily commanding the Council to restore Alderman Joseph Clegg into the place and office of one of the Common Council of the said borough.

Mandamus granted.

The record proceeds :—

> "It is Ordered that the said Joseph Clegg be now restored to his said place or office of a Common Councilman of the said borough of Liverpoole

Clegg restored.

with all the franchises, liberties and privileges thereunto belonging, and he is accordingly restored."

Immediately on his reinstatement, Mr Alderman Clegg commenced another onslaught on the jurisdiction claimed by the Council.

Mandamus for Common Hall.

1759, June 6th. A notice was served on the Mayor that the Court of King's Bench would be moved for a mandamus to compel the Mayor to hold a Common Hall of the Burgesses.

The notice sets forth the Charters of Charles I. and William III., so often referred to, claiming

"That the power to make By-laws rested with the Mayor Bailiffs and Burgesses . . that whereas there was a necessity for makeing some by-laws for want of which the rights and privileges of the Mayor Bailiffs and Burgesses are greatly incroached upon and abused. This is therefore to give you notice that unless in six days from this notice you cause a Common Hall to be summoned in obedience to the said several charters . . His Majesty's Court of Kings Bench will be moved for obtaining a rule for information in the nature of a *Quo Warranto* or for a Writ of Mandamus or other such of his Majesty's Writts or Informations as the Court shall award."

On the receipt of this notice the Council passed the resolution :—

Defence.

"It is ordered that Mr Mayor be defended against any such motion at the Corporation expence."

Nothing ultimately came of this. Mr Clegg and his friends had not the means to contend with the funds of the Corporation, which were expended without stint in support of the existing authorities, and the matter slumbered for another half century.

The following entry is not without interest :—

Duke of Athol.

"1737, Aug. 10. It is ordered that his Grace the Duke of Athol be complimented with his freedom."

On the decease of James, the tenth Earl of Derby, in 1735, his estates unconnected with the title passed by female inheritance to the Duke.

At the same time Lord Sidney Beauclerk, son of the *Sidney Beauclerk.* Duke of St. Albans, and the Rev. Jno. Norris were admitted. Lord Sidney had married the heiress of the Norrises of Speke Hall.

The proceedings connected with the rebellion of 1745 *Rebellion.* form a very interesting chapter in the records. Liverpool has always been loyal and faithful to the Hanoverian dynasty, and prepared to support its loyalty by its actions, in this respect forming a strong contrast to other towns in the North of England.

The first notice is as follows :—

"1743, Feby. 28. John Brookes Mayor.
"Ordered, that this Corporation do address his Majesty on account of *Address to Crown.* an intended invasion in favour of the Pretender's son and that the address for that purpose now read be passed under the Corporation Seal, and sent up to the members of this borough to be presented to his Majesty."

The text is not recorded.

"1745, Aug. 7. Ordered that the account of the publick Arms of this *Arms.* Corporation now read be entred in this Council book and are as follows :—
"Chest No. 1 contains sixty six Muskets
" No. 2   „   sixty five
" No. 3   „   forty seven
" No. 4   „   forty three
" in all two hundred and twenty.
" 1 Chest of Pistols containing one hundred and fifty four
" Twenty five swords."

"1745, Sept. 17. Owen Pritchard Mayor.
"Ordered That the address to his Majesty on the invasion of these kingdoms in favour of the Pretender now read to this Council be passed under the Comon Seal of this Corporation and presented to his Majestye and it is as follows vizt:—
"To THE KING'S MOST EXCELLENT MAJESTY.
"The humble address of the Mayor, Recorder, Aldermen and Common *Address.* Council of the Borough and Corporation of Liverpoole in the County Palatine of Lancaster.
"Most Gracious Sovereign.
"We, your Majesty's most dutyfull and loyal subjects, the Mayor,

Address to Crown.

Recorder, Aldermen and Common Council of the ancient Borough of Liverpoole in Council beg leave to congratulate your Majesty on your safe and happy return to your British dominions after having contributed so much to the election of an Emperor, and thereby to settle the peace of Europe.

"The taking of Cape Breton by your Majesty's forces is another event which will add to the glorys of your Majesty's reign, as it is an acquisition much wished for and of the highest importance, not only to the trade of these nations, but as it will remain a constant supply and nursery of seamen for your royal navy.

"This second daring attempt of the Pretender in Scotland we cannot think of but with the utmost abhorrence; and we do with hearts full of the warmest loyalty assure your Majesty that we will at the hazard of our lives and fortunes exert ourselves in the support of the succession in your Majesty's royal house (as this Corporation with the greatest unanimity did on the rebellion in the year one thousand seven hundred and fifteen) against all opposers whatsoever. Your Majesty's mild and prudent government calls for our earnest testimonys of loyalty as subjects; the defence of our religion and the support of our laws require them of us as men. All concur to demand our prayers for a continuance of your Majesty's reign over a free people, and that the succession may remain in your Royal and Illustrious House to the latest posterity.

"In testimony whereof" &c.

These were not vain and empty words, but were followed by active practical measures. Four days after the despatch of this address we read:—

"1745, Sept. 21. Owen Pritchard Mayor.

Grant for Defence.

"Upon intelligence being received that the Pretender's son is now invading Scotland with a great force, and a plan being now laid before this Council for raising fortifications about this town for its defence against the rebels; and a subscription being proposed to be set on foot for the defraying the expenses thereof. It is now Ordered that this Corporation do pay and contribute the sume of one thousand pounds towards the carrying on these works, and raising forces for the defence of the town; and that a Bond be passed under the Seal to any persons willing to advance 'em the money on the usual interest for a security for a repayment of the same; and that Ald. Steers have the direction of the works, and to call in any person to his assistance that he shall think necessary and proper. And the Corporation Committee to allow of and order the treasurer to pay the bills upon 'em being signed by Ald. Steers.

"Ordered, That the Constables do give a list to the Mayor the preceding day, of persons who are to watch the next night; and that

Mr Pole do now pay the watch who have watched these three nights last Watch and past twelve pence a piece ⅌ night. And for the future twenty five men to Ward. be hired to watch every night, and to be paid only eight pence a piece ⅌ night. And also that Ald Brooke be empowered to hire and set a watch of six men on the powder magazine till the powder be shipped on board Powder. some ship. And that Mr Bird may hire two small vessels to take the powder on board and hire people to guard it.

"Ordered, that Mr Deputy Mayor be empowered to dispatch Samuel Street for intelligence to Edinburgh or any other places he shall think Intelligence. proper; and that the treasurer do advance him ten guineas towards his expences."

"1745, Octr. 10. At a Special Council held this day.

"Whereas upon good advice taken it hath been found impracticable to fortifye this town to any effect, without incurring vast expences; and Mr Mayor having been empowered by His Majesty's sign manual to raise forces for the defence of His Majesty's person and government, this Council doth now order that the sume of one thousand pounds ordered last Council day to be subscribed by this Council towards the expence of raising fortifications, be now made and paid towards the expences of Regiment raising one thousand men, more or less in this town, for the defence of raised. His Majesty's person and government. And that the said commission to Mr Mayor under His Majesty's sign manual be entred in this Council Book as follows—

"George R.

"George the Second, by the grace of God King of Great Britain &c.

"To our trusty and well beloved Owen Pritchard Mayor of our town of Liverpoole in Lancashire, Greeting.

"Whereas several of our loyal subjects in our town of Liverpool have testified unto us their earnest desire in time of common danger when a rebellion is actually begun within this our kingdom in favour of a Popish Royal Pretender, to enter into associations for taking up arms for the common Commission. defence, and have desired our Royal approbation and authority for their so doing.

"We therefore having a just sense of so commendable a zeal, and being desirous to encourage this seasonable instance of their loyalty to us, and their concern for the religion and libertys of their country, have thought fit hereby to give you power and authority, and we do hereby authorize and empower you to signifye to our well affected subjects our Royal approbation of the said design, and to form into troops or companys Troops. such persons as shall be willing to associate themselves for the purposes aforesaid in our town of Liverpoole; and to grant Commissions in our name to such of them as you shall think proper to exercise and command them. And for your executing and performing the power and authority hereby given and granted to you, this shall be a sufficient warrant.

"Given at our Court at Kensington this 23rd day of September 1745 in the nineteenth year of our reign.

"By His Majesty's command
"HOLLES NEWCASTLE.
"The Mayor of Liverpoole
"to grant Commissions."

Liverpool Blues.
The regiment was accordingly raised and called the Liverpool Blues. It consisted of 648 men, commanded by Colonel (afterwards Brigadier-General) Graham, with Lt.-Col. Gordon and Major Bendish as his subordinates. They continued in pay from October 7th, 1745 to the 15th January, 1746, and were present at the taking of Carlisle. When they were disbanded, they received very high compliments from the military authorities.

Watch.
For the purposes of watch and ward, five companies of sixty men each were embodied, who kept a nightly patrol in rotation until the suppression of the rebellion.

Sermons.
"1745, Octr. 10. Ordered that the Bailiffs be desired to write to the clergy of this town who have preached loyal sermons on occasion of the present rebellion. Return 'em the thanks of this Council and desire 'em to print the sermons.

Intelligence.
"That Mathew Strong merchant, who served five years by ind're to Ald^n Gildart be admitted free gratis in consideration that he is now out on the public service of this town gaining us intelligence of the rebels."

"1745, Octr. 18. Ordered that this Corporation do pay the expence of all expresses and messengers sent for intelligence concerning the present invasion."

Freedom to Officers.
"Nov. 6. Col Wm Graham, Lieut Col Gordon and Major Richard Bendishe admitted free, gratis, in consideration of their taking upon 'emselves the comand of the forces raised by this town.

"John Amherst Esq commander of the South Sea Castle Man of War, and Wm Bladwell Esq comander of the Mercury Man of War admitted free, gratis.

Guard Room in Tower.
"Ordered, That the Leather Hall at the Tower, be fitted up for a Guard room for the Soldiers, and that a shop near the Exchange be fitted up as a Watch house for the Constables.

Precautions.
"Ordered, That Mr Mayor if he shall find or apprehend it necessary, be empowered to secure and remove the Corporation Chest with the Seal, Deeds, Charters, Records, Leases and other books and papers, and ship

them on board one of the Men of War now lying in the river, if the rebels approach near the town."

"1745, Nov. 19. James Bromfield Mayor.

"At a special Council

"Mr Mayor now representing that as His Majesty upon our humble petition had been graciously pleased to send down officers, a Colonel, Lieutenant-Colonel, and Major, to command the forces raised in this town and which said officers must be paid for their service by the subscribers to the said forces or the Corporation; therefore to prevent any disagreement or discord between the said subscribers and the Corporation about payment of the said officers, and in order to promote as far as in us lyes His Majesty's interest and welfare. It is Ordered that the Corporation do pay the said three officers their pay as comanding officers of their rank so long as they and the said forces shall be continued in this service. And it is further orderd, that for the better providing for and defraying this expence, as also the charges of paying Expresses for the gaining of more certain intelligence of the Rebels, sent and to be sent out from time to time as occasion should require—or for any other necessary expences unprovided for—during the present rebellion; this Council shall take up at interest any further sume of money not exceeding one thousand pounds, to be expended if found necessary in the above service. [*margin:* Payment of Troops.]

"And in consideration that Mr Mayor—in case any imminent danger from the Rebels should more nearly threaten or beset us—upon many unforseen accidents may'nt nor can get a Council together, it is likewise Ordered, that bonds shall be passed under the Corporation Seal to any persons willing to advance the said sume of one thousand pounds, upon the usual terms for repayment thereof with interest at four pounds and one half ℔ cent ℔ ann. And this one thousand pounds to be lodged in Mr Treasurer's hands, and the application thereof for the purposes aforesaid if required, shall be vested in Mr Mayor, the Aldermen and Bailiffs, and five of them are hereby constituted a committee with power to examine, allow, and order payment of any bills of expences to be incurred in these services on Mr Treasurer of this Corporation, to the extent and amount of the said one thousand pounds only; and the Treasurer to be allowed such payments in his accounts." [*margin:* Bonds for Money advanced.]

"1745, Decr. 24. Whereas at a meeting of several of the principal merchants and inhabitants of this town, held at the Exchange on the 19th day of December 1745, it was by them then agreed that each person present and subscribing should renew and pay one fourth part of their respective former subscriptions by them subscribed for and towards the support and maintenence of the Regiment rais'd by this town, called the Liverpool Bleus, for the defence of His Majesty's person and government, to the several collectors, who have collected their former subscriptions; but upon this condition only, vizt that the Corporation of Liverpoole should [*margin:* Subscriptions.]

pay and subscribe a proportionable and equal sume of money to what is or should hereafter be subscribed by the aforesaid subscribers for the purposes aforesaid.

<small>Further Expenditure.</small>
"It is therefore now ordered by this Council, that this Corporation out of their great zeal for, and loyalty to his present Majesty's person, family, and government, and in consideration that the money formerly subscribed is expended in the maintenance of the said troops who are now become good disciplined soldiers, and who have now join'd the King's troops and may be of great service against the rebels; shall and will, in compliance with the said recited agreement, advance and pay for and towards the further continuance and support of the said troops, any sume of money adequate to the said one other fourth part of the said subscription by them subscribed in pursuance of the said agreement. And the Treasurer of this Corporation is hereby required to pay the money now ordered to be paid, to any collector of the subscription money out of the one thousand pounds ordered by this Council to be rais'd at the last Council day. But it is upon this condition, that in case the whole money now subscribed be not expended on this account that then a proportionable part of what remains unspent shall be return'd to the Corporation."

"1746, May 9. James Bromfield Mayor.

<small>Address to Crown.</small>
"Order'd, that the Common Seal of this borough be put to the address now read in Council, congratulating His Majesty on the success of his arms against the rebels, and that the same be transmitted to the members of Parliament for this borough, to be presented to his Majesty."

The text of the address is not entered.

<small>Amount paid.</small>
The equipment and pay of the regiment thus raised amounted to £4,859, raised entirely within the town.

Some time after the suppression of the rebellion and the restoration of peace, the Council resolved to place on record the history of the proceedings in Liverpool relating thereto, which stands in the Records as follows:—

"1749, May 3. Joseph Clegg Mayor.

<small>Abstract of Proceedings.</small>
"Ordered that the minutes or abstract and account of the Common Council and town and Corporation of Liverpoole's behaviour and proceedings during the late rebellion, and the Commissions and letters which the Mayors of this Corporation were honoured with from His Majesty or His Royal Highness the Duke of Cumberland, be entred in the Council Book as a record and are as follows:—

"Whereas an unnatural Rebellion broke out in that part of Great Britain called Scotland in the year of our Lord 1745, Charles Edward, the

MUNICIPAL AFFAIRS.

Pretender's elder son came over from France with a small retinue, and landed in the Isle of Sky. The first intelligence was brought to this town by Capt. Robinson, who coming from the Baltic, put into that island a few days after the said Pretender's son landed. The account was transmitted by express to His Majesty's Secretary of State's office at London by order of Owen Pritchard Esq then Mayor.

"As the Rebels collected in great numbers, and it was imagined they intended to invade that part of His Majesty's dominions called England; the 17th day of September 1745, the Mayor, Recorder Aldermen and Common Council of this borough addressed his Majesty expressing their abhorence of such unnatural and base behaviour towards the best of princes.

"Upon the 21st day of September aforesaid, the Common Council ordered the sume of one thousand pounds to be raised and applyed to the making such fortifications and raising forces for the defence of the town as should be thought necessary, and sent Mr Samuel Street to Edinburgh to give the best intelligence possible as to the number and progress of the rebels. Narrative.

"The Worshipful Owen Prichard Esq then Mayor, received a Commission from His Majesty to raise and form into troops such persons as should be willing to associate themselves. Soon after this a Regiment of Foot was raised, and proper officers appointed; the men furnished with hatts, coats, stockings and shoes, with an allowance of twelve pence a day for each private man, and the pay of the officers in the proportion according to rank; and so soon as they were equip'd and disciplined, the Honourable Colonel William Graham—soon after created a Brigadier-General—Lieutenant-Colonel Gordon, and Major Richard Bendishe, were appointed by His Majesty to take upon them the command of the said Regiment at the request of the Corporation.

"Soon after, it being thought necessary for the good of the common cause, that the said Regiment should march out of town to any part of His Majesty's dominions where they could be thought to be most serviceable, accordingly on the 15th day of November 1745 they began their march for Warrington, and quartered in several villages in Cheshire, with an additional allowance of four pence a day to every private man during their absence from the town. March out.

"The first duty they were engaged in was taking down several bridges on the rivers betwixt Lancashire and Cheshire, to prevent the progress of the Rebels in those parts. Soon after this, when the Rebels who got into England as far as the town of Derby, retreated to return towards Scotland, the Liverpool Regiment called Bleus, (their uniform being of that colour) consisting of eight companies, joined his Majesty's forces and marched as far as Carlisle, where they did duty during the time of the siege till the place was surrendered to his Royal Highness the Duke of Cumberland, Advance to Carlisle.

CHAP. II, A.D. 1727—1760.

<small>Discharged with Honour.</small> after which they marched back by direction of his Royal Highness to Liverpoole, and were there discharged, having acquitted themselves in such a manner as gave general satisfaction to His Majesty, his Royal Highness and other general officers.

"During the whole time of their doing duty, all the officers and private men (except the said Colonel Graham, who generously refused to take any pay from the Corporation or town for his service) were duely and regularly paid out of a sume of money raised by generous subscriptions of the Common Council out of their publick stock, and the merchants and other inhabitants of the town.

"The charge of raising and paying the Regiment with other incident charges, of expresses, amounted to upwards of six thousand pounds, besides what further expence must necessarily have attended it, if the care and trouble of collecting the subscription money paying the same, and holding the necessary accounts had not been generously undertaken and executed by gentlemen of the town, without any other consideration than the pleasure of doing real service to their King and country.

<small>Volunteers.</small> "When the Regiment raised by the town was ordered to march, the merchants and other the inhabitants of the said town formed themselves, at their own expence, except a small sume which the Corporation allowed these companies; did duty in a regular manner, and thereby prevented any riots or disturbances in town during the course of the rebellion.

<small>Corporation send Supplies.</small> "When his Royal Highness the Duke of Cumberland was upon his march, pursuing the Rebels flying to Scotland, the Corporation sent an express to know if the army would want anything which they could furnish, and accordingly they sent about thirteen tons of biscuit bread after the army as far as Carlisle, under the care of the Worshipful Joseph Clegg Esq present Mayor and Mr Aldⁿ William Pole, who saw it safely delivered to His Royal Highness the Duke's orders, wherefore and upon the general conduct of the town of Liverpoole on this affair, His Royal <small>Acknowledgment.</small> Highness the Duke by letter to the Worshipfull James Bromfield Esqr then Mayor, expressed his gratefull acknowledgement for the zeal and affection shewn by the town of Liverpoole to His Majesty's person and Government. And since that time, not only his Majesty but his said Royal Highness, have on several occasions expressed and testified with Royal gratitude their remembrance of the loyal behaviour of the town of Liverpoole. And in a particular manner by his Majesty's command, His Grace the Duke of Bedford on the said present Mr Mayor's generous application interceding for a pardon for one Thomas Lawson a Rebel prisoner, who having on the like application been by a royal warrant detained in this goal to be cut for the stone, which operation he survived and then had his said pardon given him, the copy of which letter is hereinafter inserted.

"Copy of His Royal Highness the Duke of Cumberland's Letter to
"Mr Mayor &c as follows:—
"Litchfield, 29th November 1745.
"Gentlemen of the Magistracy of Liverpoole.

"The proofs of fidelity and zeal which you have given and give upon this important occasion, and of which Col¹ Grimes has made a very exact report, are as they ought to be, extreamly agreeable to me, and I must earnestly recommend you to persevere in the same laudable and honourable course, and at the same time let you know how much it will be for the King's and the nation's service that you should not be induced either by intreatys or menacys to call back the boats or vessels of what kind soever which you have sent off and put under the protection of His Majesty's Ships of War, but that you leave them there in the perswasion, that the utmost care will be had of them, and which by this messenger I recommend in the strongest manner to the commanding officer of those ships. _{Duke of Cumberland's Letter.}

"I am very sorry your courage and good affections are put to so severe a tryal, and that you are exposed to so great inconveniencies. But I hope the time of your deliverance draws nigh, and that by the blessing of the Almighty thes insolent plunderers will receive very soon the just rewards of their villanies.

"This army will be formed in a day or two, when I shall endeavour to pursue such courses as will most effectually contribute to that end.

"I can't help taking notice to you how much I am pleased with the account Col¹ Grimes gives of your regiment. Be assured I shall be glad to do anything that may contribute to your ease and contentment, and to give you the most effective marks of my esteem, and that I am truly your good friend

"WILLIAM.

"By His Royal Highness's command
"Everard Fawkener."

Then follows copy of the letter of the Duke of Bedford, containing Lawson's pardon alluded to above, dated Feby. 23rd, 1748-9. _{Pardon of Lawson.}

On the conclusion of the peace at Aix-la-Chapelle, in 1748, a resolution was passed:—

"1748, Decr. 23. Joseph Clegg Mayor.
"That this Council do address His Majesty under the Common Seal on his happy arrival and conclusion of peace." _{Address on Peace.}

The text is not given.

When the war with France broke out in 1755, fraught

with such important consequences to the future of North America, the loyalty of the people of Liverpool displayed itself conspicuously.

"1755, March 24. Charles Goore Mayor.

<small>Seamen wanted.</small>
"Whereas His Majesty's most Honourable Privy Council by their letter to the Worshipful Mr Mayor of this Corporation, have intimated the want of seamen for the speedy manning of the fleet now fitting out; and warrants haveing been sent down to Mr Mayor and the Magistrates for the impressing of seamen for the said service from the Lord Commissioners of the Admiralty; And the cause of this speedy armament being deemed to be on account of the French having attacked His Majesty's dominions in America, and having formed other designs ag^t these realms, This Council therefore, according to their usual stedy and unalterable loyalty and zeal for His Majesty, his family and government, to promote it as far

<small>Bounties.</small>
as in us lies, Do Order that a reward or Bounty of two guineas ℔ man shall be paid out of the Corporation estate to each able and experienced seaman who shall enter himself a volunteer to serve on board any of His Majesty's ships of war; with the following Gent^n of this Council vizt Mr Mayor, Messrs Aldermen Bird, Davies and James Gildart and Mr Forbes or any three of them being a Committee appointed for such purpose; which said bounty money shall be only paid to such seamen between twenty and fifty years old, and who shall be accepted of and certify^d by the regulating captain or officer at Liverpoole (except for apprentices) and to be continued till the twentieth day of April next" &c.

"1755, Octr. 6. Charles Goore Mayor.
"It is ordered that the following address from this Council on His Majesty's safe return be passed under the Common Seal and transmitted to the African Committee for this town, to be presented to His Majesty, as both our members are in the country.

<small>Address to Crown.</small>
"To the King's most excellent Majesty.
"The humble address of the Mayor Bailiffs and Burgesses of Liverpoole in Common Council assembled.
"Most Gracious Sovereign.
"We, your Majesty's most dutyfull and loyal subjects the Mayor, Bailiffs and Burgesses of Liverpoole in Common Council assembled, beg leave with the sincerest hearts to congratulate your Majesty on your safe return into your British dominions.
"Your Majesty's unwearied zeal for the welfare of Europe, your parental concern for the trade and commerce of all your subjects both here and in America call for the greatest acknowledgments of gratitude from every British breast. And we do rejoyce at this opportunity of repeating to your Majesty that we shall with the same alacrity as we have ever done,

contribute our utmost in support of the Protestant succession in your Majesty and your Royal House, and in defence of your Majesty's rights and dominions against all attacks and incroachments whatsoever."

As the war proceeded, and was carried on principally at sea, it became necessary to offer increased inducements to seamen to join. The Council acted on this occasion without any prompting from the Government. *Contribution*

" 1756, Mar. 10. Spencer Steers Mayor.
" Whereas there still wants a supply of able bodied and expert seamen to compleat the manning of His Majesty's vast fleet of ships of warr, to enable them to act with vigour, against our inveterate and perfidious enemies the French, who are making vast preparations, and daily threaten to invade these kingdoms with a powerfull army.
" This Council therefore, to contribute as far as in them lyes to enable His Majesty to oppose and frustrate such desperate and wicked attempts of our enemies, formed and designed by them against these kingdoms, in revenge for the resolute and vigourous measures His Majesty hath pursued in the defence and protection of his American dominions and subjects against the unprovoked and unjustifiable attacks and ravages of the French subjects committed on them, Do hereby order that a bounty or reward of three pounds a man shall be offered and given to every able and expert seaman who shall enter and serve as a volunteer on board any of his ships of war at Liverpoole, on or before the first Wednesday in April next, to be first examined and approved of, and to be within the description and instructions of the Comittee of this Council formerly appointed for such purpose." *Bounties to Seamen.*

It will be seen that, according to the communication from Government, warrants had been sent to the Mayor for the forcible impressment of seamen, and it does credit to the humanity and liberality of the Liverpool Corporation, that at their own expense they substituted a reward for voluntary service in place of the odious system of impressment. *Warrants.*

As the war proceeded the loyalty of Liverpool kept pace with the course of events.

" 1756, April 9. Spencer Steers Mayor.
" It is Ordered that the following Address (read over and approved) be

passed under the Common Seal and transmitted to our Members of Parliament to be presented by them to his Majesty, viz‘—

Address.
"To the King's most excellent Majesty.

"The humble Address of the Mayor, Aldermen and Common Council of the Borough and Corporation of Liverpoole in Council assembled.

"Most Gracious Sovereign.

"We, your Majesty's dutiful and loyal subjects, the Mayor, Aldermen, and Common Council of the town of Liverpoole, humbly beg leave thus to approach your Majesty, that among the rest of your faithful and loyal subjects, we may tender you our best services on the present important occasion.

"Sensible as we are of the great preparations already made and still carrying on by the French, for an unjust invasion of your Majesty's dominions, and that it is the duty of every individual who has the safety of his King, the true interest of his country, and the preservation of his libertys civil and religious at heart, chearfully to exert himself in time of tryal.

"The wise and vigorous measures which your Majesty hath taken by augmenting your naval and landed force at home, by strengthening your hands with potent and faithful allies, particularly so in your late Royal Act of Condescention to the earnest request of your Parliament in granting a considerable body of your Hanoverian troops for the safety and defence of these nations, are such peculiar marks of your paternal care and affection for your British subjects, and the welfare of these Kingdoms in this time of imminent danger, as will ever endear your Majesty to them and their latest posterity, which thro' the blessing of God will be a sure guard and defence against any desperate attempts of your enemies on the repose and quiet of this land.

Lives and Fortunes.
"We therefore beg leave humbly to assure your Majesty that both in our corporate and natural capacitys, we will heartily concurr at the hazzard of our lives and fortunes to protect and defend your sacred life, support and maintain your undoubted right to these realms and the Protestant succession as established by law in your Royal House, and vindicate the honour of your Crown against all your enemies and oppressors whatsoever.   "In testimony whereof" &c.

"1756, May 14. It is Ordered that the following paragraph in a letter to the Town clerk from Sir Ellis Cunliffe, acquainting the Council that he had (together with Mr Pole our other worthy member of Parliament) presented their address to His Majesty on the present situation of National affairs, and that in token of its gracious reception His Majesty was pleased to confer the honour of knighthood on him, be entred in the Council book and which is as follows :—

Cunliffe knighted.

"London Apr 14, 1756.

"S^r. I had this day, accompanied by Mr Pole the honour to present to

MUNICIPAL AFFAIRS.   117

His Majesty the address of the Council; in token of its gracious reception, His Majesty was pleased to confer on me the dignity of knighthood. I must look upon myself indebted for this honour to the great reputation the town of Liverpoole stands in by its loyalty in the late rebellion."

In 1759, a Baronetcy was conferred on Sir Ellis Cunliffe. _{Cunliffe Baronet.} The family is now represented by Sir Robert Cunliffe, of Acton Park, Wrexham, M.P. for the Denbigh boroughs.

"1758, Sept. 23. William Goodwin Mayor.
"Ordered, that the address now read to congratulate his Majesty on the success of his arms in the reduction of Cape Breton, and the many other important events of this year, be transmitted under the Common Seal of this borough to the Right Honourable William Pitt Esquire, by Sir Ellis Cunliffe in order to be presented to his Majesty." _{Address to Crown.}

The address succinctly sums up the events of the war in

"The reduction of the important fortress of Louisbourg, with the Isles of Cape Breton and St John's, the demolition of Cherbourg, the seizure of the settlements on the river Senegal, the destruction of the ships of St Malo; these and the other repeated blows given to the commerce and naval power of France, joined to the victories obtained by Prince Ferdinand at Crevelt, and by the King of Prussia near Custrin, are events which must ever make your Majesty's name dear to your subjects, dreaded by your enemies and glorious to future ages," _{Cape Breton, &c.}

and terminates with the usual expressions of loyalty and devotion.

"1758, Octr. 4. On a petition of several merchants and traders of this town, setting forth the danger the town is in from our enemies from its defenceless state, and for the security of the trade and shipping of this port, and praying the assistance of this Council with his Majesty's ministers herein. _{Town defenceless.}
"It is ordered by this Council that our members of Parliament be authorized and desired to report it to the Government, and pray their assistance herein in such manner and means as they shall think fit." _{Petition.}

To this application Mr Pitt (Lord Chatham) sent the following reply:—
"St James's Square Mar 16, 1759.
"Gentlemen
"I received the favour of your letter of the 13th inst with the papers therewith inclosed, setting forth the defenceless state of the town, two

Letter from Pitt.

docks and pier of Liverpoole; and I am to acquaint you that I immediately referr'd what you represent to the Board of Ordnance, and at the same time signified his Majesty's pleasure to that Board that they should direct some proper and skilfull person to repair to Liverpoole to survey the state of the said town, docks and pier, and that they should report their opinion what may be necessary and advisable to be done for the security and defence of a place of so much importance against any insult from the enemy.

"I am with great truth and regard
"Your most obed^t humble serv^t
"W. PITT."

In consequence of this communication several batteries were constructed, one in the Old Church Yard.

Further demands were made for seamen to man the Navy, and we find the following record :—

"1759, Feby. 7. Robert Cunliffe Mayor.

Bounties to Seamen.

"Mr Mayor having ordered that a special Council might be called on the 19th day of January last, as some officers of the navy now are come to town, being properly authorized by the Lords of the Admiralty to impress seamen into His Majesty's service, and in order to promote this national service, and to keep the peace of the town by encouraging volunteers to enter into His Majesty's sea service; and it was then intended to give a bounty for that purpose, but not a sufficient number of the Common Council of Liverpoole attending at that time, It is now ordered by this Council that the same bounty which was lately given by this Corporation for the like purposes to such volunteer sailors as should enter, be now revived and continued and remain in full force for the space of six months if found necessary."

The pressure still continuing, strenuous efforts were made for the defence of the Country both by land and sea.

"1759, Octr. 3. It is resolved and ordered on the motion of Sir Ellis Cunliffe Baronet, that the following proposals be made and stand as resolutions, orders and acts of this Council, to wit

Subscriptions.

"That a subscription be immediately opened at the Mayor's office for voluntary contributions, to be given in Bountys of four guineas to each able bodied Landsman as shall within two months from the date hereof inlist himself to serve his King and country as a soldier in Captain Jeffry's company of Royal Volunteers now raising at Liverpoole, and for the company of Captain Nathaniel Heywood of the Royal Volunteers; being first approved of by a Committee appointed for such purpose and Captain Jeffry or his Lieutenant.

Volunteers.

"That to promote such loyal and laudable service, Mr Alderman Pole the treasurer of this Corporation, do on the behalf of the Mayor, Bailiffs and Burgesses of this borough subscribe and pay the sum of one hundred guineas for the purposes aforesaid out of the publick estate of this Corporation. Contribution

"That no person entered on the Militia of any county shall be enlisted on this bounty."

The arms of England continued victorious, and we find recorded as follows:—

"1759, Nov. 27.   Lawrence Spencer Mayor.

"It is Ordered that this Council do address His Majesty on the many signal victories and conquests made and obtained by His Majesty's troops and naval forces, and that the following address be passed under the Common Seal and be transmitted by Sir Ellis Cunliffe Bart to Mr Secretary Pitt to be presented to his Majesty. Address to Crown.

"To the King's Most Excellent Majesty.

"The humble address of the Mayor &c.

"May it please your Majesty

"We your Majesty's most dutiful and loyal subjects the Mayor Aldermen, Bailiffs and Common Council of the Borough and Corporation of Liverpoole in Council assembled, beg leave to offer to your Majesty our most humble and hearty congratulations on the continued series of success which it has pleased the Divine Providence to bless your Majesty's arms within the compass of one year in every quarter of the world.

"The power of the French repressed in the East Indies, their fleet defeated off Cape Lagos; their armies totally routed on the plains of Minden; the islands of Goree and Guadaloupe reduced; the forts of Du Quesne, Niagara, Ticonderoga, and Crown Point taken, but above all Quebec that proud capital of the French Empire in America subjected to Brittish dominion. Victories.

Quebec.

"These signal victories and advantages obtained whilst our trade has been secured and our manufactures encouraged, must mark your reign a distinguished æra in the annals of Great Britain.

"Your Majesty's experienced paternal care and protection engage us to exert ourselves to the utmost to support your Majesty against all the attempts of your enemies. We entirely rely on the wisdom of your Majesty's Councils in the proper prosecution of this just and necessary war; not doubting but your Majesty by the divine blessing will in due time procure for us a solid and honourable peace."

"1759, Decr. 24. It is ordered that a bounty of four guineas ℔ man be given out of the subscription money raised in this town, to ten able-bodied landsmen to be incorporated in the regiment called the Old Buffs now Bounties.

Old Buffs.

recruiting at Liverpoole, it being reported to this Council that the private subscribers to this fund are willing to concur with this Council in the same."

Great alarm and consternation were caused in the town by the daring proceedings of the French squadron under M. Thurot, who had landed in Ireland and sacked the town of Carrickfergus. The following minute occurs:—

Thurot.

Freedom voted to Officers.

"1760, March 8. Ordered, that the following noblemen and gentlemen be admitted free of this borough and Corporation, being the colonels, field officers and captains in the two battalions of the Lincolnshire militia and other officers in his Majesty's military land service, in consideration of their great alacrity, chearfulness and expedition, in marching to the assistance of this town on the request of Mr Mayor and other the magistrates and gentlemen of the town, on Mr Mayor's letter to them notifying Mons' Thurot's, Comander of a French squadron landing in Ireland and taking the castle of Carrickfergus; and that we were fearfull he might visit this town and port, destroy the shipping, or lay the town under contribution. And that they be admitted gratis and without fees."

Then follows a list of twenty-five admissions to the freedom of the Corporation, commencing with the Earl of Scarborough and Sir John Cust, Bart.

In the midst of these important national affairs the self-elected Council never lost sight of their own interests, real or supposed. From the earliest records in the reign of Queen Mary, although by the charter of 1556 all restrictions on trade had been prohibited, there was a constant struggle to prevent "foreigners" settling or transacting business in the town.

Restrictions on Trade.

"1731, Nov. 12. Richard Gildart Mayor.

Prohibition of non-Freemen.

"It being represented to this Council that great numbers of artificers and handicraftsmen, foreigners not being free of this burrough, have p'sum'd to exercise and sett up their sev'all trades and to open shops, and therein to expose to sale their goods and wares, and retail the same, contrary to the ancient custom and by-laws of this burrough, in manifest violation of the known rights and priviledges of the freemen, and to the great damage of the whole body corporate.

"It is therefore Order'd That no foreigner not being free of this burrough shall on any pretence whatsoever directly or indirectly open a shop or sett up any trade within this burrough or the Liberties thereof, till he or she hath compounded with the Mayor, Aldermen Bailiffs and Comon Council for his or her liberty so to do.

Compounding.

" And to the end that such persons may now be discov'ed and presented; it is Order'd that publick notice hereof be given, and that all the freemen and burgesses be desired to attend the Comitee (which sits every Thursday in the Comon Hall at three o'clock in the afternoon) to give information of all such persons as do, or have p'sumed to exercise, any trades or manuall occupations within this burrough not being free thereof."

This order was renewed in 1734.

"1740, Feby. 9. Henry Trafford Mayor.

" Mr Aldⁿ Steers representing to this Councill that Theophilus Bent and others who are foreigners have lately imported severall quantities of corn and exposed the same for sale . . it is now order'd that the Water Bailiff do take a distress of all such corn, of one bushell for every hundred . . and that he be indemnifyed therein and in defending any action brought against him."

Foreigners importing Corn.

"1746, July 2. James Bromfield Mayor.

" Ordered that notice be given to James Rhodes of Liverpoole, gardiner to appear before the Common Council of this Corporation in the Comon Hall . . . to shew cause why he shall not be disfranchised for empowering John Rhodes a forreigner not being free of this town, to keep an open shop in this borough, and covering the said John Rhodes' goods under the pretext of his own proper goods, contrary to the ancient custom and by-laws of the said borough, and the oath of a freeman thereof."

Non-Freemen prosecuted.

1746, Oct. 8th. A proclamation was issued by the Council affirming their right by ancient custom to restrict and exclude all "foreigners" from trading in the town, but that these restrictions had hitherto proved ineffectual,

Restrictions.

" Inasmuch as divers and sundry foreigners and strangers, not regarding the said ancient custom, by-laws and ordinances, but wholly intending their private property and gain, have of late years devis'd and practised by all sinister and subtle means to defeat the said custom, and to that end do in private and secret places usually and ordinarily expose to sale and sell their wares" &c.

They therefore proceeded to denounce in the strongest terms such nefarious proceedings, and to inflict a fine of forty shillings for every offence.

Fines.

The ordinance was not to extend to business transacted at the time of public fairs and markets, nor to corn, grain, or victuals.

"1747, Jany. 21. Joseph Bird Mayor.

Fazakerley prosecuted.
"Ordered that John Fazakerley, silversmith and watchmaker be prosecuted for exerciseing the faculty of a freeman of this borough."

Mr. Fazakerley being recalcitrant, it was thought desirable Law Officers consulted. to take the opinion and advice of the Attorney General. The amended resolution, founded on this opinion, is set out at length but does not materially differ from that quoted above.

"1750, July 4. Joseph Davies Mayor.

Case stated.
"Ordered, that the Town Clerk state a new case of forreigners exerciseing their trades within the town not being free, and take Council's opinion thereon."

Notwithstanding all this blustering there seems to have been considerable hesitation in carrying the question to extremities.

"1756, May 14. Spencer Steers Mayor.

"It is Ordered on the petition of many freemen now preferred and read to this Council, complaining of a breach of their franchises by forreigners or non-freemen exerciseing and following their trades and businesses in this town; That a case be stated and laid before the Council for their approbation, and that the Attorney General's opinion be taken thereon, in order to procure the freemen redress herein."

Prosecutions.
"1756, Octr. 6. Upon Mr Attorney General's opinion that the power of making by-laws is in the Common Council under the Charter of King William the third, and that non-freemen may be prosecuted for following their trades in this Corporation. It is ordered that the Corporation will bear the expence of prosecuting such violators of the franchises of the town agreeable to the said opinion."

"1757, Mar 2. Richard Hughes Mayor.

Shoemakers prosecuted.
"Whereas a prosecution by information at the instance of the shoemakers free of this Corporation, hath been commenced in the Court of Quarter Sessions of this borough against one Frances Davies, for exercising and following the trade of a shoemaker, not having served seven years to the said trade, according to the statute of the 5th Elizabeth, and she, having submitted to the said information, and paid into court sixteen pounds for eight months penalty, one half whereof goes to the prosecutor, and the other to this Corporation as grantees under the Crown. It is therefore

now ordered that the said Corporation moiety be given to make up if any or what costs the said shoemakers have expended, and the remainder thereof be distributed among some poor freemen's familys of the said trade."

The supply of water to the town, which from the commencement of the century had been a subject of anxiety, still continued to occupy the public mind. Water Supply.

"1731, Nov. 17. Richard Gildart Mayor.

"Mr James Shaw proposeing on behalf of himself and partners to undertake and bring fresh water to town, provided they may have liberty to do, and a proper grant thereof; It is now Order'd that they shall have liberty, and a grant be pass'd for that purpose under the Corp^n Seale; they begining the undertakeing within a year now next, and being obliged to finish the same in seven yeares, and paying five guin^s rent from Mich'as next, and that they enter into proper articles for that purpose. This grant to be for nine hundred and ninety nine yeares." Shaw's offer.

"1732, July 12. A draught of a lease to Mr James Shaw for liberty to bring fresh water to town and to lay pipes &c being now read, was approv'd of, and order'd to be ingross'd and pass'd under the Corp^n Seale." Lease.

It is not stated where was the source of the supply. The subject slumbered during eight years, when it was revived.

"1740, July 23. Thomas Steers Mayor.

"Ald^n Gildart and Mr James Shaw proposeing to finish their intended waterworks in five years from Michaelmas next, if the Corporation will but enlarge their term, which was granted to the late Mr Shaw for the doing thereof for seven yeares from 12 July 1732. Lease to Gildart and Shaw.

"It is now order'd, that they have liberty according to the said lease for the term of five yeares from Michaelmas, on condition that they compleat the same within that term, and do begin and proceed effectually in two yeares from Michaelmas next, Otherwise this order to be absolutely void."

No further notice is recorded of this scheme, which like all the preceding ones collapsed.

"1748, Decr. 7. Joseph Clegg, Mayor.

"Mr Peter Whitfield having by letter remonstrated to this Council that he had a very probable scheme of finding out water, that might be easily brought, and sufficient to supply this town of Liverpoole. It is Ordered that Mr Whitfield be desired to communicate it to the Corporat^n, and if they judge it probable, then they will give incouragement to such scheme being carried into execution." Whitfield's Water Scheme.

"1749, April 5. Ordered, that Mr Pet. Whitfield be desired to confer with such of the Council as he shall think proper about bringing the water to town."

This scheme also proved abortive, nothing more being heard of it.

Several periods of great distress are recorded, which are noticeable from the earnest efforts made for their alleviation.

"1739, Decr. 10. Thomas Steers Mayor.

Distress. "Whereas it hath been represented to the Worpp^{ll} the Mayor, Ald^a, Bailiffs, and the rest of the Comon Councill of this Corporation, that great numbers of the inhabitants of this town are in great distress for want of work, which they are deprived of by and thro' the severity of the season, and reduced to great misery, and that thro' the dearness of the marketts are not able to subsist themselves and families, and must inevitably perish if not timely relieved; and that it hath been propos'd by the principall
Collection. merchants and inhabitants to contribute thereto, and that if a collection be made thro' the town amongst the better sort of the inhabitants, a competent reliefe for such poor miserable persons might be rais'd and distributed amongst them, and that severall persons haveing undertook such collection and distribution, which this Councill takeing into consideration
Corporation doe agree that the Corporation contribute thereto, and order that the
contribute. treasurer do advance the sum of fifty pounds out of the Corporation Stock for and towards such charitable contribution, and be allow'd the same in his accounts."

Again, seventeen years afterwards, distress prevailed to a much wider extent.

"1756, Nov. 17. Richard Hughes Mayor.
Distress. "Whereas corn and grain is at such an extravagant and high price in this town at present, that the poor freemen and inhabitants of the town cannot scarce from their labour get daily bread; it is therefore Ordered
Contribution that for the present relief of the poor that the Corporation do take up the sum of two thousand pounds at interest for such purpose, and that Mr Mayor and Bailiffs, Mr Steers, Mr Goore, Mr Robert Cunliffe, Mr Spencer, Mr Scrope Colquitt, Mr Clegg, Mr Manesty, Mr Carr, the Town Clerk,
Committee. Mr Pole and Mr Blundell, any five of them to be a Committee for such purpose, and to lay out and distribute the same in corn, under the direction of the Council as they shall think proper from time to time, to the poor indigent and needy housekeepers inhabiting in this town, at such prices only as to reimburse the Corporation their own money, and only such interest and charges as they shall be put to.

"1757, June 1. It is Ordered that the publick dinners made and given by the Worshipfull Mr Mayor and Bailiffs at the two fairs, to the freemen and inhabitants of this town, be now upon the motion of Mr Mayor and Bailiffs laid aside and discontinued on account of the great scarcity and dearness of every necessary of life at present, and that the moneys given them to defray the expence thereof, be for the present applied and laid out in the purchase of corn by the said corn committee and distributed in flour to poor freemen's familys and other necessitous poor of the town." *Public Dinners discontinued. Purchase of Corn.*

The Mayor of Liverpool from an early period has always had an allowance to keep up the dignity and hospitality of his office. For this purpose the whole or part of the *Prizage* on Wines, and the two best fines paid for admission to freedom, were appropriated. As the duties of the office increased, the question had to be reconsidered.

"1738, Oct. 12. George Norton Mayor.

"It being represented to this Council, that as the town and the number of its inhabitants do greatly increase; of consequence the attendance of the Mayor in discharging the whole duty of his office hath much more of late so increased than formerly, that most of his time is thereby taken up, and that he hath scarce any time to negociate his own private affairs, and that the present allowance is not adequate to the extraordinary trouble, attendance and expences every Mayor must necessarily be put unto: This Council are of opinion that such further reasonable allowance should be made, as will be sufficient to support the dignity of the office, and reimburse his extraordinary expenses. And do therefore order that the yearly allowance shall for the future be made the full sum of one hundred guineas, besides the settled yearly allowance of forty pounds in lieu of and for the two best freemen's fines." *Mayor's Allowance.*

In 1753 the allowance was increased to £110 besides the freemen's fines.

"1745, April 3. Ordered that the expence of a Quarter Sessions and Court of Tryals dinner shall not for the future exceed the sume of ten pounds if seperate, and fifteen pounds if joint." *Sessions' Dinners.*

"1733, Nov. 7. It being now represented that the late Mayor and Bailiffs did provide at their own charge 22 dozen of knives and forks to be us'd in and for the publick entertainments in the Hall, and the great necessity there is of haveing a sett of table linen for the two tables and the bench, and more knives and forks.

"It is Order'd that the Treasurer do repay the late Mayor and bayliffs the charge of those knives and forks they did provide, and take them for *Purchase of Knives and Forks.*

the publick use, and provide such linen as shall be suitable and necessary, and so many knives and forks more as will make upp the whole tenn dozen of knives and forks and four setts of lignum vitæ castors."

These knives and forks are still in existence, though not used. They have silver handles. The forks have two steel prongs each.

"1755, Oct. 6. Charles Goore Mayor.

Fair Dinners. "It is Ordered that as the entertainments of the two fair dinners since the building of the new Exchange, must of necessity be considerably encreased from the entertainment to be provided, and furnished for tables sutable to the rooms; Therefore the present and future Mayor and Bailiffs shall be allowed and paid any sume not exceeding the sume of one hundred and twenty guineas for defraying the expence of the said two dinners by the Corporation. And that in lieu or aid thereof the present and future Mayor and Bailiffs give up to the Corporation all their right, title and interest to the tolls comonly called the corn tolls; so that the Corporation are from henceforth during this agreement to receive the corn tolls and also the Ingate and Outgate tolls payable or arising within this borough and Corporation."

Riding the Liberties. On the occasion of the annual riding the Liberties or bounds of the borough, it was customary for the Mayor to provide refreshments for the cortege accompanying him, but Mr. Spencer Steers, Mayor in 1756, declined to follow this example; whereupon the following entry was made:—

"Ordered that the Corporation do pay a bill of four pounds thirteen shillings due to the widow of John Thompson, for the expence of the last Liberty Day for providing a refreshment for Mr Mayor and the gentlemen who attended him riding the boundaries and dining the constables, as Mr Mayor upon taking on him the said office, declared he would not pay any such expences."

The state and ceremony of the authorities were pretty well kept up.

Halberdiers. "1734, Apl. 3. William Pole Mayor.

"The report of the Comittee being now read, representing their opinion that the Halberteers should have an allowance of twelve pence for the attendance of two of them every Sunday att the foot of the stairs into the

Comōn Hall; it is now Order'd that they have such allowance from the 25th day of March last past, and that the Treasurer doe provide a new sett of Hallberts for them, and the old ones to be kept and made use of by the watchmen, and that the Hallberteers be obliged to take care of and keep his Hallbert clean and neat at his own expence."

"1745, Apl. 3. Ordered, that the Treasurer of this Corporation do attend at the taking up of the cloaths for the Corporation Officers to prevent 'em exceeding the limited prices, and that the Sergeant, Sword Bearer and Water Bailiff's hats and lace do not severally exceed 15 shillings, and the Bellman's and Exchange keeper's hat and lace ten shillings and sixpence, and the Halberdiers' hats four shillings each." *Clothes for Officers.*

"1760, Nov. 5. Ordered that Mr Mayor be authorised to buy cloth cloaks for all the Constables at the expence of this Corporation not exceeding five shillings and sixpence per yard." *Cloaks for Constables.*

Many notices occur of the provisions for Watch and Ward.

In 1667 the town was divided into five wards for ad- *Wards.* ministrative purpose.

In 1678 the watching was entrusted to

"Twelve sufficient housekeepers or a greater number of them as Mr *Watching.* Maior shall see cause, who shall everie night keepe watch from sixe a clock at night to sixe a clock the next morninge."

1738, October 20th. The town was divided into two *Districts.* separate districts, to wit the North and South. Each district was divided into three wards, and the Sub-Bailiffs and others *Wards.* were appointed to serve by two in each ward to summon the inhabitants appointed to watch.

1741, October, 18th. This system was revised and rearranged.

Liverpool has usually been a quiet and loyal town, but occasional émeutes have disturbed its harmony, of which several notices occur.

"1754, Nov. 6. Charles Goore Mayor.

"It is Ordered that the Town Clerk be repaid thirty six guineas which *Riots.* he paid to some persons for apprehending one John Courtney, James McHoy, and Eleanor Tobin, who with some others lately broke open in a

Prosecutions.
most bold and audacious manner the gaol of this Corporation, and thereout rescued the said Eleanor Tobin, who was confined therein for felony, and the expence of prosecuting the said offenders at Lancaster. It being a great offence at law, and insult on the magistracy of this town, and as the Gaoler Mr Hornby was not in circumstances to prosecute, and died insolvent, and being the reward advertized by order of Aldᵃ Crosbie the late Mayor for apprehending the said offenders."

Firearms.
"1758, Apl. 21. Ordered that sixty good musketts and bayonetts, cartouch boxes and accoutrements, be bought for the use of the town, to be kept in the Exchange, as the Corporation are obliged by the grant of the Castle to them, to keep up a number of arms, and the many late riots in this town, shew the necessity of them."

Arms.
"1759, Oct. 3. It is Ordered that Mr Goore, Mr Manesty, and Mr Campbell, be appointed a Committee to appraize and value the arms borrowed from Mr Spencer to defend the town from the insults of the Prescot mob."

"1760, Sept. 13. It is Ordered that Mr Adams, Gunmaker, be paid the sume of forty nine pounds for a parcell of musketts and bayonetts &c formerly sold to this Corporation, according to a Bill of Parcels now delivered in to the Corporation, when the town was threatened, and in danger of being plundered by a mob of country people and colliers in and about Prescot, and which have since been used by the Independant Company lately raised for the defence of the town of Liverpool."

Rather a singular entry is found under date of October 5th, 1748.

Rev. Thos. Baldwin.
The Revd. Thos. Baldwin was appointed by the Council one of the Rectors of the Parish in 1721, and on the 24th Sept., 1733, he was elected as a member of the Council, being the only clergyman who ever filled that office.

It seems that some objection, or at least dissatisfaction, had been expressed, from the allusion in his letter of resignation, as follows:—

"Leyland Octʳ 4 '48.

"Worthy Gentlemen

Letter.
"I should esteem myself guilty of the highest ingratitude did I refuse granting any request to that body politick which hath been so extraordinarily generous in constituting me one of their Rectors.

Resignation.
"As to oblige your Honours I consented to be a member of your society, so at your desire I now willingly resign that station, and heartily wish that you may pitch upon one to succeed as willing to exert himself

on all occasions to promote your true interest and welfare as I have been and ever shall remain.

"Gentlemen

"Y^r most devoted hum^l ser^t

"THO. BALDWIN.

"Upon which letter of resignation it is now declared that Mr Baldwin's seat as a Councilman is now vacant."

The following record requires explanation. Probably the proposal related to a provision for arbitration.

"1752, Jany. 8. Ordered that a petition be presented to Parliament for erecting a Court of Conscience in this town of Liverpoole on the plan of that of Lincoln; and passed under the Common Seal, and presented to Parliament; to be done at the expence of the Corporation." Court of Conscience.

At the date of the rebellion of 1745, and for some time afterwards, considerable alarm was excited by the proximity of the Powder Magazine, which stood on the North side of Brownlow Hill a little above the present line of Russell Street.

This was erected in 1737 according to the following record :—

"1737, Aug. 10. It being represented to this Councill that Thomas Pearse, Saml Underhill and Robt Norman of the City of London, have laid out a considerable sume in building a Powder House, and walling it about in the close in lease to Richd Gildart Esq lying on the north side of the lane leading to Brownlow Hill, and that they desire to have the lease thereof to themselves. It is now order'd that such lease be granted" &c. Powder House.

1744, April 5th. The lease was extended and divided into thirds amongst the lessees.

"1751, Octr. 18. It is ordered that Mr Mayor and Bailiffs (with seven others named) be appointed a Committee to treat for the purchase of a piece of land in Cheshire near the Black Rock, for to erect the powder magazines on, when they shall be removed from their present situation near this town . . . and this Council will confirm such agreement and carry the same into execution." Powder Magazines.

A few illustrations occasionally occur, illustrative of the customs of the period.

"1746, Oct. 18. Joseph Bird Mayor.

"Ordered upon the humble motion of Mr Bailiff Spencer, that this Corporation do patronize and qualifye the pack of hounds comonly called Pack of Hounds.

the Town's hounds, kept by subscription in this town, to hunt for the diversion of the gentlemen of this town. And that the Corporation do allow the huntsman for the time being the yearly sum of five guineas as and for a livery, and that the Treasurer be allow'd it in his accounts."

"1749, Apl. 4. Ordered that the Pillory be repaired and made fit for use."

Tower.

Derrick.

The Tower, in Water Street, was used as the Common Gaol, but the upper rooms were appropriated to festive purposes. Samuel Derrick, who gives an account of the town in 1760, states that "the proceedings are regulated by a lady styled 'the Queen,' and she rules with very absolute power."

"1748, April 13. Ordered, that the rooms in the Tower may be used by the gentlemen and ladies of this town, for their assembly grat^s during the pleasure of the Council."

Queen of Assembly.

"1754, Feby. 6. Ordered, that the Queen of the assembly have power to lock up the tea room in the Tower during the pleasure of this Council."

When in 1754 the New Town Hall, or Exchange as it was then called, was opened, the rooms in the Tower were vacated, and the following orders were passed :—

Court of Requests.

"That the rooms in the Tower be fitted up in order to hold the Court of Requests in.

Throne.

"That Mr Goore and Mr Winstanley be appointed to treat and agree with Mr Atherton for the sale of the Throne lately erected in the Assembly room.

Assemblies.

"That on the petition of the Managers of the Assemblies, the ladies shall have the use of the (new) Council chamber and furniture to hold their assemblies in during the pleasure of the Council."

"1748, Feby. 13. Joseph Clegg Mayor.

Peace Proclamation

"Ordered that Mr Mayor be desired to give a publick entertainment to the ladies and gentlemen in town to celebrate the day of his Majesty's Royal proclamation of peace, at the expence of the Corporation, under the direction of Mr Mayor and Bailiffs, Ald Pole, and Mr Forbes."

There is a subsequent entry in the margin as follows :—

Ball.

"Given by ye Corpor'on at ye Infirmary, at wch were present near 1000 Genl and Ladies and every person pleas'd." [1]

---

[1] There is a notable circumstance connected with this entertainment. Miss Martha Linaker, residing in Liverpool, attended this ball as a young lady and lived to be present at the ball given in the Town Hall on the opening of the New Infirmary in 1824, seventy six years afterwards.

"1748, March 17. The Worshipful the Mayor of this Corporation now bringing in to this Council the several bills of the charge and expence of the late Ball ordered to be given to the gentlemen and ladies upon the peace being concluded, amounting to eighty one pounds nine shillings and eleven pence, be paid by Mr Treasurer and allowed in his accounts, and that the thanks of the Council be given to Mr Mayor, Bailiffs, Aldⁿ Pole and Mr Forbes, the managers thereof for their great care and frugality therein, and also to all other persons who were so kind to lend them several requisites necessary for accomodating the company at the Ball." Cost.

The Waits as an institution were still kept up, but seem occasionally to have been a little disorderly. Waits.

"1743, Sept. 7. Edward Trafford Mayor.
"Ordered that the Publick Musick or Waits of this town be displaced or dismissed from their said offices, for misbehaviour in their places, and that Ald. Hughes be desired to consult proper persons to provide a new set for the town."

"1754, Mar. 6. James Crosbie Mayor.
"It is Ordered that two Waites or Musicians be added to the present Waites or Musick of this town, and that they all be paid and allowed four pounds a piece salary, and that the perquisites of the town be divided among them equally, and that they be each of them allowed a laced cloak in the usual form once in five years only. And that Mr Alderman Winstanley (and two others) be appointed to chuse and fix the town's Musick from time to time till further notice." Perquisites.

CORPORATE ESTATE AND REVENUES.

The Corporeal Estate of the Corporation consisted partly of lands and tenements within the ancient limits of the borough west of the Pool stream, including the old burgage tenements.

Estate.

Town Field. This estate, it appears from the older records, originally included a considerable area at the north end of the town, comprising the Great Town Field and other enclosures. How these came to be alienated there appears no evidence from the Records. From the early part of the 18th Century the bulk of the town's property consisted of the Mosslake Fields, granted by Edmund, Earl of Lancaster, in 1309, and of the Great Heath, wrested from the Molyneux family in 1672 by the courage and perseverance of the Corporation. This extensive area, extending from Islington to Parliament Street from North to South, and between Whitechapel and Crown Street from East to West, constitutes the present Corporate Estate, portions of which have at different times been conveyed freehold, but of which the great bulk is leased for terms of 75 years, the fines for the renewal of which produce a large revenue.

Moss Lake.

Great Heath.

Demand. During the period now under review this virgin soil began to be in demand, and building was rapidly extending eastward. Many notices occur of the sales of land and the management of the estate.

Survey. "1733, Sept. 10. Order'd that Aldⁿ John Seacome and Mr John Martindale, do make a new survey of all the Corporation Estate and report to the Councill what part is in lease, and what not, and what lives are in being, as soon as may be."

The inception of the Docks was undertaken by the Council, who obtained the first Act in 1709, and contributed towards the construction of the dock. Questions soon arose as to the relation of the two estates, both managed by the same authority. The good sense and sagacity of the Council is shown by the following minutes :— *Docks.*

> "1731, Jany. 5. Aldⁿ Goodwin now representing to this Councill that in his Mayoralty he receiv'd the Dock Duties from Mr Seacome, and thereout paid the sume of three hundred fifty eight pounds nine shillings and four pence on acc^t of the Corporation, and that he is now sued for misapplication thereof. It is ordered that Mr Goodwin be indemnified by the Corporation for such paym^t of the ballance of his accounts, which is seven pounds fifteen shillings and two pence, to the receiver of the Dock Duties, and that he be discharg'd from his accounts for moneys paid and received by him on acc^t of the Dock during his Mayoralty." *Dock Dues.*

This entry must be taken along with the following of the same date, which explains the nature of the transaction.

> "This Councill now takeing into consideration the order made by the Comon Councill the 8th December 1709, and the further orders made the 7th & 14th Aprill 1714, which do order that all mon^s rais'd by leaseing the ground round the dock be apply'd to the finishing of the dock. This Councill are of opinion that the same was only lent and advanc'd by the Corporation, to be repaid as could be conveniently rais'd out of the Dock Duties." *Land around Dock.*

The Old Tower in Water Street, the ancient fortified mansion of the Stanleys, where James, the tenth Earl of Derby, whilst Mayor in 1735, had exercised splendid hospitality, was sold soon after his decease to Mr. Clayton. *Sale of Tower.*

> "1737, Jany. 11th. George Norton Mayor.
> "It being now represented to this Councill that the prison or Comon Goale of this town is too small, and that there being now an oportunity of haveing the vaults and rooms late in the possession of Mr John Earle, part of the Tower at Water Street end, for a term under a reasonable rent.
> "It is Order'd that Mr Mayor be desired to treat with Mr Clayton, and obtain a lease to the Corporation on as reasonable terms as he can, and pass a counterpart under the Comon Seale for the term of ninety nine yeares." *Comon Gaol.* *Lease of Tower.*

"1737, Jany. 25. Mr Mayor now representing to this Councill, that he hath contracted and agreed with Mr Clayton of Adlington for the Tower, for the term of ninety nine yeares from the 2nd day of February next at twenty eight pounds a year clear of all outgoings. This Councill doth approve thereof and agree thereto, and it is now order'd and agreed that the back side wall be of brick and lyme mortar, and be made five yards high above the surface of the ground.

Alterations.

"Also that a Comittee be appointed, and desired to inspect the work, and to give directions for makeing the same necessary and convenient for a prison, and some apartment for a House of Correction, and that the Iron Grates, Cieling, and what is necessary, be taken and removed from the old Prison."

"1738, Octr. 12. Upon reading the report of the Comittee appointed to view the house in possession of Robert Linaker, belonging to and part of the Tower, who are of opinion that it may be inconvenient to have the same lett to any person not under the power of the Corporation, and would be proper to be added to and included in the lease agreed to be taken of the Tower from Richard Clayton Esqr, who agrees therewith at £4 a year.

"It is Order'd and agreed to by this Councill, that the same be included in the new lease from Mr Clayton, and it is also order'd : That the rooms which are lett at present for an assembly, be reserv'd to and under the order and direction of the Comon Council, and that the Serjeant at Mace shall be accountable to the Treasurer for the income arising therefrom, and that the same be paid and applyed towards the reserved rent to Mr Clayton, and that the Serj^t hold the rest of the rooms in the Tower without paying any further or other rent, and have liberty to make use of the assembly rooms at all times but when us'd for the assembly, till further order from the Comon Councill."

Assembly Rooms.

The Gaol or Prison, before this purchase of the Tower, stood in Derby Square, on part of the precinct of the old Castle.

"1741, Sept. 9. Peter Rainford Mayor.

"It being now represented in Council that Henry Winstanley, haveing purchass'd the old Prison, which was order'd to be granted to Ald^n Richard Gildart for a certain term, and undertaken to build severall messuages and make large improvem^{ts} thereon, and apply'd to the Worpp^{ll} the Mayor and Bayliffs to sett out the same, and they haveing measured and sett the same out so as not to incomode the street, and said Henry Winstanley hath sunk vaults and is erecting the walls, but is and hath been greatly obstructed in carrying on the work by Richard Mercer, Barber, tenant to Mr James Dansey of the house adjoining, and claims a right to a passage and shop which said Mercer hath lately erected, encroach'd upon the

Improvements in Tower.

town's wast' and made into the street without haveing any grant thereof, or leave or right so to do, and hath brought writts or actions at law against said Henry Winstanley and his workmen, and threatens to putt them to great expenses and to ruin them, and hath so intimidated the workmen that he cannot gett workmen to go on with the work, altho' they have not in the least intruded upon the said house or pull'd down any further than is allow'd and awarded by Alderman Foster Cunliffe Esq', who was appointed to be umpire between said Winstanley and Mercer. And hath made his award therein before the west end wall between the old prison, and the said house which jetted over the prison were laid open. And the said Henry Winstanley now praying to be defended therein at the charge of the Corporation; and this Council now takeing the same into consideration, and that the said encroachm' was made and hath been continued by him for severall yeares past, without having any grant or right so to do. It is therefore order'd that the said Henry Winstanley shall be defended at the charge of the Corporation; and that unless the said Richard Mercer do imediatly on notice to him given, open and make the passage out of his house into the street as it formerly and anciently was before the said encroachment was made, and remove and take down such encroachm', that he be presented at the charge of the Corporation, and be oblig'd to make it as it was before such encroachment." *Disputes. Award. Defence.*

The market in Derby Square proved so successful that within a few years after its establishment it had to be extended.

"1736, Nov. 19. It is order'd that Mr Mayor be desired with the Bayl* to make proposalls to the present lessees to purchase their terms and interest in the houses at the head of Pool Lane on south side St. George's Church, in order to pull them down and lay open the ground for a publick markett." *Provision for Market.*

The Fish Market has had many removals. Originally held at the bottom of Chapel Street in connection with Tarleton's "Fish Yards," it was removed to Derby Square when the Castle was demolished and the market place formed. As the market extended it became desirable to remove it. *Fish Market.*

"1750, Octr. 3. Ordered that the Committee appointed the last Council day for making or erecting a fish markett do treat with Miss Gamons for the purchas of their house at James Street end, and report their agreement to be confirmed by the next Council."

Butchers' Shambles.

The Butchers' Shambles have always had a tendency to herd together. At one period they stood on the west side of High Street, on a site now covered by the extension of the Town Hall. At another they occupied the site of the original Town Hall on the east side of the same street. Another range of shambles formed a narrow lane running with an elbow from Pool Lane to Cable Street.

Lease.

"1734, Sept. 12. Mr William Carr now proposeing to farm the Butchers' shambles and the shoemakers' shops and stalls for the term of seven years, and to pay the yearly rent of seventy pounds for the same, the Corporation allowing him five pounds for building a shop on the vacancy and paying all leys and taxes for the whole &c. It is now agreed that the same be lett to him accordingly."

Ingates and Outgates.

The Ingates and Outgates constituted a sort of octroi, consisting of a small toll on all provisions or provender entering or leaving the town. Its continued increase offers a striking indication of the progress of trade. In 1701 this revenue was farmed at £14 a year. In 1709 it was £25. In 1744 it was let at £100; and in 1760, along with the stallage rents, corn tolls, shambles and standings, it brought in the sum of £280.

Another source of income was the payment of compositions for exemption from town's dues.

Compounding Town's Dues.

"1743, Jany. 19. Ordered that John Entwistle merchant be exempted during his life from payment of any town's dutys for all goods, wares, and merchandizes of his own brought or imported into or exported out of the town of Liverpoole, paying twenty guineas fine for such priveledge."

Ship Building.

Shipbuilding also contributed to the Corporation exchequer.

"1750, Nov. 7. Ordered that Mr Roger Brooks have liberty to set a ship on the stocks on the Corporation ground somewhere between James's and Moor Street, paying the old accustomed rent of sixpence ℔ ton to the Corporation, and agreeing not to incommodate the streets or road."

"1752, April 15. Ordered that Mr Mayor have power to employ persons to remove the ship now in building on the ground or key of the New Dock, being the Corporation's land or estate, by Mr John Okill, which he hath done, and hath frequently pull'd down the dock wall in order to launch his ships, against repeated orders of Council made and notice given him not to do the like for the future, and that the Council be desired to attend Mr Mayor on this affair."

Mem. in the margin :—

"N.B. on the 16ᵗʰ April 1752 Mr Mayor attended and woᵈ have proceeded to have pulled these ships off the stocks when Mr Okill attended and engaged not to set any more on that groᵈ."

"1749, Sept. 6. Ordered that the shipbuilders who have sett ships or vessels about the new dock have a continuance of such liberty to set ships &c and launch into the said dock 'till the first day of March next, they making good all damages as shall be repaired and done by Mr Steers' order."

About 1749-50 the Cross Hall estate, extending from Dale Street to Whitechapel, was brought into the market for building, and the mansion destroyed. The Corporation levied a fine for permission to open out the streets. Cross Hall Estate.

"1749, July 11. Ordered, that Thos Cross Esq of Cross Hall shall pay twenty guineas to the Corporation for opening a passage into his field at the bottom of Dale Street upon the Corporation wast in fourteen days from this date; to be about seven yards." Opening Streets.

"1749, Sept. 6. Ordered that the fine set on Mr Cross last Council day for his opening on the Corporation be mitigated to ten Pounds.

"Ordered that an opening on the waste from Mr Cross's field at the bottom of Dale Street be granted him for ever being near 7 yards."

In laying out the land on the heath the Corporation were not unmindful of the amenities.

"1743, June 1. Ordered, that Ald Rainford be desir'd to lay out and plant hedges and make grass plots for the inhabitants of this town to dry their cloaths on, and the said heath to be made fitting for that purpose at the expence of the Corporation. Laying out Heath.

"Ordered, that two Publick Walks be made, one at the South end the other at the North end of this town, and that Mr Mayor, the Bailiffs and such others of this Council as he shall desire to attend him be impowered to treat with any persons for the purchase of two pieces of ground for such purposes, and to report the same to the Council." Public Walks.

"1753, Aug. 8. Ordered that the Public Walk leading from Duke Street up towards Quarry Hill be repaired and gravell'd and that a foot walk be made thence up to the said hill under the direction of Mr Aldⁿ Trafford, Mr Pole and Mr Bailiffe Cunliffe."

"1749, Nov. 16. Ordered, that Mr Mayor order Boundary stones to be fixed all along the edge of the banks of the ground on the North side of Mere Stones.

the town upon the strand or shore to the extent of the Corporation liberties, and that no houses shall be set within twelve yards to the westward of the said stones."

Tower.

The old Tower in Water Street originally stood on the margin of the river, the tide coming up within a few yards of the western side. There was a road along the Strand leading from Water Street to the Old Church Yard. The land along this margin became gradually appropriated.

Enclosing Strand.

"1749, July 11. Ordered that Thomas Hamlett have liberty to enclose and take the strand before his houses in Old Church Alley as it was lately set him out by the Committee, paying twelve pence ᵽ yard for the West front, and that the Parishioners of this Parish have the like liberty to carry out the Old Church Yard."

"1749, Sept. 6. Ordered that the several proprietors of the houses on the West side of the Old Church Alley have the Waste granted to them opposite their respective premisses as shall be set them out.

Extension of Churchyard.

"Ordered that all the rubbish which is carried down Water Street[1] and to the Northward thereof to the water side be laid on the ground now going to be enclosed by the Parish for an additional church yard to St. Nicholas's."

Petition of Parish.

"1752, Decr. 6. Ordered on the petition of the Churchwardens and others in behalf of the Parishioners of this Parish to this Council made; that the Corporation do convey a tract of ground which the said Parishioners by a former order of Common Council of this borough and Corporation were permitted to inclose from the sea shore or strand opposite the Old Church yard, as an additional church yard, and to be used as such by the Parishioners and inhabitants of Liverpoole aforesaid.

"And the said Churchwardens and Parishⁿ of the said Parish of Liverpoole aforesaid, having purchased from Robert Kennish a small parcel of land to the said parcel of ground above mentioned adjoining at the south end thereof, likewise inclosed by him from the sea shore and by him held by lease for the term of three lives and 21 years granted by this Corporation.

Grant.

"It is likewise ordered that upon the surrender of the said lease into the hands of this Corporacōn that this piece of land be likewise by the Corporation granted to the use of the Parish for the purpose of an additional church yard, for the term of nine hundred years or some such long term to such Trustees or in such manner as shall be most adviseable and proper, reserving thereupon a yearly ground rent of five shillings payable to the Corporation during such grant or term."

From the works at the New Exchange, the present Town Hall.

These lands thus granted, with all their erections, were <small>Re-purchase.</small> in 1883 repurchased by the Corporation for the purpose of widening the road in front. The premises between the Alley and George's Dock Quay cost £60,000. £3,000 was given for the alleged interest of the Rector in the portion of the church yard.

The Infirmary, formerly standing on a portion of the site <small>Infirmary.</small> of St. George's Hall, was erected in 1745, and removed to Brownlow Street in 1824.

The following is the record of the grant of the land :—

"1745, Apl. 3. Ordered, that the field, commonly called the Oyl Mill <small>Grant of Land.</small> field, and the waste before it formerly granted to Mr Bromfield, be granted to trustees to be appointed for the new intended Hospital for sick and wounded poor people, to be erected thereon, for a term of nine hundred and ninety nine years for the use of the said hospital, under the yearly ground rent of five shillings, and on condition that the Mayor of this town for the time being shall always be one of the trustees."

This was modified by subsequent orders, to comply with the terms of the Mortmain Act for the purpose of enrolment in Chancery. The grant was ultimately made free and unconditional.

The records contain frequent notices of Sir Thomas <small>Sir Thos. Johnson.</small> Johnson, who occupied a very conspicuous place in the Municipality during the first quarter of the eighteenth century. The following entry relates to his daughters, who it is to be feared were not very well provided for.

"1740, July 23. It being now proposed that Mrs Alice Johnson and Mrs Margaret Johnson, Daughters of Sir Thomas Johnson, will give to the Corporation one hundred pounds a peice haveing tenn pounds yearly for each hundred pounds, for the life of each. It is now order'd that the treasurer do take the moneys and pay the yearly sum of tenn pounds for each hundred pounds."

The following entry is interesting as relating to a man of whom Liverpool has reason to be proud—William Roscoe. He was born at the Old Bowling Green House at the end of

William Roscoe.

Hope Street, Mount Pleasant, on the 11th March, 1753. At that time his father had just completed the erection of another house and bowling green on the opposite side of the road, to which he afterwards removed.

"1753, Aug. 1. Ordered that William Roscoe have twenty one years added to the three lives in being in the house and bowling green by him built and made out of a field by him bought from Alderman Bromfield situate on the north side of the road leading to Martindale's house and to have a lease thereof granted to him for his own three lives and 21 years; paying a yearly ground rent of 12^d ℔ yard for the front of the house and six pence ℔ yard only for the front of the ground which is not built upon, and which six pence ℔ yard shall be made 12^d ℔ yard, when and as the said ground is built upon."

TRADE AND COMMERCE.

The original dock, opened in 1715, was soon found too small for the increasing business.

"1737, Jan. 11. George Norton Mayor.

"It having been heretofore and is now again represented to this Council Dock Extension. that there is an absolute necessity to have an addition made to the present dock or basin for light ships to lye in whilst refitting and other necessary uses, and a convenient pier be erected in the open harbour on the north side of the entrance into the present dock tow^{ds} Redcross Street end, for the safety of all ships when ready to sail from this port to lye within till a fair wind happens, and which very often are prevented when within the Wett Dock or Basin by other ships lying before at the entrance and are all pressing to gett out before them, to the manifest prejudice and frequent delay, and often loss of their voyages, and that in case of a fire happening in the wett dock (which God avert) will be of the greatest consequence and safety to the rest of the ships to fly unto and to be preserved from; and that according to a plan, computation and estimate lately made by Dry Dock. Mr Thos Steers, the same will take up at least seven acres of the adjacent wast ground of and belonging to this Corporation, and will cost at least the sum of twelve thousand pounds to make and perfect such Works and conveniences necessary. And the Mayor, Aldermen, Bailiffs and Comon Council now takeing the same into consideration, and that the makeing such addition and pier will tend greatly to encourage trade, advance his Maj^{ties} revenues, and be a publick good and safety to all ships tradeing to and from this port, do order that so much of the said wast ground as shall be sufficient for the makeing such addition and conveniences on the south side of the said entrance into the present wett dock, and for such pier and Pier. compass within as shall be necessary on the north side of the said entrance, be granted and sett apart for those purposes, and remain to and for such use and uses for ever, saveing and reserving to the Corporation the benefitt and advantage of setting, letting and granting the wast ground adjoining in such manner as they might have done in case the said addition and pier had not been made; and it is further ordered, that the Corporation doe actually advance out of their town's customs or take up upon the credit Advance of Money. thereof, the sume of one thousand pounds towards the first charge out of their publick revenues to carry on such pier, which it is conceiv'd sho'd be first made and will be of great advantage to the harbour and port, and that the Treasurer do pay the same as shall be first wanted and take it up at intrest under the Comon Seale if occasion be, and be allow'd the same in his accounts.

Application for Act.

"It is also order'd that Aldⁿ Thomas Brereton and Aldⁿ Richard Gildart Esqʳ be desired to assist in applying to the Parliamᵗ for an Act of Parliamᵗ for enlargeing the term in the present Dock Acts, and for enlightening round the Dock and thro' the whole town if it may be obtain'd, with power to assess the inhabitants towards the charge thereof and of keeping the lights in repair with proper clauses, powers and limitations to be therein inserted as shall be thought necessary."

Expenses.

"1737, Feby. 1. Ordered That the Receiver of the Dock Duties do remitt what will be wanting to obtain a new Act of Parliamᵗ for enlargeing the term in the present Dock Acts and building a Pier &c. to the Town Clerk now order'd to go to London to sollicite the same, and to defray the expence of him and his clerk."

Alderman Kelsall was also requested to go, and his expenses to be paid.

Advertising for Tenders.

"1738, June 7. The Trustees order and direct: that advertisemⁿ be putt into the publick news papers from Chester and Manchester, for any that are willing to undertake any of the Mason's Work about the new pier on the best terms for next year. That they bring or send their proposals in writing to the Comittee, who will sitt in the Comon Hall every Thursday at two a clock in the afternoon to receive the same and treat with them thereupon."

"1738, Nov. 1. Robert Armitage Mayor.

Ways and Means.

"It being represented to this Councill that money will be wanting to pay off the mason's and other workmen's bills for their work at the new Pier and other demands incurr'd on the building the outward wall of the said new Pier, and that the Corporation being to advance the sume of one thousand pounds . . . and Mr Edward Trafford haveing offered to lend the sume of eight hundred pounds at £4 10ˢ a hundred intrest a year; it is now ordered that the said sume of eight hundred pounds be taken up and applyed accordingly" &c.

These works were carried out, but occupied several years, and were extended further than was originally intended.

"1739, Mar. 12. Mr Mayor now representing that it will be necessary to carry forwards the Comon shore towards or round near to the Gallery. It is Ordered that the same be done accordingly at the charge of the Corporation as Mr Mayor shall direct.

TRADE AND COMMERCE.

"And that it will be necessary to purchase the Dry Dock[1] and appurtenance now in lease under the Comon Seale for the term of one life and 21 yeares, from the owners and proprietors in order to lay the same open to inlarge the new pier. — Additional Works.

"It is Order'd that Mr Mayor, Aldⁿ Armitage, Aldⁿ Blundell, Bailiffs Henry and Edwᵈ Trafford or any five of them be desired and appointed to treat for the purchaseing the same and report their proceedings therein from time to time to the Comon Council."

"1743, Sept. 7. Ordered that a plan of the new pier and the ground of it as intended to be built upon be drawn out against the next Council day and that the value of the said ground be then fixed." — Plans.

"1744, June 12. It is ordered and agreed by this Council that a stone pier be immediately begun and carried on in this summer of such dimensions and under the directions of Mr Ald. Steers and to be run out fifty or sixty yards or thereabouts to the westward of the new docks." — Pier.

These piers were not found sufficient for the purpose and further accommodation was required.

"1746, June 5. James Bromfield Mayor.
"Ordered, that a Dry Dock be immediately made at the north end of the new Pier under the direction of Aldⁿ Steers at the expence of the Corporation, and that Aldⁿ Cunliffe, Blundell, Armitage, Trafford, Messrs Bird Davies and Forbes be appointed a Comittee to examine and sign all bills for the said work. And three of them to make a Comittee, whereof an Alderman always to be one." — Dry Dock.

Early attention was drawn to the conservancy of the navigation.

"1755, June 4. It is ordered by this Council that a petition be prepared and passed under the Common Seal in order to obtain the Conservancy of this Port of Liverpoole vested in the Mayor of this borough and Corporation for the time being, and that the same be preferred to their Excellencies the Right Honourable the Lords of the Regency or to his Majesty's most Honourable Privy Council or other proper authority as shall be advised." — Conservancy.

"1755, June 13. Ordered, that a petition be prepared and passed under the Common Seal of this Corporation against any grant of Hoyle Lake being made to the persons who have petitioned the Crown for such purpose in order to lay any Oyster Beds therein, as such a grant might be of great detriment to the navigation of this Port and to the prejudice of the interest of the Corporation and of the inhabitants of the town in general; and that the expence of any opposition and of witnesses in this — Hoyle Lake. Oyster Beds.

---

[1] This was a small Graving Dock opening from the Old Dock Basin.

Opposition. affair be defrayed by the Corporation. And that the Town Clerk do write a letter on behalf and in the name of this Council to the Honourable Mr Herbert, His Majesty's Surveyor General, of this their resolution."

A previous attempt to enclose fish yards in the same neighbourhood had been successfully resisted.

Fish Yards. "1751, April 3. It being represented to this Council that fish yards are set up beyond the Rock within the limits of this Port to the great prejudice of the navigation thereof. It is Ordered that Mr Mayor and the Council or any of them be desired to go and view them and report the state thereof to the next Council."

Apprehensions were entertained, which have subsequently proved correct, of the danger of the sea breaking in over the Wallasey Leasowe. A communication on the subject was received from the Bishop of Chester, of which the following is the record :—

Wallasey Leasowe.

"1754, Sept. 11. James Crosbie Mayor.

Reply to Bishop of Chester. "Ordered that Mr Mayor be desired to return an answer to the Revd Father in God Edmund, Lord Bishop of Chester from this Council in regard to the apprehension that the sea is likely to make an irruption or inroad over Wallazey Leisure, vizt That there hath been a survey taken of it lately, and the Council are informed that the navigation of this Port is not in any danger as they apprehend. And if the landholders thereabouts would keep up their banks, they might easily stop the progress of the tides at a small expence now, and prevent any damage or overflowing of their lands."

Survey of Coast. "1759, June 6. Ordered that Mr John Eyes be paid by the Corporation the sume of seven Pounds for surveying the coast up the river, and takeing an account of the fish yards erected therein."

Sankey Navigation. The Sankey Navigation was projected in 1754. The proposal met with encouragement from the Corporation of Liverpool.

"1754, Oct. 25. Charles Goore Mayor.

"Whereas an application is intended to be made to Parliament at the ensuing sessions for making the river or brook called Sankey Brook and three branches thereof up as far or near St Helens in Windle, navigable, ... by certain persons subscribers for that purpose, to be named Undertakers in the said Act, at their own expence for the better supplying (amongst others) the town of Liverpoole with coals. It is now Ordered that the

Corporation do advance and lend the said undertakers thereof the sume of three hundred Pounds towards the payment of the expences of obtaining the Act, and of the survey of the said brook taken by order of this Council and all other incident charges thereon, which said sume of three hundred Pounds shall be repaid to the Corporation by the said Undertakers if the Bill pass into a law. But in case the said Act shall not be obtained by reason of any opposition, that then the Corporation shall lose the said money, as the said navigation is chiefly calculated and intended for the better supplying this town with coal, which of late years are become scarce and dear, and the measure greatly lessened to the great imposition and oppression of the trade, manufactures, and inhabitants of this Corporation, and that the said money hereby granted be paid by the treasurer to Mr Ashton for such purpose, as he shall call for it." *(Loan by Corporation. Supply of Coal.)*

This undertaking has been in its results one of the most successful of similar enterprises.

In 1737 a Bill was brought into Parliament for the improvement of the River Weaver, the important link of communication with the salt district of Cheshire. *(River Weaver.)*

This was opposed by the Corporation of Liverpool, and Alderman Steers was sent up to represent them before the Committee.

"1737, June 16. Richard Gildart Mayor.
"It being now made appear to this Council, that Mr Steers was out of pockett and at a much greater expence in attending in London on behalf of the Corporation to oppose the passing of the Act of Parliam^t for making the River Weaver navigable on the terms therein mentioned, and for so great a tunnage as was insisted on by or on behalfe of the County of Chester, than he hath received. It is now Ordered that the Treasurer doe pay him thirty pounds, in full for his expences and attendance, and all demands relateing thereto." *(Opposition.)*

The Act was obtained and the work carried out, but the result does not appear to have been quite satisfactory.

"1757, Sept. 7. Richard Hughes Mayor.
"It is Ordered on a petition to this Council from several merchants in this town, complaining of the ill management of the navigation of the River Weaver, by some persons who are concerned about the same. That this Council do bear the expences of any gentleman who shall take the trouble to go and order a survey of the said river, and to meet any gentleman *(Survey.)*

concerned in the said navigation, in order to have the inconveniences and mismanagement of the said river redressed."

Careful attention now began to be paid to the entrances to the harbour and the navigation.

Buoys and Banks.
" 1736, Nov. 19. It being represented that there is an absolute necessity to regulate the buoys on the banks off Highlake, It is Order'd that Mr Steers the Dockmaster do take immediate care thereof, and see that they be placed in proper places for the safe direction of all ships comeing in and going out of this Port, and be repaid the charge thereof out of the Dock duties by the Receiver."

" 1740, May 14. Thomas Steers Mayor.

Beacon or Landmark.
Hoyle Lake.
" It being now represented to the Trustees for the Dock the great necessity for the speedy erecting and placeing a Bacon or Landmark on the hills or near the shore at Hoyl Lake, which they did heretofore agree should be plac'd conformable to the plan of the Coast made by Messrs. Fearon and Eyes, and that Mr Charles Hough of Dublin, son of Thomas Hough, Lether dresser, who is the owner of the land whereon it is convenient to place it in the Meoles, agreeing to grant liberty to erect and place such Bacon and to repair and maintain it from time to time as there shall be occasion, and that they shall and may hold and enjoy the same for ever, with full and free liberty of ingress, egress and regress to and from the same, paying six pence a year rent to him and his heirs—upon condition that his son William Hough stockin weaver be admitted free of this Corporation.

" It is now Order'd that the said William Hough be admitted free accordingly, and that the said landmark be built imediately after the tytle is fix'd and grant executed."

Supply of Fish.
About the period now under consideration the supply of fish attracted much attention. It was brought to the notice of the Council by Capt. Wm. Hutchinson who occupied a somewhat conspicuous position in the town.[1]

" 1754, Decr. 3. Charles Goore Mayor.

Hutchinson's Memorial.
" Whereas Captain William Hutchinson mariner, hath referred to this Council a memorial or representation setting forth his discoverys and observations made on the coasts in regard to finding out a proper place for to resort to and catching cod and other fish, and that he was about to purchase a cod smack or well boat in order to establish and pursue the said scheme of bringing live fish in such vessels to Liverpoole. It is therefore Ordered, that Mr Mayor and Bailiffs, Mr Ald^n Goore, Pole,

[1] See Memorials of Liverpool, Vol. I. p. 188.

Davies, James Gildart, M. Forbes, Ellis Cunliffe and the Town Clerk be appointed a Comittee or any five of them to consider of proper means to encourage so laudable a design and report their resolution to the Council." <small>Committee appointed.</small>

The Committee met, and after due deliberation presented the following report :—

"1756, Feby. 4. Spencer Steers Mayor.

" Mr Mayor having reported to this Council from the Committee appointed to meet Capt. Wm Hutchinson in regard to the giving him some encouragement towards establishing a live fishery at Liverpoole Markett. <small>Report.</small>

" That it is their opinion a bounty of ten shillings a ton by the year for three years certain of Carpenter's measure, shall be given to all owners of vessels which shall be employed in the said fishing trade, and that such vessels to be entitled to such bounty, shall not be less than twenty five tons each, of the same measure, and to be equip'd with all necessary and fit tackle and furniture for this fishing trade; and no vessel shall be deemed to be entitled to such bounty but such as have wells thro' their bottoms. And that all persons who shall apply for this bounty shall enter their names and the names of their vessels with the Mr Mayor of this Corporation for the time being, in a book to be kept for such purpose. <small>Bounty.</small> <small>Well Boats.</small>

" It is therefore Ordered that this Council will give such bounty upon such vessels to be employed and equipped for the fishing trade as aforesaid. And this Council further recommends it to the said Committee to draw up proper articles for such persons to sign, to be first laid before the Council, to be approved and confirmed by them before the same take place. And that all fish catched by such vessels shall be bro' to this Market." <small>Articles to be signed.</small>

" 1756, Sept. 10. Whereas Capt Wm Hutchinson has preferred his petition to this Council, setting forth that he hath found out a place or fishery, from whence he can certainly and plentyfully supply this town with fresh sea fish, but that it is absolutely necessary to bring the said schem to perfection that he should have another cod smack and he having already expended the most part of his fortune in building one cod smack, purchasing other conveniences and making tryals on the said fishery, and that he hath not money to build another smack, and therefore praying the assistance of this Corporation ; this Council now taking the premisses into consideration are of opinion that a constant and regular supply of fish will be of great utility to the freemen and inhabitants of this town, and that the said Captn Hutchinson ought to be encouraged by the Publick. It is Ordered that this Corporation do, and shall, advance him the sume of four hundred pounds for building him another cod smack, free of any interest for three years, and also that he shall be allowed the same bounty money on this smack as was heretofore ordered to be given him; he being the first Undertaker of the fishery, and having lost and expended a <small>Hutchinson's Report.</small> <small>Cod Smack.</small> <small>Advance of Money.</small>

considerable sume of money in finding out and settling this fishery, and that upon his giving security to the Corporation to repay them the said money."

Further Application.

After a two years' trial the scheme was found not to answer the sanguine expectations of its promoter. He therefore again approached the Council.

"1758, Decr. 6. Robert Cunliffe Mayor.

Further Grant.

Conservancy.

"It is Ordered on Capt Hutchinson's petition to this Council setting forth his great loss in his fishery, and that he cannot proceed in it without the further aid of this Council; that in order to encourage the said fishery the said Hutchinson be allowed a further bounty of ten shillings per ton for each of his two cod smacks for the space of two years, and he submitting himself to the Council whether it would not be for the intrest of the Corporation to endeavour to obtain the conservator*p* of the river Mersey for the preservation of the navigation of the river and fishery and for laying and breeding of oysters; and that the Town Clerk write to our members for their sentiments and advice hereon, and report his proceedings to this Council."

Scheme abandoned.

The scheme was abandoned. Capt. Hutchinson turned his attention to privateering, but was again thwarted.

In 1760 he was appointed dock master, which situation he filled until his decease in 1801.

Excise Bill.

In 1733 considerable agitation arose in Liverpool owing to Sir Robt. Walpole's Excise Bill of that year. The duties on wine and tobacco had previously been levied by the Customs, and it was notorious that an enormous amount of corruption and fraud prevailed. The correspondence of the period shows that a large proportion of the profits in the tobacco trade were made by defrauding the Government. It was stated in Parliament that the gross produce of the duty should have been £754,000 whereas all which reached the Exchequer was £161,000. The Government measure transferred the duties from the Customs to the Excise, reduced the amount and remodelled the whole system, introducing the bonding principle.

Tobacco Trade.

Bristol and Liverpool offered the most strenuous opposition to the measure. *Opposition.*

"1733, Feby. 12. Thos Brereton Mayor.

"It being proposed that a letter should be wrote to our representatives in Parliam' to oppose any new Excise, or any extension of the Excise laws, which it is apprehended will be of great consequence to the trade in gen'all, and to the manufacturers of this town and port, of tobacco, and dealers in wine in particular.

"It is Order'd and agreed, that such letters be immediately wrote to the representatives, earnestly recomending their utmost care to oppose it."

In April the bill was postponed to the 12th June, whereat there was great rejoicing. *Postponement of Bill.*

"An express conveying the agreeable news reached Bristol at 11 o'clock at night, when in spite of the lateness of the hour, the merchants and principal traders assembled at the Council house, and drank healths to the worthy 204 and other gentlemen who opposed the Excise Bill. Bonfires were lighted and rejoicings were made throughout the City . . . the joy has been universal, particularly at Liverpool where a 'Courant' containing some severe reflections on the merchants was publickly burnt."[1] *Rejoicings.*

In spite of all this opposition the Bill ultimately passed. *Bill passed.*

About 1750 a silk throwing manufactory was set up in a lane leading from Tithebarn Street, which therefrom acquired the name of Silkhouse Lane. *Silk Works.*

The following reference occurs:—

"1753, May 2. Ordered that Mr Thomas Hopkins of London, silk throwster, Proprietor of the silk works here be admitted free gratis."

In 1757 public affairs were in a very depressed condition and great distress prevailed, which produced its usual results. *Distress.*

"1757, Oct. 18. The Mayor and Bailiffs being alarmed that a great mob were coming up to the Exchange, they were obliged to adjourn the court of election (for Mayor) or defer the election of sub-bailiffs till the next day." *Riots.*

"1757, Nov. 2. Ordered that the windows of the Exchange which were broke last Election day, the eighteenth day of October, be immediately repaired by Mr John Eden glazier at the Corporation expence." *Windows broken.*

[1] *Gentlemen's Magazine,* 1733, p. 212.

The commerce of the port required protection, both from foreign and domestic enemies.

"1759, Apl. 21. Robert Cunliffe Mayor.

Erection of Batteries.
"It is now Ordered upon the representation of Captain More one of His Majesty's Engineers by him most graciously sent to survey the town and port of Liverpoole, that several pieces of the waste land belonging to this Corporation on the sea strand, or shore, as also some particular parts or places on the new Dock keys or walls already enclosed, will be wanted for the use of erecting Batterys on, for the immediate and future defence of this town in such proper places thereof as he has remarked to this Council, and that in case the Trustees of the Dock or the Corporation of Liverpoole shall at any time hereafter be minded and shall actually take in or inclose any part of the sea strand from the west and north walls of the present Dry Pier, that then His Majesty, his heirs and successors shall have free liberty to take in or erect any necessary Batterys or fortifications for the defence of this port and town, not incroaching private property

Grants of Land.
already granted by the Corporation, nor to encroach upon or prejudice the safety and use of the publick docks or harbour of this town or port, and to hold and keep to his Majesty, his heirs and successors such parts and portions of land necessary to be used in fortifications and batterys as long as he and they shall keep and use them for such purpose only, and that when any such batterys or fortifications shall be removed or disused, they shall severally become again the property and revert to the Corporation of Liverpoole and their successors for ever."

"1760, Aug. 6. Lawrence Spencer Mayor.

Grant of Money.
"Ordered, That for the better defence and security of this town, harbour and the trade and shipping thereof, this Corporation do give any sume of money not exceeding one hundred pounds, in aid of, and to be added to the savings of moneys lately ordered by His Majesty for fortifying

Battery. James Street.
this town; to be employed in erecting another Battery on part of the sea shore at the bottom of James Street. And that the Engineer have liberty to take and enclose such part of the strand or shore there as shall be necessary to erect the same on, according to the plan now laid before this Council, not encroaching upon, or prejudiceing private property, the safety and use of the publick docks or harbour of this town. To hold such parts and portions of the said strand or shore, necessary and requisite to be taken and enclosed for erecting the said Battery on, unto His Majesty, his heirs and successors, so long as he and they or any of them shall employ, use and keep the same land for that purpose only. But if the said Battery or fortifications shall at any time hereafter be removed or disused, in such case the same land shall immediately from thenceforth in the condition it may then be in, revert to and be reinvested in the said Corporation of Liverpoole, and their successors for ever.

"It is also Ordered that the Corporation do grant the reversion of the Hogshey fields at Hogshey Nook (now held by lease for three lives and twenty one years by Mr Alderman Goodwin under this Corporation) to the Crown; and which said land the said Mr Goodwin has agreed to sell to the Crown for to erect a fort on for the defence of this town, which reversion is to be granted to the Crown in like manner and on the same conditions as mentioned in the last above order of this Common Council."

STREETS AND BUILDINGS.

At the commencement of this period (1727) the town, considerably extended since the beginning of the century, formed an irregular triangle, with its base along the margin of the river from Oldhall Street to Mersey Street, and its apex at the east end of Dale Street. There was also an outlying portion across the site of the Pool, clustered round St. Peter's Church, recently erected. Within this limit there were many open spaces. The streets were narrow, tortuous, and ill-paved, most of them without footwalks; the dwelling-houses, with a few exceptions, mean and poor, built principally of brick.

Site of the Town.

A few extracts from the records relative to the condition of the streets and buildings, may be interesting.

Paving.

That the paving was in a very primitive condition may be inferred from the following entry:—

Contract.

"1750, Decr. 5. Ordered that upon Mr Mayor's now reporting to this Council that the Committee had agreed with Edmund Parker, paviour, the lowest proposer, to keep the pavement of all the streets of the town in repair at ninety pounds a year for the term of seven years, allowing him the boon and statute work of the town, according to the printed proposals; and thirteen pence a yard for all new work; that the said Agreement be confirmed by this Council on behalf of the said Committee."

Prescot Road

Down to the middle of the 18th century the road from Liverpool to Prescot and Warrington, being the highway to London, was impassable for carriages. An Act of Parliament was obtained in 1720 for repairing, widening, and extending it, but the measure remained dormant for many years. The Corporation at length took the matter up.

"1745, Mar. 5. James Bromfield Mayor.

"Ordered that Mr Mayor and Ald Pole be indemnified by the Corporation for all money by them borrowed to defray the expence of the application to Parliament for renewing the Act for repairing the road to Prescot, &c and for any other sume they shall have occasion to borrow for that account." <small>Application to Parliament</small>

This improvement was not completed until 1760. In July of that year the first stage coach to London was advertised.

The scavenging arrangements may be judged of by the following records :— <small>Scavenging.</small>

"1731, Feby. 10th. Mr Mayor now propounding that a proper person be appointed to take away the dirt out of the streets; it is now Ordered, that if any person will undertake to carry away the dirt in the streets twice a week he shall have the muck for his pains and two or three guineas a year, and that every inhabitant shall be oblig'd to clean their respective streets every Wednesday and Saturday, whereof publick notice to be given; and Mr May^r is desir'd to agree with and impower such proper person as farr as he can."

"1742, Octr. 22. Edward Trafford Mayor.

"It being now represented to this Council the great necessity of the imediate takeing some proper method for cleansing the streets within this town, which are at present very much neglected; this Council have and do order and establish that Mr William Hornby the present surveyor of the publick streets and highways, shall be appointed and impower'd to supervise all the streets and lanes within this town, and take care that the same be cleansed of dirt and filth, and that all the dirt and filth shall be imediatly carried away and not suffer'd to lie and remain in the streets, and to that end. <small>Cleansing Streets.</small>

"It is now ordained and established by the Mayor, Bailiffs, Aldermen and Comon Council of this burrough or town of Liverpool in and for the same burrough in Council assembled; That all the former by-laws and ordinances made for cleansing the publick streets of this town, be, and are hereby confirmed. And that every housekeeper or occupier of ev"y house, warehouse or other building fronting the street, shall be obliged under a certain penalty, to sweep their street twice every week, and imediatly carry the dirt away, and that in case of failure therein, the publick carts which shall be imployed for that purpose shall and may carry the same away; and that the said Wm Hornby shall provide two proper carts at the charge of the Corporation, and shall and do hire and imploy two or more sufficient persons to cart and carry away all such dirt and filth or other soil as the inhabitants shall have so swept together and not carried away, and that imediatly on the ringing of a bell which those persons so imployed are to ring to give notice to the inhabitants, every person may <small>By-Laws. Householders to sweep. Carrying away.</small>

CHAP. II, A.D. 1727—1760.

then bring out his and their ashes and dirt to the cart, and that the carters shall and do carry it away, and lay all the dirt, filth and ashes in some convenient place out of town to be set out for that purpose, and that the said Wm Hornby may dispose thereof to the best advantage," &c.

Lighting. The lighting of the town was a matter of considerable anxiety. In 1718 forty-five lamps were ordered, and a contract was made to light and keep them in order for ten shillings a year each. This does not seem to have been satisfactory, for we subsequently read as follows :—

"1738, Nov. 1. Robert Armitage Mayor.

Inhabitants provide Lights. "Forasmuch as the lighting of the streets of this town would be of great importance, and tend to the preservation of the persons and properties of the inhabitants and other persons resorting thereto, and that to encourage so good and necessary a work severall persons have propos'd to be at the charge of lighting and maintaining one lamp a peice if they can have such lamps plac'd at or near their dwelling houses free of the charge thereof, and the Councill being of opinion that such lamps sho^d be provided and fix'd up at the charge of the Corporation.

"It is now Ordered, that the Treasurer do provide and cause lamps to be fix'd up for such persons as will engage to light and maintain the same at their own charge, and plac'd in such places at the charge of the Corporation as the Worship^{ll} the Mayor for the time being shall from time to time order and direct. And Mr Mayor now proposeing to send for a quantity of oyle proper from London at a much cheaper rate than sold here; it is order'd that he be desired to send for a quantity."

"1749, Novr. 16. Joseph Davies Mayor.

Stations of Lamps. "Order'd That this town be enlightned for this winter by the Council as usual and that lamps be provided and set up at the following places, at ye Corporation expence, vizt at the North-west corner of the Exchange, at Mr Markland's, the corner of Edmund Street, at the corner of Hackinshey in Tithebarn Street, at the bottom of Lord Street at John Colquitt's Esqr, at Mr Bank's in Pool Lane, at corner house where Clark lived, at the corner of Preesons Row next Pool Lane, at Mr Reid's end, Castle Hey."

Horse Causeway. "1756, Sept. 10. Ordered, on the petition of the several landowners in Pinfold Lane (Vauxhall Road) setting forth that the horse causeway is in a ruinous state therefore that it be repaired at the expence of the Corporation so for as it extends within our liberties; and to be stoop'd out."

Doghouse Lane. "1758, July 14. It is now ordered that a horse causeway be made from the Doghouse Lane to the township of Everton near the Loggerheads to meet the horse causeway there."

It appears from this and other entries that many of the roads leading into Liverpool had merely a narrow strip of paving in the middle for pack-horses but were impassable for wheel carriages. Doghouse Lane, the present Richmond Row, so called from the kennels of the town's pack of hounds being situated there.   *Richmond Row.*

The Loggerheads was the ancient tavern at the corner of the present Soho Street.   *Loggerheads.*

The Ladies' Walk, at the north end of the town, has been mentioned above.   *Ladies' Walk.*

"1755, Octr. 6. Ordered that the stones of the fence wall at the end of Water Street, or so much thereof as shall be wanted be used in the building a breast wall and pair of steps from the shore or road up to the Ladies' Walk on the North side of the town, under the direction of the present Mayor and the Committee appointed for the said Walk."

There anciently existed three crosses in the town; the High Cross at the intersection of Water Street, Dale Street, and Castle Street, now occupied by the Townhall; St. Patrick's Cross at the east end of Tithebarn Street; and the White Cross at the intersection of Tithebarn, Chapel, and Oldhall Streets.   *Crosses.*

The following entry relates to the last mentioned :—

"1746, May 14. Whereas the White Cross at the top of Chaple Street, was lately pulled down by som evil minded persons, it is ordered to be rebuilt at the Corporation expence."   *White Cross.*
"Sept. 10. The ruins and steps ordered to be taken away."

It was never rebuilt.

In 1684 twelve Almshouses were built by Mr. David Poole at the east end of Dale Street.   *Almshouses.*

Subsequently several other foundations of a similar character were erected by different individuals.

In 1739 Mr. Thos. Steers, the Mayor at the time, made an offer to the Corporation as follows :—

"Decr. 10. Mr Mayor now proposeing the building a number of houses for habitations for poor decay'd seamen and such as shall happen to be maimed in the publick service or otherwise, and thereby rendred incapable of maintaining themselves and families, upon some part of the wast belonging to the Corporation; to encourage so good and laudable an undertaking this Councill do unanimously concurr therein, and recommend to Mr Mayor that he will be pleased to take such of the Com̄on Councill and view such part of the wast as will be most com̄odious and report the same to the Councill."

Report.

Poole's Almshouses. In 1748 Poole's Almshouses, at Dale Street end, had become dilapidated, and stood in the way of the improvement of the neighbourhood. They were dealt with as here recorded :—

Removal. "Ordered that this Council do agree with Mr John Livesey for pulling the Corporation Alm houses down at the bottom of Dale Street and carrying the materials off, and building the like number of Almshouses on such waste ground in this Corporation as the Council shall give and assign for that purpose, of the same dimensions and form as those Almshouses of Mr Scarisbrick's, in consideration whereof the Council agree to pay him the sume of seventy pounds, and allow him the old materials, and to grant him a lease for three lives and 21 years of the scite or ground where the said Almshouses stand, paying twelve pence ⅌ yard ground rent yearly for the front to Dale Street end. And this ground to be set out by Mr Mayor and Bailiffs for Mr Livesey."

Scarisbrick.

Brown Low. Mention is made in the early records of the *Brunelagh* or Brown Low, a rocky eminence on the east side of the town, at the foot of which extended the Moss Lake southward. This from time immemorial was worked as a freestone quarry, and, together with the lake adjoining, formed a barrier against the extension of buildings eastward. In 1732 this barrier was broken through.

"1732, May 3. Richard Gildart Mayor.

Quarry. "It being represented to this Councill that the quarry or delf att Brownlow Hill sho'd be cut thorow to make the highway below, and that the same sho'd nott be gott deeper than will be convenient for such way. It is order'd to be view'd and that the getting stone att the Quarry hill delf be stopp'd and not permitted to be open till that way be cutt thorow on Brownlow Hill, and that Mr Litherland pay a rent for that delf att Brownlow Hill."

"1732, July 12. Mr May', sev'all of the Ald", Mr Bayliffe Hamilton and others haveing view'd the delf att Brownlow Hill and Mr Ed. Litherland proposeing to cutt it thro' in two yeares from Mich' next so that a convenient highway will thereby be made that way on condicōn that he have the stone he getts for his pains. It is Order'd accordingly he entring into a contract to perform it under a penalty of one hundred pounds, and not to make it broader than it now is till cutt thorow, and to carry it straight and lay all the wast stuff in the low part of the lane eastwards and the Corporation to have what stones they want." _{Road cut through}

The buildings erected during this period were much superior to anything previous. Hanover Street and Common Shore (altered to Paradise Street) were lined partially with noble mansions, with others scattered in the older parts of the town. _{Buildings.}

The public buildings also began to assume an architectural importance not known before. St. George's Church was a vast advance upon St. Peter's, and St. Thomas's in its original condition with its noble tower and lofty spire was a fine structure. _{Churches.}

The most important and imposing building of the age is undoubtedly the Exchange, now the Town Hall, of the erection of which the records give us an ample history.

The first Exchange stood in High Street, which was superseded by the second, built in 1673, which stood in the recess at the angle of Castle Street and Dale Street. Not more than seventy years from its erection it had become ruinous. _{Exchange.}

" 1740, Octr. 24. Henry Trafford Mayor.
" The Mayor now representing that the Exchange is become decay'd, and that the pillars and one of the arches below have given way and are lately shrunk, and that it is apprehended the great weight of the turrett doth greatly tend thereto. It is now order'd that the turrett be imediatly taken down, and that Ald" Steers, Mr John Martindale and Mr John Brooks be desired to survey the whole building and roofe, and that Mr Mayor will give imediate directions therein for securing the same. _{Decay.} _{Survey.}
" That the Bailiffs do take an account of the weight of the lead taken off."

"1748, Octr. 18. Ordered, that Mr Mayor be desired to employ some able workmen to view the 'Change, and take any stones &c down for the safety of it if they shall judge necessary."

"1747, June 15. Joseph Bird Mayor.

Site for Exchange.
"Ordered, that Mr Mayor, Ald. Carr and Brooks be empowered to treat with Mr Fazakerley of Ormskirk for the purchase of his houses and ground on the north side of Water Street upon the best terms they can, not exceeding nine hundred pounds for the same, and that a plan for a new Exchange be drawn and laid before the Council."

The purchase was made, and immediate steps were taken to acquire possession.

Buildings removed.
"1747, Sept. 16. Ordered that notice in writing be given by the Town Clerk to the tenants of the houses in Water Street and High Street lately purchased by the Corporation, that they are severally to quit their possessions on or before the twenty fifth day of March now next ensuing."

Sale of Materials.
"1747, Decr. 7. Ordered that the Town Clerk with the approbation of Mr Mayor and Bailiffs do sell in three lotts the materials of the houses standing where the Exchange is to be built on, at publick auction to the highest bidder, a month's notice being first given and advertized of the sale."

Building Stone.
"1748, Feby. 13. Ordered, that stone be got ready for the building a new Exchange, which shall be built with an area."

Committee on Plans.
"1748, March 1. Ordered that Mr Mayor and Bailiffs Ald^n Shaw, Steers and Brooks, Messrs Davies, Winstanley, Forbes, Goore and the Town Clerke be appointed a Committee to draw up and agree upon two plans for a new Exchange, and to report and lay them before the Councel at their next meeting; any five of which gentlemen to constitute a Committee and to receive proposals for doing the whole work necessary and requisite to be done, in and about it. And that all proposals be given in to them at their meetings sealed up."

Resolutions.
"1748, Mar. 17. Upon the inspecting and considering the two plans of the intended new 'Change now laid before this Council; it is Ordered that there be two grand rooms, one for the Court room and another for an Assembly room in the intended building; and this resolution to be an instruction to the Comittee in ordering or receiving any plans."

After ample consideration the following conclusion was arrived at :—

"1749, July 11. Joseph Clegg Mayor.

Wood's Plan approved.
"Ordered that the plan of the new intended Exchange now laid before this Council by John Wood Esq Architect (of Bath) being approved of,

be carried into execution under his direction. And that the said Mr Wood shall be allowed and paid for his services in the planning and structure of the said intended Exchange, the sume of five pounds ⅌ cent on the money which shall be laid out on the said building. And that whenever the said Mr Wood shall come to Liverpoole to direct the carrying on the said building, his travelling charges are to be paid by the Corporation. Commission.

"And in consideration of which payments or allowance, the said Mr Wood agrees to leave his son Mr John Wood at Liverpoole during the summer seasons to superintend and carry on the said building." Clerk of Works.

The selection of the Architect proved a wise and successful measure. John Wood was the architect of the fine crescents and squares of Bath, and his buildings display much taste and skill. Wood Architect.

"1749, July 5. Ordered that John Wood Esquire Architeck for the new intended Exchange be admitted free, gratis.

"Ordered that John Wood Junior Gentleman be admitted free, gratis."

The first stone of the new building was laid on the 14th September, 1749, by Mr. Joseph Clegg the Mayor.

"1752, July 3. The Committee appointed for building the new Exchange, having now laid before this Council designs of work in Basso Relievo for the Pediment thereof to Water Street for their approbation ; it is Ordered that the said Pediment be ornamented with such work and that the Committee be empowered to agree with a Statuary to do the said work." Sculpture. Pediment.

"1753, July 10. Henry Winstanley Mayor.

"It is by this Council Ordered, that Mr Stephenson the statuary be paid the sum of eighty guineas and no more in full for the statuary work by him executed in the Pediment of the new Exchange, they thinking it a sufficient and full pay for the same." Payment.

Mr. Stephenson was not satisfied, and petitioned for a further grant, which was met by the following resolution :— Stephenson, Sculptor.

"1756, Nov. 17. It is Ordered, that Wm Stevenson's petition to this Council praying the payment of twenty pounds, which was by agreement with the Council for doing the sculpture work of the Pediment of the Exchange left to the discretion of the Council according to his performance of the work; the Council, to former petition by him to them preferred for the same, gave him for answer that the work is ill executed, and they think he is already paid more than it deserves, being paid eighty pounds, and therefore they'l pay him no more."

Removal of Books.
"1753, Octr. 19. Ordered that the Town Clerk be authorized and empowered to remove the Corporation books, records, papers and writings under his care into the proper places provided in the new Exchange for the reception."

Chandelier.
"1754, Feby. 6. Ordered that a glass lustre or chandelier be bought by the Corporation for the Merchants Hall in the New Exchange not exceeding sixty guineas price."

Opening.
The building was soon afterwards publicly opened with great rejoicings, but no record is to be found in the books.

Sale of Old Exchange.
"1754, Feby. 6. Ordered, that the Old Exchange of this town be putt up to sale at auction to the highest bidder and fourteen days notice be given of the sale, and that the purchaser of the said building shall pull it down, and the ground cleared at the expence of the purchaser within one month from the sale, and that it be sold under such other proper conditions of sale to be agreed and settled by Mr Mayor. And that Mr Mayor first order what will be necessary and fitting to be putt up in any part of the New Exchange to be removed from the said old building. Also that the room under the Mayor's office in the New Exchange be immediately fitted up to hold the Court of Requests in."

Workhouse,
In 1731 an effort was made to provide a permanent workhouse for the poor, who had up to that time been temporarily provided for in various localities.

"1731, Mar. 1. Richard Gildart Mayor.

Parish Meeting.
"The proceedings of the Trustees or Comittee appointed by the inhabitants of the Parish of Liverpool att a generall meeting in the Comon Hall on the 16ᵗʰ day of February last past to fix on and treat for a proper place to build a workhouse upon wherein to imploy the poor of this Parish and thereby to ease the inhabitants of the great burthen the poor are at present, and likely to encrease, being now read and approved of by this Councill, and the ground adjoining to the back wings of the Charity School now in lease to Mr John Brooks for three lives and 21 years being thought most convenient to build such Workhouse upon, and

Grant of Land.
the said John Brooks now consenting and agreeing to transferr his term and intrest in the piece of ground fix'd on for that purpose on reasonable terms;

"This Councill doth agree thereto, and it is now ordered that proper conveyances be passed under the Comon Seale of this burrough and Corporation to such person or persons as Councill shall advise, of the reversion and inheritance thereof, and of all the buildings, courts and yards thereto belonging, to that use and purpose for ever."

STREETS AND BUILDINGS.

In 1770 the site of the Workhouse was transferred to Brownlow Hill.

The old Infirmary, formerly standing on a portion of the site of St. George's Hall, was erected 1745-50. The following entry relates to its inception:— *Infirmary.*

"1748, Apl. 13. Thomas Shaw Mayor.

"Whereas by several Orders of Council heretofore made the 3rd April 1745 and 16th August in the same year.

"It is Ordered that the field commonly called the Oyl Mill field and the Waste before it at the bottom of Dale Street shall be granted to the Trustees to be appointed for erecting an Infirmary for poor persons, sick and wounded, for 999 years without any reserved rent or conditions of forfeiture pursuant to the Act made in the 9th year of his p'sent Majestye King George the second, entitled an Act to restrain the disposition of lands whereby the same become unalienable; And by another order of Council made the eleventh day of March 1746, it is Ordered that the date of the lease of the said Oyl Mill field granted by the Corporation to the Trustees of the said Infirmary shall be altered and changed to the said eleventh day of March 1746, on account that the said lease was to be enrolled in the High Court of Chancery within six months from the date thereof, pursuant to the above mentioned Act. And whereas a lease and counterpart were accordingly made and executed and were sent up to London in order to have been inrolled in Chancery, pursuant to the said Act, but by mistake of the attorney they were inrolled in the Court of King's Bench instead of the Court of Chancery. *Grant of Land. Lease.*

"It is therefore now Ordered that all the above recited Orders of Council be, and they are each of them renewed and continued and that a new lease be now granted to the Trustees of the said Infirmary of the said Oyl Mill field pursuant to the severall Orders above mentioned, and that the said lease shall bear date from this 13th day of April instant and be inrolled in Chancery pursuant to the directions of the above mentioned statute, and that at the execution of such new lease, the lease and counterpart of the said Oyl Mill field and premises already executed shall be cancelled and destroyed." *Enrollment.*

Oldhall Street originally terminated at the Ladies' Walk, now the Canal Basin; beyond this the strand of the river was the only way northward. In 1749 an effort was made to carry the street forward. *Oldhall Street.*

Road Northward.
"1749, July 11. Ordered that the Mayor and Mr Aldⁿ Cunliffe be desired to acquaint the landowners who petition to have a road made from the Mile house to the upper end of Oldhall Street, and to bring in an estimate of the expence, and the Council will then consider what allowance will be given towards the expence of making the road."

ECCLESIASTICAL.

The building of St. George's Church was commenced in 1726.[1]

"1728, Novr. 6. John Hughes Mayor.

"Ordered. That all the mon' due by contract or otherwise be call'd in and apply'd towards carrying on the new church, and that the sev'all leases be p'pared for y^t purpose and such as refuse to pay be sued." St. George's Church.

"1729, May 7. Order'd that the flaggs for the new church be gott out of the delf over ag^t Robert Wilson's Ropery, when and as the Comittee shall direct. Flags.

"That the new church in Derby Square be vaulted and arched with brick." Vaulting.

"1731, Nov. 3. Order'd that the Comittee for building the new church be desired to carry on the same with all speed."

"Nov. 12. Order'd that the present Baylives be added to Comittee for carrying on the new church, and that as many of the Aldermen as please to attend, be of that Comittee." Committee.

"1732, Mar. 1. Order'd that the Comittee for building the new church in Derby Square doe view and consider of what stepps or bench may be conveniently made on the north side of the said church for the use of the markett people and report their opinion thereon next Council day." Market.

"1732, Mar. 23. Richd Gildart Mayor.

"It being represented to this Councill that Mr James Shaw hath been very much in advance for materials found and work done att the new church in Derby Square and praying to have intrest after a certain time. Shaw's claim.

"It is Ordered that he be allow'd intrest at 5 ⅌ cent from the expiration of nine months after the work done and materialls deliv''ed, to be settled by the Comittee and to be paid accordingly by the Treasurer."

"1732, May 3. Then appointed Mr Mayor and Baylives (and others) any five to be the Comitee for carrying on and finishing the new church in Derby Square, and are desir'd to meet every other Thursday at three a clock in the afternoon in the Comon Hall." Committee.

"1732, Decr. 18. Ordered, that the Treasurer do pay to Mr Ed Litherland sixty pounds tow^{ds} his work in the steeple to the new church in Derby Square." Steeple.

[1] See *ante* p. 70.

"1734, July 26. William Pole Mayor.

Consecration. "It being signify'd to this Council that the Right Reverend the Lord Bishop of Chester intends to consecrate the new church or chappell lately erected and built by the Corporation upon the scite and soile of the late Castle, on Thursday the first day of August next, and that it will be necessary that a fitt person be now elected and chosen to be the first

Chaplain. curate or chaplain thereof, and that the presentation or nomination be prepared in the mean time.

"It is now resolved and Ordered that it will be expected from such curate or chaplain, that he perform divine service and preach every forenoon and afternoon on every Sunday in the year, and morning and evening prayers every Tuesday and Thursday in the week, and every holiday in the year, and that all the rights of the Mayor Bayl^s and Comon Councill be reserv'd to them according to the Act of Parliam^t made in the first year of his late Maj^{tie} King George the first.

Wolstenholme. "The Reverend Henry Wolstenholme is now elected and chosen to be first curate or chaplain of the said new church or chappel.

Sewell. "Mr Mayor now also recommends that an assistant to Mr Wolstenholme be now appointed, and nominates the Reverend Cuthbert Sewell to be assistant to the said chaplain, which this Council agree to and recomend

Lectures. him accordingly, and that the chaplain or his assistant do preach a lecture sermon on every other or second Thursday in the afternoon throughout the year, and that the prayers in the weekdays be at tenn aforenoon, and six a'clock in the evening dureing sumer season and at three in the afternoon in the winter season."

"1736, Nov. 3. Richd Gildart Mayor.

"Whereas by the Act of Parliam^t for building and endowing St George's church or chappell, the Mayor Bayl^s and Comon Councill for the time being or the major part of them have the full and free disposition of all and every the seats and pews in the said church or chappell, and that in

Letting of Pews. pursuance thereof they did on the 15th day of Augt 1734 agree to sett and lett the same (the publick seats for the Mayor Ald^n Bayl^s and Comon Councill and their wives only excepted) and that the severall persons who have agreed to take seats in the said church or chappell have respectively subscribed a contract for each seat, and that the Comittee having agreed with them for a certain yearly rent for each particular seat, and which this Council do approve of, ratify and confirm.

"And that on the 12th day of September 1734, the Mayor Ald^n Bayl^s and Comon Councill in Council assembled takeing the same into con-

Salaries. sideration, did order that the severall and respective yearly sallaries or stipends hereafter mentioned sho'd be paid to the minister, curate or chaplain of the said church or chappell and to the minister assistant and to the clerk and sexton to witt—

"To the Rev'end Henry Wolstenholme not less than £50 a year.
"To the Rev'end Cuthbert Sewell assistant £40.

"To Edward Green clerk £20.
"To John Nicholls sexton £10.
"And this Councill now takeing into further consideration the report made this day by the Comittee, appointed to manage and attend the setting of the said seats and other purposes relateing to the said church. It appears that there are — Pew Rents.

"31 seats below on the south side lett which make £42 12 0
"35 on the north side lett which make 43 8 0
"35 seats in the Gallery on the south side 34 10 0
"34 ,, in the Gallery on the north side 33 17 6

and that the back long seat intended for the Bayliffs Peers might be sett, which is now order'd to be divided and sett, and that there are some few back seats yet unsett and it also appearing that the income of the seats already sett for this present year ending at Christmas next will make above £30 more than the above yearly sallaries or stipends, and that the stipends to Mr Wolstenholme and Mr Sewell are not adequate to the trouble they have; it is Order'd by this Councill that the said overplus be paid to the said Mr Wolstenholme and Mr Sewell, that is to say, to Mr Wolstenholme two third parts thereof, and to Mr Sewell one third part thereof." — Arrangements.

The church continued to prosper, and the Committee reported on the 6th Sept., 1738, that there was a further surplus, which the Council agreed should be paid over to the two incumbents as before. — Surplus.

Mr. Wolstenholme was a very popular preacher.

"1740, May 14. Ordered that the Rev'end Mr Henry Wolstenholme be desired to print his sermon preach'd on the last fast day in St George's."

Many entries occur relating to the letting of the seats, the Bailiffs appearing to have the care and responsibility.

"1743, Feby. 2. John Brookes Mayor.
"Whereas it hath been represented to the Worshipfull the Mayor, Aldermen, Bailiffs and Common Council in Council assembled, that the present stipend of salarys of the Rev^d Mr Hen. Wolstenholme and the Rev^d Mr Maddock the Chaplain and Lecturer at St George's Church, are not adequate to the constant attendance required, not only in the performance of their duty in the publick service of the church, but also in preaching lectures every fortnight, &c they determine to raise the salaries to £100 for the chaplain and £80 to the lecturer." — Raising Salaries.

It appears from an entry about this date that the vaults under the church were let for storage purposes and brought in a revenue, notwithstanding the consecration of the edifice by the Bishop.

The pews seem to have been in great demand.

Disputes about Pews.
"1748, April 13. Whereas a dispute hath arisen between the late Alderman Coore's Ex^r and Mr John Atherton about the right of possession of the seats in St George's Church of Ald Coore. It is now Ordered, that the said seats shall be continued to the said Aldⁿ Coore's daughter Mrs Pickersgill, in the same manner as other tenants hold them. And that the said Mrs Pickersgill shall be defended and maintained against any persons disturbing her in the peaceable possession thereof at the expence of the Corporation, she paying the rent in arrear for the said seat before said Mr Atherton occupied the same.

"And Aldⁿ Gildart now proposing to give up his own seat in St George's Church to accommodate Mr Jno Atherton, in consideration that the Corporation will grant him the last of the Bailiffs Peers seats in the said church. It is therefore accordingly order'd that Aldⁿ Gildart have the said seat upon the same rent he paid for the other seat."

Raising Salaries.
"1750, Octr. 3. Ordered that a list of the rents of the seats in St George's Church be laid before the Council at the next meeting, and that twenty pounds a piece a year be added to and paid to the two ministers of the said church which is to be raised and laid on the seats."

Arrangement of Pews.
"1751, Sept. 4. Ordered that the Town Clerk have one side of the Bailiff's wife's seat, and that the other be reserved for the Corporation use, he paying such rent as Mr Mayor and Mr Bayliffs shall fix, and that Mr Green (the clerk) have notice to forbid any other persons having no right from coming and using the seat, as they now do."

"1752, April 15. Upon the petition of Mrs Kaye to this Council setting forth her right; it is Ordered that she have the seat in the gallery in St George's Church late Mrs Winstanley's, and to which the Widow Cheshire hath laid some claim. But that it appears to this Council that Mrs Cheshire gave it up or quitted the said seat the next year after the said church was consecrated, and hath now another seat in the said church."

Winstanley and Cheshire.

"1754, Aug. 7. Whereas it hath been represented to this Council that many persons who rent seats in Saint George's Church from the Council, after they quitt sitting in them by themselves or familys, do take upon them to sett the said seats for an over-rent to themselves, or do assign or otherwise transfer the same to some other persons without any order of Council.

Prohibition against Sub-letting.
"It is therefore now Ordered, that no tenant or other occupier of any seat, pew or sitting in the said church shall have any right, power, or authority to assign, transfer or sett any such seat, pew, or sitting to any persons whatever . . but that every such seat shall revert and come

into the hands of the Council to all intents and purposes, as if the same had never been sett or enjoyed."

These orders are subsequently repeated, and sufficiently indicate the popularity of the church, owing no doubt in great measure to the ministrations of Mr. Wolstenholme and his assistant, as we do not find the same eagerness in relation to St. Nicholas', the old Parish Church, or to St. Peter's.

The mode of conducting the service caused some difference of opinion.

"1751, Octr. 18. It is Order'd upon the motion of Mr Aldⁿ Shaw that chaunting divine service, or such parts thereof as are usually thus performed, be introduced and performed in the said service in St George's Church. And that the management thereof be left to the direction of Mr Shaw, who is to agree with some proper persons to instruct some persons in the knowledge and exercise thereof." *Chanting.*

After a few months' trial this innovation was not generally approved.

"1752, July 3. Ordered, that chaunting the publick service in St. George's Church be for the future discontinued, and that Mr Aldⁿ Pole pay Mr Brett, the master, five guineas for his trouble in instructing persons to chaunt." *Discontinued*

"1745, Apl. 3. Whereas an Order of Council was made the 2nd November 1743 that there should be two brass branches or chandeliers provided for St Geo^s Church, and nothing done therein. It is Ordered that Mr Mayor and Bailiffs do write to London to buy 'em." *Chandeliers.*

"1748, Nov. 2. Ordered that the Comittee for making an altar piece in St George's Church do agree with Mr Coppuck to paint an Altar Piece in such scripture—historical manner as the said Comittee shall fix, and that Mr Mayor, Bailiffs and Mr Goore be added to s^d Comittee." *Altar Piece.*

"1751, July 3. Ordered that Mr Mayor Aldⁿ Shaw and Mr Goore be appointed a Comittee to treat and agree with Ralph Holland to take down the Weathercock of St George's Church to raise the steeple and put up the Weathercock." *Steeple.*

At the time of the rebellion, in 1745, the clergy did their duty in aiding and stimulating the loyalty of their flocks.

"1745, Octr. 10. Owen Pritchard Mayor.
"Ordered, that the Bailiffs be desired to waite on the Clergy of this town who have preached loyal sermons on occasion of the present *Clergy.* *Thanks to*

rebellion, return 'em the thanks of this Council, and desire them to print the sermons."

Thanks to Maddox.

"1746, Octr. 18. Ordered, that the Reverend Mr Maddox have the thanks of this Corporation returned him for the loyal and good sermon he preached on the thanksgiving day, the ninth instant, for the signal victory obtained by His Royal Highness the Duke of Cumberland over the rebels, and that he be desired to print the same at the expence of the Corporation."

Heskain's Lecture.

"1752, Sept. 18. Ordered that the Rev^d Mr Heskain of this town, have liberty to have a lecture every other Thursday evening (not being the present lecture evening) at Saint George's Church and that the lecture now had there on Sunday mornings be not continued in the morning any longer till Sunday next, but be postponed till after evening service of that day."

Extra Service discontinued.

"1752, Octr. 16. Ordered that the extraordinary service performed at St George's Church be discontinued at Christmas next on account of the many complaints made by the owners of the seats in the said church of great inconveniencies occasioned thereby."

St. George's was the Corporation church *par excellence*, and long continued to be the resort of the Liverpool aristocracy. St. Peter's, though built by the Corporation, being a Parish Church, was not so much under their control. They possessed, however, certain rights which, with their usual tenacity, they were not slow to defend.

Disputes about Seats.

"1744, Octr. 11. Ordered that the Town Clerk be empowered to defend on behalf of the Corporation of Liverpoole, their right to the seat in St Peter's church comonly called Lord Molyneux's seat agst any persons claiming the same, at the expence of this Corporation."

Thanks to Rector Stanley.

"1750, Apl. 4. Ordered that the thanks of this Council be given to the Honourable and Reverend Mr Stanley one of our late Rectors upon his cession now made of this his cure, for his diligent faithfull and able discharge of his ecclesiastick function, for his kind and early letter of resignation thereof to this body his patrons, on his being inducted to the Rectory of Halsall in this county, and for the pious and gratefull orthodox and instructive sermon of farewell which he preached and delivered to his congregation last Sunday at St Peter's church in this town. And that Mr Mayor be desired to waite on him in the name of the whole Corporate body for this purpose."

At the beginning of the century Liverpool had only a single chapel of ease, under Walton. Before the middle of the century there were three large churches, all well filled. A fourth was now called for.

"1747, Jany. 27. Thomas Shaw Mayor.

"Whereas several well disposed persons have lately subscribed the sume of two thousand three hundred pounds and upwards towards the building a new church or chapel in Mr Okill's ground near Park Lane in Liverpoole, the ground for the building which upon, the said Mr Okill hath promised to give, and the presentation and advowson to which said church or chapel is to be vested in the Mayor, Aldermen, Bailiffs and Common Council of this Corporation. St. Thomas's Church.

"Upon this consideration that the Corporation will grant their reversionary interest or inheritance of the said ground on which the said church is to be built for that purpose. And to be at the expence of obtaining the said Act of Parliament for building the same—which is therefore now accordingly Order'd by this Council. Grant of Land.

"And that the following gentlemen be appointed a Comittee to draw up a petition to Parliament, for the obtaining an Act for building the said church viz' Mr Mayor and Bailiffs, Ald" Cunliffe (with ten others).". Act of Parliament.

The Act was obtained, and the church (St. Thomas's) commenced.

"1748, Jany. 4. Joseph Clegg Mayor.

"Ordered That Mr Goore and some of the Commissioners for the church now in building be desir'd to meet Mr Okill and confer with him about the price of his ground in Park Lane, and which is intended to be bought from him for a church yard to the said church and report it to the Council." Land.

"1748, Mar. 1. Ordered that Mr Mayor and Bailiffs, Ald" Steers, and Brooks be appointed a Committee to view the delf at Quarry Hill where it is feygh'd for the Docks, in order to allow the contractors for the church to take of it for the use of the church and to fix what price they shall pay for it in case they allow them to get stone where feigh'd." Stone for Church.

The church was completed in 1750.

"1750, July 4. Whereas the Lord Bishop of Chester is to come to this town the next week, to consecrate St Thomas's Church, and confirm in this town. It is Ordered that Mr Mayor be desired to entertain him at the expence of the Corporation in such manner as he shall think proper." Consecration

"1751, Apl. 3. Ordered that the Treasurer do pay Mr Goore the expences of consecrating St Thomas's Church amounting to the sume of eighteen pounds sixteen shillings and sixpence."

"1753, Nov. 7. It being proposed and agreed by the Parishioners to

Churchyard. purchase a church yard on a Lych Ley for St Thomas's Church out of ground belonging to Mr Okill adjoining thereto held by lease under the Corporation.

Grant of Land. "It is ordered that this Corporation do grant their reversionary interest therein for a church yard."

"1757, April 21. Ordered that the Council do give the Commissioners of Saint Thomas's Church the sum of five hundred pounds towards the purchasing of a church yard to the said church."

St. Thomas's Church, in its original condition, was a handsome structure, with a lofty spire. Unfortunately the stone of which it was built was soft and friable, and not many years elapsed before serious repairs were required.

"1757, Apl. 19. It is Ordered, that whereas the top part of the steeple of Saint Thomas's Church was in the late storm blown down, and it falling into or upon the body of the said church beat through the roof and did considerable damage to the same, and to the seats and gallerys in the said church. That the same be repaired at the expence of this Corporation, and that Mr Mayor and Bailiffs (with 8 others) be appointed a Committee or any five of them."

Steeple rebuilt. "1759, Aug. 15. Ordered that Thomas Wainwright, mason, be paid the sum of forty five Pounds, for the rebuilding the top of the steeple of Saint Thomas's Church and that Mr Ald^n Pole, the treasurer take credit for the same."

The time had now arrived when a fifth church was called for; this time at the north end of the town, which was then the most fashionable district.

"1753, Nov. 7. James Crosbie Mayor.

St. Paul's Church. "It is Ordered that an Act of Parliament be applied for this session at the Corporation expence, for the building a new church in this town, on the plan and scheme lately proposed and agreed on at the vestry, and, on the petition of the parishioners of this parish now read to the Council; upon the condition and agreement that the Common Council be vested with the perpetual advowson of the said church, and also to have nomination of the clerk and sexton of the said church, after the first presentation of the minister and nomination of the first clerk and sexton."

"1760, Octr. 10. Lawrence Spencer Mayor.

Resolutions of Parish. "Whereas it has been resolved by the Parishioners of the Parish of Liverpoole to build one or more church or churches within this town by a general levy or tax on real and personal estates of the inhabitants, the body of which churches are to be laid open for the benefit of the poor, but the seats in the gallerys are to be appropriated for or towards the paying the ministers stipends and other officers and uses of the said churches. And whereas one of the said churches is imediately intended to be erected on a piece of land formerly purchased by this Parish from Mr Ralph Earl, being part of the Dog field on the north side of the town, but that the other is to be postponed for some years till this is finished and paid for, and another is found to be necessary and wanted. And whereas it has been proposed and agreed to that the next presentation and perpetual advowson to and of such churches shall be vested in the Mayor, Bailiffs, and Common Council of the said borough and Corporation of Liverpoole in the like manner as those to the other churches in this town are by Parliament settled and invested. And whereas there has been and still are subsisting some differences and disputes between the Corporation and the Parish in regard to some claims of moneys which the said Parishioners alledge the said Corporation owe the said Parish, but which said claims this Council do not admitt to be just, or that such moneys are so owing by them; but for the considerations aforesaid and in lieu of such claims and demands and to promote an agreement and unanimity between the Parish in general and the Corporation. It is now therefore Order'd that this Corporation shall be at and pay the charge and expence of obtaining an Act of Parliament this next session for the building one or more church or churches in the town of Liverpoole. And that the said Corporation shall pay and allow unto the minister for the time being of the said North Church and his successors, the yearly sume of thirty pounds, first saving, reserving and excepting out of this agreement to the said Parishioners, all legacies and other sumes of money now in ye hands of the said Corporation which they now acknowledge or pay interest for the same, due, owing or in any wise belonging to the said parishioners of Liverpoole or their poore." Dog Field.

Disputes.

Act of Parliament.

Contribution

The further proceedings will be referred to in the next chapter.

References have been made in the preceding chapter to the Free Grammar School, dating from the time of Queen Elizabeth. It was still continued, but never appears to have been in a very flourishing condition. Free Grammar School.

"1745, April 10. Upon a representation that the Free School of this town is attended with an annual expence to this Corporation of sixty two pounds. Ordered that Mr Mayor be desired to take the Council with him to visit the said school." Visit.

"1748, Jany. 4. Whereas Mr Mayor with several of this Council have lately visited the free school of this town, and found the same to have very Report.

Order.

Instruction.

few scholars in it, the reason whereof, as appears to this Council, that the inhabitants or freemen have neglected their children. Therefore this Council doth order that publick notice be given to the inhabitants or freemen, that for the future there will be taught in the said school the Latin and English tongues, as also Writing and Vulgar Arithmetick, as an inducement to them to send their children in; thereby effectually to answer the good intent of the said school in giving sutable education to the children of the poor freemen, who could not without this assistance have done it, and that the Comittee be appointed to draw up proper rules and regulations for the better government of the said school."

Rules.

"1748, Mar. 1. Ordered that the Rules now read to this Council for the government of the Free School of this town be establish'd and entred in this Council book, and that all schoolmasters of the said school for the future shall observe them. And whereas the Rev^d Mr Martin, school-master of the said school, by the Rev^d Mr Baldwin, one of the Rectors of this Parish having left or not being resident in this Parish, and who hath not provided any curate to officiate for him, whereby a double duty is devolved on the said Mr Martin his curate, from which it is not possible he can attend the duty of the school as he otherwise might or would do.

Master to surrender.

It is now further Ordered that in case the said Mr Martin will surrender up the said school to the Council now, That they will as a gratuity give him the sume of forty guineas; and it is likewise Ordered, that for the future no clergyman shall be admitted Schoolmaster or Usher of the said school in any capacity whatsoever."

No Clergyman to be admitted.

Rules.

Here follow the Rules, the main features of which are the following:—

Subjects taught.

The Head Master was to instruct the scholars in Latin and English; the Under Master to teach writing and arithmetic.

Hours.

That both masters attend between Lady Day and Michaelmas from seven in the morning until noon, and in the afternoon from two to five. During the remainder of the year the attendance was to be from eight to twelve, and from half-past one to four.

Payments.

Every scholar to pay one shilling entrance money, one shilling at Shrovetide, one shilling fire money, and one shilling at Christmas. These perquisites to be divided, two-thirds to the Head Master and one-third to the Usher.

The vacation time to be three weeks at Christmas, a Vacations. week at Easter, a fortnight at Whitsuntide, and the church holidays.

No scholar to be admitted till he is able to read in the Qualifications. Psalter, and their parents to send them in clean and decent dress, and free from offensive and catching disorders.

The school to be visited the first Monday in every month Visiting. by at least three members of the Council, who were to examine and report, and to give such orders as might be necessary.

The schoolmaster having made some demur as to his resignation, his gratuity was increased to fifty guineas, which he accepted and resigned.

"1749, Apl. 5. Ordered that whoever shall be elected schoolmaster of this school shall before he is admitted give a bond to the Mayor, Bailiffs and Burgesses in the sume of five hundred pounds conditioned that he Bond for will resign the school and license, whenever the Common Council shall resignation. request the same into their hands.

"Ordered that the vacancy for a Head Master be advertized in some Vacancy publick newspapers; that the Rev^d Mr Bardesley and Mr James Ansdell advertised. shall be excluded from offering themselves or being either of them chosen, and that a Committee be appointed to inspect and revise the rules."

No record is extant of the appointment of the Master.

"1752, Decr. 6. Ordered that Mr Mayor and such others of the Mayor, &c. Council as please, be authorized and desired to visit the free school and to visit. take an account of the scholars and to distinguish therein, who are the sonns of freemen and who are not, and which of the parents of such scholars are able to pay a quarteridge to the Masters, or which of them do."

"1753, Aug. 1. On a representation made to this Council that the Report. Free School of the town is crowded and fill'd up with a great number of scholars who have no right to the benefit of the said school; It is Ordered that the masters of the said school shall not admitt or receive any scholars into the said school till he hath received an order under the Mayor and hands of the Mayor and Bailiffs directing and authorizing the admission Bailiffs to direct. of every person or scholar so applying."

"1759, Apl. 9. Ordered that Mr John Baines be elected the head John Baines master of the Free School of this town in the room of Mr Abram Ashcroft elected Master.

who has resigned it into the hands of this Council, with the same salary, during the pleasure of the Council only, and to be subject to the Rules already established or any other Rules which may be established by the Council for the government of the same, and give a like bond to the Council as Mr Ashcroft did."

Last appointment. This was the last appointment made. On Mr. Baines's decease, about 1802, the school was closed. After an interval of more than twenty years it was revived by the establishment of elementary schools by the Corporation, in the north and south districts of the town, which were subsequently made over to the School Board.

CHAPTER THIRD.

FROM THE ACCESSION OF GEORGE III. (1760) TO THE END OF THE EIGHTEENTH CENTURY.

MUNICIPAL AFFAIRS.

The loyal Corporation were not tardy in presenting their congratulations to the youthful successor to the throne.

"1760, Nov. 5. John Blackburn Mayor.

"Ordered that the present Address of condolance and congratulation on the death of his late Majesty and the accession of his present Majesty to the throne of these kingdoms, as now read to this Council, be fair copied, passed under the Common Seal and transmitted to our members to be presented to his Majesty. Address.

"To the King's Most Excellent Majesty.

"The humble Address of the Mayor, Aldermen, Bailiffs and Common Council of the Borough and Corporation of Liverpoole.

"Most Gracious Sovereign.

"We, your Majesty's ever dutyfull and loyal subjects, the Mayor, Aldermen, Bailiffs and Common Council of the town of Liverpoole in Common Council assembled humbly beg leave to approach your Royal and sacred person, with this, our most sincere address of condolance on the death of our late august and well beloved sovereign, your illustrious grandfather ; a Prince in whom were united all the virtues, which constitute a brave, wise, humane and pious ruler ; whose government over a free and gratefull people was so equitable and just, that during his long and glorious reign, the prerogative of the Crown and the rights and liberties of the subject went hand in hand, sacred and inviolable. George II.

"At the same time, Great Sire, we most humbly beseech you to permit us, with the same warm affections, to congratulate your Majesty on your accession to the Empire of these realms, your native country. And although your Majesty ascends the throne in the midst of the rage and calamities of war, yet, from the natural and royal magnanimity of soul, inherent in the ancient and illustrious House of Hanover—from the many shining virtues and powerful abilities which have so conspicuously adorned your early part of life, cultivated and encouraged under the best of Royal Congratulations.

Declaration. mothers, the arduous task of Government will be easy to yourself, and happy to your subjects.

"Your royal and voluntary declaration issued immediately upon your accession to the Crown 'That you would preserve and strengthen the present happy constitution in church and state' must endear your Majesty to all your subjects, and afford them a pleasing confidence, that in you, the Almighty has rais'd up another indulgent Father of their country—another George—auspicious name to Britons! a king who will reign in the hearts of a great and powerfull nation;—ready and willing to defend them against all their enemies, to protect, encourage and maintain them in all their legal rights, possessions and commercial interests.

Allies. "The wisdom and integrity of your Majesty's ministers, the fortitude and bravery of our fleets and armies, under whose directions and by whose valour, so many noble victories and wide extended conquests have been acquired, will we trust in God, with the concurrence of your steady allies, enable your Majesty to triumph over the inveterate enemies of your kingdom, and compel the rivals of our trade to accept from your Majesty's hand a peace upon terms honourable, just and permanent, to these kingdoms.

"May it please God, of his great mercy and kindness so often shewn to these nations, to grant to your Majesty health and long life, a happy and glorious reign, and that the Imperial Crown of these realms may descend from you to the latest posterity of your Royal House with additional lustre and glory. And that your Majesty will be graciously pleased to accept this Address as the sincere pledge of our allegiance, fidelity and zeal for the welfare and service of your royal and most illustrious family and government.

"By order of the Council."

King's Birthday. "1761, June 3. Ordered that Mr Mayor be desired to invite the Gent. of the town to the Exchange to-morrow, being his Majesty's birthday, to drink the king's health at the Corporation expense."

Election. The election of members to the New Parliament was stiffly contested. The number of freemen admitted preparatory thereto according to the records was 743. This seems almost incredible, as the whole number polled only amounted to 2164, but the particulars are set forth with the amount paid by each: 3s. 4d. by those free born, 6s. 8d. from those free by servitude, and from those free by purchase sums varying from £3 3s. up to £15 15s.

Candidates. The candidates were Sir Ellis Cunliffe, Sir Wm. Meredith, and Mr. Chas. Pole, of whom the two former were elected. After the election, the following entry occurs :—

"1761, Decr. 2. Ordered, that the Treasurer do pay John Blackburn Esq (the late Mayor) the sum of one hundred and eleven pounds for so much money by him paid for a councel to assist and advise him at the late Counsel. election of Members of Parliament for this Borough and Corporation and be allowed it in his accounts."

"1761, June 3. Ordered that Mr Mayor be authorized and empowered Arms. to call in the arms belonging to this Corporation and to prosecute any persons refusing to deliver up the same to him or his order."

Reference was made in the last Chapter to the law proceedings arising out of the disputes with Mr. Clegg, Mayor in 1748, and his expulsion from the Council.

"1761, Sept. 9. Ordered that Mr Ald^n Clegg be paid the costs he was Disputes put to in bringing a mandamus to be restored to his seat in Council; to with Clegg. be taxed by the Master."

Mr. Clegg was still restless and dissatisfied, as appears from the following record :—

"1762, Octr. 6. Ordered that an opinion of Councel be taken on a publication of Mr Alderman Clegg's in the Manchester newspaper relative to the Corporation credit."

The King's Marriage and Coronation took place in King's September, 1761. Loyal addresses were presented to each Marriage. of the Royal pair, and the following resolution adopted :—

"1761, Sept. 9. It is Ordered, that Mr Mayor be authorized and empowered to entertain the Gentlemen, Merchants, and Tradesmen of this Corporation, with a dinner or otherwise, and to give the Ladies a Ball Dinner and in the Exchange on the day of their Majestys' Coronation, at the publick Ball. expence, and that the Treasurer be authorized and is hereby, to pay the charge thereof, and to be allowed it in his accounts; and that the following Gent. be appointed a Committee to order, conduct and to regulate the same vizt Messrs the Mayor and Bailiffs, Goore, Hughes, Trafford, Colquitt, Powell, Manesty, Johnson, Halliday, Parr, Williamson, Strong, Earle, and the Town Clerk, any three of whom to make a Committee and act. And that they have power to do any other act for the more splendid celebration of that glorious and happy day, as they shall see requisite and necessary.

"And that the Treasurer do repay Mr Mayor two guineas by him given

Invalids. to the Company of Invalids at Liverpoole, to drink his Majesty's health on his late birthday."

Contest for Mayoralty. The election of Mayor in October, 1761, was strongly contested, and occupied four days. It resulted in the choice of Mr. John Williamson, a brewer, residing in Lancelot's Hey, a member of an old Liverpool family.

"1762, Sept. 28. John Williamson Mayor.

Birth of Prince. "Ordered that the Address now read to the Common Council on the safe delivery of the Queen and birth of his Royal Highness the Prince of Wales be passed under the Common Seal and be presented to his Majesty."

Here follows the address, which is couched in the usual high flown phraseology of such documents, proving at all events the steady loyalty of Liverpool to the Hanoverian succession.

"1763, June 7. William Gregson Mayor.

Address. "Ordered, That the Address to his Majesty now read on the conclusion of peace, and to assure him of our inviolable attachment to his person and family, be immediately transmitted to Sir Ellis Cunliffe in order to be presented to his Majesty."

The address expresses

"The unfeigned acknowledgments of the Council for the constant and effectual support granted to our commerce, by means whereof it has flourished in an extraordinary degree during the course of a dangerous and extensive War."

A very significant allusion is made to the Wilkes and Luttrell disputes, which then agitated the political world.

"We are glad on all occasions to declare our zeal and attachment to your sacred person and government and shall be always ready to express our disapprobation and abhorence of the least spirit of discord or faction which may tend to alienate the affections of your Majesty's subjects from the best of Kings."

In 1769, when these disputes had reached their climax, the following loyal and dutiful address was presented by the Council to the King :—

"1769, March 13. Matthew Stronge Mayor.

"Ordered that the Address now read and passed under the Common Address. Seal be presented by Owen Salusbury Brereton Esquire, our Recorder, who is desired to take along with him Alderman Sir Robert Cunliffe Baronet, and John Tarleton and Richard Hughes Esquires and Mr Town Clerk.

"To the King's most Excellent Majesty.

"Most gracious Sovereign.

"Filled with a grateful sense of the blessings this nation has enjoyed under your Majesty's just and mild administration (of which the trade of this commercial place has felt the happy influence) we beg leave to represent to your Majesty that we cannot hear your Government so insolently maligned, nor see a torrent of sedition so violent and rapid as Sedition. to endanger the overthrow of our civil and religious rights, without expressing our utmost abhorrence on so alarming an occasion.

"Nothing but a faction of licentiousness under the mask of liberty would attempt to weaken the cement of your people's duty and affection to your Majesty, and to relax the sinews of your Government by misconstruing the proceedings of your Parliament, and groundlessly diminishing the authority of your courts of justice, which in no age were more uprightly or ably filled.

"By the outrages they have so daringly committed, these enemies of Outrages. their Country, at the same time they are undermining the foundation of our excellent constitution are rashly attempting the destruction of that valuable privilege they profess for their object, of which your Majesty's subjects have had the full fruition during your auspicious reign.

"When your Majesty's peace has been so violently disturbed and the distribution of justice so daringly impeded (though void of all foundation in reason or policy) our attachment to your sacred person and regard for our happy constitution, impel us thus to approach your Majesty, to express our apprehensions, that these invasions of the public tranquillity Apprehen- may be productive of the greatest evils to the state, and, if not timely sions. restrained, be attended with most dangerous consequences to the community.

"Firmly confiding in your Majesty's wisdom, that such prudent, just and reasonable measures will be taken, as may tend to re-establish due order and obedience among your subjects, and stop the progress of these factious combinations, and fully convinced that every thing valuable to us is inseparably connected with the stability of your Majesty's Government, we are resolved, at the risque of our lives and fortunes to second your Lives and Majesty's efforts to dis-countenance and repel these disorders which must Fortunes. needs disturb the repose of your Majesty's reign, and affect the interest and prosperity of your kingdoms."

On the breaking out of the war of independence in War with America.

America, the same spirit of devoted loyalty manifested itself in an address, expressing the Council's

"Abhorrence and detestation of all traitorous and rebellious disturbers of your Majesty's peace and Government, and assuring your Majesty that we shall ever be ready and willing to exert our utmost endeavours for the discouragement of all such illegal proceedings."[1]

Their loyalty was practically shown in the following minute :—

"1775, Nov. 1. James Clemens Mayor.

Grant to Army.

"Ordered, that this Corporation do give out of the public Estate of this town the sum of one hundred guineas to the subscription now set on foot in London and elsewhere, for such occasional acts of benevolence as may be useful to the soldiers who are or may be employed in his Majesty's service in America, and for affording relief to the widows and orphans of such brave men as have fallen or may fall in defending the constitutional government of these realms, in which we are convinced the welfare, well-being, and safety of this town and the trade thereof is greatly concerned; and in part performance of, and conformity to our late address to his Majesty on the present rebellion existing in America. And that the Treasurer of this Corporation do pay unto Mr Mayor the said sum of money to be remitted to the said Committee for this purpose, and be allowed it in his accounts."

Press Warrants.

1770, November 7th. The Mayor having received Press Warrants to impress seamen into the Naval Service, the Council offered one guinea bounty to each able seaman, and half-a-guinea to each able-bodied landsman voluntarily entering the service.

Bounties to Seamen.

In 1776, similar Press Warrants being issued, the Council offered an increased bounty of two guineas for each able seaman, and one guinea for each landsman volunteering. This it was stated

"Would be for the common profit and advantage of the town and the trade thereof, and would be lessening the great hardships and inconveniences which must of course be brought on the freemen and inhabitants."

[1] The address will be found at length in Troughton's History p. 159.

In 1779 the bounty was increased to ten guineas for each seaman and five guineas for the landsmen.

In 1787 the terms were reduced to forty shillings and twenty shillings respectively, which was renewed in 1793.

Steps were also taken towards the defence of the port.

"1773, Feby. 3. Thomas Golightly Mayor.

"Mr Mayor having received a letter from the Board of Ordnance intimating that they would send for the Government great guns, gunpowder, and stores from the town, provided the gentlemen of the Corporation have no objection thereto. It is Ordered that Mr Mayor be desired to write in the name of this Council to desire that they may be continued here for the defence of the town; and also that they would appoint a proper person to take care of the same, and the magistrates will see that such person does his duty; as they were granted for the security and defence of the town and trade thereof." *Cannon and Stores.*

In 1776 more active efforts were made with the same object.

"1776, Nov. 6. William Crosbie Mayor.

"It is Ordered that the petition to his Majesty now read for erecting a fort at Hog's Hey Nook, be referred to a Committee vizt Mr Mayor, Mr Recorder (and others) the Town Clerk to settle the same and transmit it under the Common Seal.

"The Petition sets forth that in the year 1759 a petition was presented to the Crown setting forth the defenceless state of the town and harbour, and praying that some Batterys, Forts or other works of defence might be provided; that an Order in Council was thereupon issued to the Board of Ordnance directing several Batterys to be erected at or near Liverpool; that Plans of the intended Batterys were soon after sent down, and one Battery erected at a place called the Old Church yard, which then commanded a part of the river Mersey and secured the docks from the attacks of the Enemy; but a Fort which was then intended to be built at a certain place called Hogs Hey Nook which was pointed out as the best situation for the safety and defence of the town, was never erected by reason of some difficulties which arose between the landowners of the scite and the said Board respecting the price, and Peace having been soon after made, the design was no further prosecuted. The petitioners represent that the town and port are still in the same defenceless state and that in consequence of the extension of the docks, the Battery in the Old Church Yard is no longer of any use. *Petition for Batteries. Old Churchyard. Hogs Hey Nook.*

"The petitioners submit to his Majesty's Royal wisdom whether there is not now a like or a greater necessity to have the battery with proper

Barracks. Barracks and other appendages made and constructed, seeing that the trade, buildings, properties and persons of the inhabitants are far greater and more numerous than they were at the former period, and that they remain exposed to the ravages of privateers or other armed vessels of any enemy of these realms.

"They therefore pray that a proper fort and barracks for the accommodation of a company or two of soldiers may be erected."

Inquiry. The prayer of the petition was granted. Major Dawson was sent down to inquire and report.

1777, February 22nd. A Committee was appointed to confer with Major Dawson and to treat with the landowners so as to determine the best site for the erection.

Report. 1777, March 5th. The Committee having reported, the Council agreed to the following resolution :—

"The Mayor, Bailiffs and Burgesses of the town of Liverpool in Common Council assembled being informed of our most gracious Sovereign's intentions to erect some proper fortifications and barracks here with a competent armed force, and it being represented to us by Major Richard Dawson one of his Majesty's Engineers, who has been appointed for the purpose that a certain piece of ground on the north side of Clegg's Bath, would be the most proper place for erecting one of such fortifications likely to be of the greatest utility.

Grant of Land. "We the said Mayor &c, impressed with a dutiful and grateful sense of his Majesty's design, and being desirous to ease our beloved Sovereign of some part of the expence, do most cheerfully offer to grant to his Majesty the inheritance of the said piece of ground, and at our common expence to erect and back the intended walls thereof, and to fill up the said ground when his Majesty's Royal Mandate shall be issued for the erection. The work to be done under the inspection of Major Dawson, together with the Engineer by us employed for the docks and other sea works at Liverpool."

Troops required. "1778, Nov. 4. It is Ordered, on Col. Gordon's letter of the state of the Fort now building in this town and concerning the number of soldiers or men which it will be necessary to ask from Government for the manning and defence thereof, that the Mayor be desired to wait on Colonel Gordon to consult and advise with him thereon, but not to ask for a less force than four or five hundred men for such purpose."

Paul Jones. Whilst these negociations were proceeding, the town was thrown into a state of alarm from the redoubtable Paul Jones, who, with his small squadron, was hovering about the channel.

"1779, Sept. 13. At a special Council held for the particular purpose of taking into consideration the best means of putting this town into a state of defence at this alarming juncture a letter having been received by the Mayor that Paul Jones with several ships of force and troops on board are now on the coast. On the Coast.

"Ordered that application be made to remove a quantity of gunpowder to be lodged for the use of the forts and batteries if there shall be occasion.

"That the Mayor apply to the Board of Ordnance for a thousand stands of arms for the use of such gentlemen and private men who may offer to serve as independent volunteer companies, in case of an enemy's landing upon this coast, which is now much to be feared. Arms: Volunteers.

"That the Mayor apply to the Secretary of State to remove the French and Spanish prisoners now confined in the gaol at Mount Pleasant to Chester or elsewhere.

"That a Pilot Boat be sent out to ply as far as Point Lynas, to give intelligence upon the appearance of an enemy, and to station Boats at the different buoys." Precautions.

"1780, Feby. 2. Ordered, that a petition to Lord North be immediately prepared and passed under the Common Seal, praying his assistance to have the Fort and Barracks completed upon the plan approved by the Board of Ordnance, and that the same may be forthwith put upon the establishment."

The undertaking did not proceed very rapidly, for four years after its inception we find the following record:—

"1781, Jany. 3. Ordered that a petition be immediately prepared, and the Common Seal affixed to the King in Council, praying that he will be pleased to give directions for the finishing the Fort at the north end of this town setting forth the encreased danger to this port, from the intimate knowledge which many of the Dutch captains and seamen trading to this port may have of the same. The petition to be presented by the members of Parliament for this town, and Mr Bamber Gascoigne senior." Petition to complete.

"1783, Decr. 3. It appearing to this Council by the representation of Harry Gordon Esq Engineer of the Fort here, that the Barracks are now completed for the reception of one hundred men. Fort completed.

"Ordered that an application be made to the Secretary of War to furnish them with that number.

"And that the present Batteries called George's Battery and Queen's Battery be taken down and the timber sold, and the money arising therefrom be appropriated for the use of the Docks." Batteries removed.

The Fort or Battery, thus completed after so tedious a

delay, stood on the margin of the river, nearly opposite the end of Denison Street, with an esplanade opening from Bath Street. Its site was absorbed into the Prince's Dock after an existence of a little more than thirty years.

The Corporation however did not merely hang on the Government for assistance, but vigorously applied their own shoulders to the wheel. Not long after the petition for the erection of forts and batteries, on the 15th December, 1777, the Council passed a resolution in substance as follows:—

Action of Council.

"We, the Mayor, Bailiffs and Burgesses in Council assembled taking into our most serious consideration the present state of publick affairs in America, and from the Declarations of Independence made, and hostile measures taken in that quarter, reflecting on the danger there may be of disuniting the continent from the British Empire if a speedy and vigorous support be not given by his subjects to his Majesty's endeavours to continue that Union.

"Knowing that our ships are frequently taken even in these channels and our coast annoyed by American Privateers—actuated by the importance of the American trade as by law established—aware that the low ebb of the African trade, principally owing to the revolt in America has in some measure cramped divers of our good brethren the Freemen from being as individuals so liberal in their offerings to our King and country at this juncture as their experienced loyalty and publick spirit incite them to; As upon the fullest conviction that we cannot employ a part of the Corporate revenue more beneficially for the general good of this town than for the following purpose—

Grant of Money.

"We do order and enact that the sum of Two Thousand Pounds be by this Corporation subscribed for raising a regiment for his Majesty's service on the foot of the said subscription, to be paid by the Treasurer, in the proportions and subject to the conditions and regulations therein mentioned."

Maj.-Gen. Calcraft.

"1778, Feby. 4. Ordered that Major Gen. Thos Calcraft Colonel of the Royal Regiment of Liverpool Blues, be complemented with, and made a freeman."

Liverpool Blues.

The regiment of the Royal Liverpool Blues was raised 1100 strong, and sent on foreign service. After the lapse of six years, in 1784, the poor remnant, reduced to eighty four in number, returned to Liverpool, and deposited their colours in the Exchange.

The martial ardour of the inhabitants was by no means exhausted, but revived with a spirit equal to the occasion when called for.

"1794, June 12. Henry Blundell Mayor.

"At a special Council this day held it was Resolved unanimously, That this Council doth most heartily approve of Captain Blair's patriotic offer of raising a Regiment for the purpose of strengthening the hands of Government . . . and doth most willingly comply with the prayer of the petition for his regiment having the name of 'The Royal Liverpool Volunteers.'" Volunteers.

"1794, Octr. 1. Resolved and Ordered that the sum of One thousand pounds be subscribed by this Corporation, agreeable to the resolutions adopted at a meeting of the 22nd September last called by the High Sheriff of the County to take their sense respecting the propriety of making an offer to his Majesty to raise a regiment of Fencibles." Fencibles.

A letter was read from Lt.-Col. Isaac Gascoyne (afterwards M.P. for the Borough) claiming the honour of raising the regiment, and expressing his desire that it should take the title of the Royal Liverpool Volunteers, and a resolution was passed

"That the Council highly approve of the name so propounded, and request the Mayor to sign a copy of the proceedings and forward it to the Secretary of War, with a request that he would assist in obtaining the name for the regiment so to be raised."

In the year 1797 another scare alarmed the inhabitants, arising from the French expedition to South Wales.

"1797, Mar. 1. George Dunbar Mayor.

"Upon the Mayor's statement of his having received a letter on Saturday last from Lieut Gen. Whyte with an account of a French force consisting of two forty four gun frigates, a corvette and a lugger having appeared in Cardigan Bay, and landed about twelve hundred troops, and the probability of their proceeding to this port, and that he had used every exertion in his power with the advice and assistance of the Navy and Army officers in town, and the Magistrates and merchants, immediately upon the spur of the occasion to adopt such measures as were thought most adviseable for putting the town into the best possible state of defence; and had called a general meeting of the inhabitants upon Sunday the 26th instant, which meeting had appointed the following merchants and other gentlemen a committee for that purpose (here follow Landing of French. Measures of Defence.

Pilot Boats.

Removing Powder.

Batteries.

Funds.

Ships of War.

French Prisoners.

the names of the Mayor and forty others) which committee had proceeded (with the particular countenance of the Mayor as the proper ostensible person) to give and sign the orders for carrying their resolutions into effect, to direct Pilot boats to go out to the westward for the purpose of descrying the Enemy if any should appear upon the coast and making signals accordingly . . and had also proceeded to give directions for taking possession of the Cannon and Ammunition at the fort (two distinct applications having been made by the Mayor so long ago as the 14th January and 14th February last to the Board of Ordnance respecting the same without any reply or notice thereof) and for the removal of the powder from the Magazines in Cheshire into Flatts to proceed with the same up the river above the town . . And also for the erecting and forming Batteries with the guns belonging to the Corporation at different places upon the Dock Piers and proper commanding points of the river, and particularly in a field or close of land at Hog's Hey Nook belonging to Thomas Plumbe Esquire, and in every other particular used all possible exertion which the time and circumstances would admit for the safety and defence of the town, its docks and shipping.

" Resolved and Ordered

" That it is the unanimous opinion of this Council that the Mayor shall and he is hereby indemnified and kept harmless out of the Corporation funds and estate from all losses, costs, charges, damages and expenses occasioned by reason of the steps which have been or shall be adopted by the said Mayor during the present alarming crisis for the safety and defence of the town, its docks and shipping."

The gun-carriages belonging to the Corporation were ordered to be repaired. Possession was taken of the land at Hog's Hey for a battery, and an apology and explanation sent to the owner. The Mayor was desired to write to the Admiralty requesting that two ships of war of not less than forty-four guns each with proper mooring chains, should be immediately ordered to Liverpool.

The Mayor was also desired to continue the application already made by him to the Duke of Portland, the Home Secretary, for a reinforcement of troops for the defence of the town, and the safe custody of the French prisoners now confined in the new gaol, and for the removal of the whole or part of them to places of safety in the interior of the country.

The scare having passed over, on the 3rd May the following resolution was passed :—

"Ordered, that the freedom of this borough be presented to Lieut Gen. R^d Whyte late commander of the Northwest district for his watchfulness and attention to the welfare of the town at the time of the late alarm, by sending the most early intelligence, and afterwards coming over to Liverpool himself to examine into the state and situation of the fort and batteries, and giving the necessary directions for putting the town into the best possible state of defence." Thanks to Gen. Whyte.

"1797, Novr. 1. Thomas Staniforth Mayor.

"Ordered that Mrs Ann Cheyné widow of the late Mr John Cheyné who was a Lieutenant in his Majesty's navy at this port at the time of the general alarm of the French having landed, be complimented with a sum of fifty guineas out of the dock fund as a mark of the respect the Council bears to the memory of Lieut Cheyné for the very spirited and enterprising manner in which at the instant he offered himself as a volunteer to take the charge of a Pilot-boat to go out and watch the motions of the enemy had any appeared, and also to arrange the signals and for the very able and seamanlike conduct which he displayed in the execution of that service. Lieut. Cheyné.

"Also ordered that John Cheyné, the son of Lieut Cheyné, who was born in Liverpool on the 8th August 1797, be complimented with the freedom of the borough when he shall attain to the age of twenty one years as a testimony of the grateful sense which the Council entertain of the meritorious service of his father."

To strengthen the hands of the Corporation in the defence of the town, the following resolution was adopted by the Council :—

"1798, May 17. Thomas Staniforth Mayor.

"Resolved That it is the opinion of this Council, that application be immediately made to Parliament for an Act to enable the Council, the Trustees of the Docks and the Churchwardens and Overseers of the Parish, jointly to raise a competent sum of money for putting the town and port of Liverpool into a proper state of defence and security against the threatened invasion, one half to be levied and raised by a tax upon the inhabitants, and the other half in equal proportions from the general Corporate fund and from the Trustees of the Docks." Provision for Defence.

During these stirring times, addresses to the Crown became very frequent.

On March 14th, 1789, on the occasion of the recovery of the King from his mental aberration, an address of congratulation Address to Crown.

was prepared, and forwarded to the borough members for presentation, and a Committee appointed to carry out the celebration of the day.

In June, 1792, when the revolutionary proceedings in France found an echo amongst the advanced reformers in England, the Council presented an address to the King in which they express

<small>Support of Government.</small>

"Their assurances of fidelity and attachment to his Majesty's person and government, and thank him for his recent proclamation against seditious meetings and writings. They observe with concern the wild and delusive theories tending to weaken the sentiments of obedience to the laws, and veneration for our happy constitution both civil and religious. They assure his Majesty that they are truly sensible of the invaluable blessings we of this nation enjoy, and declare that, sensible of his Majesty's never ceasing endeavours to promote the happiness and prosperity of his subjects, they will ever be found zealous in the support of the constitution of these realms, so deservedly the envy and admiration of surrounding nations."

In December, 1792, on the eve of the war with France, another address was presented

<small>Address of Attachment.</small>

"Lamenting with the most sincere concern that the time should ever have arrived when it seems no longer superfluous to express the firm allegiance which we bear to your Majesty's person, and our unshaken attachment to our invaluable constitution. . . Observing by your Majesty's late proclamation that the utmost industry is employed by evil disposed persons within the kingdom acting in concert with persons of foreign parts, we beg leave to represent to your Majesty the abhorrence with which we regard, and are determined to resist at the hazard of our lives and fortunes, all attempts that are so obviously and vitally repugnant to every principle of reason, gratitude and duty."

And concludes with the usual expressions of attachment to the principles of the constitution.

In February, 1793, after the commencement of hostilities, another address was presented to the King assuring him of the loyal support of the inhabitants.

At the same time an entry is made as follows:—

"The Worshipful the Mayor having reported to this Council that in consequence of a letter from Bamber Gascoyne Esq' one of the representatives in Parliament of this borough, written at the request of the Right Hon. William Pitt, he had caused a general meeting of the merchants and others for the purpose of appointing a delegation to represent to the Government the necessity of a naval force being despatched for the protection of the British Shipping now on the coast of Africa, and for the convoy and protection of every branch of their trade, and such meeting having deputed George Case Esq. (with others). "Ordered that the grateful thanks of the Council be presented to the said gentlemen, and that their expenses be paid." Naval Force required.

In May, 1795, an address to the Crown was presented on the marriage of the Prince of Wales (George IV.) Marriage of Prince of Wales.

Another in November of the same year, on the supposed attempt on the King's life on his way to Parliament.

Another in November, 1797, on the Naval victory of Admiral Duncan at Camperdown. Battle of Camperdown

One in 1798 on Nelson's battle of the Nile; and in 1800 one on the shooting at the King, in Drury Lane Theatre, by Hatfield. Battle of the Nile.

The freedom of the borough was frequently conferred on distinguished Naval and Military commanders. In 1784 Lord Hood was entertained at a banquet and the freedom bestowed. In 1794 the freedom was conferred on Lord Howe, Sir John Jervis and Sir Charles Gray; in 1795 on Sir Edward Pellew; in 1797 on Admiral Lord Duncan and Sir Richard Onslow; in 1798 on Lord Nelson and Sir John Borlase Warren; in 1799 on the Marquis of Buckingham for his services in Ireland at the time of the rebellion. Grant of Freedom. Lord Hood.

"1789. Ordered that the thanks of this Council be given to the Earl of Westmorland and Lord Walsingham and that they be severally presented with the freedom of this Corporation for the eminent services they have rendered to the community by establishing a post directly over the Mersey to convey in a few hours the letters to and from Liverpool and Chester." Lords Westmorland and Walsingham.

A similar compliment had been paid in 1786 to Mr John Palmer, the Post Office reformer, "as a mark of respect to him for the evident advantages arising to the commercial Palmer.

part of this kingdom from his late adopted plan of a more speedy conveyance of the mails."

Earl of Liverpool.

In May, 1796, the title of Earl of Liverpool was conferred upon Charles Jenkinson, Lord Hawkesbury, who subsequently held the post of Prime Minister from 1812 to 1827. The announcement in the *London Gazette* was read at a meeting of the Council on July 6th, when the following resolution was passed unanimously :—

Title.

"That this being the first instance within the knowledge of this Council of the name of Liverpool having ever appeared amongst the titles of the Peers of this realm, the choice made by the Right Honourable the Earl of Liverpool is considered by this Council as an honour conferred upon the town, and that the thanks of the Council be therefore respectfully presented to his Lordship for so distinguished a mark of his attention and notice.

Arms of Liverpool.

"That as the title of Earl of Liverpool is thus annexed to the Peerage of Great Britain, the present Earl be invited to accept of the authority of this Council for himself and his heirs, to quarter the arms of this Corporation with his Lordships own arms; and if this shall be found to be agreeable to his Lordship, that his Majesty's consent thereto be immediately applied for, and his concession and declaration registered in his College of Arms, a due exemplification being first had according to the laws of Arms, and recorded in the Herald's Office.

"That the Mayor be desired to transmit a copy of these proceedings to the Right Honourable the Earl of Liverpool with a request that his Lordship would signify his pleasure respecting them; and that the Mayor, Recorder, Aldermen (with others named) be a committee with full power and authority . . to give effect to this resolution."

A letter was accordingly written by the Mayor embodying the resolution, and transmitted through Mr. Owen Salusbury Brereton, the Recorder, to which the Earl returned the following reply :—

"Addiscombe Place, July 16, 1796.

"Thos Naylor Esq
"Mayor of Liverpool
"Sir

Letter from Earl of Liverpool.

"I received yesterday evening through the hands of the Recorder your letter of the 10th instant enclosing an extract from the Minutes of the Common Council of Liverpool held on the 6th inst.

"It is impossible that I should not be highly sensible of the great compliment paid me on the present occasion, by a Corporation so respectable as that of Liverpool, for it affords a proof of their approbation of my endeavours to be of service to the commerce and navigation of this country in the office which I have now held for several years, as well as of the honour which his Majesty has been graciously pleased lately to confer on me.

"The motives which you assign for this compliment, and the unanimity with which it has been conferred, add very much to the value of it; and I shall feel a pride in bearing with the arms of my family, those of a Corporation composed of many wealthy, intelligent and respectable merchants, who by their extraordinary industry and enterprise have contributed in so great a degree to augment the commerce and navigation of Great Britain, and who have thereby in a short period of years raised the town to a most distinguished state of maritime importance, and of population, affluence and prosperity.

"I beg Sir you will yourself accept my sincere thanks, &c.

"Your faithful and obedient humble
"Servant
"LIVERPOOL."

1797, May 3rd. The Committee reported progress that the exemplification had been obtained, allowing the Earl to quarter the Arms of Liverpool with his own, and were further authorized to apply to the Earl Marshal for his warrant for the Corporation to bear and use supporters to the Arms as an honourable distinction. The expense of the whole to be borne by the Corporation. *Supporters to Arms.*

The Council had previous reasons for gratitude to the Earl when Lord Hawkesbury, as appears from the following entry :—

"1788, June 20. Ordered that the Freedom of this borough be presented to the Right Hon. Charles Lord Hawkesbury in consideration of the important advantages resulting to the nation at large from his Lordship's great attention to its commercial interests, and more particularly in gratitude for the essential services rendered to the town of Liverpool by his Lordship's late exertion in Parliament in support of the African Slave Trade, and that the Mayor be requested to communicate the same by letter to Lord Hawkesbury." *Freedom to Lord Hawkesbury.*

At the periods of distress amongst the poor, which occurred

from time to time, the Corporation were never wanting in liberality.

Relief of Poor.

"1774, Feby. 2. Whereas a publick collection hath been made throughout this town for the relief of the poor freemen and their families and other very necessitous poor of this Parish among the inhabitants. It is Ordered that Mr Treasurer of this Corporation do pay Mr Mayor the sum of One hundred Pounds out of the publick Corporation stock to be by him disposed of for such good and charitable use."

"1776, Feby. 2. James Clemens Mayor

Distress.

"At a meeting of several of the Parishioners called by the Mayor and the other Magistrates to take into consideration the deplorable case of the poor of and in the said town, occasioned by the severity of the weather, it was then and there unanimously agreed and undertaken as hereafter set forth . . That the Mayor, Bailiffs and Burgesses of this Corporation would advance to Mr Chaffers and others the present Churchwardens and Overseers of the Poor, the sum of Six hundred Pounds to be laid out and distributed by them in conjunction with the Magistrates for the relief of the Poor; but in such case they the said parishioners whose names are thereunto subscribed, did thereby promise and undertake to repay the said sum within twelve months from the date thereof, out of some future Parochial Ley to be raised by the inhabitants of the said Parish.

"We the Common Council of this borough taking the said charitable and good work of the said Parishioners so assembled into consideration, do hereby agree and order, that the Treasurer do immediately advance to the Churchwardens and Overseers on the credit of the said undertaking the said sum of Six hundred Pounds."

Relief of Poor.

"1784, Feby. 4. Ordered that the sum of one hundred guineas towards the relief of the Poor during the late inclement season be paid to the Treasurer of the Charitable Association Committee by the Treasurer of the Corporation and allowed in his accounts."

Grant of Money.

"1792, Dec. 5. On the motion of Mr Mayor stating that there might probably during the ensuing winter be a scarcity of coals and other necessaries of life, it is hereby ordered that a Committee consisting of the Mayor, the Bailiffs (with others named) with full powers to enquire into and ascertain the stock of the several articles enumerated, and to adopt such measures as the occasion may seem to require, and that they are hereby empowered to draw upon the Treasurer not exceeding the amount of Seven hundred Pounds, who shall be allowed the same in his accounts."

"1795, Aug. 3. At a special Council held this day pursuant to special summons; present John Shaw Esq Mayor and 27 others.

Purchase of Grain.

"In consequence of the present high price of grain, it is thought expedient by this Council, that a quantity of oats and barley, oatmeal and barley flour, and such other articles as may be judged necessary be purchased at the lowest prices possible.

"Ordered that One thousand Pounds be subscribed towards the above purpose by this Corporation, and that the Treasurer do advance the same at such times and in such proportions as the following Committee shall judge proper (here follow the names) which Committee are hereby requested to act in concert with such merchants or other persons as may be requested by the Mayor or Magistrates to give their advice and assistance." *£1000 Subscribed.*

"1800, Decr. 3. Upon the motion of the Mayor, seconded by Mr Alderman Naylor, that owing to the dearness and scarcity of provisions, he had thought proper to call a public meeting for the purpose of considering the best means to be adopted for alleviating the distresses of the Poor, and that a general subscription had been entered into by way of loan and also as donations for the raising a fund to be under the direction and management of a Committee of the subscribers for the purchasing Potatoes and other necessaries of life, and selling the same at reduced prices. *Distress and Relief.*

"Resolved and Ordered

"That the sum of Two Thousand pounds be subscribed by the Treasurer as a loan from the Corporation for the above laudable purposes, to be advanced by installments or as a per Centage agreeable to the orders of the Committee, in proportion to the sums to be advanced by the other subscribers of loans, and that the same or the eventual loss be allowed the Treasurer in his accounts." *Loans.*

The charity of the Corporation was not always restricted within its own borders. We read under the date of November 6th, 1765:—

"Ordered that the sum of twenty guineas be repaid Mr Mayor for so much money given by him to a poor Prince of Palestine, dispossessed of his dominions by the Grand Signiors Officers there, and recommended by his Excellency General Conway, one of his Majesty's principal Secretaries of State." *Prince of Palestine.*

In 1784 the Sunday School system, recently commenced by Robert Raikes of Gloucester, was introduced into Liverpool. A minute of the Council, December 1st, orders *Sunday Schools.*

"That the sum of twenty guineas per annum be paid during the pleasure of the Council, towards the support and encouragement of the Sunday Schools lately instituted in this town, the same having been found to be of very material advantage to the morals of the children admitted and instituted there." *Grant.*

Admission to the freedom of the borough was obtained in several ways : by birth, servitude, purchase, or gift.

Franchise by birth. Every son of a freeman, born within the borough bounds, was entitled to the privileges of a burgess on attaining the age of twenty-one, and retained it wherever he might reside.

By servitude. Every youth, wherever born, serving an apprenticeship of seven years to a freeman within the borough, was equally entitled.

By purchase. Freedom by purchase was exceedingly arbitrary, the Council fixing the sum at their pleasure. As the freedom exempted from payment of town dues, it was worth the while of a merchant to pay a considerable sum for the privilege. £100 was not unfrequently paid.

On the 4th June, 1777, the following resolution was passed :—

Purchase prohibited. " Whereas it has been represented to this Council that the admitting persons to the freedom of this Borough and Corporation by purchase for any sum of money is attended with many great inconveniences and losses to the publick estate and revenue, by greatly lessening the town duties and customs, it is now Ordered and Agreed, that from henceforth no person shall be admitted a freeman of this borough and Corporation upon purchase, for any sum of money or other valuable consideration for granting such freedom."

Mayor's Freeman. It was the privilege of every Mayor on retiring from office to name some friend to be admitted gratuitously to the franchise, but a few months previous to the order just quoted the following resolution was passed :—

" 1776, Decr. 4. It is Ordered that when any future Mayor of this Corporation nominates his gratis or Mayor's freeman, every such Mayor shall be confined to nominate a gentleman, or person not in trade, or following any merchandize or trade in or out of this town."

Honorary Franchise. The honorary freedom was usually conferred on public and distinguished men. It conveyed the same privileges as the ordinary franchise. Many famous statesmen and warriors have been thus enrolled on the list of the Liverpool freemen. The Stanleys, Earls of Derby, and the members of their family were in this way intimately connected with the borough down to the death of James, the tenth Earl, who died during his mayoralty in 1735. After his decease, the title and estates passing to another branch, the intimacy was gradually allowed to lapse. *James, Tenth Earl of Derby.*

In 1774, Nov. 3, we read

"It is Ordered that the Right Honourable Edward, Lord Stanley (afterwards the 12th Earl) be admitted to the freedom free gratis." *Edward, Twelfth Earl.*

The oaths taken by the Burgesses and Officials have been given in a former chapter of this work.[1]

In 1767 a resolution was passed relaxing the obligation as regarded the Quakers.

"1767, Decr. 1. It is Ordered, that the people called Quakers be at liberty to affirm to the Freeman's oath, with the words struck out as relative to the payment of church taxes, as was usually done and permitted before the late restraint in this respect put on Messrs Rawlinson and Chorley, two Quakers, notwithstanding these two persons did affirm to the whole of the oath." *Quakers.*

This obligation was further relaxed in 1792 owing to the circumstances recorded as follows:—

"1792, Decr. 5. Clayton Tarleton Mayor.

"The Mayor having reported to this Council that Mr Henry Butler, whose claim to the freedom of this borough by servitude to Richard Heywood, Banker, had been received and regularly admitted, and whose title had been ratified and confirmed by the Council, had on the 15th day of November last past presented himself to the Mayor and Bailiffs demanding to be sworn a free burgess upon barely taking the oath of a free burgess of this borough, and that in consequence of such demand the said Mayor and Bailiffs have directed the Town Clerk to investigate on what ground persons before their taking the oath of a free burgess had uniformly taken the oaths to the Government, and that the Town Clerk upon such investigation had discovered in the ancient records of this Corporation, two several Orders of Council, the first made at a Common Council held on the third day of April 1679 in the words following— *Oath of Allegiance.*

[1] Vol. I, 121-3.

"'Ordered by this Assembly *(nem con)* that all persons that are or shall be admitted freemen in this Corporation, shall take the oaths of allegiance and supremacy before the oath of a freeman, in the presence of the Mayor, or his deputy and one of the Bailiffs.'

"And the other of such Orders of Council made at a Common Council held on the 4th day of March 1712 in the words following—

Oath of Abjuration.
"'Ordered, that every person petitioning to be free of this borough shall take the abjuration oath before the oath of a freeman.'

"And the Mayor having further reported to this Council that he had caused a case to be stated to Messrs Law, Hargrave, Wood, and Peters for their seperate opinions.

"1st Whether the above By-laws were intrinsically and in themselves valid or bad?

"2nd Supposing they should be intrinsically bad, then whether by any Act of Parliament, persons before they took the oath of a free burgess of a borough were bound to take the oaths to the Government? . . and that the said Messrs Law, Hargrave, Wood and Peters had seperately

Counsel's opinion.
given it as their opinion—first that the said By-laws were in themselves and intrinsically bad and void; and 2ndly that there was not any Act of Parliament which obliged persons claiming the freedom of a borough to take the oaths to the Government previously to their taking the oath of a free burgess.

"This Council therefore seriously and maturely weighing the premises, and taking also into their consideration that in the body of the oath itself of a free burgess of this borough is contained a clause of allegiance to the

By-laws bad.
King, do now declare that the above By-laws are as in themselves and in the subject matter of them intrinsically bad, and that in conformity to the above opinions, no person whatever is either by the said By-laws or by the general law of this kingdom bound to take the oaths to the Government previously to his taking the oath of a free burgess of this borough.

Oath abrogated.
"And this Council do therefore recommend to the present and future Mayors and Bailiffs of this Corporation, that they do not demand from any persons who shall hereafter apply to be sworn free of this borough that they do take the oaths to the Government previously to their taking their said oath of a free burgess."

In 1782 Mr. John Brown, who had been elected Mayor, refused to serve. The Council thereupon instituted a prosecution (presumably a mandamus) in the Court of King's Bench. In 1783, October 1st, occurs the following entry:—

"Ordered that the Town Clerk be directed to prepare an account of the expences of maintaining a prosecution in the Court of King's Bench and also at the last Lancaster Assizes, against John Brown Esq for refusing to take upon him the office of Mayor of this borough and Corporation, having been unanimously elected thereto on the 18th day of October last; and also for asserting and maintaining the just rights and privileges of the freemen of this borough at large; all of which have been attempted to be invaded in consequence of the above refusal. And that the Treasurer do pay a sum of money not exceeding the sum of seven hundred and fifty pounds in consequence of such prosecution, and be allowed the same in his accounts."

<small>Mr. Brown prosecuted.</small>

"1783, Decr. 3. William Hesketh Mayor.

"Mr Brown having made an apology in Council for the trouble and expence to which this Corporation was put on account of his refusing to take upon himself the office of Mayor, Ordered that such his apology be accepted of."

<small>Mr. Brown apologizes.</small>

The proceedings in Council during this period were regulated as follows:—

"1794, July 2. Henry Blundell Mayor.

"Ordered that upon every matter of debate or election which shall in future be put to the vote, the order of proceeding to take such votes shall be as follows—that is to say—it shall begin with the youngest Council-man who has not served the office of Mayor, and so to the eldest, then the Town Clerk, then the Bailiffs, then the Aldermen beginning with the youngest and so proceeding to the oldest, then the Recorder, and last of all the Mayor."

<small>Order of Debate.</small>

Numerous references are made in the records to the gowns worn by the members of the Council from 1558 downwards. In the earlier records a distinction is made. Down to the end of the 17th century gowns were only worn by the Mayor, Aldermen, Bailiffs and their Peers. The Common Councillors were to provide themselves with short cloaks under a penalty, but subsequently all wore gowns.

<small>Gowns.</small>

"1767, June 3. Thomas Johnson Mayor.

"It is Ordered that the new gowns provided by Mr Mayor for the Council be received and worn by all the members of the Common Council for the time being, and that it be the future dress or habit for the Aldermen, Recorder, Town Clerk and Common Council of the borough and Corporation of Liverpoole to be by them worn only on the Waiting Sundays and other public state days, and occasional days at the discretion of the Mayor for the time being; and that the old gowns be worn on other Sundays or common days as usual; that such gowns (patterns of which

<small>New Gowns</small>

are now produced) for all the said several members of this Corporation be paid for at the expence of the several members of the Common Council and their successors, and not at the expence of the Corporation; and that the new gowns be worn to-morrow for the first time."

Blue Silk Gowns.

"1772, July 1. Ordered that the Corporation Treasurer do pay Messrs Parr, Wilson and Allen for certain new Councilmen's blew silk gowns, which have not yet been taken up, till they can be disposed of to any gentlemen who are or may come into Council and are not provided with such gowns; amounting to fifty pounds and eight shillings and be allowed it in his accounts."

During this period a small addition was made to the Regalia.

Regalia.

"1763. George Campbell Mayor.

Sword and Maces.

"Ordered that a new Corporation Regalia *(sic)* vizt a sword, sergeant's mace, and two sub-bailiff's maces be provided at the expence of this Corporation, and that Mr Mayor be desired to order the same according to the models thereof sent him from London."

In 1785 a portion of the Regalia was stolen, comprising the large mace presented by the Earl of Derby in 1666, two smaller maces, and the silver oar emblematical of the jurisdiction over the waters of the Mersey.

The large mace and one of the smaller ones were recovered; the silver oar and the missing small mace were replaced. The thief, one Charles Coney, was captured,

Thief executed.

tried at the ensuing Assizes at Lancaster, and executed.

Replacement

"1785, Feby. 2. Ordered that the Mayor and Bailiffs replace the Regalia which were lately stolen in such manner and stile and at such expence as they may think proper, and that such expence be defrayed by this Corporation."

Plate.

The Plate received attention from time to time.

"1773, Octr. 18. John Parr Mayor.

"Ordered that any sum not exceeding two hundred pounds be granted to be laid out in useful Plate for this Corporation, to be used by the Mayors for the time being of this borough, as complaints have been made by gentlemen who serve this office, that there is not a sufficiency of useful Plate belonging to this Corporation and that they are oft put to great expences herein, and therefore is a discouragement to gentlemen to accept of said office of Mayor."

"1775, Oct. 18. James Clemens Mayor.
"Ordered that Mr Mayor be desir'd to order a handsome silver Epergn, two silver bread baskets and eight silver salts for the Corporation, at the public expence and the Treasurer be allowed it in his accounts." Epergn and Salts.

These articles are still in existence. The epergn, in the style of the period, is a very handsome and elaborate piece of work.

The allowance to the Mayor, for hospitality, naturally increased with the progress of the times.

"1797, Nov. 1. Thomas Staniforth Mayor.
"Ordered that Mr Alderman Dunbar the late Mayor, be requested to accept the thanks of this Council for his very spirited, active, and upright conduct during his Mayoralty, and that he be paid the sum of eight hundred pounds towards the expences of his Mayoralty by the Treasurer, and that Alderman Dunbar be also allowed the nomination of his Mayor's freeman according to ancient usage." Mayor's allowance.

In addition to the annual allowance, special banquets were occasionally paid for by the Council.

"1773, Mar. 3. Thomas Golightly Mayor.
"Ordered, that the expence of the entertainment given the Lord Bishop of this diocese by Mr Mayor on his late visitation be paid by the Treasurer." Dinner to Bishop.

"1777, Feby. 3. William Crosbie Mayor.
"Ordered that the sum of thirty pounds be allowed to the late Mayor Mr Alderman Clemens towards the extra expence he was at, in entertaining the Honourable Mr North, son of the Right Honourable Lord North, when he was lately in town and in his Mayoralty." Dinner to North.

"1780, Feby. 2. William Crosbie Jun' Mayor.
"Ordered that Mr Mayor, the Bailiffs (with others named) or any gentlemen of the Council who please to attend, be appointed a Committee to inspect and regulate the expence of the dinners at the Courts of Quarter Sessions and Passage, and to report to the next Council at what they conceive a dinner for the Court, the two juries, and the necessary attendants on the Mayor at those Courts may reasonably be furnished, one court with another; and that the allowance to be fixed by the Council, of the four Annual dinners after hearing the Committee's report, be deemed (as it is) a part of the expences of supporting the dignity of office of the Chief Magistrate, so important to the peace and good government of this town, and be considered in the Annual allowance in that behalf to be made Expenses of Dinners

to the Mayors, who are meant to defray the costs, and to have the sole direction of and invitation to such dinners."

Sessions' Dinners.

" 1780, April 5. Upon hearing the report now read of the Committee which met the third of April instant, respecting the regulation of Session dinners, this Council do approve thereof and do order that the orders, regulations and articles therein contained be from henceforth carried into execution, and that the expences of the Sessions dinners upon the foot thereof be experienced for a few Sessions, and afterwards that a standing sum for the expences of such dinners be ascertained upon that foot to be allowed as part of the expences of office of Mayor for the time being, or that such further regulations be afterwards made respecting such dinners as in experience shall be found useful.

" It is the opinion of this Committee that suppers for the Magistrates, for either Jury, Officers or any other company in the evenings at Session times, are inconvenient, retard the attending at Court next morning, are rather a restraint upon the Mayor and Bailiffs, and that it would be of utility to abolish them."

One Dinner only.

" 1793, Dec. 4. Ordered that in future only one dinner be allowed at each Quarter Sessions for this borough at the charge of the Corporation, and that the Treasurer take upon him the particular direction and management respecting the expences of such dinner."

Emeutes and riots against the Corporation were not frequent, but they occasionally occurred.

" 1768, July 6. Charles Goore Mayor.

Riots.

" Ordered, that Mr Alderman Campbell be paid the expences he was at in defending his house and the Exchange from the mob in the year 1757; who assembled and threatened to pull the said Exchange and buildings down; and in prosecuting the said rioters; being about the sum of forty two pounds."

" 1777, Feby. 5. William Crosbie Mayor.

Outrage on Clarke.

" Ordered, that what money shall be collected by the voluntary contributions of well-disposed persons for the relief of one Mary Clarke, who was lately sett upon, assaulted, and cruelly and barbarously ducked in the docks, so as to endanger her life, and thrown her into violent convulsions, so as to incapacitate her (in all probability) for getting her future livelihood (for which several of the rioters have been lately convicted and ordered to be fined and imprisoned by the last Court of Quarter Sessions for this

Grant of Annuity.

borough) be taken in by this Corporation on an annuity for her life, and that she be allowed and paid for the same at the rate of ten per cent for such money, and that a bond be passed under the Common Seal for payment thereof, to be made to Ralph Peters and Joseph Brookes Esquires in trust for her sole and seperate use, as Mr Peters shall settle and fix it."

It has not happened very frequently that the higher officers of the Corporation have had to be dismissed for misconduct. Such an occurrence however took place in 1789.

"Aug. 5. John Blackburne Mayor.

"On the motion of Mr Mayor and his having stated to the Council that John Crosbie Esquire, the Treasurer of this Corporation (and who was suspended from his office of Treasurer by the order of a special Council held on the 14th day of July last) has been guilty of very improper and unjustifiable conduct in his said office of Treasurer. Dismissal of Treasurer.

"It is Ordered that the said John Crosbie be dismissed from his said office of Treasurer, and that another be appointed to such office in his stead."

In 1786 the adminstration of justice and the state of the Police attracted the attention of the Council. By a supplementary charter, granted in 1751, the four senior Aldermen were appointed Justices in addition to the Mayor and the ex-Mayor, who up to that date alone possessed the privilege. Charter for Magistrates.

1787, March 7th. James Gildart, Jun., Mayor.

On the recommendation of the Mayor and acting Magistrates certain resolutions tending to the improvement of the Police were passed.

"At a meeting of the Magistrates held 22nd Feby. it was resolved that in the opinion of the Magistrates that the very great increase of the town renders it necessary that some alteration should be made in the Police, and that for the better and more effectual exercise of their jurisdiction the town should be divided into four districts to be fixed agreeable to the division made for the watchmen. Each district to be under the regulation and government of the Magistrate who shall be appointed for such district at a subsequent meeting. Police. Districts.

"That to effect a regulation which promises such salutary advantages it is proposed to have a person of good and unexceptionable character in each district to act as Head Constable, and among other branches of his duty inspect the conduct of the other Constables; such Head Constable to give security in the sum of £ (blank) for the faithful discharge of his duty and reside in the district to which he is appointed. Head Constable.

"It is not intended by these regulations to lessen the consequence of the Chief Magistrate, as all complaints will be heard and determined at Chief Magistrate.

the Mayor's office in the same manner and form as hitherto been the custom and practice.

"That previous to these regulations being carried into execution, the Publick shall be made acquainted with the plan by advertisement, and requested to assist the Magistrates by giving information of disorderly houses, irregular publicans, nuisances, and cellars where Vagrants are encouraged and harboured, to the Magistrate who shall be appointed to such district."

These regulations were well intended but failed to produce the desired effect. There was no day police perambulating the streets. The night watchmen were old and feeble, and the evil continued to increase until the introduction of the new Police force by the Reformed Council in 1836.

Night Watchmen.

Some reform in the system was sorely needed, to judge by the following record:—

"1780, Decr. 6. It is ordered that the Mayor be permitted to offer and advertize a reward of twenty pounds to be paid and given to any person apprehending any felon guilty of any highway robbery within this borough or the neighbourhood, for the space of one month from this day; it appearing to this Council that the Post has been lately stopped upon the highway near this town, and footpads having been also in several parts of the town and neighbourhood. Such reward to be paid upon conviction."

Highway Robberies.

Footpads.

The extension of public houses and taverns has always been a source of complaint.

"1772, Mar. 4. Thomas Wilson Mayor.

"This Council doth now recommend it to the present and future Magistrates of this borough to reduce the number of Alehouses in this town, particularly about the several docks and piers of this town, as many acts of wickedness, licentiousness, and other immoralities committed in this town, are attributed to this growing evil."

Taverns.

The old institution of the "Waites" or Town's Musicians was still kept up, but the last entry which I can find relating to them is as follows:—

Waits.

"1764, Novr. 7. John Tarleton Mayor.

"Ordered that John Bolton and John Langhorn be appointed two publick Waites of this town, with the usual perquisites and salary during the pleasure of the Council."

The conduct of the self-elected Council in setting at nought the provisions of the charters, and denying to the body of the Burgesses any rights or influence in the Corporate affairs, with the simple exception of the annual election of Mayor, had repeatedly been called in question and efforts been made to assert the rights of the Burgesses. This usurpation took place in 1580, and in the applications for subsequent charters attempts were made to obtain legal sanction, but without success. Nevertheless, the Council having possession, and the command of the funds, managed to defeat every attempt at reform by wearing out and disheartening their opponents, whose impecuniosity placed them at a disadvantage. *Struggles of Burgesses.*

During the early part of the 18th century several attempts, already alluded to in a previous chapter, were made to shake off the yoke, but without success.

"1768, Mar. 2. Wm Pownall Mayor.
"Ordered that the following Rule being lately served on Mr John Knight one of this Council to show cause why he acted as one of this Council and the said Rule on his shewing cause to the Court of King's Bench being discharged, that the expences to which Mr Knight hath been put to on this prosecution be paid by the Treasurer." *Knight attacked.*

In 1790-1 a more systematic and vigorous effort was made which is recorded at length in the records.

On October 5th, 1790, a memorial was addressed to the Mayor and Bailiffs signed by a number of the leading merchants, both Whigs and Tories, in which they say:—

"We hereby take the liberty of expressing our disapprobation not only of the mode of election of Councilmen, but of the persons who are frequently chosen into that body . . We think we are warranted in saying that the Council, in choosing their own body, do not consult the wishes or interests of the burgesses . . We presume to desire that you will not hold a Council to-morrow, but take into consideration the propriety of summoning a Common Hall, at which the burgesses may have an opportunity of electing the guardians of their own estate." *Memorial for Common Hall.*

Mr. John Sparling, who was elected Mayor a few weeks afterwards, was favourable to the movement. The further proceedings are set forth in the records as follows :—

Mayor favourable.

"1791, Feby. 2. At a Common Council held in the Council Chamber within the Exchange this 2nd day of February 1791 being the first Wednesday in the month, according to ancient custom;

Council Meeting.

"Present John Sparling Mayor.

"15 Aldermen 2 Bailiffs & 13 Councillors.

"At which time also appeared Mr Richard Walker, Mr Charles Caldwell, Mr Peter Ellames and Mr Willis Earle, and claimed their seats as Common Councilmen, having been as they alledged, and which was admitted by the Mayor, unanimously elected by the Burgesses at large at the Common Hall called by the Mayor and Bailiffs, and that they had taken the necessary oaths to qualify them for the office of Common Councilmen.

Intruders.

"Upon which Mr Alderman Case rose, and after a preface upon the subject, moved—that Mr Walker, Mr Caldwell, Mr Willis Earle, and Mr Peter Ellames, not being considered as duly elected according to the ancient custom of this borough and Corporation, be requested to withdraw, which was seconded by Mr Staniforth.

Motion to withdraw.

"Mr Ellames moved, whether it is proper to proceed to the general business of leasing and other public business in preference to Mr Case's motion, which was seconded by Mr Willis Earle. And Mr Ellames, as also Mr Walker, Mr Caldwell and Mr Willis Earle, declared that if there could be any doubt of their having taken the oaths, they were ready to take and subscribe the same.

"Mr Smyth moved that it be put to the vote whether Mr Case's motion should now be proceeded in, which was seconded by Mr Blundell, and the same being accordingly put to the vote, was carried in the affirmative.

"And upon Mr Case's motion being also put, the same was likewise carried in the affirmative.

Motion carried.

"Mr Case then moved that the following declaration and protest be entered in the Council Book, which was seconded by Mr Alderman William Pole, and Mr Case accordingly read the declaration and protest which was as follows :—

Declaration and Protest.

"Whereas since the holding of the last Common Council, to wit on or about the seventeenth day of January last past, the present Mayor John Sparling Esq, and Robert Moss and Clayton Tarleton Esqrs the present Bailiffs of the said borough and Corporation of Liverpool, did take upon themselves in an illegal manner to summon and hold a meeting or Assembly at which were present the said Mayor and Bailiffs and a number of the burgesses of this Corporation, which meeting they thought fit to call a Common Hall, and then and there pretended to make a certain By-law,

Common Hall.

thereby enacting, ordering or declaring that all By-laws, Resolutions and Agreements at any time theretofore made by the Mayor, Bailiff, and Burgesses of this Borough . . whereby power was given to the Mayor and Council to elect any persons to fill up any vacancy in the Council, . . should be repealed, abrogated, annulled, and made void.

"And whereas the same Mayor, Bailiffs and Burgesses at the same meeting, did take upon them in the like illegal manner to elect Richard Walker, Charles Caldwell, Willis Earle, Peter Ellames and Joshua Rose to be five of the Common Councilmen of this borough in the room of others deceased, resigned or removed. *Election of Councillors.*

"And whereas the said Mayor &c did at the same meeting or assembly in the like illegal manner make another certain By-law ordering that the Town's Treasurer should draw out an accurate account of all the monies by him officially received, and deliver the same to the Mayor, that he might order the same to be properly audited by four of the Council and four burgesses not of the Council to be named at the Common Hall along with the Mayor. *Treasurer.*

"And whereas the same Mayor &c did at the same meeting or assembly make another certain By-law, ordering that a Committee should be named to inspect all the By-laws theretofore made, consisting of the Mayor (with others named) and that they should proceed to the inspection of all such By-laws, and whether any and which of them were necessary to be repealed and which continued, and if necessary, to make other By-laws to be confirmed by the Mayor, Bailiffs and Burgesses in Common Hall to be assembled. *Committee on By-laws.*

"And whereas the same Mayor &c did at the same meeting take upon them in the like illegal manner to elect and nominate different persons to constitute the aforesaid Committee so illegally appointed.

"All which Acts and proceedings are contrary to the Charters and constitution of this Corporation; which illegal proceedings the Common Council taking into their serious consideration. It is hereby declared that the said meeting or assembly and all its proceedings were and are illegal and contrary to the immemorial usages, customs, charters and to the very constitution of this borough and Corporation, and that they are hereby declared to be absolutely null and void." *Declaration.*

With much more to the same effect, against all which the majority of the Councillors enter their solemn protest. *Protest.*

These resolutions were carried by the majority of the Council; against which the Mayor, the two Bailiffs, and six Councillors entered the following protest :—

"That the aforesaid motion was made and seconded and afterwards passed contrary to the will of the said Mayor, Bailiffs and the several persons whose names are hereunto subscribed, and they, the said subscribers hereto do hereby express their dissent from and protest against the said order and declaration.

"Signed   "JOHN SPARLING, Mayor
"ROBT. MOSS
"CLAYTON TARLETON } Bailiffs
"THOS. EARLE
"HENRY BLUNDELL
"RICHARD WALKER
"P. ELLAMES
"CHA. CALDWELL
"WILLIS EARLE."

This minority comprised the existing Mayor and Bailiffs, two Aldermen, and four of the Councillors recently elected, as alleged, illegally.

Alderman Case.

It is remarkable that Alderman George Case, Mayor in 1781, and the leader of the strong opposition to the proceedings in question, lived to witness the passing of the Municipal Reform Act (1835) forty-five years later, by which he and his party were ousted from the management of affairs. Mr. Case entered the Council in 1775 so that he continued a member for 60 years.

Committee appointed.

"Mr Case then moved that a Committee of seven members should be appointed with full powers to do and transact under the direction of Counsel, every thing necessary to protect and defend the rights, privileges and immunities of this borough and Corporation from the illegal attacks now made upon them, and that all expenses be paid by the Treasurer. The motion, seconded by Mr Edmund Rigby was then put, but the Mayor with the following gentlemen, Mr Walker, Mr Caldwell, Mr Ellames, and Mr Willis Earle, left the room, and the vote was proceeded with, and afterwards carried in the affirmative.

"In a few minutes (before the vote had actually passed) Mr Ellames returned to the room, and said that the Mayor had directed him to acquaint the gentlemen that if they would proceed to the reading of the minutes of the last Council and the leasing business, he would return. He was then told, that there was a motion before the Council which had been seconded and must be disposed of.

"In a few minutes afterwards the Mayor himself returned into the

Council room and said 'Since you are upon business which I think very imprudent and very improper, I discharge you all' . . and left the Council room, the other Councilmen still remaining to go on with the public business." Secession of Mayor.

"1791, July 6. John Sparling Mayor.

"Messrs Peter Ellames and Willis Earle appeared and claimed their seats as Common Councilmen, having been as they alledged, unanimously elected by the Burgesses at large, at the Common Hall called by the Mayor and Bailiffs on the 17th day of January last. Council Meeting.

"Messrs Willis Earle and Peter Ellames being now present and claiming a right to vote and act as Common Councilmen of this borough and Corporation . . . this Council again taking their claims into serious consideration, doth hereby further declare such their pretended Election to be illegal and void to all intents and purposes whatever, being contrary to the immemorial usage, customs and charters, and the very constitution itself of this borough and Corporation; And this Council doth therefore again most solemnly protest against all, each, and every of the acts and doings as Common Councilmen of them the said Willis Earle, and Peter Ellames. Intruders. Protest.

"And whereas doubts have been entertained concerning the validity or legality of such of the proceedings of this Council on the 2nd day of February last as were done and transacted after the Mayor had left the Council room and taken upon him contrary to the sense of the majority of the members present to dissolve the meeting; the whole of which proceedings being recorded in this Council book and having been now read. Resolved, that the said Proceedings on the 2nd February last be and they are hereby fully ratified and confirmed in like manner and to all intents and purposes whatsoever, as much as if the same had formed a part of the business of this present Common Council." Confirmation of Proceedings.

Here the record in the Council Book terminates, but a few words may be added as to the ultimate result.

At a Common Hall of the Burgesses called by the Mayor on January 17th, 1791, a By-law was passed requiring the Treasurer's accounts to be audited and published.

On June 16th of the same year another Common Hall was held, at which a By-law was passed inflicting a penalty of forty shillings for every refusal of the Treasurer to allow the auditors to inspect his books. Mr. Thomas Golightly, the Treasurer, acting under the authority of the majority of the Council, refused such inspection, upon which a technical Common Hall.

action was brought against him in the Court of King's Bench for a recovery of the penalty, which, if successful, would have established the legality of the Common Hall and the right of the Burgesses to manage their own affairs.

Action at Law.

The action was tried at Lancaster before Baron Thompson. The judge ruled in favour of the plaintiffs, the Burgesses, and the jury pronounced accordingly.

A motion was made in the Court of King's Bench for a new trial, which was granted, and a verdict was again given against the Council.

New Trials.

Another motion was made for a third trial on technical grounds. It became now evident that the Council were prepared to use every possible effort and to spend any amount of money to defeat the action of the Burgesses, and being unprepared to meet on equal terms, the plaintiffs reluctantly abandoned the prosecution, and so the matter slept until revived in 1835.

Prosecution abandoned.

Water Supply.

The supply of water to the town at the latter end of the century began to assume a serious aspect. The shallow wells in the outcrop of the sandstone, which had afforded an ample supply for the sparse population, began to be exhausted.

The Bootle scheme, which had been propounded by Sir Cleave Moore, and for which an act had been obtained in 1709, after slumbering for nearly seventy years was revived.

Jordan's Scheme.

"1774, Nov. 2. Peter Rigby Mayor.

"Whereas, Mr John Jordan who is, or pretends to be assignee under the late Sir Cleave More, Bar^t. and to have a right of bringing and supplying the town of Liverpoole with fresh water from Bootle Springs by virtue of and under the Act of Parliament made the 8th of Queen Anne, hath lately served this Council with notice that he is now proceeding to put the powers of the said Act into execution; And this Council being of opinion that the powers of the said Act with respect to the supplying the town of Liverpoole with fresh water are become forfeited by the wilful default or neglect of the said Sir Cleave More, his heirs and assigns in not

Powers forfeited.

perfecting the said work for so many years and according to the limitation prescribed by the said Act, and therefore, that such right or powers are become re-invested or returned into the Corporation of Liverpoole,

"Therefore it is now ordered, that the Town Clerk do serve the said John Jordan with a proper notice to be settled by Mr Recorder Peters or other counsel learned in the law, that the Corporation of Liverpoole will not at present admit the said Mr Jordan to enter into any of their lands, tenements, streets, roads, ways, waste or other lands within the town and liberties of Liverpoole for the supplying the said town, inhabitants and shipping thereof with fresh water, and also attend at the inquisition to be taken the 29th instant before the Sheriff of Lancashire and to give such notice of this our order, and to do further therein as he shall be advised by counsel learned in the law, shall be necessary in the premisses." *Inquisition.*

After the lapse of eleven years the subject again came before the Council.

"1785, June 1. John Gregson Mayor.
"Ordered, that a case respecting the right of Owen Bowen Esq and others, to break up the streets and highways of this town under an Act passed in the eighth of Queen Anne for the purpose of conveying into this town water from the Bootle Springs be stated, and laid before Mr Peters, and that what shall have been done in pursuance of this order be reported by the Town Clerk to the next Council." *Case for Counsel.*

Another twelve years passed without anything being done.

"1797, May 3. George Dunbar Mayor.
"Upon reading a letter to the Mayor dated the 29th of April from Mr Thomas Bryer and Mr James Jones, as proprietors of the Bootle Springs, inclosing their proposals for supplying this town, the public buildings and shipping with fresh water by virtue of the Act of Parliament of eighth Anne, Chap 25, and upon reading such printed proposals—and upon searching the minutes of the Council at different periods respecting the same, and particularly the Minutes in the year 1718. *Bryer and Jones's Scheme.*

"Resolved and Ordered. That the Mayor and Bailiffs attended by the Town Clerk be requested to wait upon Mr Bryer, and Mr Jones, and deliver the following answer—

"That it is the opinion of this Council that they, Mr Bryer and Mr Jones have no powers under the Act to carry their proposed plan into execution." *Powers void.*

"1797, Oct. 4. Upon reading Mr Bryer's letter respecting the Bootle Springs, Ordered, That the select Committee be desired to fix a time for Mr Bryer to attend them upon the subject of his letter, and that they confer with him and make their report to the Council." *Bryer's Scheme.*

"1798, Octr. 3. Thomas Staniforth Mayor.

Bryer's application.
"Upon the statement of Mr Bryer's application respecting the Bootle Springs, and particularly the intention of the persons calling themselves the proprietors of those springs to apply to Parliament to amend and extend their present Act as expressed in his letter to the Mayor of the 12ᵗʰ Sept 1798.

"'Sir

Letter.
"'The Proprietors of Bootle Springs being determined at all events to apply to Parliament to amend and extend their present Act, have directed notices agreeable to the Standing Orders of the House to be given.

"'They however, desire me to communicate to you that by those steps they do not wish to break off all negotiation with the Corporation, but are still anxious and at present desirous of entering into, in handsome and liberal terms.

"'I have the honor to be &c
"'THOMAS BRYER
"'To the Worshipful the Mayor.   "'19 Basnett Street
                                          "'Sept 12, 1798.'

"Resolved and Ordered

Resolution.
"That the full consideration of this business be referred to the select Committee, and that that Committee have full power to watch and oppose the motions of the said persons calling themselves the proprietors, in their applications to Parliament. And that the Town Clerk or his deputy be, and they are hereby directed to signify to Mr Bryer that the Council purpose as soon as it may be convenient to put in force the powers they are invested with to supply the town of Liverpool with water."

"1799, Mar. 25. Thomas Leyland Mayor.

"Special Council.

"The following draft of a Petition to Parliament having been read, it was approved, and ordered to be transcribed and transmitted to Colonel Gascoyne one of the members, to be by him presented to the House.

"To the Honourable the Commons &c

Petition against Bill.
"That your petitioners have seen a Bill intituled a Bill for better supplying the town and port of Liverpool with water from certain springs in Bootle," &c.

The petition then refers to an Act passed in 1786, by which the Council were invested with powers to make several improvements, and also to dig for springs and fountains, and make reservoirs, and all other requisite works for raising, conducting, and conveying water into the town for the use and benefit of the inhabitants.

"The petitioners further state that by the powers and provisions of the said Act, they will be fully enabled to supply the town with water, and that they have actually purchased a spring in the said town and have made other preparations for that purpose, and have in contemplation the purchase of other springs within the said town. *Corporation Works.*

"That the petitioners are humbly of opinion, that the Springs at Bootle are inadequate to supply the town with a sufficient quantity. *Bootle Springs.*

"That the Bill would if passed be prejudicial to the rights and interests of the petitioners and inconvenient to the inhabitants of the said town.

"The Petitioners therefore pray that the Bill may not pass into a law and that they may be heard by Council against it."

Ultimately powers were obtained for carrying out both schemes. The Corporation transferred their interest under the Act to a Company called the "Liverpool and Harrington Water Works Co." *Both schemes adopted.*

Matters thus remained until 1846, when both Companies were superseded by the sale to the Corporation under the Rivington Water Works Act.

Whatever might be the state of parties, and however high disputes might run, the Council had always a keen eye and prompt action in everything which they considered affected the interests of the town and port. Thus—

"1778, Apl. 1. Thomas Birch Mayor.

"Upon a report from the Committee of Trade that a Bill is moved for in Parliament for the uniting the kingdom of Ireland with this kingdom and putting it upon the same footing with Scotland in respect of exports and imports.

"It is Ordered that a petition be drawn as soon as the copy of the Bill can be got, or the Bill is ordered to be brought into the House, in the name of this Corporate body with the Common Seal affixed, to be heard at the bar of the House against the said Bill." *Petition against Union with Ireland.*

In accordance with this resolution, petitions were prepared and presented "in opposition to the Bills before Parliament for enlarging the trade to and from Ireland, called the Exportation and Importation Bills."

When the Union actually took place, twenty-two years *Union Act.*

afterwards, it does not appear that the Corporation presented any petition against it.

Menai Bridge In 1785 a proposition was made for building a bridge over the Menai Strait to connect the island of Anglesey with the main land, which was twenty years later successfully carried out by Telford. For some unexplained reason the Corporation of Liverpool set their faces against the proposal.

Petition against.
"1785, Mar. 2. John Gregson Mayor.
"Ordered, that the Common Seal of this Corporation be affixed to a petition against the building of a bridge over an Arm of the Sea called the Straits of Menai, the same being recommended by the Board of Trade."

The same year the Corporation came into collision with the County Magistrates.

County Magistrates.
"Ordered, Whereas it appears to us that there is an attempt now set on foot by the Justices of Peace for the County to intermeddle with the acting Magistrates of this town in respect to the power of passing vagrants.
"Resolved, that the Corporation do dispute such right and that proper measures be forthwith taken in order to prevent such or any other intermeddling, and maintain their own exclusive privileges."

City of London. In 1798 several entries occur relative to the disputes with the City of London on the subject of the Liverpool town dues on goods passing through the port.

Disputes. The citizens of London claimed exemption arising out of early grants from the Crown overriding the claims of the provincial Corporations.

In the same year the matter came to an issue in the Court of Exchequer in London. The claim of exemption by the *Trial.* resident freemen of the City of London was not disputed, but that of those residing outside in any other part of the Kingdom was resisted.

"1798, Octr. 3. Thomas Staniforth Mayor.
"Upon reading a letter from Mr Henry Brown respecting the state of the important cause now depending between the City of London and this Corporation relative to the town and port duties.

"Resolved, That this Council have great satisfaction in expressing their approbation of Mr Brown's continued exertions for the real interests of the Corporation in his searches and investigation of the important materials by him discovered in the examination of the Records of the City of London, and very much approve of his caution in not attempting to bring this cause to trial until his searches and examination into those records shall be perfectly complete both in his own judgment and that of the Recorder." *Thanks to Brown.*

On the 20th April, 1799, the cause was decided by a verdict "that the citizens of London were entitled to the exemption for their goods and wares, but that it belonged exclusively to such as were resident freemen within the liberties paying scot and lot." *Decision.*

This was a verdict decidedly in favour of the Corporation of Liverpool, and was received with great rejoicing.

During the flourishing and progressive period comprised in the present chapter, there were two blots on the fair fame of Liverpool commerce which could not but have a demoralizing tendency on society generally. I allude to privateering and the slave trade.

Privateering, though practised to a considerable extent, was in private hands, and did not come within the purview of the Corporation, hence there is no allusion to it in the records. The African slave trade, on the other hand, was continually before the public in the way of attack and defence, and the Council, consisting to a great extent of merchants engaged in the trade, felt themselves bound to defend it to the utmost of their power. *Privateering.*

The first slave ship from Liverpool was a barque of 30 tons which carried fifteen slaves across the Atlantic. At first the trade progressed slowly, but by the middle of the century it had acquired large dimensions, and increased rapidly towards the end. In 1771, 105 slave ships sailed from Liverpool and carried to the West Indies 28,200 negro slaves. *Slave Trade.*

First move for abolition.

The first movement towards the abolition of the slave trade was made in 1787, when a petition was presented to the House of Commons, signed principally by members of the Society of Friends, praying for its suppression; and in the following year the Anti-Slavery Society was instituted by Wilberforce, Clarkson, and Granville Sharp.

The Liverpool Common Council immediately took the alarm.

"1788, Feby. 14. Thomas Earle, Mayor.

Petition against abolition.

"At a special Council held this day in the Council Chamber within the Exchange, pursuant to special summons, for the purpose of considering the propriety of affixing the Seal to a Petition to Parliament against the abolition of the slave trade, present the Mayor, two Bailiffs, and twenty four Councillors.

"Ordered that the Common Seal be affixed to a petition now read, for the above purpose; that the same be immediately presented to Parliament and that the thanks of this Council be given to Mr Statham for his services in drawing it up, which petition is as follows—

"To the honourable the House of Commons &c.

"The humble petition of the Mayor &c sheweth

"That your petitioners as Trustees of the Corporate fund of the ancient and loyal town of Liverpool have always been ready not only to give every encouragement in their power to the commercial interests of that part of the Community more immediately under their care, but as much as possible to strengthen the reins of Government and to promote the public welfare.

Trade of Port Acts of Parliament. Docks.

"That the trade of Liverpool having met with the countenance of this honourable House in many Acts of Parliament, which have been granted at different times during the present century, for the constructing of proper and convenient wet docks for shipping, and more especially for the African ships, which from their form require to be constantly afloat, your Petitioners have been emboldened to lay out considerable sums of money and to pledge their Corporate Seal for other sums to a very large amount for effectuating these good and laudable purposes.

Canals.

"That your Petitioners have also been happy to see the great increase and different resources of trade which has flowed in upon their town by the numerous canals and other communications from the interior parts of this kingdom, in which many individuals, as well as public bodies of proprietors are materially interested.

"And that from these causes, particularly the convenience of the docks, and some other local advantages, added to the enterprizing spirit of the people, which has enabled them to carry on the African Slave Trade with vigour, the town of Liverpool has arrived at a pitch of mercantile con- Importance sequence which cannot but affect and improve the wealth and prosperity of the Port. of the kingdom at large.

"Your Petitioners therefore contemplate with real concern the attempts now making by the petitions lately preferred to your honourable House to obtain a total abolition of the African Slave trade, which has hitherto received the sanction of Parliament, and for a long series of years has Sanction of constituted and still continues to form a very extensive branch of the Parliament. commerce of Liverpool, and in effect gives strength and energy to the whole; but confiding in the wisdom and justice of the British Senate,

> "Your Petitioners humbly pray to be heard by their Counsel against the abolition of this source of wealth before the Honourable House shall proceed to determine upon a point which so essentially concerns the welfare of the town and port of Liverpool in particular, and the landed interest of the kingdom in general, and which in their judgment must also tend to the prejudice of the British manufacturers, must ruin the property of the English merchants in the West Indies, diminish the public revenue and impair the maritime strength of Great Britain.
>
> "And your Petitioners will ever pray" &c.

"1788, June 4. It having been reported to this Council that attempts have been lately made in Parliament to abolish the African Slave Trade, and Messrs John Tarleton, Robert Norris, James Penny, John Matthews Deputation and Archibald Dalzell having been deputed by the Committee of the to London. Liverpool African Merchants to attend in London on this business, Ordered that the thanks of this Council be given to the above mentioned gentlemen for the important service rendered by them to the town of Liverpool on this occasion, and that the Mayor be requested to communicate the same to them.

"Ordered that the freedom of this borough be granted to the above Freedom named gentlemen for the very essential advantages derived to the trade of granted. Liverpool from their evidence in support of the African Slave Trade, and for the public spirit they have manifested on this occasion."

In 1788, Mr. Wm. Roscoe issued a pamphlet entitled "a Roscoe's general view of the African slave trade, demonstrating its Pamphlet. injustice and impolicy, with hints towards a Bill for its abolition."

A reply was immediately put forth by the Reverend Raymond Harris, entitled "Scriptural researches on the Rev. Harris.

licitness of the slave trade, showing its conformity with principles of natural and revealed religion, delineated in the sacred writings of the Word of God."[1]

He did not go unrewarded, as will be seen from the following record :—

Grant to Harris.
" 1788, June 4. Ordered that the Mayor be desired to communicate the thanks of this Council to the Reverend Raymond Harris for his late excellent publication on the subject of the Slave Trade; and that he be requested to accept the sum of One hundred Pounds as a mark of the high sense this Council entertains of the advantages resulting to the town and trade of Liverpool from the said publication, and that the Treasurer pay the said sum.

Payment of Expenses.
"Ordered that the Board of Trade [2] have power to defray the expenses attending the opposition to the measures now pursuing in Parliament relative to the Slave Trade.

1788, June 20th. A Petition was also presented to the House of Lords in somewhat varied terms. It set forth :—

Petition to Lords.
"That your Petitioners are informed that a Bill has passed the Honourable House of Commons, and is now submitted to your Lordship's consideration, imposing a variety of unnecessary and grievous restrictions upon the African Slave Trade.

Trade legal.
"That the trade has been legally and uninterruptedly carried on for centuries past by many of his Majesty's subjects with advantages to the country both important and extensive; but has lately been unjustly reprobated as impolitic and inhuman.

Inquiry.
"That a Resolution has been passed in another House of Parliament to institute a very strict inquiry into the nature of this trade, in the ensuing session; and your Petitioners therefore were little aware of any attempts being intended hastily and injudiciously to force upon the African merchant such a train of crude and indigested restrictions and alterations

Bill.
as those contained in the Bill now before your Lordships, which if passed into a law cannot fail of indirectly amounting to a direct abolition of the African trade.

"That the importance of the subject to the revenues, navigation, and commerce of the country, does as is very humbly conceived deserve a

---

[1] Father Raymond Harris was a Jesuit Priest, of English extraction. He officiated at the Catholic Church in Edmund Street, now removed. He was born at Bilbao, 4th September, 1744, admitted S.J. 1758, expatriated from Corsica, April 1st, 1767, was afterwards Chaplain at Walton Hall, removed to Liverpool, and died in 1789. Whilst here he was thrice suspended by his Bishop.

[2] A local Committee of the Council.

more serious and deliberate consideration than can possibly be bestowed on it in the present expiring session of Parliament, during which your Petitioners cannot fairly be expected to prepare themselves with such counsel and evidence to prove the allegations they have here set forth, as are suited to the dignity of your Lordship's proceedings, and consistent with their own interests, upon an occasion of so much consequence to them and to their posterity. *Plea for postponement.*

"They therefore, relying upon your Lordships acknowledged wisdom and justice, do, on behalf of themselves and the freemen and traders of Liverpool whom they have the honour here to represent, humbly implore your Lordships that the Bill now complained of may not pass into a law, or that they may be heard by themselves or counsel against it.

"And your Petitioners as in duty bound will ever pray" &c.

In April, 1789, a petition was presented to the Commons, verbatim with that of the previous year, and on July 1st another, similar in most of its statements, and praying that the further inquiry and the examination of witnesses may be postponed for another year. *Petitions to Commons.*

"1789, December 2. The thanks of the Council are presented to Messrs Norris and Penny for their diligent attendance on the House and otherwise respecting the business of the African Slave Trade Bill." *Thanks to Delegates.*

"1792, May 24. Henry Blundell Mayor.

"At a Special Council another petition against interference with the Slave trade was approved and ordered to be transmitted to John Barnes, Richard Miles and Peter Brancker Esquires, who are desired to wait upon his Royal Highness the Duke of Clarence (William 4th) and request that he will present the same to the House of Lords." *Petition.*

"1792, Decr. 5. Clayton Tarleton Mayor.

"A Committee having been appointed to consider the services of the late Mr Robert Norris, Mr Jas Penny and Mr Saml Green in reference to the African Slave trade, report that the object of their appointment was both important in its nature and delicate in the result. *Services of Delegates.*

"They have been more than satisfied that the duties during a four years appointment have been discharged with unremitting labour, assiduity and diligence, being evidently instrumental in a most eminent degree in obtaining that temporary success which has thus far attended the measures of the African Merchants. The Committee have uniformly been of opinion that a considerable part of the Corporation estate consists of that kind of property which is inseparably connected with the *Temporary success.*

Committee favourable.
prosperity of the trade in question, and they cannot help thinking that a direct abolition of it would greatly injure the Corporation's future revenues themselves; on this account the services of the late Mr Norris will be allowed to have been important indeed."

The Committee so conclude a very lengthy report, entering minutely into the services of each of the gentlemen, and making certain recommendations, which, with some modifications, were adopted by the Council as follows :—

Grants.

Norris.
An annuity of £100 ℔ annum to the widow of Mr. Norris during the term of her natural life.

Penny.
A piece of plate of the value of £100 to be presented to Mr. James Penny.

Green.
The sum of £300 to be paid to the widow of Mr. Samuel Green for the benefit of his surviving family. £42 for his public services during the preceding two years, and £75 for expenses disbursed.

Case.
It was further resolved that the thanks of the Council be given to Alderman George Case and the rest of the members of the Committee, for their very full and accurate reports on this business.

Delegates.
Delegates were sent up from the various ports interested, who sat in London to take charge of the opposition. Messrs. John Barnes and Peter Whitfield Brancker represented Liverpool.

"1796, Mar. 12. Thomas Naylor Mayor.
"At a Special Council.

Letters.

Petitions.
"Upon reading the letters from the Delegates in London on the subject of the Bills before Parliament for the abolition of the African Slave trade recommending petitions from the Merchants and Corporation against the said Bills, it was unanimously agreed that petitions be sent up on behalf of the Corporation against the Bills, and praying to be heard by Counsel."

The petitions were merely an echo of those previously presented.

"1798, Octr. 3. Thomas Staniforth Mayor.
"It being now stated to this Council that great advantages have been

derived to the trade of this town from having thus far succeeded in defeating the repeated attempts in Parliament to obtain an abolition of the African Slave trade; and it being also suggested that Peter Whitfield Brancker Esquire a member of this Council, in his official character of Delegate had been very instrumental in securing a continuance of this trade under proper restrictions and regulations, and that he had been under the necessity of attending Parliament every session for several years past with considerable inconvenience to his own private affairs. _{Brancker.}

"Unanimously Resolved. That the thanks of this Council be presented to Mr Brancker for his very great attention to the laborious duties of his office; and as a lasting mark of the high sense entertained by the Council of his services, he be requested to accept of a Piece of Silver Plate of the value of One hundred guineas, the same to be provided, inscribed and presented under the directions of the Committee of Trade." _{Thanks.} _{Plate presented.}

"1799, April 1. Thomas Leyland Mayor.

"A Petition to the House of Commons was presented, stating that the Council observed with great concern a Bill introduced entitled a Bill to prohibit the trading for slaves to the coast of Africa within certain limits. _{Petition.}

"That your Petitioners humbly conceive the principle of the Bill to be full of the most dangerous consequences to the Navigation, Commerce and Manufactures of this country; and with almost incalculable injury to the estates and revenues of your petitioners in their Corporate capacities. _{Injury to Property.}

"That your petitioners beg leave humbly to represent the utter impossibility of carrying some parts of the said Bill into effect, and they consider the remainder so injurious, partial, and oppressive, that the general trade to Africa and consequently the interests of the Merchants, Artificers and others concerned therein as well as the holders of landed and all other descriptions of property within the town and port of Liverpool will be greatly affected thereby."

1799, May 1st. Another Bill was introduced into the House of Lords "for regulating the shipping and carrying of slaves in British Vessels from the coast of Africa." _{Bill.}

A Petition was sent up against it by the Council, stating amongst other arguments, _{Petition.}

"That by the regulations already adopted, 'the health and comfort of the slaves are proved to have been effectually secured. . . that the Bill now proposed departing from the principle of the existing regulating Bill, is founded upon a most fallacious theory and if passed into a law will have the certain effect of grievously oppressing the merchants, traders and others concerned in the African trade.'" _{Comfort of Slaves.}

"1769, July 3. Resolved and Ordered.

"That the thanks of this Council be presented to Col Gascoyne for his _{Thanks to Gascoyne.}

general attention to the concerns and interest of this town and port during the late Session of Parliament particularly for his assiduity and unwearied exertions on the slave carrying and limitation Bills respecting the African trade &c."

"1800, Decr. 3. John Shaw Mayor.

Freedom to Duke of Clarence.

"Mr Alderman Case reported that pursuant to previous instructions of the Council, the Recorder accompanied by the Committee had attended his Royal Highness the Duke of Clarence for the purpose of presenting him with the Freedom of the Borough in a Gold Box at St James's Palace on Tuesday Octr 14ᵗʰ with an address expressing 'the just and grateful sense which the Council of Liverpool have of your Royal Highness's active and able exertions in Parliament for the trade and commerce of the kingdom (as it is euphemistically expressed), in points in which the town of Liverpool is particularly interested.'"

Reply.

His Royal Highness, in his gracious reply, does not "put too fine a point on it," but boldly states that "the sense the Corporation has entertained of my exertions in Parliament, on the discussion of questions relative to the African Slave Trade, is highly flattering to me . . I am happy if my feeble efforts have succeeded in defending an interest which I felt it my indispensable duty to support, and which was suffering from the exaggeration of facts and the prejudice of opinion."

Gold Box.

The cost of the Gold Box is recorded at £226, paid to Messrs. Rundell and Bridge, and twenty five guineas for the illuminated Address.

The subsequent proceedings relative to the slave trade will come in review within the next chapter.

THE CORPORATE ESTATE AND REVENUES.

The Corporation at this period began to realise the benefits of the courage and resolution of their predecessors, particularly in reference to the land eastward of the Pool, secured by the treaty with Lord Molyneux in 1667. [Landed Estate.]

The town was rapidly extending and land was in demand.

"1764, Octr. 3. Ordered that Mr Eyes do plan the Corporation Estate, and colour it under the direction of the Committee of views, for the time being." [Plan.]

The present Corporate Estate lies almost exclusively to the south of the line of Islington, except in the case of purchases comparatively recent, but in the older records we read of large tracts at the north end belonging to the Corporation. How or when these lands were sold or otherwise disposed of there is no record. Some of the last references to this portion of the estate are the following:— [Boundaries.]

"1773, March 3.
"Ordered, that the Proprietors of the Canal making from Leeds to Liverpoole have liberty to cut through two lands of ground in the old Townfield belonging to the Corporation, paying after the same rate for this ground as they pay Mr Ralph Williamson for the remainder of the field." [Leeds Canal.]

Again, 1774, February 2nd,

"Ordered on application of Mr John Seacome to this Council, acquainting them that a valuation had been fixed by the Commissioners of the Leeds and Liverpool canal for the ground they have cutt thro' in his fields held by lease from this Corporation for the term of three lives and twenty-one years amounts to Fifty Pounds eleven shillings and sixpence, and desiring to know what part of the said money he is to have for his possession . . that Mr Treasurer do allow him two-thirds of the said money and receive one-third part thereof for the loss of the Corporation reversion in the said premises," [Seacome. Land taken.]

"1776, Jany. 3. Ordered, that the Mayor and Bailiffs (with nine others named) be appointed a Committee to treat with the Proprietors of the Leeds Canal upon the subject of the late Notice given to the Mayor dated the 9th of December last, and that it be given in instructions to the said Committee to accommodate the said Proprietors so as not to injure the Navigation of this port, and that the Committee report their proceedings to the next Council."

Treaty with Canal Co.

The following documents are important, as exhibiting very graphically the state of the Corporation affairs at the close of the 18th century, and explaining the alienation of a considerable amount of their property.

"1798, Feby. 7. Thomas Staniforth Mayor.

Report on Estate.

"Report of the Select Finance Committee to the Council upon the general state of the Corporation affairs, Accounts and Finances, referred to their consideration by an order of Council dated the 4th day of October 1797.

"Your Committee has held several meetings upon the very important matters referred to their consideration, during which time they have found it necessary to call for a variety of accounts relating to the general state of the finances of the Corporation. These accounts have been regularly produced, and having every appearance of authenticity and correctness they enable the Committee to report the following facts; which for the sake of conciseness and perspicuity, they arrange under three different heads or divisions.

Debt. "1st. The sum total of the Corporation Bond Debt on Jany. 1st 1798.

Income. "2nd. The amount of the annual Income of the Corporation for seven years from 1790 to 1796 both inclusive.

Expenses. "3rd. The amount of the annual Expenses of the Corporation during the same period.

Debt. "First the sum total of the Corporation Bond Debt on Jany. 1st 1798 appears to be £453,528 17s. 1d. and as five per Cent is paid for interest it creates an annual charge of £22,676 8s.

"The Corporation is also under engagements for the payment of Life Annuities to the amount of upwards of £2,800 more. On the 1st Jany. 1786 these Bond debts were only £51,625 and as they very rapidly increased to their present almost unmanageable extent, it will be a satisfaction to the Council to have the general causes somewhat explained.

Annuities.

Improvement Acts. "In 1786 the Act of Parliament for the improvement of the town was obtained, under the authority of which heavy expenses have been incurred in opening of new streets and the enlargement of old ones, with all their consequent charges of pavements and repairs. Nearly at the same time, the erection of the New Gaol commenced, as well also as the additional

Gaol.

buildings at the Exchange. Many extensive purchases have also been made, with a view to a proper situation for a new Dock; as also in other parts of the town for a variety of public purposes, particularly near St James's Walk, Quarry Hill, and Wapping. During this intermediate space since 1786, new Graving Docks have also been erected, and the old ones improved; a Quay for the accommodation of the river flats has been made; the Alms-houses removed; the Tobacco Warehouse has been built, and commodious Public Baths have been introduced. The dignity of the Corporation and the loyalty of the town have likewise been manifested upon several public, and it may be said national, occasions, more especially at the time of the recovery of the King; in the granting of bounties to seamen &c entering into his Majesty's service; and by a subscription to the raising of the Lancashire Fencibles; all of which have considerably encreased the general expences. Many unforeseen and heavy charges have also been incurred in law, by defending the rights of the Corporation in regard to its Port Duties and its disputes with the burgesses; and in carrying on a suit with his Grace the Duke of Bridgwater. In Parliament by supporting the commerce of the town and the Estate of the Corporation as connected with the continuance of a well-regulated African Slave Trade. *[margin: Exchange. Dock. Walks. Graving Dock. Tobacco Warehouse. Public occasions. Bounties. Volunteers. Disputes. Bridgwater. Slave Trade.]*

"Second, the Amount of the Annual Income of the Corporation for seven years from 1790 to 1796. *[Income.]*

"It is not possible to ascertain the precise amount of the annual income of the Corporation, on account of the fluctuating state of its several branches of revenue; particularly during the contested situation of a part of its Port Duties; but your Committee has collected sufficient information upon that head for their present purpose.

"It appears by the accounts produced to the Committee that the Corporation annual income in the year 1790 was about £19,206 and in the year 1796 about £28,000. This flattering addition to its income seems to have arisen from increased Port Duties, increased rents of houses and lands, increased fines for the renewal of leases and increased Graving Dockage. *[Duties, Rents Fines.]*

"Third. The amount of the annual expences of the Corporation during the like period. *[Expences.]*

"The annual expences, depending as they necessarily must, upon its engagements and public undertakings, cannot be fixed at any given sum, or confined to any particular description. There are however, various heads of expence which are annual and certain, but unavoidably differing in their several amounts in different years according to circumstances. These principally consist of Interest on the Bond debt, Life annuities, Salaries, Taxes lately made very considerable, Repairs &c., Establishment of St George's Church, and the charges of maintaining an effective Police for the good government of the town. These different expences amounted *[Interest. Repairs. Police.]*

in the year 1790 to about £20,638; but in 1796 they are found to have increased to a sum not less than £33,305, arising from the mortifying addition to the annual interest of the Bond debt, annuities, Taxes, Salaries and Repairs.

Necessity for change

"Remarks. By an attention to these general statements sufficiently particular however, to form general conclusions, the necessity of an immediate and decisive alteration of system in the mode of conducting the Corporation affairs will evidently appear. The alarming fact of its annual expences having far exceeded its annual income since the commencement of the present inquiry, is fully established. The Council will please to observe, that this has arisen altogether from an injudicious, uniform, annual increase of the Bond Debt during that period, thereby fastening upon the Corporation estate a consequent proportionate increase of annual interest. By a reference to the accounts produced, it will appear that there has been a constant yearly taking up of money upon new bonds, yet as constant a discharge of old ones for the convenience of individual creditors, but that the yearly sums taken up have regularly exceeded the yearly sums discharged, in the proportion of £27,000 ⅌ annum; the Corporation thus exposing itself to the mischievous consequences of borrowing money to pay its annual interest.

Expense exceeding Income.

Remedy.

"The Remedy.—Having advanced thus far in reporting the present state of the finances of the Corporation as they appear to your Committee from an attentive perusal of the accounts produced to them under the authority of the Council, they will now proceed to point out what they conceive would be the wisest if not the only mode of relieving the Corporation estate from its insupportable load of Bond Debt from whence arise all its difficulties. In vain will the Committee have formed the preceding statement of affairs if the Council should not speedily adopt a well digested and effectual plan of greatly diminishing this intolerable burthen. Your Committee presume to state, that if there were no other motives for such a plan than what arise from common prudence, it ought not to be any longer neglected. But when the pressing demands of many of the Bond creditors for their money, some of whom have resorted to legal measures to recover it, are considered, it becomes absolutely and indispensably necessary; especially as there is reason to believe these demands may greatly increase, and if the Corporation should not be able to discharge them, the greatest inconvenience will be occasioned.

Sufficient Property.

"Your Committee is fully persuaded of their being abundance of property to resort to for the raising of the money now wanted, and they have bestowed much of their time and attention on the consideration of what particular part of such property is the fittest to be used on this occasion. They have at length formed a decided opinion that a sale of the reversionary interest of the Corporation in houses and buildings would not only be the most productive but in itself the most expedient to be

Sale of Reversions.

sold. The annual rents of this property are estimated at £98,270, and if wholly disposed of, would, in the opinion of your Committee, extricate the Corporation from all its difficulties; if sold only in part, yet its present wants may be fully supplied.

"As an argument in proof of the propriety of recommending the sale of this part of the Corporation Estate they have to remark, that the average produce of it in Fines for the renewal of leases for the last 14 years as appears by the office statements is only £2,378 ⅌ annum. Whereas if the reversionary interest was itself sold your Committee has little doubt of its bringing into the Corporation Funds a sum of money the annual interest of which would be more than six times the annual average produce of the fines. Average produce.

"The Committee presume also further to state that upon an arithmetical calculation founded upon the data before mentioned, it would be unwise in the Corporation even in the most flourishing condition of their affairs, any longer to keep this description of property, except in particular cases; for it evidently appears that a very serious sum is annually lost by retaining it; inasmuch as is the difference between the annual interest of the money it would sell for, and the annual average produce of the fines. Unwise to retain.

"This is the Remedy, which your Committee strongly recommends to the Council for the purpose of relieving the Corporation from its present difficulties.

"Although prejudices may be entertained against the disposal of a property which the Corporation has long possessed and to which it has been in the constant habit of affording every encouragement in its power, yet it is apprehended no substantial reasons can be given for the selling of any other part of the estate in preference to the reversionary interest in houses and buildings. Money must be raised; there is no alternative, or the Corporation credit already wounded will be shaken to its centre. By this exertion which will not affect the improving staple branches of the revenue, your Committee are of opinion the Corporation may be relieved from its present intolerable load of Bond Debt, and be left in possession of a larger nett annual income, for the support of its own dignity and for the general purposes of public good than it would ever expend with propriety at any former period. Prejudice. Money must be raised. Relief.

"Your Committee likewise further report, that they conceive a sinking fund may be established with effect by the annual appropriation of a moderate sum with a view to the creating of the means for the future discharge of a further part of this heavy debt, and they are also of a confirmed opinion that the annual income of the Corporation may be greatly increased and the annual expenditure much diminished by a strict examination into the particulars. They are not yet, however, prepared to report upon them, but will reserve these three last important articles for future consideration and for the subject of a future report. Sinking Fund.

Resolution.

Reversions to be sold.

Foster Agent.

" Resolved Unanimously

"That it appears to this Council from the before mentioned Report, that it is absolutely necessary to raise a considerable sum of money with all possible despatch to extricate the Corporation from its present pecuniary embarrassments; and therefore Resolved

"That the Reversionary Interest of this Corporation in Houses and Buildings as stated and recommended in the Report shall forthwith be sold and that the Select Finance Committee be fully authorized and empowered to proceed to the sale thereof upon such terms and conditions as they may think adviseable; at all times however giving a preference to the proprietors respectively."

"1798, May 3. The Select Finance Committee reported that having taken into consideration the necessity that the agency of carrying into effect the sales of the Corporation Reversions should be transacted by one person only; they do appoint Mr John Foster Jun' to be such agent and do direct that in that capacity he alone receive the returns of the printed forms and certificates—and that he be granted for such additional labour an extra allowance of £150 per annum."

Purchases.

At the time the Council were thus engaged in parting with their freeholds in order to raise money, they very prudently made purchases where it appeared the money could be advantageously expended.

Tower.

The old Tower in Water Street had been sold by the Earl of Derby to the Clayton family about fifty years previously.

1774, November 2nd, occurs the following record :—

"On a proposal made by Sir Richard Clayton, Baronet and his brothers, to the Council that they are willing to sell the Old Tower (now the Gaol) with other premises now in lease, to the Corporation, also the house now in possession of Mr Brownell &c. . . it was agreed to leave the price to arbitration."

Purchase.

"1775, Aug. 2. The valuation of £1535 10 0 for the purchase of the Tower and other premises adjoining was confirmed."

Another purchase was made at this time of the greatest importance, and of a very beneficial nature.

Reference will be found in the former volume to the settle-

Lord Sefton's Reversions.

ment of the disputes with Caryl, Lord Molyneux, in 1672, by the purchase of all his rights and claims as Lord of the

Manor, including the wastes and commons, on a lease for 1,000 years, at £30 per annum.

"1774, Nov. 2. Peter Rigby Mayor.

"It being mentioned to this Council that Lord Sefton is willing to sell to the Corporation the stallage Rents and other reversionary interest leased by his ancestors to the Corporation for a term of nine hundred and ninety nine years, or some such long term, and all other (if any such there be) royalties of this town together with the reversions of all the houses in and about Lord Street in Liverpoole as also the Ferries and Burgage rents of the town; it is Ordered, that Mr Mayor (with seven others) be appointed a Committee to treat with his Lordship about the purchase thereof, except the reversions in and about Lord Street." *Purchase.*

The bargain was ultimately struck on the 4th September, 1776, for the sum of £2,250, which has been the most lucrative investment the Corporation ever made.

"1772, Feby. 5. Ordered that Mr Mayor, Bailiffs and the Council or any twelve of them be appointed a Committee to set out the quantity and boundaries of the land necessary for the New Poor House and its conveniences, and the term, rent, or consideration they shall pay to the Corporation for the same, and report it to the Council; and that Brownlow Hill Mill and house and premises be lett to the present tenant at the present rent during the pleasure of this Council; And that Mr Mayor be empowered to employ persons to feigh a post of stone at the said quarry for the use of the docks." *New Poorhouse.*

"1776, Jany. 3. Ordered that this Corporation do allow five hundred pounds to be abated of the debt the Parish owe them, towards the erecting of a House of Correction near the Workhouse on the plan now produced; provided the Parish choose to be at the rest of the expence thereof, and provided also that the Justices in Sessions shall order the same to be erected." *Parish Debt.*

"1779, June 2. Ordered that the Treasurer do treat with the Chancellor of the Duchy of Lancaster, for the purchase of the Chantry Rents payable by the Corporation to the Duchy." *Chantry Rents.*

"1796, Mar. 12. Thomas Naylor, Mayor.

"Upon the motion of the Worshipful the Mayor for a Committee of the Council to meet the Committee of the Parish appointed at the Annual Vestry respecting the settlement of accounts between them. Ordered that the following gentlemen viz Aldermen Earle and Gregson, and Messrs Brooks, Statham, and Brown be appointed a Committee to meet the gentlemen appointed by the Vestry to take into consideration the accounts and differences between the Parish and the Corporation, agreeable to the *Parish Accounts settled.*

terms and powers of the order made at the last public Vestry, viz on the claim of one thousand pounds made by the Corporation against the Parish for rent of the Workhouse and other general accounts, but exclusive of the Four thousand pounds borrowed by the Parish and laid out in building the Workhouse, which is clear and undisputed."

Origin of Disputes.

The differences arose in this way. The Parish claimed rates from the Corporation property, including the tolls and dues. On the other hand, the Corporation claimed rent or interest from the land in Brownlow Hill, on which the Workhouse now stands, from the year 1769. The Corporation had also expended the sum of four thousand pounds in the erection of the Workhouse, for which the Parish stood indebted.

The original Minute of the Council was as follows:—

Workhouse.

"At a Special Council held 17th May 1769.

"It is Ordered. That a Poor House be built on part of the field called Brownlow Mill Field according to a plan drawn and laid before the Council by Mr Joseph Brooks on the application of the Parishioners at their Annual Vestry, the said Parishioners undertaking to pay the Corporation the sum of Four Pounds ten shillings per cent per annum clear of all repairs, insurance and other charges, until the said Parishioners shall pay off all such principal money and interest as the Corporation shall lay out on such building, under the direction of the said Mr Joseph Brooks."

The two Committees met in the most friendly spirit, and agreed on the following terms, viz. :—

Agreement.

"That the Parish pay the Corporation One thousand and fifty Pounds besides their liability to the Four thousand pounds expended on the buildings; that a lease of the whole site be granted by the Corporation for 1000 years at a pepper corn rent, subject to various conditions and provisions; that the said sum of £1050 shall be taken and considered on account and in part of the Taxes now due from the Corporation to the Parish and that the interest likewise of the said sum of £4000 now due shall also be taken and considered on account and in part

Payment.

reduction of the taxes due; and the remaining balance be forthwith paid by the Corporation; that the Parish Committee shall use their best endeavours to pay off the sum of £4000 so due, with interest at 5 per cent, and that the accruing interest shall be deducted from the future taxes upon the Corporation Estate."

CORPORATE ESTATE AND REVENUES.

Down to the end of the 18th century the Corporation paid Parish Rates on all their property, including Tolls, Dock Dues and Town Dues.

"1800, May 7. Pudsey Dawson Mayor.
"Ordered that the Report of the Select Finance Committee of the 24th December last upon the letter from the Churchwardens of the 5th November to the Council respecting the Parish Rates claimed by them to be due from the Corporation, viz 'that Mr Henry Brown be requested to inform the Churchwardens and Parish Treasurer that this Committee do not consider the Port duties to be liable to be rated to the Poor of this Parish, and therefore they advise the Common Council not to pay the same at present;' and the same is hereby ratified and confirmed." — *Rating of Corporate Property.*

The Corporation therefore ceased to pay.

In 1806, a decision of Lord Kenyon's, in a parallel case, confirmed the exemption so claimed. In 1825, the case of the liability of the Dock dues to be rated came before Lord Tenterden, whose decision, based upon the previous one of Lord Kenyon, was in favour of the exemption. — *Lord Kenyon's decision. Lord Tenterden.*

In 1848 the subject was revived and a Rating Bill was proposed, but afterwards dropped.

In 1858 a serious attempt was made to deal with the matter by legislation, but in vain. The Parish then took legal proceedings to enforce the rate. They were defeated in the Court of Common Pleas, and again, on appeal, in the Exchequer Chamber, but the House of Lords, after four days' argument by counsel, and after taking the opinion of the Judges, decided against the exemption of the Dock duties. The tolls and Town Dues as incorporeal hereditaments still retain their exemption. — *Trials. Final decision.*

1781, February 7th. A portion of the Corporation property on the East-side of Castle Street, consisting of seven shops, was put up by auction, for three lives and 21 years, and one shilling per yard of frontage ground rent. — *Sales in Castle Street.*

The premises were divided into four lots, and realized

£3,181, being—the record states—more than the valuation fixed thereon by the Committee.

This was before the widening of Castle Street in 1786.

The following notices of two names of high appreciation in Liverpool are interesting:—

William Roscoe.

"1781, March 7, Ordered that a lease be granted to Mr William Roscoe Jun' to add one life to two lives and twenty one years in being in a messuage with two small gardens and a bowling green adjoining thereto situate on Mount Pleasant, paying an annual ground rent of one shilling per yard for the whole front to the lane."

"1786, Nov. 1. Ordered that the petition of Mr William Roscoe, Attorney, for liberty to get stone out of the quarry on the east side of Rodney Street for the use of the buildings in the said street be granted."

John Gladstone.

"1798, Feby. 7. Ordered that John Gladstone, Merchant, have leave to add one life and to change the two lives in being, and to have a building lease for three fresh lives and twenty one years in a piece of land on the west side of Rodney Street adjoining on the south side to the house and garden of the said John Gladstone, and containing in front to Rodney Street thirty four yards, on paying a fine of three guineas, and twelve pence per yard rent for the front."

W. E. Gladstone.

In this house, on the 29th December, 1809, was born the Right Honourable William Ewart Gladstone, a man of whom, all will admit, Liverpool has reason to be proud.

Wm. Rathbone.

The name of William Rathbone is one of high reputation in Liverpool, having been borne by several generations of a family distinguished for public spirit and philanthropy. The name frequently occurs in the records in various relations with the Corporation, both friendly and the reverse.

The following entry occurs during the period now recorded:—

Encroachment.

"1776, June 5. It being now reported to this Council that Mr William Rathbone is still going on with making an encroachment or inclosure upon the river Mersey opposite or to the westward of his premises, west of the Salthouse Dock, notwithstanding his petition to the last Council for liberty to inclose or take in the same ground from the said river, was rejected or refused by the said Council to be complied with, and of which the said William Rathbone, his Clerk or Agent was acquainted.

"It is therefore Ordered, that the Town Clerk give him the said William Rathbone notice to desist going on therewith, and to take the same down; otherwise in case of refusal or neglect, then that the Mayor be authorized to cause such incroachment to be forthwith prostrated." Notices.

"Also a like notice for him the said William Rathbone to take up the causeway made by him running from his yard, to or on a certain place called Pluckington's Bank, in the said river Mersey, as the same inclosure or causeway, it is feared, will be of great disservice and an obstruction to the free navigation of the river Mersey and Port of Liverpool."

On a petition being subsequently presented by Mr. Rathbone, a compromise was effected; the causeway or projection to Pluckington Bank was undertaken to be removed, and the enclosure was allowed to remain. Compromise.

This projection into the river, somewhat resembling the piers at Brighton, Southport, &c., is shown on one of the views of Liverpool, from the river, at this period. It was removed very soon afterwards.

"1772, Feby. 5. Thomas Wilson Mayor.

"A complaint being made to this Council that the sea has made several breaches in the wall of the New Kay, which has washed the publick road over the said Kay in some places entirely or nearly away, so as not to leave a cart road over the same, and is become very dangerous to passengers; and it being also mentioned now in Council that no persons can at present be found out who are the owners of the said land, to call upon them to repair the said road. Breaches in Sea Walls.

"It is Ordered that the said breaches of the said wall be made and built up at the expence of the Corporation; but an exact account of that expence is to be kept, in order to charge the owners of the said land with, when they appear or shall be found out."

The Salt Works of Mr. Blackburne, which gave their name to the Salthouse Dock, were continued down to the year 1796, when the works were dismantled and the land laid out for building, under a lease from the Corporation. Salt Works.

"1797, Nov. 17. At a meeting of the Dock Committee of the Council the Surveyor laid before them a plan for laying out the site, in which the main street, running from east to west is laid down for 12 yds wide and proposed to be continued in a straight line from the Dock Quay to Hurst Street. Docks and Street.

232   CHAP. III, A.D. 1760—1800.

"Resolved that the said plan would in the opinion of this Committee be sufficient for publick purposes; for although the Order of Council of the 6th June 1770 directs all main streets hereafter to be fourteen yards wide, yet it leaves an opening for discretion to be exercised in particular cases where such a width would bear hard upon the parties concerned, and the Committee are of opinion that the present is one of such cases."

"1798, March 22. At a special meeting of the Dock Committee, the plan being reconsidered, it was resolved unanimously that the said plan be finally fixed upon and reported to the Council.

Arcade. "The above mentioned plan having annexed to it an arcade to the front of four yards wide, forming a most important part of the design, inasmuch as the safety and convenience of persons employed in transacting their business there are more effectually secured, it is unanimously resolved that the said arcade be provided as explained upon the plan and that the front part be immediately erected at the expence of the Docks."

Goree. This arcade was only partially carried out, and was never completed. The arcade of the Goree warehouses had been erected in 1793.

The Council during the 18th century were always very jealous of any interference with their right of markets and tolls.

Butchers' Stalls. Market. "1763, Oct. 3. Ordered that no Butchers stalls be suffered for the future to be erected on the ground at the top of Pool Lane belonging to this Corporation, but that it be kept for a Country Market, and that Mr Tillinghurst be defended as the Corporation Lessee of the Tolls, Rents, Dues and Stallage against persons refusing to pay the same. And that all persons erecting stalls in any part of this town do pay the customary stallage rents to the Corporation, or their Lessee, or be sued for the same."

The original Market of Liverpool was held at the intersection of Chapel Street, Oldhall Street, Tithebarn Street White Cross. and High Street, called the "White Cross" from the monument there erected. After the purchase and dismantling of the castle at the beginning of the 18th century, the main Derby Square. market was removed to a portion of the site called Derby Square. There it continued until the end of the century. The following entry will explain the action then taken.

CORPORATE ESTATE AND REVENUES. 233

"1800, Aug. 6. Pudsey Dawson Mayor.

"Upon reading the proceedings of the Select Committee it was Resolved,

"That whereas the Corporation of Liverpool are entitled to hold and have held, an ancient Market within the town of Liverpool for the buying and selling of all sorts of Goods, Merchandizes and Provisions whatsoever upon the Saturday in every week of the year; And are also entitled by Patent to hold another market within the same town for the buying and selling therein of all sorts of Goods and Merchandizes upon the Wednesday in every week of the year, which said Saturday and Wednesday's Markets have for many years last past been held in and near unto a place in Liverpool aforesaid called Derby Square. Patent of Markets.

"And whereas from the great concourse of late years of persons resorting to the said Markets for the purpose of buying and selling provisions serving for the food of man, it has been and is found greatly incommodious that any other kind of goods save only those which shall serve for the food of man shall be bought and sold in or near to the said place called Derby Square. Inconvenience.

"Therefore it is by this Council ordered and enacted that from henceforth the said Ancient Market, and the said Patent Market shall not any longer be held in or near unto the said place called Derby Square, but that the same shall henceforth be held at a certain place or square within the town of Liverpool called Clieveland Square. Partial Removal.

"And whereas by a certain Act of Parliament passed in the 26th year of the reign of his present Majesty entitled *inter alia* an Act for opening certain streets, for appointing additional Market Places &c, it is enacted that the Common Council shall have the power of directing and ordering such public squares or parts of streets to be used for public Market Places for such sorts and species of goods and provisions only as they shall think proper. . . Now this Common Council, by virtue of the power so delegated to them, do hereby order and enact that the said place called Derby Square and such parts of the avenues as have been lately used for a market, shall from henceforth be used for a public Market Place on the Saturday and on the Wednesday in every week of the year for the purpose of buying and selling such goods and provisions only as are for the food of man, and not for any other goods or merchandizes whatsoever." Powers of Council.
Derby Square.

In 1788, the mind of the Council was exercised by what was considered an infringement of the exclusive privilege of holding public markets. Mr. Thomas Dobb erected a building in Richmond Row, surrounding an open area, with galleries in two stories, intending to appropriate the galleries for the sale of woollen goods, and the area for a market. Market, Richmond Row.

G G

The Council took the alarm and passed the following resolution :—

Counsel's opinion.

" 1788, April 2. Ordered, that the Records be searched and a case be stated for the opinion of Counsel respecting the proper mode to be pursued in order to suppress the attempt now making to hold a Market or Fair for the purpose of vending different manufactures at a place erected by Messrs Dobb and others near St Anne's Church called the Woollen Hall."

" 1789, April 1. The cases and opinions respecting the Fairs held at a place called Richmond in this town, whereby a breach has been committed on that franchise of the Corporation having been read to this Council; it is their opinion that another case more fully stated under the inspection of the following gentlemen (the Mayor and Bailiffs with others) be drawn up, and that they be requested to produce the same at the next Council."

Market abandoned.

Nothing came out of this enquiry. The open market was abandoned, but the woollen trade was there successfully carried on for fifty years. It then began to decline, and was finally abandoned and the buildings converted into cottage tenements.

Gaol.

The Gaol erected by the Corporation in 1786 was soon after its erection rented by the Government as a depôt for French prisoners. In the year 1798 there were 4,000 prisoners interned within its walls. The following entry refers to this.

" 1799, July 3. Thos Leyland Mayor.

Rent.

" Upon the motion of Mr Alderman Earle, seconded by Mr Brooks, with respect to the propriety of giving notice to the Commissioners of the Transport Office, that the Corporation were inclined to think themselves well justified in calling for an increase of rent of the new Gaol now occupied by the French prisoners, and other prisoners of War under the direction of that Board, not only on account of the very great injury done to the building by persons of this description, and under these particular circumstances, but on account of the very great loss as well as inconvenience, which the Corporation suffered and were and are put to from their own prisoners for debt and on prosecutions at suit of the Crown being now confined in a very close and improper building, which nevertheless on account of its advantageous situation for warehouses &c close to the present Georges Dock must be extremely valuable.

Prisoners.

" Resolved and Ordered, that the consideration of this subject be referred to the Select Finance Committee, with power to act as they shall see fit."

Much has been written on the origin of railroads and the date of their inception. The following entry will be interesting.

"1800, Dec. 3. Upon reading the report and recommendation of the Dock Committee, that Mr Foster jun^r had laid before them a scheme and estimate for forming a waggon way or *Railed Road* for conveying stone from the quarry down Parliament Street to the south end of the Queen's Dock to be conveyed from thence in boats to such docks or places on the river as might be required, and also an estimate of the probable saving that would arise from this mode of conveyance.

"And upon due consideration of the said scheme and estimates, and the advantages likely to arise to the general Corporation estates in regard to the injury done to the pavements of the streets through which the carts conveying the stone had usually passed, as well as to the dispatch and great saving in point of expence to the particular fund under the direction of the Trustees of the Docks.

"Resolved and Ordered, that the said scheme be carried into immediate effect."

TRADE AND COMMERCE.

The period now under review was a prosperous one for the commerce of Liverpool. New openings continually presented themselves, which were eagerly availed of. The rising manufactures of Lancashire and Yorkshire found an outlet in Liverpool superior to any available elsewhere.

Rising importance.

The merchants and local authorities were keenly alive to their own interests, perhaps not always wisely, but according to their light earnestly, and generally successfully.

" 1766, June 17. John Crosbie Mayor.

" Ordered that the following noblemen and gentlemen be complimented with their freedom of this borough :—The most honourable the Marquis of Rockingham; the Right Hon. the Earl of Dartmouth (with ten others), with a letter of thanks for their services in obtaining the free Ports in the West Indies during the last Session of Parliament."

Freedom to Lords Rockingham and Dartmouth.

" 1774, Feby. 15. John Parr Mayor.

" Whereas a petition hath been read to this Council purporting to be a petition to Parliament from the Merchants and Traders of Liverpoole, praying liberty to bring in a Bill this session for imposing a tax on the importation of all goods into the port of Liverpoole according to a printed table of rates delivered into the Council, alledged to be for the support and benefit of trade and any other publick occasion, or to that purport. And whereas the said Merchants, at a late publick meeting of them held in the Town Hall of this town did then openly declare that no such application was intended or should be made at this session for such Bill.

Proposed Town Imposts.

" And whereas no such Bill or draft hath been prepared or laid before the public or this Council, who conceive from the general purposes of their petition that such Bill may affect the rights, interests, good order and government of the town. It is therefore now Ordered that in case any such application be made or Bill brought into Parliament that an opposition thereto on the behalf and at the expence of the Corporation be made this session of Parliament against the same passing into a law; and that the Mayor (with fourteen others) be appointed a Committee to manage such opposition in Parliament. And that a petition be prepared and presented to the House of Commons."

Bill opposed.

TRADE AND COMMERCE.

"1774, Feby. 22. On a representation made to the Committee by several very respectable merchants and burgesses that it is necessary to send up deputies, and that resources are wanted to pay the expenses, the Council consider that it is for the interest of the town and Corporation that a competent fund out of its Corporate revenue be dedicated to the service of that commerce from whence the far greater part of such revenue immediately springs. *[Payment of Expenses.]*

"It is therefore hereby ordered that after such part of the Trade duty which has been levied for the support of trade for many years last past shall have been applied and expended for the purposes to which it is now applicable, any sum or sums of money not exceeding the sum of £250 a year of this Corporation revenue shall be annually set apart and paid by the Treasurer to such Committee of Commerce, to consist of such number of Merchants, Burgesses of this Corporation, provided an equal part of them respectively be persons chosen by the Mayor, Bailiffs and Burgesses of this town in Common Council assembled, and an equal part of them by the Merchants and Traders, Burgesses of this town, subject to such rules and regulations for the common good of this town as the Corporation Committee appointed at the last Council, of whom the Mayor and one Bailiff shall be two." *[Committee of Commerce.]*

"1774, Feby. 26. It is resolved that several of the proposals now offered by the Committee and proposers of the intended Bill for a tax on trade now read to and considered by the Mayor, Bailiffs and Burgesses in this Council assembled, being in their opinion not proper to be complied with by them, they declare they cannot comply with the said proposals, and that if the petition to Parliament for bringing in the said intended Bill is or shall be presented contrary to the intent of the order of the last Council, the fund thereby established is or will be thereby void. Nevertheless the Mayor, Bailiffs and Burgesses in this Council assembled still retaining and meaning in all things to shew a due regard to the Commonwealth of this town, will always on proper occasions administer such aids to the commercial interests of this town as in the discretion of the Mayor, Bailiffs and Burgesses from time to time in Common Council assembled, and in experience shall be found expedient for the advancement of the Comon good of Liverpoole. *[Objections.]*

Here follow three pages of objections under seven heads.

"The foregoing objections or proposals being this day brought on by Mr Sparling, as he declared, from the assembly of the petitioners on the business therein contained, after being deliberately read over by the Town Clerk three several times to the Council, and many debates thereon, and the question put thereon, Whether this Council do now agree to accept them or not; Carried *nem. con.* against accepting them." *[Discussion.]*

"1774, Decr. 7. It is now ordered—That a Committee of Commerce *[Committee of Commerce.]*

be appointed out of the body of this Council, to consist of such number, to be subject to such orders and regulations as shall be established at the next Council, and that Mr Peters be desired to draw up some proper rules and orders for such purpose."

"1775, April 5. Peter Rigby Mayor.

"It is Ordered that the following Instrument or Deed now reported from the Committee and read to the Council be confirmed and made an Act and Order of this Council to be in force from this time, and is as follows vizt—

Act of Council.

Deed.

"The Mayor, Bailiffs and Burgesses in this Common Council assembled, taking into their consideration the great emolument which has arisen and is likely to arise, to the estate and revenue of this Corporation from the trade and commerce of the town, and being well satisfied that they cannot do anything which will more tend to the furtherance and advancement of the common profit and commodity thereof than by using their reasonable endeavour for the protecting and advancing its trade and commerce, and they having the prosperity thereof at heart, do hereby declare it to be their resolution to extend their Corporate aids for the defence and promotion of all such trade and commerce as do and shall concern the interest of this town, in such manner and measure as exigencies shall from time to time require, and as the Mayor, Bailiffs and Burgesses in Common Council to be assembled shall in their discretion seem meet and expedient for the common wealth thereof.

Recital.

"And for the better and more speedy execution of all such matters and things as relate to such trade and commerce, it is by the authority of the Mayor &c in this Common Council assembled, Ordained and enacted; that from henceforth there shall be every year seven Common Councilmen appointed or continued, on every first Wednesday in April yearly, who shall be called The Committee of Trade of the Town of Liverpool and shall continue in office for one whole year. . . . And such Committeemen for the time being shall be invested with full power during their continuance in office to order, make, and execute, all such acts and orders for sending up deputies, agents and witnesses, to attend Parliament and elsewhere, and the soliciting or opposing any Acts of Parliament or any clauses therein, or any other commercial purpose, and all such matters or things as shall in any way tend to the protection, increase, or advantage of such trade and commerce as it is to the interest of this town to support, acquire or augment as they in their discretion shall think meet, making entries from time to time in books to be kept for the purpose, to be reported every year to the Council and presented for their inspection.

Committee to be appointed.

Powers and Functions.

"For which purpose a grant of £250 a year, was placed at the disposal of the Committee."

Grant.

The acts of this Committee were not always as liberal as

TRADE AND COMMERCE.

their professions. In 1778 a Bill was brought into Parliament for the purpose of giving facilities for enlarging the trade with Ireland. This measure met with the most strenuous opposition of the Liverpool Corporation. *Trade with Ireland.*

"1778, April 1. Thos Birch Mayor.

"Upon a report from the Committee of Trade that a Bill is moved for in Parliament for the uniting the kingdom of Ireland with this kingdom, and putting it upon the same footing with Scotland in respect of exports and imports,

"It is Ordained that a petition be drawn as soon as the Copy of the Bill can be got, or the Bill is ordered to be brought into the House, in the name of this Corporate body with the Common Seal affixed; to be heard at the Bar of the House against the said Bill." *Petition against.*

1778, May 6th. It was reported that the petition had been prepared and the seal affixed.

It was agreed and ordered that if necessary a similar petition should be presented to the House of Lords. *Petition to Lords.*

"1778, Octr. 7. It is ordered that the thanks of the Council be presented to Bamber Gascoyne Esq (of Childwall, M.P. for Truro) for his many great, important and eminent services done this town and the trade thereof in the Honourable the House of Commons during the last session of Parliament on the Irish Trade Bills in particular, and also for the many other like services by him rendered the same in his publick characters of a Lord of Trade and Plantations, a member of Parliament, a ready and constant friend, ready on all occasions to promote the true interest and common welfare thereof; and that the Town Clerk do wait upon him with a copy of this order, and desire his acceptance thereof, as a small testimony of our gratitude to him." *Thanks to Gascoyne.*

Whilst thus opposing the grant of commercial privileges to Ireland the Council were ready to grasp at any advantage which trade with Ireland would afford.

"1778, Nov. 4. Ordered and agreed, that petitions be drawn up and prepared for liberty to be granted to merchants to export to Ireland or carry coastwise, great guns, small Arms and Ball." *Exports to Ireland.*

Considerable attention has always been paid to the state of the river and estuary, and everything pertaining to the navigation.

"1761, Sept. 9. John Blackburne Jun Mayor.

Conservancy of Navigation
"It is Ordered that a Committee be appointed to consider of the preservation of the Navigation of this Port and Harbour, and that the Town Clerk be ordered to advertize the Vessel called the Floating Light for sale. And also for all persons who have sustained any losses in their shipping or vessels &c by the fish yards &c erected within the limits of this port, that they be desired to send to the Town Clerk such proper and authentick proofs thereof as can if necessary be established before Parliament, sealed up, directed to the said Committee at the Mayor's office in the Exchange."

"1761, Oct. 10. Ordered that the Committee lately appointed for preserving the navigation of the river Mersey, be empowered to employ Mr McKenzie to survey this river, and to take such measures as to them
Survey by McKenzie. shall seem meet for preserving the said navigation; and that their expences be paid by the Corporation and they indempnifyed for any Acts they may do herein."

"1762, Aug. 10. It is Ordered, that publick notice be given to all Lords and Ladies of Manors and other proprietors of lands on the river Mersey, and their tenants, owners of land lying on the river Mersey, who
Obstructions to be removed. have set up any fish yards, cheverons, or other obstructions to navigation in the river Mersey, that they do take the same down in two months from this time, and that the notice now read in Council be published in the Liverpoole and Chester papers, and printed and delivered out. And in case they refuse to take such fish yards down, that they be cutt down, and that the persons authorized by the Council and Mr Mayor and Justices directing the same be indempnifyed at the expence of this Corporation for any act they shall do or order therein."

These measures do not appear to have been immediately successful.

"1771, Nov. 6. Ordered that the Committee have power to look into
Fish Garths. and take proper means to remove the several fish garths erected within this Port to the annoyance of the navigation thereof and destruction of the brood of fish, and to report their proceedings first to the Council before any peremptory measures are taken to have their authority and sanction."

In 1776 Mr. McKenzie's Survey was published, as appears from the following entry.

"1776, June 5. Ordered, that the Corporation do subscribe for ten setts
McKenzie's Survey. of Mr. McKenzie's survey of the sea coasts, this Corporation taking into consideration the great profit and emolument daily arising to the publick estate of this Corporation from a safe navigation to this town."

The question of the fish garths and their obstruction still

remained unsettled, and connected itself with the supply of fish to the town.

"1789, Mar. 4. John Blackburn Jun Mayor.

"The Mayor having stated to the Council that with a view to increase the supply of salt-water fish to this market, he had called several meetings in the nature of a Committee of Council to take into consideration the propriety of applying to the several Lords of Manors and other proprietors of lands on the Cheshire as well as Lancashire shores of the river Mersey for liberty to inspect and eventually to destroy the Fish Yards now set upon the same, as the most effectual means to obtain so good a purpose; and that he had sent circular letters upon the subject to the different parties interested; from several of whom he had already received very favourable answers. And now moving for a confirmation of the Council of what had been done, and to have a Committee appointed for carrying this laudable scheme into execution, and also stating the necessity of the same Committee's having powers to enquire into the situation of the Ferries upon the river Mersey, and the interests of the several proprietors, and to take measures for the better ascertaining the tolls now demanded and paid for crossing the said river and for regulating the ferrymen and other boatmen employed upon the same. *[margin: Committee on Fish supply. Ferry rights.]*

"Ordered that the Mayor and Bailiffs with nine others be appointed a Committee to enquire and report, and to take such steps as they shall think advisable in order to invest the Common Council with the conservancy of the River Mersey." *[margin: Committee on Conservancy.]*

The Ferry rights here alluded to had already been the cause of litigation.

"1774, Sept. 7. Ordered that Mr Treasurer do pay into the hands of Mr Richard Statham the sum of One hundred Pounds in order to sue out and proceed in a Commission of Chancery for the perpetuating the testimony of ancient witnesses in a cause depending in the Court of King's Bench wherein Richard Parry Price Esq' is Plaintiff and Robert Ellison is Defendant, for demanding one penny for each person landing on the Cheshire shore within the Plaintiff's alleged Manor of Birkenhead, and which demand of the Plaintiff's we apprehend he hath no right to, and if this demand is established it would greatly affect and prejudice the trade interest and the common wealth of this town of Liverpool in many instances." *[margin: Litigation with Price. Levy on Passengers.]*

It may be incidentally mentioned that if such a right could have been established, it would have amounted at the present day to an annual income of many thousands.

Lighthouses. The question of Lighthouses began to attract attention.

Act. "1761, Decr. 2. It is ordered that an application be made this Sessions of Parliament for an Act to erect Light houses or other lights at the mouth of this harbour, and for laying a duty on shipping for defraying the expence thereof, and for proper powers to remove any obstructions in the channels to preserving the navigations and fishery of the river Mersey."

The Act was obtained.

1762, August 10th. A Committee was appointed to carry out the provisions of the Act.

"1763, May 11. Ordered, that a signal house for shipping be built on the rock land in Cheshire at the expence of the Dock duties according to the plan now laid before the Council by Mr Lightoller; and that Robert Gwyllim Esq be admitted to fit up and have such rooms therein as he shall think proper during the pleasure of the Council, not prejudicing the said building nor the uses thereof."

Hoylake Lights. "1764, Apl. 16. Ordered, that a Special Committee be appointed for settling the expence of compleating the Lighthouses with power to appoint and remove the Lightkeepers and to control the receivers of the dues at Chester and Liverpool and the Inspector at Hoyl Lake."

These entries have reference only to the Lighthouses at Hoylake.

Lighthouse, Bidston. 1771, June 5th. The Dock Committee were authorized and appointed to treat with Mr. Vyner about the site and erection of a Lighthouse on Bidston Hill, and to build a Lighthouse thereon.

"1772, July 1. Ordered that the sum of twenty guineas be given to Mr Holden for his invention of the reflecting lights fixed up at the Lighthouses for this Port, and to be paid him by Mr Gerard in full of all his demands on the Trustees of the said duties.

"Ordered that the Treasurer do pay Robert Blackburne, a poor ingenious mathematician of this town with a numerous family, the sum of ten guineas, being in great distress in London, finding out the Longitude."

Point of Air Lighthouse. "1776, Jany. 3. It is Resolved and Ordered by this Council that this Corporation as Trustees of the Docks and Light-houses do oppose a Bill intended to be brought into Parliament by the Citizens and Traders of Chester for erecting Lighthouses on the Point of Air and other purposes, the same being detrimental to the navigation of this town, and that the Committee of Trade be desired to watch the motions of the promoters of such Bill."

TRADE AND COMMERCE.

The latter half of the 18th century was the period for the construction of canals and inland navigation, and Liverpool had its full share in the enterprise.

In 1755 the Act was obtained for constructing the Sankey Canal. In 1761 the Duke of Bridgewater obtained Parliamentary sanction for his canal, which brought out the genius of Brindley. The following Minute introduces him to Liverpool :— *Sankey Canal. Bridgwater Canal.*

"1764, June 27. Ordered that the Town Clerk do write to Mr Brindley, Agent to the Duke of Bridgwater, to desire he'll come over to Liverpoole in order to take a survey of the Docks about some method of cleansing the docks one by another, and that he be paid for his trouble; his scheme or method to be reported to the Council." *Brindley.*

"1765, May 1. John Tarleton Mayor.

"Mr Mayor having reported to this Council that he has been applied to by Mr Wedgwood of Staffordshire, acquainting him that some gentlemen there intend to apply to Parliament for an Act to enable them to make a navigation from the river Weaver to the river Trent, and desiring the countenance and assistance of this Corporation. It is therefore Ordered that Mr Mayor be desired to correspond with him on this subject, and if thereon the Council shall find it to be a scheme for the encouragement and promotion of trade, that they shall contribute what they shall judge necessary towards obtaining the said Act." *Wedgwood. Trent Canal.*

"1765, July 3. On a further representation made to this Council by Mr Wedgwood respecting the intended navigation from the Trent to the Mersey; It is now Ordered that this Council do make up the former order for fifty guineas to the sum of two hundred pounds, to be paid by the Treasurer in such sums and calls as shall be made for such purpose." *Council contribute.*

"1765, Decr. 11. John Crosbie Mayor.

"It is Ordered that a publick letter be wrote from or in the name of the Council to the Members of Parliament in this and the adjacent Counties, to desire their concurrence and assistance in Parliament on a Bill intended to be brought in during this sessions for making an inland Navigation from Wilden Ferry in Derbyshire into the River Mersey, or to join the Duke of Bridgwater's Canal, and that this Council will give the Undertakers all the interest and assistance they can." *Canal to Derbyshire.*

A bold scheme was broached by Brindley for carrying the canal over the Mersey and continuing it to Liverpool, which it is to be regretted was not carried out. *Canal across Mersey.*

244   CHAP. III, A.D. 1760—1800.

"1768, Novr. 23. Matthew Stronge Mayor.

Trent Canal. "It is desired by this Council on a letter from the Proprietors of the Trent Navigation to Mr Alderman Tarleton (the Mayor during the previous year) acquainting him of a meeting intended to be held at Trentham on the 29th inst. concerning carrying on or continuing the said Navigation by a Bridge Acqueduct and path or road from Runcorn over the Mersey to Liverpoole, and also from the said Staffordshire Canal to Chester; that John Tarleton and Richard Hughes Esq^{rs} be desired to attend the said meeting on behalf of the town and trade of Liverpoole, to hear the result,

Continuation to Liverpool. and to know whether the Duke of Bridgewater will join his Canal to this intended Navigation and upon what terms and conditions; and that Mr Brindley be desired to survey the land which this intended Canal to Liverpoole is to go through from the said bridge, and to make and give in estimates of the charge of building the said bridge, and compleating the said Canal, and that the following gentlemen Mr Mayor, Mr Tarleton and Alderman Hughes be appointed a Committee to write or wait on the landowners and make their report."

Nothing more is found in the records relating to this subject except the following entry:—

Trent Reservoir. "1796, Octr. 24. A petition was presented by the Corporation to the House of Commons setting forth that the Canal from the Trent to the Mersey, which was executed at great hazard and expence, has been productive of very important advantages to the town and port of Liverpool; that a Bill was being promoted for enabling the Proprietors to form a reservoir and make a branch to the town of Leek, and praying that the said Bill may pass into a law."

The connection of the East and West Coasts by means of a navigable canal attracted considerable attention at this time, and was brought under the notice of the Corporation as follows:—

"1767, Novr. 4. Wm Pownall Mayor.

Grant for Canal to Hull. "It is Ordered that the sum of two hundred pounds be paid or given to the persons concerned in promoting a navigable Canal from the port of Hull to the port of Liverpoole according to the plan laid before the Council—£100 on the bill being brought in, and £100 on its being passed into an Act."

This was the precursor of the Leeds and Liverpool Canal, which has been so successful an undertaking.

"1768, July 6. Charles Goore Mayor.

Grant for Canal survey. "It is Ordered that this Corporation do give the sum of fifty pounds towards the expence of a resurvey of the intended navigation from Leeds to Liverpoole, and as the Committee for the said Navigation by their agents now appearing, request it, we recommend that Mr James Brindley one of the surveyors thereof, be paid to the order of the said Committee when such survey is finished and laid before the Council. This grant is exclusive of the sum of £200 voted by this Council formerly for this intended Navigation."

Brindley.

"1769, Jan. 11. It is now ordered on reading a petition to Parliament praying for liberty to bring in a bill to make a navigable canal from the town of Leeds to terminate at or near the North Lady's Walk and to communicate with the new dock now making in the town of Liverpoole, that this Council will give their assistance, on condition that it be provided that the said canal shall terminate at or near the said Lady's Walk, and they to lock down to the sea shore there at their own expence, and the Trustees or Commissioners in the said Bill do undertake not to come on the said sea shore there, but that powers be reserved and vested in the Trustees for the Docks at Liverpoole to make a cutt or canal from the new dock now in making at Liverpoole, to join, open, and communicate with such navigable canal, and which additional cutt shall be done at the expence of and out of the Dock Duties, having such a reasonable or moderate tonnage or duty as shall be granted them for this purpose by Parliament."

Leeds Canal.
Lady's Walk.
Cut to Dock.

"1769, Jan. 20. Ordered that the petition now read for making the cutt or canal, and the agreement thereupon be engrossed and passed under the Common Seal."

Petition for Canal.

The Act for constructing the canal was delayed for a time.

1771, December 20th. The following entry occurs:—

"The sense of this Council is desired to be taken on this question. Whether the intended canal from Liverpoole to Wigan will be of publick utility to the town or not?

"Agreed, 'that it is of such utility.'"

Resolution.

A Committee was then appointed to examine and report on the Bill, which was passed in the ensuing session.

"1774, Octr. 5. John Parr Mayor.

"It is ordered on reading the petition of several of the proprietors of the Canal from Leeds to Liverpoole, that this Council as Trustees for the docks at Liverpoole will not admit of the said proprietors or company of the said canal making any canal of communication into any of the said docks at Liverpoole, nor will or legally can the said Trustees make any such canal, docks or works for them upon or through any part of the

Objections to Canal to Dock.

North Shore lately by the Council set apart for the use of the said docks. But that the Company must make (if they will have any such) all such docks or works on the sea strand to the northwards of the said ground so laid out for the use of the docks aforesaid at their own expence, as any such communication with the docks might be attended with many and great inconveniences and interruption to the trade of the town and port, and to the use of the docks by such ships and vessells as pay dock duties for the same."

"1776, Feb. 7. James Clemens Mayor.

Conferences. "Whereas the Committee appointed to meet the Commissioners of the Leeds Canal have now brought into the Council the plan of the works intended to be made on the sea shore below the Lady's Walk at the north end of the town, by those gentlemen according to the plan now produced, for the use of the said canal.

Bridge. "It is Ordered that the said Committee of the Council have power to meet and agree with them to or on the said plan now produced. Provided that the said Leeds Commissioners agree in the first place to build a good capacious and sufficient stone bridge and arch over the publick road on the said shore, and leave the road on or along the same shore twenty yards wide; and report their proceedings to the Council to be confirmed."

Decision against Junction. "1776, April 3. It is Ordered that this Council do abide by their former Order made on the 7th day of February last in respect to the application concerning the locking down and making a bridge and other necessary works for the canal on the sea shore. And that on further application by certain others of the said proprietors for more works to be done at the publick expence by this Council thereat, and according to a certain written paper dated the 1st day of April 1776, stiled 'At a Committee Meeting held at Mr Wrigley's the Golden Lyon in Liverpool on Monday the 1st day of April 1776' requesting the same. Wherefore we say and give 'em for answer: We shall abide by our said former order of Council and shall not recede from the same to comply with such unconditioned requisitions."

The scheme was therefore abandoned, but at a subsequent period resumed.

"1790, April 7. Thos Smyth Mayor.

Opposition to Canal to Dock. "It appearing to this Council that a Bill is now depending in Parliament to enable the proprietors of the Leeds Canal to vary the line of their navigation, and there being no restraining clause inserted preserving the rights of the Corporation; It is Ordered, that the members for this town be instructed and requested to attend the Bill in Committee and take care that a clause be inserted reserving to the Corporation all their franchises, liberties, privileges, tolls, customs, rights, estates and interests whatsoever."

This communication by a cut and locks down to the river was never carried out, but under the powers of an Act passed in 1844, access was provided more to the northward. *Withdrawn.*

In 1790 the Corporation came into collision with the great Duke of Bridgewater. The Duke had purchased an extensive site, south of the Salthouse Dock, where he had constructed docks and warehouses as the river terminus of his navigation. Mr. Wm. Rathbone possessed on lease from the Corporation premises immediately adjoining on the north. Both the Duke and Mr. Rathbone carried out works projecting into the river, which were deemed objectionable by the Council and ordered to be removed. Subsequently an arrangement was come to with Mr. Rathbone, by which a portion of his alleged encroachment was allowed to remain. His Grace felt aggrieved at this, and commenced a suit against Mr. Rathbone, which led to the following letter, couched in a much more humble style than that usually affected by the Corporation. *Dispute with Duke of Bridgewater.*

"1790, June 2.
"A copy of a letter dated the 12th day of April last addressed by the Mayor to his Grace the Duke of Bridgwater, being laid before this Council and which letter is couched in the following terms, vizt—
"'My Lord.
"'I am directed by the gentlemen of the Corporation of Liverpool to request your Grace will allow me on their behalf to represent to you the extreme concern which they feel that the slightest misunderstanding should ever have arisen between them and a nobleman whom they regard with such sentiments as they do your Grace. They beg leave to assure your Grace that they entertain a due sense of the number and importance of the advantages which this town and neighbourhood derive from that extensive and well directed spirit of enterprise and liberality by which your Grace has been so eminently distinguished. Conscious as they are at the same time of having no possible interest to serve, or aim to attain but the public good, and unable as they are to see in what respect the advantage of that public can run counter to the interests of your Grace, they flatter themselves and believe no difficulty whatever could remain if your Grace was once in possession of their real wishes and sentiments. They have *Letter.*

Apology.

248   CHAP. III, A.D. 1760—1800.

Deputation. therefore commissioned me to request that your Grace will permit a deputation from their body, vested with ample powers to treat for them, to wait upon your Grace at Worsley or elsewhere ; as they hope that by an interview the interests of each party would be immediately and essentially served, and that they should no longer have to lament an interruption of that harmony which the high opinion and very sincere respect they entertain for your Grace makes them peculiarly solicitous to obtain and preserve.

"'I have the honour to be with all possible respect
"'My Lord
"'Your Grace's most obedient and humble servant,
"'THO. SMYTH Mayor.'"

The Duke's reply is in a somewhat lordly strain.

"'Mr Mayor

Letter from Duke. "'Since the application I made to the Corporation in 1776 for the extension of my premises, which was refused me as not consistent with the safety of the Port of Liverpool, and which at that time was also refused Mr Rathbone for the like reasons, but afterwards it being granted him I applied a second time to Mr Birch the then Mayor, but from that application I received no answer. The expence Mr Rathbone's extension has occasioned me, and the apparent disposition of the Corporation has prevented my applying any more except for that I had a right to demand, and, notwithstanding the safety of the river above alluded to, another extension has been granted Mr Rathbone and others, made still more to *Declines Deputation.* my prejudice. For these reasons I beg to be excused from complying with your request, being determined to take the opinion of a Jury.

"'I am your Hble Serv'
"'BRIDGEWATER.'

Rathbone. " And the Trustees of the late William Rathbone having presented a petition to this Council, stating that his Grace has instituted a fresh suit against them, and praying to be defended at the expence of the Corporation."

Resolution. "It is therefore Ordered that the former Committee be, and they are hereby authorized and empowered to take such steps for the defence thereof by Mr Statham the attorney for the said Trustees, as may be thought advisable, this Council thinking themselves aggrieved by the former suit, and that the expenses thereof be paid by the Treasurer."

The various purchases of lands for the extension of the docks are duly recorded, but need not here be specified.

Strand. The strand forming part of the site of the Prince's Dock came into the possession of Lord Derby, as a portion of the manorial estate of the Moore's, in 1712.

TRADE AND COMMERCE.

"1790, Feby. 3. A letter from Mr Waring, Lord Derby's steward respecting the strand and premises on the side of the New Quay and Bath Street having been read to the Council,

"Ordered, that the Mayor (with four others) be appointed a Committee with full powers to treat for the absolute purchase of the same on the best terms they can either by reference or otherwise." Purchase.

"1790, March 4. Ordered that in consequence of the Committee appointed by the last Council having agreed with Lord Derby for the purchase of the land and premises in question for the sum of three thousand pounds, the said sum be paid by the Treasurer and allowed in his accounts provided a good and sufficient title be made to the satisfaction of the Council." Lord Derby.

The Rating of the Docks at this time occupied considerable attention, but it has been referred to in the previous pages. Rating of Docks.

In 1794 an effort was made on the renewal of the Charter of the East India Company, to have the trade thrown open. Mr. (afterwards Sir John) Gladstone came forward prominently in support of the measure, which had to wait forty years before it was conceded. The only notice in the records is the following:— Gladstone.

"1794, Feby. 5. Ordered that the application of Messrs Gore, Billinge and Fergusson to this Council for the payment of their bills for advertizing and printing upon a late intended application to Parliament to lay open the East India trade, amounting to £79 5s. be referred to the Committee of Trade, who are hereby empowered to make such order therein as to them shall seem meet." East India Trade.

In 1793 the declaration of war with France on February 11th, and the commencement of the revolutionary struggle, most seriously affected the commerce of Liverpool. A general panic set in, and numerous mercantile houses of the highest standing were prostrated in ruin. Confidence was at an end. Produce could not be disposed of, and bills could not be met. A run upon the banks took place, one of which, that of Caldwell, Smyth & Co., succumbed to the pressure. Commercial Panic.

The measures taken by the leading men, acting with the aid and support of the Council, were prompt and successful. Measures taken.

The entries on the records are very full and complete.

"1793, March 20. Clayton Tarleton Mayor.

Failures. "The Mayor having reported to this Council that the late extensive failures, particularly of some great Commercial and Banking Houses in London were almost immediately followed with the failure of a very old and principal Banking house in Liverpool; that the latter failure had now caused such an alarm in this town and its neighbourhood, that not only *Banks.* the other Banking-houses were greatly distressed, but there was an apprehension of a general calamity to the merchants, traders, and inhabitants of this place, and to the County of Lancaster at large, from the shock to public confidence, and from the want of immediate pecuniary resource. *Meeting.* That under this impression he had this day held a meeting of some of the principal merchants in the Exchange, at which several resolutions were entered into, and they had unanimously subscribed the following paper earnestly requesting him to convene the Common Council, to consider *Application to Bank of England.* whether it might not be proper to offer the Corporate Seal to the Bank of England for a loan of money to assist the credit of this place by an application under the direction of a Committee, composed of an equal number of Members of the Common Council and of respectable Merchants out of the Council, or to consider whether it was possible for the Common Council by taking measures in their Corporate capacity to avert the common ruin that seemed to threaten the commerce of the town.

"It is therefore now unanimously resolved by this Council, that the very unprecedented and truly alarming state of the public credit of this country and of this town in particular, does in the opinion of this Council well *Council Meeting.* justify the Meeting of the Merchants held here this day and the requisition made for the convening of this Special Council.

"That the representations now made of the distresses of all commercial persons in this town, do well deserve the very serious attention of this Council so as to induce them to consider whether any and what effectual *Question of Relief.* relief can be afforded in their Corporate capacity. That they therefore do now nominate the following six members, viz' the Mayor, Mr Ald^a Earle, Mr Ald^a Wm Crosbie Junr, Mr Ald^a Case, Mr Brooks, and Mr Statham a *Committee.* Committee to confer with the same number of gentlemen appointed by the Merchants at large at their meeting held this day in the Exchange; that such Committee be requested to prepare themselves with a report of what they may consider proper to be done; the same to be made at a further Special Council which the Mayor is now requested to call to be held to-morrow evening at six o'clock."

Requisition. The requisition was signed by 112 of the leading merchants of the town, amongst whom we find John Gladstone, John Bolton, Sir George Dunbar, Edwd. Falkner, William Harper,

William Earle, William Rathbone, and many others of the highest standing.

No time was lost in taking immediate measures.

A special Council was held on the following day, March 21st, when a report, hastily drawn up by the Committee, was presented. <small>Special Council.</small>

It set forth,

"That they found after an interview with the four existing Banking-houses in the town that the sum of a hundred thousand pounds was wanted and would be sufficient to answer the present exigencies. . . . that it was expedient for the preservation of public credit that some speedy method should be adopted of raising the money. . . . that the most desirable mode would be by an application from the Corporation to the Directors of the Bank of England through the medium of Mr Pitt, the Chancellor of the Exchequer, and of the Lords of the Treasury. . . . that such loan when obtained should be advanced under the direction of the Committee through the local Bankers, on satisfactory securities within the space of fifteen months, beyond which period it was their opinion no further advances would be required." <small>Report. Second application to Bank of England.</small>

The Report further suggests that the loan should be advanced on the Bond of the Corporation, subject to such conditions as may be found necessary. <small>Loan.</small>

The Report having been read to the Council, it was ordered:—

"1793, March 21st.

"That such Report be confirmed; and a deputation was nominated to proceed to London to wait on the Chancellor of the Exchequer and the Bank of England." <small>Council confirm.</small>

The application was not successful. <small>Application declined.</small>

"1793, April 15. At a Special Council.

"It having been reported by the Mayor that the negociation with the Bank of England for the loan of £100,000 on the Bond of this Corporation not having been successful, he and the other delegates from the very urgent necessity of removing with the greatest expedition possible the present stagnation of credit in Liverpool, thought it their duty to apply, and accordingly have applied to Parliament by petition in the names of the Mayor and others of the Common Council then in London on behalf of themselves and the rest of the Council, for leave to bring in a Bill for <small>Petition to Parliament.</small>

the purpose of empowering the Corporation to issue negociable notes to a certain amount and for a given period, on the credit of the estate of the said Corporation.

Delegation. "This Council do fully in all respects ratify and confirm every step which has been taken, and hereby fully empower the delegates to take every measure which shall seem to them expedient and necessary in order to carry into effect the said petition."

Then follows the text of the petition which sets forth

Petition. "That the trade and commerce of the town have of late years greatly increased, and were continuing to do so till the stagnation of credit which has lately taken place both here and in other parts of the kingdom checked the same, and occasioned serious alarms of further inconvenience.

Danger. "That in the event of such a want of credit being even of a short duration, your petitioners have great reason to apprehend the town of Liverpool will be greatly injured thereby, and that the manufacturers and traders throughout the County of Lancaster will feel the effects of it to a very great extent, by which the interest of the public and of individuals will be materially affected and the estate of the Corporation of Liverpool will be much lessened in its value.

Proposed issue of Notes. "That this alarming evil may, your petitioners humbly conceive, be remedied by authority being given to the Corporation to issue negociable notes for different sums of money, in the whole considerably below the value of their estates after making allowance for their present debts, the notes to be payable with lawful interest thereon or otherwise, at a time to be limited; provision being made that the estate of the said Corporation shall be subjected to the discharge of the said notes at the period at which they shall become payable.

"With this view your petitioners are desirous of laying before the House a precise statement of their property and of the engagements to which it is liable in order to enable the House to judge of the grounds of this application."

Act passed. An Act was accordingly brought in and passed, giving power to the Council to issue during two years, for value received, Notes payable to Bearer for the respective sums of £50 and £100, with interest not exceeding legal interest, and *Amount of issue.* without interest notes of £5 and £10 respectively. The amount of the notes not to exceed £300,000.

There were various minor regulations as to the issue and withdrawal of the notes. The amount of the notes issued was to be laid annually before Parliament.

The Council were prohibited from trading in Merchandize, but might, during the three years of the Act, buy or sell bullion or Bills of Exchange, and might sell any goods deposited with them as security for money lent. *Regulations.*

A joint Committee of Councillors and outside merchants was appointed to conduct the business.

The scheme was fully carried out and proved a success. *Success.*

1795, March 12th. John Shaw, Mayor.

The Annual Report of the Negotiable Note Office was presented by which it appeared that the notes issued up to the 25th February amounted to £140,390, and the value of the securities deposited to £155,907 16s. 6d., that the value of the notes then in circulation was £35,315. The report stated that much essential good had been derived from the institution and the Committee were of opinion that an extension of the Act for three years longer would be a further benefit. *Annual Report. Notes and Securities.*

The extension however was limited to one year only.

1776, Sept. 7th. Thos. Naylor, Mayor.

The Loan Office Committee presented a report of their proceedings preparatory to the final winding up of the operations under the Act, which appear to have been eminently beneficial and satisfactory, the loans having all been paid off and the notes withdrawn. *Report. Winding up.*

The whole transaction reflects great credit on the public spirit and sagacity of the Liverpool Merchants of the day, in warding off a great public calamity, and tiding over an unprecedented crisis in the commercial world.

STREETS AND BUILDINGS.

1761, March 4th. The following record requires an explanation which is not forthcoming.

Fortifications

"Mr Dawson, his Majesty's Engineer for the fortifications now making at Liverpoole signifying by letter to Mr Mayor that the Honourable Board of Ordnance had been informed by some persons that the people in Liverpoole did not desire any further fortifications to be made to the town than what are already contracted for, and desireing to know Mr Mayor's sentiments hereon; which letter being now laid before this Council, they are unanimously of opinion that the said fortifications be compleated according to the order of his late Majesty and the plan settled for such purpose; and that this our intention be signifyed to the said Captain Dawson, to be transmitted to the said Board of Ordnance."

It is difficult to see where these projected fortifications could have been placed. In Perry's Map of 1769 the only indication of any fortifications is a 14 gun battery on the west side of St. Nicholas's churchyard, to which the minute may possibly allude.

Powder Magazines.

"1761, Sept. 9. Ordered that a piece of land or ground, part of the Wast of this Corporation be given to his Majesty, his heirs and successors to build Magazines on, under the like conditions the land for the fortification is given."

The land in question was situated at the top of Duke Street near the North end of St. James's Walk.

The Council at this period were not unmindful of the amenities of the town.

"1762, March 3. Ordered that the Walk, Cop, or Road, at the top of Quarry Hill be repaired under the inspection and direction of Thomas Johnson Esquire, a gentleman of this Council."

"1763, March 2. William Gregson Mayor.

"Ordered, That Mr Mayor and Bailiffs, Mr Johnson and Mr Manesty be appointed a Committee to go to Mr Alderman Gildart and talk with

STREETS AND BUILDINGS.

him about the purchasing of the Rope-walk at the top of Duke Street, or such part thereof as is not sold, and report the price he asks for the same to the Council to make it into a publick Walk, if it shall be thought proper to buy it . . And it is also Ordered that an Estimate of finishing the Walk at the Quarry Hill be laid before this Council next Council day, and that £20 be laid out thereon in the mean time." Public Walks

The arrangement was made, and the public walk was constructed, at first named Mount Sion, but afterwards St James's Walk, in the Mayoralty of Thos. Johnson in 1766. St. James's Walk.

"1768, Decr. 7. It is Ordered that John Bridge have liberty to enclose and take in a piece of ground to the South and eastwards of his house on Sion Walk on Quarry Hill Waste according to the plan now produced, and to take down the present Powder Magazine and Watch house, and rebuild the same in some other convenient place as shall be fixed by the Mayor and the Committee of Views with the consent and approbation of his Majesty's Board of Ordnance [1] and to convert the said land into a Bowling Green, but not to be suffered to build any houses or other buildings except an alcove on the said Green." Magazine removed. Bowling Green.

"1771, June 5. John Sparling Mayor.
"Ordered that John Callender be allowed the sum of £20 a year, to look after and take care of the North and South Public Walks; finding all trees, gravel, labourer's tools, and all other things relative thereto for such yearly sum to the satisfaction of Mr Mayor and Bailiffs for the time being and during the pleasure of this Council." Public Walks.

"1777, June 4. William Crosbie Mayor.
"It is ordered that Mr Mayor and the before-mentioned gentlemen do purchase at a fair price a Windmill and Premises on Quarry Hill, from Mr Drinkwater, to prevent its being purchased by others who are about buying it and might convert it into some use that might detriment the Public Walk." Windmill.

Up to this date Oldhall Street terminated northwards at the Lady's Walk, now the site of the Canal Basin. Beyond this extended a narrow occupation road called Mile House Lane, leading into the fields. Oldhall Street.

"1777, Nov. 5. It is Ordered that the Corporation do purchase Mr Richard Gildart's interest in Mile House Lane and Maiden's Green for the sum of £164; and this land to be applied for making publick Mile House Lane, Maiden's Green.

---

[1] It was built on the slope of Brownlow Hill, where it remained until the construction of the Magazines at Liscard.

roads thro' and for other the purposes and uses mentioned in the Committee's report; viz¹ ' The Committee appointed to treat with Mr Rich⁴ Gildart for the purchase of his interest in Mile House Lane, to lay or make a publick road through it, report : that they think it greatly for the interest of the town to have a road thro' it and have agreed with him for the purchase of his interest therein, but recommend it to the Council not to open any road &c there 'till they see what the landholders adjacent will do for making the road from the North Lady's Walk to this land; then to lay out a sufficient road thro' it, and sell the remainder to the adjoining landowners.' "

In this new street it was proposed to build a new Gaol.

New Gaol. "1777, Feby. 5. Ordered that Mr John Hope Architect be authorized to send for the plans &c of the New Gaol in London called Newgate as lately rebuilt; but the cost thereof not to exceed Seven Guineas."

Gaol insufficient. "1783, Feby. 4. The Grand Jury at the last Quarter Sessions of the Peace held for this borough on the 29ᵗʰ January last, having reported that the present Common Gaol of this town is totally insufficient for the purposes intended; and that there is great reason to dread the most alarming consequences from its present confined situation ;

Committee. "It is Ordered, that a Committee consisting of the Mayor, Aldermen, Bailiffs and the Town Clerk be appointed to consider and report on the most proper place whereon to construct a new gaol with a plan, estimate and such other observations as may occur."

Purchase of old Lady's Walk. "1784, March 8. Ordered that a Committee, consisting of the Mayor, Aldermen &c be authorized to treat with Lord Sefton for the purchase of his reversionary interest in the old Lady's Walk, and also with the owners of the ground to the North and South thereof for the purpose of building a new and compleat gaol; that they in the meantime furnish themselves with the best plans that can be procured, and be likewise empowered to do every other Act which may tend to facilitate so good and necessary a work."

Purchase of Land. "1784, Aug. 4. On the Motion of Mr Mayor signifying that two fields near the Canal, the one belonging to Mr Jackson, the other to Mr Waterworth were to be sold, and the same having been purchased by the Committee appointed, viz Mr Waterworth's at the rate of £300 per customary acre and Mr Jackson's at the sum of £735 for the whole of the field ;

"It is Ordered that the purchase money be paid by the Treasurer on a good title being made."

Gaol. "1785, Feby. 2. Ordered, that the Committee before appointed be again to proceed in carrying on a plan for building a gaol within this town."

STREETS AND BUILDINGS.

"1789, Apl. 1. John Blackburne Jun Mayor.

"Ordered, that the Overseer of the New Gaol do produce to the next Council such plans and sections thereof as are now in his possession together with the present state of the said gaol, and that the Treasurer do likewise produce an account of the expences already incurred in the erection thereof." Plans of Gaol.

Before the gaol had been well completed, it became necessary to divert it from its original purpose.

"1793, June 5. Mr Foster Jun' reported to the Council that under the direction of the Mayor he had entered into a contract which the Mayor had signed for letting certain parts of the new gaol for the purpose of detaining therein the French prisoners of War on terms and conditions approved by the Council." (¹) French Prisoners.

The roads giving access to the town received attention at this time. In 1760, the turnpike road to Prescot and Warrington was completed, and not long afterwards the subject of the North road was taken up. Roads.

"1770, Decr. 10. John Sparling Mayor.

"It is Ordered that this Council do give the sum of One Hundred Pounds towards obtaining an Act of Parliament for making a Turnpike Road from Patrick's Cross or opposite the Flashes in Liverpoole through Ormskirk to the town of Preston in the County of Lancaster upon these conditions; that on account that the town of Liverpoole has already made a good pavement on this road as far as their liberties extend, be excused from doing any statute work on this road during the turnpike term, and that the like clause of exemptions be inserted in the intended Bill as is in the Prescot &c Turnpike Bill, and that no gate shall be erected nigher Liverpoole than the four mile stone from Liverpoole towards Ormskirk, and that the said One Hundred Pounds shall be paid to the agents or managers when the said Bill shall be brought into the House of Commons and not before. And on this further express condition, that the Trustees of the said Bill shall, after passing of the Bill begin with repairing the said intended Turnpike road at the said Patrick's Cross and proceed with the repair thereof as far as Ormskirk as fast as the money to be taken on this part of the road between Liverpoole and Ormskirk will admit of, any thing in a late Order of Council to the contrary notwithstanding. And if any differences should arise in respect to such clause of exemption or other matters not being principal things that can much affect the rights or North Road.
Prescot Road.
Contribution.
Provision for Differences.

(¹) *Vide supra*, p. 234.

interest of the town of Liverpoole, the Mayor and any six of the Council be appointed a Committee for such purpose, and to agree upon a list of tolls to be taken and to ascertain the toll upon turf carts, with the promoters of the said Bill or their Agents."

Streets.

The improvement of the Streets began to force itself upon the notice of the Council. They were originally narrow, tortuous, and ill paved, and have cost enormous sums to place in proper condition.

The first movement was to widen Castle Street.

"1774, Sept. 7. John Parr Mayor.

Proposed Widening.
"Ordered that the plan of widening Castle Street be postponed and taken into consideration against the next Council day."

"1774, Octr. 5. It is Ordered, that Mr Mayor and Bailiffs for the time

Committee. being (with 14 others) be appointed a Committee to consider of ways and means of raising money for defraying the expence of taking down one side of Castle Street &c according to the plan produced in Council for such purpose, reporting their proceedings from time to time to the Council."

"1782, April 3. George Case Mayor.

"It is Ordered that the Mayor and Treasurer be empowered to agree

Purchases. for the purchase of the premises of Robt Moss, contiguous to the West side of the Exchange, agreeable to the plan now produced, so as such purchase money does not exceed the sum of £2800, and a good and sufficient title being made."

"1782, May 1. Ordered that the contract made with Mr Moss for the purchase of the houses and shambles adjoining to the Exchange for

Confirmed. £2700, is hereby ratified and confirmed."

The subject slept for three years longer when it was revived.

"1785, Decr. 20. Improvement Committee.

"It is the unanimous opinion of this Committee that an application be made to Parliament for the improvement and better government of the said town.

Isolating Exchange.
"It being the opinion of this Committee that it would greatly tend both to the ornament and improvement of this town if the Exchange was insulated.

"Resolved that every necessary step be taken for that purpose.

"It is likewise the unanimous opinion of this Committee that the open-

Widening Castle Street.
ing and widening of Castle Street from Saint George's Church to the Exchange and from the Exchange northward, and from the Exchange to

the eastward down Dale Street, and also Fenwick Street would be highly beneficial.

"Ordered that an advertisement be inserted in the Liverpool Papers, setting forth that a Committee will sit in the Exchange on Tuesday next and on every subsequent Tuesday untill further notice to consider of the best methods of improving the town; and that such Committee will be ready to receive and inspect such plans from any persons who may please to offer the same." — Committee.

"1786, Jany. 10. Charles Pole Mayor.

"Resolved, that it is the unanimous opinion of this Council that a Bill be drawn and brought into Parliament for the purpose of improving and widening the streets. — Bill.

"Resolved also, that this Council do concur in opinion with the Committee this day held for the above purpose, that the improvement of this town be confined to the plan then laid before the Committee, with the further addition, that the intended street from Castle Street to Fenwick Street be continued from thence to Goree Causeway, and also to open the whole extent of Dale Street not exceeding 20 yds in breadth, and that the widening of Tythe Barn Street to Patrick's Cross be dropt at present.[1] — Brunswick Street. Tithebarn Street.

"Resolved, that it is the unanimous opinion of this Council that in the reselling of the Freehold land of inheritance, to be purchased for the purpose of widening the streets, that each owner or occupier shall have the election of having his ground again, either as land of inheritance, or as leasehold under the Corporation, at his option." — Reselling Land.

"1786, Feby. 1. Ordered, that Mr Statham, Mr John Gregson and Mr Brooks do, as soon as they conveniently can, go up to London to solicit the intended Bill for improveing the streets, and to prefer the petition for that purpose, and that they have a discretionary power to alter, defeat, or add such other clauses to such Bill as they may be advised, or as may be thought proper. — Improvement Bill.

"Ordered also, That the petition and Bill, together with an abstract thereof, be laid upon the table in the Town Hall for the inspection and perusal of the inhabitants, and that an advertizment to the above effect be published on the next Monday's Liverpoole paper."

1786, Feby. 6th. The petition was read and the Common Seal affixed:

"Ordered unanimously. That the thanks of this Council be given to Mr Richard Statham for the very great professional services he has rendered to this Corporation as one of the Select Committee in the purchasing of houses for the purpose of widening the streets in this town, — Thanks to Statham.

---

(1) Dale Street was only widened under this Act from the Town Hall to Moorfields.

and for the improvement thereof, and that Mr Statham receive a reasonable recompense for his trouble and attendance, and for his journey to London."

Committee. "1786, Apl. 8. Resolved and Ordered that the following gentlemen to wit William Crosbie Jun' (with seven others) be appointed a Committee to carry into execution the purposes and designs of the said Act so far as the same relate to the opening, widening, purchasing and selling the several streets and passages, to the supplying the town with water, to the levelling of the streets, and altering and amending the common sewers. And also to the elevation of any future buildings.

Thanks to Lord Derby. "Resolved unanimously, that the thanks of this Council be given to the Right Honorable the Earl of Derby (12th Earl) for his Lordship's great attention and support to the Bill for the intended improvements in this town."

Sewerage. This Act amongst a multitude of other provisions, gave power to improve the sewerage. The necessity for this had assumed a very serious aspect. The course of the old Pool stream along the present Paradise Street and Whitechapel had been filled in and converted into streets under the names of Frog Lane and Common Shore. The level being very little above the tideway of the Mersey, any high tide stopped the flow and inundated the tenements along the line.

Before the passing of the Improvement Act of 1786 some steps had been taken to give relief.

Eyes's Plan. "1785, Decr. 20. Resolved, that a Plan be provided by Mr Eyes setting forth the best methods of carrying off the water from different parts of the town; the present tunnels and water courses being in the opinion of the Select Committee very insufficient and inconvenient."

Some action was taken immediately after the passing of the Act.

Flooding. "1787, Octr. 23. Ordered that Mr Eyes do immediately take every necessary measure in order to prevent the water in future incommoding the tenants of the houses in Paradise Street, by flowing into the cellars on the occasion of the fall of rain."

Blackburne's Plan. "1788, Sept. 16. Mr Blackburne the Architect from London appeared, and promised to furnish this Committee with the most complete plan possible of improving our present Tunnells."

STREETS AND BUILDINGS.

Nothing came of this project. Three years afterwards we find the following record:

"1791, March 22. This Committee having taken into consideration the necessity of making such additional Sewers and other alterations as would be most likely to prevent the overflowing of Whitechapel and Paradise Street &c, and having examined the plans and the following report made to them by the Surveyors, vizt— [Committee.]

"'To Wm Crosbie Junr Esqr Chairman of the Select Committee

"'Sir

"'We beg leave to inform you that in consequence of the heavy rains which fell last night and this morning, and the inadequate state of the sewers to carry off the water, Whitechapel, with the lower ends of all the streets communicating with it, was overflowed from the bottom of Lord Street to the Haymarket as also the lower end of Cable Street and Thomas Street, by which the inhabitants of the cellars in those streets were reduced to the greatest distress, and it is a lamentable truth that many of the people were not acquainted with their situation till they found the water coming into their beds. We should be wanting in duty if we did not in the most earnest manner point out the means by which this dreadful evil may be remedied, which can be by no other method than by enlarging the sewer in Whitechapel and Paradise Street, and carrying it through Cooper's Row to join the sewer already made along the North side of the Old Dock; to make the Tunnel proposed some time since from the bottom of Richmond Row under the new Gaol to the River Mersey near the Fish Dock, and to raise the present pavement in Whitechapel, Paradise Street, and the ends of the streets communicating with them so as to make a gradual descent from the Haymarket to the Docks in which distance there is a fall of at least five feet. [Report. Recommendation.]

"'We are still of opinion that notwithstanding the proposed new sewers, it is possible that in very heavy rains, they may not be able to carry off all the water which will be brought into them from the new streets and roads which are accumulating round the town, with that rapidity which may be wish'd for, owing to the want of a proper descent as there is scarcely a perceptible fall from the bottom of the watercourse near the Dog Kennels where it empties itself into the Dock. But if it should so happen that by excessive rains at tide time the water could not be convey'd thro' the sewers, it would—when the streets are raised as proposed rise through the gratings, and run over the surface of the pavement into the dock, by which means it is impossible that a similar accident can again happen in those streets.'" [Results.]

Notwithstanding this alleged impossibility, the overflow of

water when the rains and the tides acted in combination continued for another half century to do serious mischief.

Bold Street. "1786, Feby. 1. Ordered that a Special Committee be appointed for the purpose of surveying Bold Street and the several cross streets leading into it, as they are at present laid down in the plan on the lease lately granted to Mr Jonas Bold, and of considering whether any and what alterations ought to be made in the situation of such cross streets so as to form a direct communication from Bold Street through Mr Thomas Seel's *Slater Street.* field to Suffolk Street, and also for the purpose of considering and of recommending such a situation as they may think eligible for the erecting other Almshouses in the room of those now at the upper end of Hanover Street and in Dale Street, and at the back of the Infirmary."

Almshouses. "1786, Sept. 6. Ordered that the Committee for removing the present Almshouses and fixing upon a situation where they may be built to the best advantage be empowered to proceed in the erection of such buildings as they may think most proper and convenient for the intended purpose, and to enter into such agreements as they may think most conducive to carry their removal into effect."

Dog Kennels. "1788, May 13. Ordered that in consideration of the Gentlemen of the Liverpool Hound Hunt removing their Dog Kennels from Sick Man's Lane to Bank Hall Marsh they be allowed old materials not exceeding the value of ten pounds."

"1788, Octr. 1. Thomas Earle Mayor.

"Ordered that the sale or otherwise of the field at the top of Duke Street in possession of Mr Wagner be referred to Messrs. Mason and *Gallows Mill.* Bourne's Committee, and that the Mill called Gallows Mill be taken down, and that the Trustees of the Prescot Turnpike Road be applied to for allowing a proportionable part of the expence, as it will be of great benefit to that part of such road."

Providing Work. "1789, Jany. 9. John Foster Jun' having reported that a considerable number of Bricklayers, Masons, Plaisterers and Carpenters now out of work—in consequence of the present inclemency of the weather—might be employed in pulling down several buildings within the line of improvement, Ordered that such of these men as are proper and willing be employed in the above business, the artificers to be allowed eighteen pence per day, and every able labourer twelve pence per day under the direction of John Foster Jun' and that a letter be written to each master tradesman in the above branches to recommend such men now out of employ as they think deserving."

"1790, Feby. 3. Thos Smyth Mayor.

Flashes. "Mr Harrison's petition respecting a lease to be granted him of the Watering Place called the Flashes for the purpose of opening a communication between Dale Street and Tythe Barn Street according to a plan annexed, having been read: it is Ordered that the same be referred to the gentlemen of the Select Committee, who are requested to make their report to the next Council."

This refers to the formation of the street now called Hatton Garden.

"1764. The intended Market place at the upper end of Pool Lane having given great disgust to the inhabitants of this town on account that it would enclose that space of ground which ought to lye open and for other causes; It is now ordered that the said work be stopped and pulled down, and that the contractors be paid for what work and materials have been done and found by them, to be valued on the Corporation behalf by Mr Eyes. And that the plan now laid before the Council by Mr Mayor of another more usefull design for a lodgement of fire engines and other utensils necessary for extinguishing fires with a Watch-house and Market-house and also of a cistern or reservoir for water be made in the area near the said buildings, be carried into execution under the direction of Mr Mayor and Bailiffs at the expence of this Corporation." Market Place. Alterations. Market House.

In 1762 the Act was obtained for constructing George's Dock, which was opened in 1771. The original scheme embraced a plan for the erection of Warehouses along the east quay, to be called "*Goree*," in commemoration of the capture of the island of Goree from the French in 1759. George's Dock. Goree.

"1768, July 6. Charles Goore Mayor.
"Ordered that John Hope be paid the sum of twelve guineas for copying and altering the drafts or plans of a set of warehouses intended to be built between Water Street and Moor Street end or thereabouts and for all materials and things appurtenant thereto or found thereon, or such further sum as the Committee shall see fitting.
"Ordered that Mr Mayor and Bailiffs (with ten others) be appointed a Committee to take into consideration the plan of the said warehouses and carrying the said buildings into execution, and to report their proceedings to the Council as to the mode and terms of disposing of the said ground and building the said warehouses before any sale, contract, or agreement shall be entered into concerning the same." Goree Warehouses. Committee.

Nothing seems to have been done under this resolution.

"1771, Jany. 7. Ordered, that Mr Mayor and Bailiffs (with seven others) be appointed a Committee for the getting a plan for a sett of

Goree Warehouses. Warehouses to be erected on the land to the southward of Water Street along the Key of the new dock and report their proceedings to the Council at some future Council day."

A further postponement of five years took place.

"1776, Octr. 2. James Clemens Mayor.

"Ordered, that the plans of the vacant ground opposite the east quay of Goree Street be looked for and produced and laid before the next or other Council in order to consider of and fix on the sale of the said land, or a proper part thereof for the scite of warehouses to be built thereon, according to an order of Council of the 6th October 1773."

Bow Windows.
"1765, March 6. It having been represented to the Council that Mr Pickance and Mr John Parr are going to project out Bow windows from their houses in Water Street, which designs if carried into execution may be attended with great inconveniences and annoyance to the town and inhabitants from the narrowness of the streets. It is Ordered that the Town Clerk do write to these gentlemen or any other persons who have formed such designs, desiring them to desist carrying the same into execution."

Town Hall. The Town Hall, originally called the Exchange, was opened in 1754. No long period elapsed before alterations were found necessary.

"1764, Novr. 7. John Tarleton Mayor.

Dome.
"Ordered that a survey of the Doom of the Exchange be made as to the expence of taking it down, and fitting up a lanthorn in lieu thereof to give light into the Court room as it is represented to the Council that a continuance of the said Doom may endanger the building."

"1766, Decr. 3. Thomas Johnson Mayor.

Strong Room.
"Ordered, that Mr Hope be desired to draw a plan of an arched room or rooms to be made in the Exchange to keep the charters, books, records and leases and other papers in belonging to the Corporation, and that Mr Mayor, Bailiffs and any gentlemen of the Council be appointed a Committee for this purpose."

"1779, Octr. 6. Ordered that the two rooms in the Exchange commonly
Card and Assembly Rooms.
called the Card and the Assembly room be furnished at the expence of this Corporation, and that the ladies and gentlemen of the town have the use thereof for their public nights of assembly; and that the Treasurer do pay the sum of £230 for that purpose."

North Wing. The North Wing was added in 1786.

"1786, Decr. 18. James Gildart Junr Mayor.

"The proceedings of the Select Committee up to the 12th instant being read to this Council, the same were approved of and they having produced plans of such additional alteration in the Exchange together with the estimate for completing the same. It is Ordered that such alteration be carried into execution under the direction of the Select Committee." Completed.

Besides this addition, considerable alterations were made in the main building at this time.

"1786, Sept. 12. At a meeting of the Select Committee.
"The Committee having surveyed those parts of the Exchange proposed to be altered, have ordered that the following alterations and improvements be immediately carried into execution." Alterations.

Here follows a list — principally interior alterations. One of the resolutions appears a little singular.

"Ordered, That Mr Robinson be employed to plaister the west front with composition plaister, and that it be painted once over with oil colour, and that the design No 4 be adopted for the centre part of the said front." Plastering West Front.

These proceedings were confirmed by the Council, with the following addition :—

"It is the opinion of this Council and it is hereby ordered, that the present Dome of the Exchange be removed and that the same be carried into execution under the direction of the same Committee." Dome.

It would appear from this record that the west front, being at the time of the erection in 1750 blocked with buildings immediately contiguous, had been left in rough brickwork. The plastering was not carried out. A better taste prevailed.

"1787, Apl. 24. Ordered that Mr Foster prepare the necessary plans and elevation of the Exchange, in order that the same may be sent to London for the opinion of some eminent architect as to the propriety and best mode of covering the area, and erecting a dome or other suitable object over the area or some other part of the Exchange." Plans.

"1788, Jany. 15. Ordered that Mr Foster write to Mr Leverton and Mr Whetton, architects in London that he will send the plans of the Liverpool Exchange in its present state for their inspection, and to make such necessary additions and alterations thereto as are wanted." London Architects.

"1788, Feby. 25. Ordered that the plans of the Exchange now produced be taken up to London and laid before Mr James Wyatt, Wyatt.

architect by John Foster Jun', and that Mr Wyatt be requested to give his opinion upon, and make designs for the intended improvements to the North side of the Exchange."

Whetton. "1788, Octr. 21. Ordered, that Mr Whetton be paid his bill amounting to thirty guineas for his designs for the Council room."

"1789, Feby. 24. Resolved, that a letter be written to James Wyatt Esq accompanied with the corrected plans of the Exchange and the intended improvements, requesting that Mr Wyatt will be pleased within three months from this time to furnish the Committee with the further necessary plans and sections for the purpose of carrying on the building with all possible expedition and to acquaint the Committee with the compliment he expects for the plans already furnished."

Estimate.

Commission.
"1789, Mar. 30. Mr Wyatt the Architect having by letter of the 20th instant stated that his estimate of the expence of the internal and external alterations and additions to the Exchange will be between nine and ten thousand pounds, and that his charge for designs and other information which may be required from him during the course of the business will be five pounds per cent upon that sum, including every expence of time employed on the subject except what shall be actually employed in travelling and for travelling expences and time on the road separately at the rate of two shillings and sixpence per mile.

"It is now ordered that Mr Wyatt be allowed the sum of five hundred pounds for his plans and designs, also the aforesaid further charges."

Purchase of Timber.
"1790, July 13. Resolved that the Surveyor of the buildings with the assistance of Mr Foster Sen' be empowered to purchase the necessary oak timber for erecting the Dome over the area of the Exchange agreeable to Mr Wyatt's design now produced."

Ballroom. "1791, Nov. 8. Ordered that the Plans now produced for increasing the height of the new Ball room be sent to Mr Wyatt for his opinion upon them."

Dome. "1792, Jany. 10. Ordered the Skeleton or Carpentry of the Dome intended to be erected over the Area of the Exchange, agreeable to the models and designs made by Mr Wyatt, be immediately proceeded upon by Mr Foster Sen' in order that it may have the opportunity of being properly seasoned before it is required to be put upon the building."

Statues. "1792, Feby. 14. Ordered that the Surveyor of the buildings consult Mr Wyatt the Architect as to the propriety of getting the four figures for the North front of the Exchange executed in artificial stone; and also of the expence of the same, together with the cost of them if executed in Portland stone in order that they may be executed and ready to be put up that they may harmonize as much as possible as to colour with the stone of the building."

"1792, Mar. 10. The Surveyor of the buildings laid before this Committee a letter from Mr Rich[d] Westmacott offering to execute the four statues for the North front of the Exchange in Portland stone, and to deliver them at his own expence on board a vessell in the Thames for a sum not exceeding one hundred and twenty-five guineas each, and also offering to abate from that sum if he can possibly afford it when they are executed."

Price.

The statues were ordered and executed, and still decorate the façade. They represent the four seasons.

"1792, Octr. 2. Ordered that the elevation for the West front of the Exchange now produced by the Surveyor of Buildings be sent to Mr Wyatt and if approved by him, that it be adopted and carried into immediate execution."

"1792, Nov. 6. Ordered that the elevation of the West front received from Mr Wyatt be adopted, and that it be carried into immediate execution. *West Front.*

"Upon the solicitation of Mr Richard Westmacott as also upon the recommendation of Mr Wyatt the Architect

"It is Ordered that the figure of Britannia designed for the termination of the intended Dome of the Exchange be contracted for with Mr Westmacott, he engaging that it shall be a twelve feet figure executed in a masterly manner in antique green Bronze, according to the design and to the entire satisfaction of Mr Wyatt, and also upon his engaging to deliver it in perfect good order in this town at his own risque and charge, and to send at his expence a proper person to superintend the fixing up of the said figure, the whole of which he engages shall not exceed the sum of Four Hundred Pounds, and the Committee rely upon his own offer to reduce the cost below that sum, if in the event he can afford it."

Britannia.

Price.

In connection with the Exchange or Town-hall, the following forms rather an interesting episode in our local history.

"1791, Nov. 22. The Mayor and a number of gentlemen of the Council met at eleven o'clock in the Council Room agreeable to a card sent them by the Mayor, when two pictures were exhibited which were presented to the town of Liverpool by Mr William Martin, Historical Painter, and at which meeting his letter to the Committee was read."

Martin, painter.

The letter is too long for insertion, but its substance is as follows :—

"'Gentlemen,

"'The encreasing consequence of the town of Liverpool having become for some years past a subject much spoken of, I was induced some time since, on a tour I was then making in the North to pay it a visit; and experienced that pleasure which arises from having our expectations

Letter.

Improvements.

more than gratified. The improvements going on in the town astonished me not less by their magnitude than it pleased me by their utility. Amongst the additions making to the Exchange the intended Dome as proposed by Mr Wyatt attracted much of my attention, but I could not help being anxious that in the present state of the fine arts in this country, the department which I profess, should lend its aid to ornament so elegant an edifice.

Assembly Rooms.

"'On enquiry I found that the principal part of the additional building was intended for an Assembly room to be finished from a design of Mr Wyatt's, and that the present Assembly room was to be appropriated for an entertaining room, and no plan fixed upon for its decoration. As the room was necessarily to be altered, it occurred to me that without any encreased expence it might be adapted to receive pictures. On my return to London I communicated my idea to some friends intimately connected with Liverpool, and encouraged by their approbation, I sat down and made the design which I now present for your inspection . . . My intention is, to present to the Corporation four large historical pictures, to be placed agreeable to the plan; the subjects as follows: Lady Macduff surpriz'd in her castle at Fife—Cleopatra arming Antony—Queen Katharine's Vision—and Ferdinand's first interview with Miranda. In addition to these I intend also to present six smaller ones to be painted in chiaro 'scuro intended to fill the compartments as express'd in the drawing; the subjects I would propose for four circular ones over the doors, should be History—Painting—Sculpture and Architecture; over the niches, Astronomy and Geometry.

Offer of Pictures.

Subjects.

Circular Pictures.

"'I have delivered to your Surveyor the estimates ready for your inspection, which I flatter myself will be found to meet your approbation.

Engravings.

. . . Your Surveyor has likewise for your inspection engravings from two pictures which I lately presented to the city of Norwich. These engravings have met a very favorable reception from the Public and the pictures have, I hope, advanc'd my professional character.

"'If my proposal meets your approbation I have only to request you will pay the expence of the frames, packing cases and carriage; and as the four large pictures are intended to be engraved by Mr Bartolozzi, that I may have this permission. . . .

"'Any further explanation which may be thought necessary I shall be happy to give and have the honour to be

"'Gentlemen

"'Your most obedient Servt

"'WILL^M MARTIN.'

" Resolved—

Resolution of Acceptance.

"This Committee sensible of the very handsome and liberal manner in which Mr Martin has so highly contributed to the embellishment of the Exchange

STREETS AND BUILDINGS.

"Do Order the Secretary to return Mr Martin their acknowledgments in writing, and request to be furnished with the expense. _{Thanks.}

"Ordered that to preserve the pictures from damage they be immediately hung up in the Assembly room under the direction of Mr Martin, and that coverings be made for them out of the curtains formerly belonging to the Assembly room."

Within less than four years these pictures were destroyed by the fire of 1795.

On the erection of the North Wing an open space was cleared round it.

"1793, Feby. 6. Ordered that a petition of the Merchants, Bankers and underwriters of this town, stating that their business renders daily attendance on the Exchange necessary and the expediency of appropriating to the use and accommodation of the trade of the town (in addition to the present area) the lower part of the new building adjoining to and communicating with the North Walk of the Exchange and requesting that the same may be accordingly appropriated under such regulations as may be adopted by this Council, be referred to the Select Committee who are requested to make their report thereon to this Council." _{North Walk of Exchange.}

It was well that by the order of 1766 a strong room was provided for the reception of the muniments, otherwise there would have remained no archives to record.

1795. On Sunday, January 18th, the whole of the interior was destroyed by fire. The inquiry into the origin and circumstances of the fire was very searching and lengthy, and occupies a large space in the records. I can only give a few of the leading features. _{Fire in Exchange.}

"1795, Jany. 20. John Shaw Mayor.

"At a Special Council held at the house of Daniel Dale in Water Street pursuant to a special Summons, to take into consideration and determine upon the measures proper to be adopted in consequence of the dreadful conflagration which on Sunday morning last took place in and destroyed the Exchange of this town. _{Special Council.}

"Present the Mayor and 28 others.

"Ordered that a Committee be appointed for the following purposes— _{Committee.}

"(1) To make a strict inquiry into the cause of the fire. _{Cause of Fire.}

"(2) To take account of the state of the building &c.

Reports.	"(3) To take reports from the officers as to the state of the papers belonging to their several offices.
Provision.	"(4) To provide proper places, in order to prevent the interruption of public business.

"Such Committee to consist of the Mayor, Bailiffs, and Magistrates with 10 others."

The charters, council books and deeds were reported safe.

Report.	"1795, Feby. 4. The report of the Committee was presented. It states that they had examined strictly into the general conduct of the Exchange keeper, as well as his particular situation previous to the commencement of the fire.
Examinations.	"They also examined such persons as were the first alarmed and had been witnesses of the progress of the fire, as well taking the opinion of
Rapidity of Flames.	experienced workmen respecting the unusual rapidity of the flames, both with regard to the satisfying of their own minds as to the cause of such appearances, as well as to enquire whether the apprehensions are well founded that the fire could have been wilfully occasioned.
Fire accidental.	"The result of such enquiries has led the Committee to conclude and they have been unanimously of opinion, that the fire has been accidental arising from causes not possible to ascertain.
Coating of Turpentine.	"But they cannot help adverting to the very singular cause of the extraordinary rapidity of the flames, which evidently arose from the circumstance of the Architect employed in building the Exchange having, to prevent decay, payed the timber with a composition chiefly turpentine as appears more particularly explained by the examinations.

"The Committee congratulate the Council on the safety of the valuables of every description in the respective offices, and pay a tribute of acknowledgment of the services of the respective officers.

Ellis Jones.	"Mr Ellis Jones the Keeper who lived on the premises testified that all was perfectly safe up to half-past ten on Saturday night when he retired to bed. About half-past four on Sunday morning his wife awaked him by her coughing and immediately said 'Ellis, good God what is the smoke there is something on fire.'—He got up and went into the Loan Office where he found a great smoke but no appearance of fire. From thence he went into the vaults and cellars, then into the Assembly room and tried to get into the Council room but found it blocked. Thence he proceeded up the great stairs into the Town hall, and found it so full of smoke that he could not breathe; thence to the Loan Office where he found the ceiling on fire. He then opened the gates, rushed out and gave the alarm of fire.
Evidence.	"Various persons in the neighbourhood gave evidence as to the first appearance and progress of the fire. They all concur that there was a great want of water and great difficulty in obtaining any supply.

"Several working carpenters testified that the timbers of the building were payed over with rosin.

"Mr John Foster, Surveyor, stated that when the alterations were made in the cupola preparatory to fixing the clock in 1769, he frequently remarked the circumstance of the timbers being covered with a strong coating of rosin, turpentine or other such inflammable composition. Foster.

He also presented a written report as follows :—

"' In obedience to your orders I beg leave to report that I have at various times since the late melancholy fire took place in the Exchange surveyed the building, and I beg to state that the fire has destroyed the whole of the principal and attic story floors and the roof of the old building together with the interior parts and finishing of all the rooms on those stories. Foster's Report. Extent of Fire.

"' The rooms in the basement story with the great stairs and the Assembly room stairs, have escaped the devastation, and the new building on the North side has not sustained any injury.

"' In respect to the furniture that was within the building at the time of the fire; all that which belonged to the Council room, Assembly room (except the covers to the seats) the principal part in the Mayor's Office, and all in the Attick stories is destroyed. The furniture in the rooms on the basement story was all carried out and saved. Furniture.

"' Respecting the present situation of the building, I beg leave to state that I am humbly of opinion that the exterior walls have not sustained any material damage, or have the interior walls that formed the area received any considerable injury beyond the destruction of the bond timbers and ties that were placed upon the top of the Doric columns in the basement story. External Walls.

"' I respectfully beg permission to add, that for the security of the walls, I am humbly of opinion it is essentially necessary as soon as possible that all the interstices which are formed by the burning of the bond timber, beams, and other timbers that lay within the walls, should be very securely closed up, to prevent any incumbent weight giving way; and that all the chimneys or other parts whose foundations have been injured or in part removed, should be taken down to prevent any accident in case they should fall. Timber in Walls.

"' I am Gentlemen
"' Your obedient very humble servant
"' JOHN FOSTER JUN^R
"' Surveyor to the Corporation Buildings.'"

No books or papers were found to be missing. The Corporation Seal was safely lodged in the iron chest.

The Council gave immediate directions to Mr. Foster to prepare plans for the rebuilding and refitting of the Exchange.

"1795, March 12. John Shaw Mayor.

Plans for Rebuilding.
"Alderman Clayton Tarleton, the Chairman of the Exchange Committee having produced to this Council a plan for the refitting the Exchange, made by the Surveyor of the Buildings, accompanied by a Report from the said Committee that it was their unanimous opinion 'that the general dispositions of the whole, and the particular arrangements of the various rooms and offices are highly proper and commodious, and such as will afford the most desireable conveniences for the public and private business of the Mayor and Corporation and their respective officers, and very ample accommodations for the merchants and the public at large.'

Wyatt, Architect.
"And the said plan having been submitted to the inspection of James Wyatt Esquire Architect, and having met with his fullest approbation: This Council do therefore unanimously resolve that the same be adopted and signed by the Mayor and Bailiffs as approved by this Council, and that the Exchange Committee do forthwith take the necessary steps for carrying the same into immediate execution; and that the said Committee do continue to superintend and direct the completion of the same."

Widow Maddocks.
"1797, May 3. Ordered that the sum of ten guineas be paid to Agnes Maddocks, Widow, on account of the expence of the funeral of her late son, whose death was occasioned by an injury he received at the late fire at the Exchange."

Theatre.
The theatre in Liverpool has had different localities from time to time. The following entries relate to the building in Williamson Square.

"1768, Dec. 7. Matthew Stronge Mayor.

Gibson's Petition.
"It is Ordered that the Mayor, Magistrates and Council of this Corporation agree to Mr Gibson's petition for erecting a Playhouse in Liverpoole, upon the same terms, conditions and agreement as was entered into with the Magistracy of the City of Norwich in the like case, and that Mr Gibson be desired to send Mr Mayor copys of all Acts necessary to be done previous to obtaining the Act of Parliament, and that the Lord Chamberlain be prayed to grant the same Licence and no other, as was granted to Norwich, and all proceedings to be done at Mr Gibson's expence. And to acquaint him that the Magistracy will not have the present House licensed, as it's in a very dangerous place for company to resort to on account of the narrow streets and avenues leading thereto." [1]

"1769, Aug. 29. It is Ordered that this Council will petition the

---

[1] The theatre referred to was in Drury Lane, Water Street.

STREETS AND BUILDINGS. 273

Parliament the next session, for an Act to enable his Majesty to grant his
Letters Patent to Mr William Gibson Comedian, his executors adminis- Petition for
trators and assigns, for the term of twenty-one years, to build a theatre in Letters
Liverpoole, on condition that the said Mr Gibson do pay all expences Patent.
attending the obtaining such Act and Letters Patent, and shall also build
the said theatre at his expence on such piece of ground as shall be
agreeable to the Mayor and Magistrates of this town."

"1770, Feby. 14. It is Ordered that the petition of the Mayor Aldermen
&c to the Right Hon. the Earl of Hertford, Lord Chamberlain of his
Majesty's household, for his Lordship's intercession with his Majesty that
a Patent may be granted to Mr William Gibson for opening a Playhouse Patent.
in Liverpoole now read, be passed under the Common Seal upon the terms
heretofore agreed upon with the said Mr Gibson and be forthwith presented
to his Lordship."

The paving of the streets at this time attracted consider- Paving.
able attention. Mr. George Byrom, who gave his name to
Byrom Street, was the person employed by the Corporation,
but he fell into disgrace, as appears from the following
minute:—

"1776, April 3. On a complaint this day made by Mr Mayor to this
Council against George Byrom Paviour for great misbehaviour and abuse Hanover
given to Mr Mayor and other gentlemen of the Committee appointed for Street.
repaving Hanover Street. It is Ordered that the said George Byrom be Byrom
discharged from his employ as Paviour to the Corporation and that Mr dismissed.
Berry be at present employed to superintend the pavements and roads of Berry
this town. employed.

"And that the said Mr Berry be authorized to buy in paving stones and
materials for paving the west side of George's Dock and to get the same
paved this summer at the Dock expence."

The old Fall Well on the Heath (near the corner of the Fall Well.
present Roe Street), which for ages had been the principal
supply of water to the town was drawing near its end, as the
following entry indicates:—

"1778, Decr. 2. It is Ordered, that the Fall Well (being a dangerous
place as the walls of it are thrown down) be viewed by Mr Mayor and
Committee, and that they report to the Council what is proper to be done
to it."

"1797, Feby. 1. Upon the petition of J T Serres, Marine Painter to Serres,
his Majesty, stating that he had made several views of the town and Painter.

M M

shipping and proposed publishing prints of them, and praying leave to dedicate the same to the Mayor Bailiffs and Burgesses.

"Ordered that the said J T Serres be permitted to dedicate the same accordingly, and that (blank) sets be taken for the Council, to be paid for by the Treasurer."

1798, Decr. 7th. Thomas Leyland, Mayor.

A petition was prepared and ordered to be presented to the House of Commons setting forth :—

Petition.

New Streets. Old Streets narrow.

No Sewers.

"That the commerce and population of the town had been progressively and considerably increasing; that as a necessary consequence a great number of new streets had been laid out and buildings erected; that many of the old streets were narrow, dangerous, and inconvenient, and the levels of many of the new streets improperly and irregularly laid out, and no common sewers made through them, and also that many Wind Mills, Lime Kilns and other annoyances were erected too near the streets and highways.

Pavement in bad repair.

"That the pavement and common sewers of the streets, lanes, and public passages and places within the said town, are in many places kept in bad repair and condition, and it would be a great safety and convenience not only to the inhabitants but to all persons resorting thereto if the streets &c were properly paved, and the old streets were made wider, and more safe and convenient; and the levels of such new made streets properly laid and common sewers made and the nuisances and annoyances removed and for the future prevented."

Hotel, Castle Street.

In 1798 an hotel was built in Castle Street by the Corporation, on the site subsequently occupied by the Branch Bank of England.

"1800, May 7. Pudsey Dawson Mayor.

"On reading the proceedings of the Select Committee

Consideration of Hotel.

"Ordered that the same be confirmed except as to the report relative to the letting the new Hotel in Castle Street, and it having been the opinion of the Council that it would be a public benefit to have such hotel erected, and the Select Committee being in the possession of the expence of erecting the same and of the probable expence of erecting stables and other requisite outbuildings, as also of purchasing suitable furniture; it is therefore referred to the said Committee and they are hereby authorized and empowered to enter into such contract for letting the same at such rent and upon such terms and conditions as to them shall seem most expedient and advantageous to the Corporation Estate. And if it shall be thought advisable by the said Committee to go to the expence of

STREETS AND BUILDINGS.

furnishing the same, they are hereby authorized to call upon the Treasurer to advance money for that purpose under their directions, or to let the same unfurnished as they shall see fit."

"1800, Aug. 6. Upon reading a letter from Mr R Horwood, Land Surveyor and publisher of a plan of London, wishing to obtain the patronage of the Corporation for his executing a similar plan of this town, should he meet with sufficient encouragement; and upon the Mayor's statement that he had enquired into Mr Horwood's merits which were found to be worthy the attention of the public, and which was confirmed by several other gentlemen of the Council who had seen his plan of the city of London. *[Horwood's Survey and Map.]*

"Resolved and Ordered, that it is the opinion of this Council that encouragement should be given to an artist of Mr Horwood's merit, and that he be therefore permitted to take the plan of the town and port of Liverpool, and have the assistance of the Corporation Surveyors in such his undertaking; and that he be permitted to dedicate this Work to the body Corporate of this town; and also that ten copies of this Plan which the Mayor has thought proper to subscribe for on behalf of the Council as an encouragement to the Scheme be paid for by the Treasurer." *[Ten copies taken.]*

ECCLESIASTICAL AFFAIRS.

The control of the Council over the Churches and Clergy became gradually relaxed as the Parish acquired more influence, but as the builders and patrons of the new churches, the Council still exercised considerable influence.

Two new Churches. In the year 1760 the Parish determined on building two new churches, and arranged with the Council that an Act of Parliament should be obtained at the expense of the Corporation, to whom the next presentation and perpetual advowson should belong, and that the Corporation should make an allowance of £30 per annum in perpetuity to the successive ministers of the North Church (St. Paul's). [1]

"1760, Decr. 3. John Blackburn Mayor.

Minister's Salary.
Ground floor free.
"Ordered on a memorial now presented and read to this Council from the Parish Committee that the stipend or salary lately voted by this Council for the Minister of the new intended church be made up the sume of £50 a year, upon condition that the whole body of the Church except two seats be laid open for the use of the poor."

Application to Parliament.
"1761, Decr. 23. Ordered that an application be made this Sessions of Parliament for building one or more churches in Liverpoole and for obliging all persons keeping carts to have six-inch Wheels."

St. Paul's. St. Paul's Church was commenced in 1765 and completed in 1769. The second church authorised by the Act was delayed for some years.

"1765, Feby. 6. John Tarleton Mayor.

Patten's Garden.
"Whereas Mr Mayor now reports to this Council, that he has applied to Mr Samuel Shaw, merchant, who has purchased the present term and interest in the ground called Patten's Garden [2] to give up his purchase of the said ground on being paid the money and interest he gave for it, in

---

[1] *Vide supra*, p. 171.
[2] Patten's Garden was at the bottom of the present St. John's Lane, fronting the Haymarket.

order that this Corporation might then give and appropriate the said ground to the Parish for a scite for a new church and a publick burial place for the Parish, which the said Mr Shaw declines.

"Therefore it is now Ordered by this Council in order to accommodate the Parish with a proper scite for a church and a publick burial place, which is most manifestly wanted, that this Council will now, and do hereby give the said Parish for the above uses the field called the Great Heath for the term of nine hundred years, but on this condition, that it be only applied by the Parish for the above uses, and as there have been some disputes between the Corporation and Parish about the right to the reversion of the said Patten's Gardens, the above grant is on this express condition that the Parish shall never trouble or molest the said Corporation about the possession of the said land, and release the rent charge of nine pounds a year payable thereout to the poor of this Parish for and during the present lease, and acquit the Corporation, their successors and assigns therefrom for ever." *Grant of Land for St. John's.* *Great Heath.* *Conditions of Grant.*

"1768, July 6. Charles Goore Mayor.

"Ordered that the Reverend Mr John Henderson be elected and appointed the first Minister or Chaplin of Saint Paul's Church, with the salary as allowed by the Council and prescribed by the several Acts of Parliament made for building two churches in the town of Liverpoole, with all the rights, priviledges, and emoluments thereto belonging, on condition that he shall reside in town during his ministry, and give security so to do in £500, and perform the duty in person unless sickness or other providential accident hinders him, and to resign it into the hands of the Council when he shall voluntarily quit the same. *Henderson, Chaplain.*

"Ordered that the Reverend Mr James Hogarth be appointed second Minister, subject to the same terms and conditions." *Hogarth, second Minister.*

Matters do not appear to have gone on very smoothly according to the following record :—

"1771, Aug. 7. John Sparling Mayor.

"In order to prevent any lawsuits between the Rectors of this Parish and the Clergy of the several Assistant or Under Churches or Chapels of this town, we do recommend and strongly insist on it, that the said several parties do state their reasons and arguments in writing pro and con to the town clerk, from whence and from the several Acts of Parliament for building such churches, that he do state a case to be approved of and laid before Mr Recorder and Depy Recorder and after their settlement to be laid before this Council, and then to take some one or two civilians' opinion thereon, which we do expect that the Clergy do severally abide by, if they intend to preserve peace amongst themselves, and their congregations. And that each of them be served with a copy of this Order." *Disputes amongst Clergy.*

Bells of St. Paul's.

"1777, March 5. Ordered that the Treasurer do pay to John Foster his bill for finishing joiners' work in raising the great bell of St Paul's Church out of the roof into the cupola, making a Sounding Board and some inward doors and other work there, amounting to £82 18s 4d.

"And also one other bill to Christopher Holding for a small or Ting Tang bell amounting to £18 14s 0d."

Some differences arose as to ringing the bells of St. Peter's.

Ringing Bells.

"1763, Decr. 22. Ordered that four ringing days on publick days (*sic*) which Mr. Wolstenholme (the Rector) has paid to or is liable to pay to the Ringers be now paid at the expence of the Corporation, as they had no notice of the late order of the late Committee against such ringing days being paid for by the Council. And that for the future the Corporation will only pay for ringing on the King's Birthday and Coronation day and no other without an order from Mr Mayor for the time being."

Organ. St. Nicholas'.

Down to 1764 there was no organ in St. Peter's Church. An organ was first provided for St. Nicholas's in 1684.

"1764, Novr. 7. John Tarleton Mayor.

St. Peter's. Organist.

"Upon a representation of the Churchwardens and Sidesmen of this Parish, setting forth that they have got a Subscription of about £400 for erecting an organ in St Peter's Church, and praying this Council to settle a Sallary on the Organist of the same, when finished.

"It is now ordered that this Council will give a Sallary of forty Pounds a year to such person as this Council shall appoint Organist thereof, to commence from the finishing and opening of the said organ, and to be continued during the pleasure of this Council only. And that Michael Williams be appointed the organist thereof, and on condition that he do extra duty by playing on the organ at the Charity School every Sunday night till further orders."

"1762, July 7. Ordered that Mr Mayor and Bailiffs (with three others) be empowered to consult with proper persons and workmen to view St

St. George's Spire.

George's Church steeple and spire, it being represented to this Council that it is in a ruinous condition and in danger of falling. And that they do contract with persons for securing the same immediately."

In 1789 the spire was again surveyed; and in April, 1790, a report was presented, signed by seven architects, that no perceptible alteration had taken place, and that there was no immediate risk of the structure falling, but that certain repairs were necessary. It was stated to be 3 ft. 2 in. out of perpendicular.

"1791, March 22. Ordered, that the repairs of St George's Church **Repairs.** steeple be immediately recommenced, and that the Surveyor of the buildings be directed to cause the same to be finished in an effectual manner agreeable to the report of April 1790."

1792, June 19. Another report was presented by the same parties. They say:—

"'We concur in opinion that there is no immediate risque of the steeple falling. We beg leave to decline giving any opinion upon the expediency of taking down or of repairing the present steeple. But with great defer- **Report.** ence we take the liberty to state the absolute necessity of immediately determining upon taking it down, or of causing an effectual repair to be proceeded upon in the manner described in our former surveys.'

"It is therefore Ordered that an effectual repair of the steeple be immediately proceeded with in the manner recommended."

1786, April 8th. In consequence of a petition from the present Rectors of Liverpool requesting an increase of salary:

"It is Ordered that the sum of One hundred pounds a piece per annum **Rectors'** be paid to them, being similar to the addition lately made by the Parish; **Salaries.** the payment to commence at the time of the Parish's additional salary."

"1772, March 4. Ordered that the acts of the Mayor, Recorder, Bailiffs and Town Clerk giving the Corporation's assent to a draft of a Bill for building a new Church (St. Anne's) near the Loggerheads and within this **St. Anne's** Parish by Mr Dobb and others, the consideration of which Bill was **Church.** referred to them by a majority of the Common Council be and such assent is hereby ratified and confirmed."

"1788, Decr. 3. A proposal having been made to this Council for the purchase of Mrs. Plumbe's Church, commonly called the Octagon, or St. Catherine's, in this town: **St. Cather-**

"Ordered that the same be referred to a Committee consisting of the **ine's,** Mayor, Bailiffs (with six others) and that they make their report to the next Council."

"1791, July 6. John Sparling Mayor.

"Ordered that the petition of the subscribers to the new Church now building for the Reverend Richard Formby at the South end of St. Anne Street (Trinity Church) now read to this Council for stone from some of **Trinity** the Corporation quarries to complete the Church with, and the Elevation **Church.** of such intended building produced, be referred to the Select Committee."

"1791, July 16. The Select Committee having reported that as the **Committee's** petitions of Messrs Harvey and Waln and of the subscribers to the **Report.**

Church now building for the Reverend Richard Formby in St. Anne Street are of the utmost importance, they beg leave to recommend to the Council to take the same again into their consideration, and to determine upon them in such manner as they shall think most expedient.

Conference with Rector.
Vestry.

"It is therefore ordered that the Mayor and Bailiffs be appointed a Committee to confer with the Rectors and Churchwardens of the Parish of Liverpool, and if necessary to request that a vestry may be called to take the sense of the Parish respecting the propriety of building the said two new Churches or otherwise."

"1792, Apl. 26. Henry Blundell Mayor.
" Report of the Select Committee.

Trinity Church.

"The Bill intended to be brought into Parliament for building a new Church or Chapel in Spring Fields near St. Anne Street being now read to this Committee,

Bill.

"Resolved, that agreeable to an Order of Council made the seventh day of March last, this Committee did report that having carefully examined the said Act, and proposed certain amendments, which the proprietors of the Church have consented to; do recommend it to the Council, that the Corporate Seal be put to a Bill as petitioned for by the said proprietors,

Steeple.

they having reserved liberty for the Corporation to erect a steeple upon the tower of the said Church, which tower the proprietors have agreed to enter into a contract to make sufficiently strong for that purpose.

"Several estimates having now been laid before this Committee for building a steeple; Resolved that it be recommended to the Council to

Contract.

agree to the proposal of Peter Grant and Company (being the lowest) to complete the same for the sum of £320 including the materials, vane &c, and that the same be carried into execution under the immediate direction of the Surveyor of the buildings."

1792, June 26th. The Surveyor of the buildings produced the following report respecting the steeple of the new church in St. Anne Street:—

Report.

"We whose names are hereunto subscribed, having surveyed the tower of the New Church now erecting near St. Ann's Street are clearly of opinion that it is not sufficient to support the spire proposed to be erected thereon, and in our opinion any additional strength which may be given to the parts now building or to be added would be inadequate to the purpose.
"JOHN HOPE.
"JOHN FOSTER, JUN[R]."

St. Stephen's.

"1792, March 7. The petition of the proprietors of a Church or Chapel intended to be called St. Stephen's Church in Byrom Street being now read, praying for this Council's acquiescence to a deed which has been executed by the present right reverend Father in God the Bishop of Chester, by the present Rectors of this Parish, and by them the aforesaid proprietors, respecting the presentation of the Curate of such Chapel, and other matters in the same deed contained. Ordered that such deed be, on behalf of this Corporation, inspected by the Town Clerk, and that he do make his report thereon to the Mayor, Bailiffs and Treasurer, and that if they shall approve of the same they do in that case affix the Common Seal of this Corporation to the same deed, the aforesaid proprietors first executing a counterpart of such deed and leaving such counterpart with the Corporation."

"1793, Jany. 2. Clayton Tarleton Mayor.

"The Mayor having reported to the Council that being of opinion that the present Churches in this town are wholly inadequate to the great number of inhabitants professing the doctrines of the Church of England, he had requested a meeting of the Parliamentary Committee and the Parish Committee, in order to consult together on the propriety of obtaining an Act for building two Churches in Liverpool, the one at the expence of the Parish, and the other at the expence of the Corporation; and that it had been unanimously resolved at that meeting that it was the opinion of those Committees that from the rapid increase of the town there was a necessity for building one or more churches for the accommodation of the inhabitants, but principally of the poorer class; and further resolved that a Vestry should be called for the purpose of taking the above resolution into their consideration. *Mayor's Report on Churches. Act applied for. Two new Churches. Vestry.*

"This Council doth approve of the above steps, and resolutions, and do order and resolve, that this Corporation will be at the expence of erecting one Church in this town if the Parish will be at the expence of erecting another, and do authorize and request the Mayor to make this proposal to the Parish at the Vestry to be held for taking the above subject into consideration." *Resolution.*

1793, Feby. 6th. A petition was prepared and presented setting forth :—

"That from the great increase of the Commerce and of the population of the said Town and Parish of Liverpool, the inhabitants thereof are now become so very numerous that the present churches therein are by no means sufficient to contain the inhabitants desirous to attend religious worship according to the rites and ceremonies of the Church of England, and that therefore the Corporation of the said town are willing and desirous to erect at their own proper expence one other Church in the said town, and the inhabitants of the said town and parish are also willing and desirous to erect at their expence one other Church in the said town and parish. *Petition. Corporation and Parish.*

St. Catherine's Church.

"That the said Corporation have lately purchased a certain building in the said town and parish called St Catherine's Chapel sometime since erected at the expence of a number of private persons in which Divine Service is celebrated, and the right of appointing the Chaplain thereof, is by law vested in the Rectors, of the said parish, which Rectors and also the Ordinary of the Diocese of Chester in which the said town and Parish are situate are willing and desirous that the property of the said Chapel should be vested in the said Corporation, and that the presentation or appointment of the Chaplains to the said Chapel of Saint Catherine should be vested in the Mayor, Bailiffs and Common Council of Liverpool for the time being . . . with other recitals.

"Your petitioners therefore humbly pray that leave may be given to bring in a Bill for the several purposes aforesaid."

The Bill was passed accordingly.

St. Matthew's

The Nonconformist Chapel in Key Street, erected in 1706, on the removal of the congregation to Paradise Street in 1791, was purchased by members of the Established Church.

Petition for Consecration.

"1794, Octr. 1. Ordered that the petition of the proprietors of the Chapel in Key Street to this Council to request the Bishop of Chester to consecrate such Chapel be referred to the Select Committee and that they do make their report thereon to the Council."

The Church was subsequently consecrated under the name of St. Matthew.

"1800, Feby. 5. Pudsey Dawson Mayor.

Letter from Vestry Clerk.

"Upon reading a letter from Mr Edward Blackstock the Vestry Clerk, to the Mayor, of the 31st Decr 1799, adverting to the circumstance of the Corporation and Parish having it in contemplation in the years 1792 and 1793 to join in the erecting two new churches for the general accommodation of the inhabitants, and also intimating that the Parish Committee were of opinion that the same reason still existed for the adopting and carrying such plan into execution, and that the ground between St James Street and Great George Street, was in their opinion

St. Michael's.

proper for the erection of one of such new Churches upon, and that if the scheme still continued to meet the approbation of the Council, they would recommend it to the consideration of the next Annual Vestry.

"Resolved and Ordered, that the subject matter of this letter be, and the same is hereby referred to the Select Committee to consider and report their opinion upon."

The Church was built accordingly, after long delay, and completed in 1825, consecrated to St. Michael.

"1800, Feby 5. Upon reading the petition of Mr John Houghton of the 3rd February instant, stating that he had erected a Church or Chapel upon a piece of ground on the south of Hunter Street, and that he was desirous of having the said Church or Chapel placed upon the establishment of the Church of England, for which purpose he had obtained the consent of the Right Reverend the Bishop of Chester, and desired the concurrence of the Common Council. And also that he had caused a Bill to be prepared for Parliament, a copy whereof he begged leave to submit to the perusal of the Common Council and humbly hoped for their approbation. {Christ Church.}

"Resolved and Ordered, that the said petition and the Copy Bill be, and the same is hereby referred to the Select Committee to consider and report."

The Church was consecrated and opened in 1800, under the name of Christ's Church.

"1800, Aug. 6. Upon reading the petition of the Reverend Mr Thomas Jones for liberty for himself and friends to build a church at the top of Duke Street, if the Corporation and Rectors shall be pleased to give their countenance to the same: {St. Mark's Church.}

"Resolved and Ordered, that the consideration of the said petition be referred to the Select Committee to consider and report."

The Church was erected and opened in 1803, dedicated to St. Mark.

In the foregoing pages, several extracts have been given from the records bearing upon the Free Grammar School, founded by John Crosse before the Reformation, and at the Dissolution vested in the Corporation. {Free Grammar School.}

"1774, Decr. 7. Peter Rigby Mayor.

"It is now Ordered, that Mr Mayor and Bailiffs and any other gentleman of the Council who will attend Mr Mayor, be appointed a Committee to view and return a state of the present Free School and to take the petition of Mr Baines the Head Master thereof into consideration respecting a new School and report their proceedings to the next Council." {Committee} {New School.}

"1775, Apl. 5. On the report of the Committee to whom the state of the Free School was referred, they now report that the School is very sufficient for the Scholars save that the same wants some additional or enlarged lights to be made therein and other small repairs which the Mayor, Bailiffs and Treasurer are ordered to get done at the Corporation expense, if the Trustees of the Charity School are not obliged by their contract to do them." {Report.} {Repairs.}

It should be explained that the Grammar School was kept in a room in School Lane, rented from the Trustees of the Blue Coat Hospital.

Petition from Baines.

"1786, Feby. 1. Ordered, on the petition of Mr Baines Head Master of the Free Grammar School, that his annual stipend shall be increased in consideration of his long and faithful services, to the sum of One hundred and five pounds, to be paid yearly during the will and pleasure of the Corporation."

Sunday School.
Inquiry.

"1788, Sept. 23. Upon the consideration of a petition presented to the Council by the Reverend Mr Hodgson for a piece of land whereon to erect a Sunday School. It is the opinion that the first object is to take into consideration the present state of the Free School and it is now accordingly ordered that the Town Clerk do forthwith by search of the Corporation Records and by such other means as shall be necessary inquire into the endowment of the said Free School and make his report to the next Committee."

Free School.

"1789, May 12. The Committee proceeded to view the land and building in Orange Street in consequence of the Reverend Mr Hodgson's memorial for the purpose of erecting Public Schools. As it is the intention of this Committee to recommend to the Council to establish the Free School upon a more liberal and extended plan, they cannot at present see the necessity of any further Day Schools, and are of opinion that the Sunday Schools properly attended to by the Clergy and Laity are amply sufficient for the education of the lower class of children."

"1793, Jany. 2. Clayton Tarleton Mayor.

Mayor's Report.

"The Mayor having reported to the Council that the scholars resorting to the present Free School within this town, had from the great increase of the town and from the circumstance of the Schools being free to the children of all the freemen, become so numerous as totally to preclude from the benefit thereof the sons of persons who were anyways able to bear the expence of paying for their education elsewhere; and that the number and reputation of the private schools within this borough for the education of youth of the established church by no means keep pace with the growth and consequence of this flourishing town: by reason whereof many persons were obliged at a great expence added to the inconvenience of removing their children from under their own eye to send them to schools at a distance, and others were induced to submit education to persons not of the established church.

Private Schools deficient.

"This Council, taking the above representation into their most serious consideration and being of opinion that the education of youth and the superintendance of their moral and religious principles are matters of the highest concern both to the present and rising generation, and as such are

ECCLESIASTICAL AFFAIRS.

objects deserving the utmost care and attention, and well worthy of the munificence and liberality of this opulent Corporation. Doth therefore resolve and order that a Committee be now appointed for the purpose of providing a school or schools for the education of youth, with full powers to erect such building as shall seem to them to be expedient and necessary, and to frame such a code of rules and regulations as shall appear to them to be requisite for the good government of the same, and that the said rules and regulations be reported to Council and entered on the Council Book. *Committee to provide Schools.*

"Ordered that the following gentlemen do compose such Comittee. The Mayor, Bailiffs (with ten others) and that the said Committee have likewise power to examine into the state of and make such regulations and alterations in the present Free School as shall be necessary to render it more commodious for the education of children of the poorer class." *Committee.*

Notwithstanding this metaphorical flourish of trumpets, nothing came of this record. Matters remained the same until the death of Mr. Baines, the Head Master, in 1803, when the School was closed, to be revived again after twenty years' suspense. *Decease of Baines.*

In respect to MANNERS and CUSTOMS, there is very little in this portion of the records differing materially from those of the present day. There is, however, one record of a piece of ruffianism publicly perpetrated which happily would be now almost impossible.

"1777, Feby. 5. William Clarke Mayor.

"Ordered that what money shall be collected by the voluntary contributions of well disposed persons for the relief of one Mary Clarke, who was lately sett upon, assaulted and cruelly and barbarously ducked in the dock, so as to endanger her life, and thrown her into violent convulsions so as to incapacitate her (in all probability) from getting her future livelihood (and for which several of the rioters have been lately convicted and ordered to be fined and imprisoned by the last Court of Quarter Sessions for this borough) be taken in by this Corporation on an annuity for her life, and that she be allowed and paid for at the rate of ten per cent for such money, and that a Bond be passed under the Common Seal for payment thereof, to be made to Ralph Peters and Joseph Brooks Esquires in trust for her sole and separate use, as Mr Peters shall settle and fix it." *Mary Clarke ill-treated.* *Rioters punished.*

CHAPTER FOURTH.
FROM A.D. 1800 TO THE PASSING OF THE MUNICIPAL REFORM ACT, 1835.

PUBLIC AND NATIONAL AFFAIRS.

The times were stirring, England was engaged in a spasmodic struggle with the French under Napoleon for very existence. War abroad and sedition at home were severely trying the endurance and loyalty of the nation. Liverpool was faithful to its ancient loyal traditions, and bravely supported the Government in its arduous contest.

Col. Despard. In February, 1803, Col. Despard and his accomplices were brought to trial at the Old Bailey for high treason. Despard and six others were found guilty and executed.

"1803, March 2. Jonas Bold Mayor.

Address. "Resolved that an Address be presented to his Majesty 'upon his escape from the late traitorous conspiracy against his sacred person and government,' and that the same be transmitted to the members for the borough, Lieut.-Gen. Tarleton and Major-Gen. Gascoyne for presentation."

The address was as follows:—

"Most Gracious Sovereign.

"We, your Majesty's dutiful and loyal subjects the Mayor, Recorder, Aldermen, Bailiffs and Common Council of the town of Liverpool most humbly approach the throne to tender to your Majesty our sincere and heartfelt congratulations on the detection and failure of the late atrocious and treasonable conspiracy against your Majesty's sacred person and Government; fully convinced that the diabolical machinations, even of the few, which through the interposition of Divine Providence have again been happily frustrated, serve only to prove more decisively the mischievous tendency of those pernicious doctrines and principles, which are equally destructive of all true and genuine liberty, and of that real comfort and security which every class of society may enjoy under the best of Kings. And we beg leave most respectfully to assure your Majesty of our determined resolution to adhere to and support the present Assurances. glorious constitution as by law established, and which we hope and trust will long continue to flourish under the paternal auspices and protection of a Sovereign so truly religious and virtuous, and so highly deserving the unfeigned regard and inviolable attachment of a grateful people."

This was followed by an energetic movement for the defence of the Port. *Port Defences.*

1803, July 10th. A public meeting of the inhabitants was held, at which an Acting Committee was appointed, who presented the following report:—

"1803, July 18. The Committee appointed to consider what measures it might be necessary to adopt for most effectually putting the town of Liverpool and its Harbour into the best state of defence against an enemy, having taken the several matters into serious deliberation, do report—

"That it is our decided and unanimous opinion that the present force is quite inadequate to the defence of the town and Harbour against any attack which the enemy may make, and which there is great reason to apprehend he meditates.

"And that we are of opinion it is absolutely necessary for the preservation of the said town and harbour, and for the security of the lives and property of the inhabitants, and of every thing held dear in society, that prompt and efficacious measures should be instantly adopted for the Immediate defence of the place, to guard against surprize and to avert the general Steps. devastation, horrors and massacres, the constant and well-known attendants on every successful attempt of the vindictive and merciless foe.

"And that it is our opinion that an armed association of the inhabitants Armed of this town is indispensably requisite to aid the force now here, and such Association. further force as may be stationed here by Government, in defence of the said town and harbour.

"And that the Plan which has been delivered by Major-General Benson to your Committee for the defence of the harbour, appears to us to be excellently calculated for that purpose, and is recommended by us to be adopted.

"And that the Chief Magistrate should be requested to press for the Measures. naval force promised by Government, and also to renew his application for a Signal Officer.

"And that we are of opinion the expenses of carrying Major-General Cost. Benson's plan into compleat effect (with the aid of the guns and stores

Ordnance.	now deposited in this town) will amount to £1600 or thereabouts (as per estimate No. 1) which we beg may be taken as a part of this our report. "And that it appears to us, that in addition to the four field pieces now at the disposal of the Parish of Liverpool, it is expedient to provide six other Field pieces, to be used as Flying Artillery, and to be formed into a Brigade, together with the necessary apparatus. And that the cost of the above additional six Field pieces and the hire of horses to draw the same for one year, may be computed at £1390 as appears by Estimate No. 2 which we beg may be taken as part of this our Report.
Gunboats.	"And that we are of opinion that two Gun boats, of a construction suitable for the river Mersey, should be provided as soon as possible, each mounting an 18 Pounder on the bow, the expence of which will be—if two of the Fort guns are appropriated to that service—about £800, as will appear by the said estimate No. 2.
Men.	"And that it is our opinion that the number of men necessary to manage the said respective Field pieces, Batteries, Guns and Gunboats will be as under viz—

```
                                                                "MEN
      " For 29 Guns in the different Batteris..................  290
        —  10 Guns in the Fort .................................  100
        —  10 Artillery Guns 13 men each  ..................  130
        —   2 Gunboats 40 men each..........................   80
                                                                ———
                                                                "600
```

Estimate.	"And that the above number of men should be paid, clothed in uniform, exercised and trained to the perfect use of the said Artillery, Great guns, and Gunboats as well as to the use of Pikes, the expence of which may be estimated at £1620 or thereabouts as appears by the said estimate No. 2.
Volunteers.	"And that we are unanimously of opinion and earnestly recommend that a further Volunteer force of at least two Regiments of Infantry, to consist of 560 Rank & File each, should be immediately raised for the defence of this town.
Cost.	"And that we are of opinion the expence of raising and cloathing such two regiments will be about £4000 provided Government will make the usual allowances, but if this is refused, a proportionate increased expence will have to be provided for.
Powder.	"And that in addition to the Amunition, the property of the Government and of this town, which remained unexpended at the conclusion of the last war, it will be proper to procure an immediate supply of 200 barrels of Powder, 20 tons of Cannon Shot, as well round as grape, and 4 tons of Musket Ball, the expence of which may be estimated at £1620.
Depôt.	"And that it appears to us highly desirable that a Depôt for Gunpowder should be immediately formed on the Lancashire side of the river Mersey

for the better protecting and securing a supply of Amunition, the expence of which it should seem will not exceed the sum of £500.

"And that a general Subscription be entered into to carry out the objects of this report." <small>Subscription.</small>

The Estimates are set forth at length, and amount to the sum of £11,530.

"1803, July 12.

"Resolved and Ordered that a Sum of not less than £2000 be laid out <small>Funds.</small> by the Corporation, and that the Dock Committee be also authorized to advance and lay out a Sum of not less than £1000 from the Dock funds for carrying out some one or more of the objects of the said Report."

July 28th. At a Special Meeting of the Council, a Committee was appointed as a Committee of Defence for the <small>Defence Committee.</small> Town and Port during the continuance of the war, with power to expend the money voted.

The Mayor was requested to write to Lord St. Vincent, First Lord of the Admiralty, requesting that two ships with heavy metal might be immediately sent to the Port, one to be a block ship, the other to be stationed at the mouth of the Harbour, and to act in conjunction with the Batteries on shore.

"1803, Sept. 7. Resolved and Ordered, that his Royal Highness Prince <small>Prince Frederick William (of Gloucester) who is lately come to this town as William.</small> Lieutenant General and Commanding Officer of the district, be requested to accept the Freedom of the Borough, and that the Mayor, Bailiffs and Town Clerk be desired to wait upon his Royal Highness with the following address."

This is couched in the high-flowing language common to such productions. He was also entertained at a public dinner, which was given in the Union Newsroom in Duke Street, then recently erected.

The cost of the dinner is set out in the minutes as being £246 14s.

1803, Sept. 19th. Jonas Bold, Mayor.

Public Meeting. Subscription.
A Public Meeting was held in the Town Hall, when the Mayor subscribed £3000 on behalf of the Corporation, and £2000 on behalf of the Dock Trustees, towards the defences of the Port during the war, in addition to the sum of £3000 previously subscribed, a portion of which had already been expended. One principal object is stated to have been the purchasing and fitting a number of Gun Boats, the guns and ammunition to be provided by the Government. Another, the erection of Fortifications on the Lancashire and Cheshire shores, the Government providing the men and arms.

Duke of Gloucester.
1804, Sept. The Duke of Gloucester, brother of George III., and father of Prince Frederick William, paid a visit to the town. He was, according to ordinary custom, presented with the Freedom, and an address, followed by a public dinner.

Barracks.
1804, October 3rd. A scheme propounded by Prince Frederick William was laid before the Council for the erection of Barracks in Great Howard Street, near the Gaol, for the accommodation of 1000 men. This was not looked on favourably by the Government, and came to no result.

Admirals.
About the same date the town was visited by the two naval heroes, Sir Thomas Trowbridge and Sir John Jarvis (Earl St. Vincent), who were welcomed with the usual honours.

1805, Nov. 14th. Henry Clay, Mayor.

Death of Nelson.
After the victory of Trafalgar and the death of Nelson, an address was presented to the Crown, of congratulation and condolence.

At the same time the sum of £1000 was voted by the Council towards the erection of a monument to the memory of the hero.

Prince of Wales.
1807, April 18th. The Prince of Wales, accompanied by

the Duke of Clarence (William IV.), visited the town, with the usual festivities and addresses. It was also

"Resolved, that the Town Hall and other public offices be illuminated in a style of extent and grandeur, similar to those upon the King's recovery, and that the Mayor and Magistrates be desired to recommend a general illumination through the town.

Illuminations.

The Town Hall being at the time under alteration and repair, the dinner was given in the large room of the Liverpool Arms Hotel in Castle Street. The report states:—

Dinner.

"Your Committee provided an elegant gold box to be presented to the Prince with the Freedom of the town; they also procured for this occasion a Service of Plate and other articles for the Prince's table, and they directed every delicacy of the season to be provided for the tables, and by every exertion in their power they procured the choicest wines of every sort, as well from the cellars of private gentlemen, who cheerfully and liberally supplied them as from public vaults.

"Your Committee selected the company to the dinner by inviting the Earl of Derby and all the visitors at Knowsley, all the principal Military and Naval Officers in the town, several of the principal gentlemen in the county, the principal clergy — the Members of the Council and others."

Company.

A deputation assembled at the Mayor's house and proceeded in carriages to Knowsley, where they presented the address, and received a written reply, which is inserted.

Deputation.

1807. On Saturday, April 19th, their Royal Highnesses again visited the town, and were taken to view the Docks and other objects of interest, and finally took leave amidst the most enthusiastic demonstrations of loyalty, after presenting three hundred guineas to the charities.

Prince's Visit.

1807, April 16th. An address was adopted for presentation to the King, setting forth that:—

"Amidst the ruin of institutions once deemed sacred and the demolition of empires which promised to resist innovation, it is the pride and happiness of Britons that the integrity of this empire is preserved, that its establishments civil and religious still exist, unshaken by the convulsions of Europe and that the sceptre is swayed by a monarch who under Providence is destined to be the watchful guardian of those invaluable

Address.

and constitutional rights which we trust will be preserved inviolate to the latest posterity by successors in your Majesty's illustrious family to the throne of these realms."

1808, Jan. 27th. An address, breathing the same sentiments, was presented, concluding with the assurance that :—

Address.

"So long as injustice and oppression continue the common practice and pursuit of our enemy, your Majesty's Government may firmly rely upon our best endeavours to meet every emergency, satisfied that the ultimate and only object of the war, with your Majesty, is an honourable and secure peace."

Some difficulties appear to have arisen as to the payment of the expenses, for more than three years afterwards we find the following entry :—

Expenses.

"1811, May 15. Upon the motion of Mr Alderman Dawson as chairman of the Committee to whom the consideration of the accounts delivered in by Messrs Perrin, Geddes & Co, Glass Manufacturers at Warrington, for the different articles of Glass presented to His Royal Highness the Prince of Wales was referred,

"Resolved and Ordered that the sum of £706 18s. 0d. being the balance of the account still remaining due to them be paid."

Jubilee.

The Jubilee of the reign of King George III. was celebrated with great éclat.

"1809, Octr. 17. James Gerard M.D. Mayor.
"Resolved and Ordered, that a respectful and dutiful Address be presented to his Majesty upon his entering into the Fiftieth Year of his reign on the 25th of October instant."

1809, Octr. 21st. John Clarke, Mayor.

A Special Council was held to take measures for carrying out the celebration in a becoming manner. Amongst other resolutions was one

King's Statue.

"For permitting the statue intended to be erected to his Majesty to be placed in Great George Square and of subscribing to the erection of the statue out of the funds of the Corporation and of co-operating with the general Committee outside."

An address was prepared, which expressed the sentiments of the Council as follows :—

"We your Majesty's most dutiful and loyal subjects the Mayor, Alder- Address. men &c. of your Majesty's Ancient Borough of Liverpool . . beg leave to approach the throne at this particular period, with the most heartfelt emotions of joy and gratitude, and to be permitted to express our deep and awful sense of the goodness of divine Providence to this highly favoured Kingdom in the continuance of your Majesty's long and glorious reign.

"Impressed with the inestimable value of your Majesty's life, we are particularly anxious to offer our renewed assurances of fidelity and attachment to a sovereign not less to be revered for his domestic virtues than honored for the practice of those principles, which as they cast such resplendent rays on the morning of your Majesty's reign do also gild the evening of it with increasing lustre.

"We earnestly and devoutly supplicate the great Disposer of all events, that your Majesty may long live to enjoy the blessings of your pious and patriotic conduct, and continue the happy instrument of preserving in the most exalted degree the civil and religious liberties of a free, loyal, and grateful people."

It was proposed to have a Ball at the Town Hall, but the alterations to the building were not in a sufficient state of forwardness to allow it.

It was resolved, that the sum of £500 be given towards the erection of the intended statue in Great George Square. Statue.

1816, Novr. A resolution was passed at a meeting of the Committee of Subscribers " That the Council be respectfully requested to permit the statue to be placed in the centre of the wide part of London Road."

This request was complied with and the statue erected accordingly.

"1821, March 7. It having been represented to this Council that there is a deficiency in the amount of the subscriptions for compleating the Subscrip- erection of the statue of his late Majesty, . tions.

"Resolved that the Treasurer be authorized to pay the sum of two hundred guineas for this purpose."

The town was brilliantly illuminated on the 21st October, Illumina- the day of the King's accession, and an entertainment was tions.

given by the Mayor at the Town Hall. Towards the expense of this the Council voted the sum of £120.

Sir Sydney Smith.

1811, May. Admiral Sir Sydney Smith visited the town and was entertained by the Mayor. The recorded expense was as follows:—

" For the Dinner	£61	2	0
,, Wine	74	17	2
,, Lamps and Lights	170	10	0
	"£306	9	2"

"1811, May 10. James Drinkwater Mayor.

Prisoners in France.

"Resolved and Ordered on the motion of the Mayor that a handsome and liberal sum of money be subscribed by this Corporation towards the relief of the British prisoners in France, which sum—in consideration that there may be a great many of the Freemen of this borough and other inhabitants and persons belonging to the same in the number—was fixed at £500, to be transmitted to Thomas Ferguson Esq Secretary to the Committee appointed for this purpose, who have advertized that they have secured a safe conveyance for such sums as are to be remitted to France for the use of the prisoners."

"1811, Decr. 12. John Bourne Mayor.

"The Mayor having laid before this Council a letter received from Major Gen. Dirom commanding the district, representing the dilapidated *Batteries.* state of the three Batteries erected by the Corporation in 1796 for the general defence of the town and Shipping.

"Resolved and Ordered that the subject be referred to the Select Finance Committee, with instructions to combine if possible with this *Site to be procured.* business the obtaining possession of the present Fort and Battery now wanted for the scite of the New North Dock called Prince's Dock."

The negotiation went on for twelve months, and ultimately possession was obtained.

Perceval shot.

1812. On Monday, the 11th May, Mr. Spencer Perceval, the Prime Minister, was shot in the lobby of the House of Commons by Bellingham, previously a Liverpool merchant.

Address.

An address to the Prince Regent was adopted by the Council, expressive of their sorrow and indignation at the atrocity, and offering their strongest assurances of loyalty and attachment, and their fixed determination to support on every occasion the honour and dignity of the Crown.

1813, January 13th. Great sympathy was excited on behalf of the Russian people at the time of Bonaparte's advance on Moscow.

"It was Resolved and Ordered that the sum of two hundred pounds be subscribed by this Corporation towards the relief of the Russian people who have so severely suffered by the French invasion." Subscription to Russia.

1813, Nov. 29th. When the reaction took place, and the rising in Germany led to the success of the Allied Armies, there were great rejoicings.

At a Special Council, held for the purpose of taking into consideration the best manner of expressing the gratitude and exultation on the great success of his Majesty's arms and those of his allies, it was Resolved:— Rejoicings.

"That an address be presented to the Prince Regent expressive of the high sense entertained by this Council of the late glorious achievements of his Majesty's Arms, and of the happy result by the attainment of an honorable and permanent peace." Address.

A public meeting of the inhabitants was held, which determined on celebrating the joyful occasion by a general illumination, but to this serious objections were raised. Public Meeting.

It was resolved, that should the illumination take place, the south front of the Town Hall should be brilliantly illuminated. Illuminations.

A public dinner and ball were held at the Town Hall. Dinner and Ball.

1815, July 5th. Thomas Leyland, Mayor.

The Mayor having stated to the Council that in compliance with a requisition, he had convened a public meeting for the purpose of affording an opportunity to the town at large of testifying their admiration of the conduct of the British army under the command of Field Marshal the Duke of Wellington in the splendid victory of the 18th June, by instituting a subscription for the widows and children of Meeting.

Subscription.

those who had fallen on that memorable day, and in the battles immediately preceding:

"Resolved that the Mayor be authorised at such meeting to subscribe the sum of two hundred guineas."

<small>Nelson's Monument.</small> "1815, October 10. The request of the Committee for the erection of the Monument to the memory of the late Admiral Lord Viscount Nelson that the Council would be pleased to take upon itself the perpetual repair of the Monument upon receiving from the Committee the sum of one hundred Pounds having been signified to the Council.

<small>Maintenance.</small> "Resolved, that the offer of such sum be declined to be received, but that the Council with a view to the protection and security of a Work so honourable to the country as a work of Art, and to this town as a splendid instance of its patriotism, liberality and taste, do take upon itself the perpetual repair of the monument, and that the expense of such repair from time to time be defrayed out of the Corporation estate."

"1815, Novr. 7. William Barton Mayor.

<small>Freedom to Wellington.</small> "Resolved, that the Freedom of this borough be presented to Field Marshal his Grace the Duke of Wellington in testimony of the high admiration, and grateful sense entertained by the Council of the signal and eminent services so repeatedly rendered by his Grace to the country at large, and more especially of the last glorious victory obtained on the plains of Waterloo; a victory adding fresh lustre to the splendid achievements of the British Arms, but attributable principally to the consumate skill and personal valour displayed by the great Commander himself."

1816, May 11th. At a Special Council, an address was adopted for presentation to the Prince Regent on the occasion <small>Marriage of Princess Charlotte.</small> of the marriage of the Princess Charlotte, with corresponding addresses to the Queen and to the Princess, and to Prince Leopold. The Mayor and Bailiffs, with the Recorder, were deputed to repair to London for the purpose of presenting the addresses in person, accompanied by the members for the Borough. On this occasion the Mayor, Mr. William Barton, received the honour of knighthood.

A ball was given at the Town Hall. The expense of lighting the rooms is stated to have amounted to £53.

1817, Nov. 6th. Thomas Case, Mayor.

An address of condolence was adopted, to be presented

to the Prince Regent, on the lamented decease of the Princess Charlotte. Princess Charlotte's Death.

1818, Decr. 5th. Jonathan Blundell Hollinshead, Mayor.

An address of condolence was presented on the decease of Queen Charlotte. Queen Charlotte.

1819, Octr. This period was one of great distress and discontent amongst the manufacturing population. Soon after what was called the Peterloo Massacre, at Manchester, an address to the Prince Regent was adopted, setting forth that:— Distress.

> "At a period when sedition under the imposing mask of reform, and tumult under the specious pretext of legal assemblage are rapidly combining to alienate the affections of the people from their sovereign, and to endanger the existence of all civil and religious rights, we feel it to be a duty imperative upon us to express in the strongest terms our abhorrence of such pernicious doctrines as are daily and industriously promulgated amongst those who are totally incompetent to discuss their merits, or to decide upon their truth, and which are alone calculated to bring into contempt the constituted authorities of the realm, to spread more widely the spirit of disaffection and discord, and to kindle more fiercely the flame of insurrection and rebellion in the country.
>
> "Deprecating alike all premature judgments and all precipitate enquiries we feel the most perfect confidence that such temperate, firm, and seasonable measures will be adopted, as may tend to bring to justice all who have really offended against the law, to preserve due order and obedience amongst the people, and to allay the progress of those factious and alarming combinations, which have of late so essentially disturbed the comforts and happiness of society and so vitally affected the welfare and prosperity of the kingdom at large."

Address.
Measures adopted.

1820. King George III. died on the 29th January. Death of George III.

February 2nd. John Tobin, Mayor.

An address was adopted for presentation to the new monarch, who was publicly proclaimed in front of the Town Hall on February 4th. On February 12th a grand procession of the inhabitants took place to celebrate the event.

On the presentation of the address, the Mayor received the honour of knighthood.

1821. Measures were taken to celebrate the forthcoming coronation with brilliancy and éclat. A Committee was appointed under the presidency of the Mayor, to make the due preparations.

Coronation.

June 11th. At a Special Council, it was Resolved :—

"That a sum of £1500 be presented by the Corporation on the day of his Majesty's coronation to be distributed amongst the public Charities of the town, and that a Committee, to consist of the whole Council be appointed to consider of the best mode of distributing the same; and also that the Committee be authorized to consider the propriety of the application of a further sum for the entertainment of the various classes of tradesmen or Societies of the town on the day of the coronation.

Preparations.

"Resolved also that the Prince's Dock be publicly opened on the day of the coronation by the Mayor and Common Council."

Opening of Prince's Dock.

1821, June 13. Thomas Leyland, Mayor.

By order of the Council, a letter was addressed by the Mayor to the members for the borough expressing a desire that the Body Corporate should attend by deputation at the King's coronation, and proposing to send in a petition to this effect to the Court of Claims. This proposal met with no encouragement and was not pressed.

Proposed Deputation.

"1821, July 4. Resolved that the Mayor be requested to communicate to Sir Thomas Laurence the great dissatisfaction felt by this Council at not having been yet furnished with the portrait of his late Majesty, and particularly so as from the strong and repeated assurances of Sir Thomas Laurence they have been induced to believe it would have been finished a long time since.

Portrait by Laurence.

"Resolved that his Royal Highness the Duke of York will be graciously pleased to honor the Common Council of this borough with his portrait by one of the most eminent artists of the day, and that the Mayor be requested to obtain his Royal Highness's consent."

Duke of York's Portrait.

An unpleasant little contretemps occurred in reference to the preparations for the Coronation day.

"1821, July 4. Thomas Leyland Mayor.

"Resolved, that in case application be made for the use of the public rooms in the Townhall for a Ball on the evening of the Coronation day

Misunderstanding.

the Select Finance Committee be authorized to grant the same; the rooms to be lighted at the expence of the Corporation."

This was thought by the Mayor to be an infringement of his jurisdiction, and he invited a dinner party for the same evening.

1821, July 17th. A Special Council was held,

"To take into consideration the following advertisement, issued by the Coronation Ball Committee, which, in consequence of the unjustifiable representation made therein, has determined the Mayor not to allow his dining apartments in the Townhall to be taken from him without his consent. {.marginnote}Coronation Ball.

'Advertisement
'Coronation Ball

'The Mayor having unexpectedly invited a party to dine with him on Thursday next the 19th July at the Townhall, the Committee for conducting the festivities of his Majesty's coronation regret that they are under the necessity of postponing the Ball to the following evening, Friday the 20th instant. {.marginnote}Mayor's Refusal.

'By Order of the Committee

'Jos. LANGTON, Secy.'

"Resolved unanimously, that the Mayor be requested to grant the use of the rooms in the Town Hall for the purposes of the intended Ball on the evening of the 20th instant."

The Mayor thereupon declined to give his consent. The ball, therefore, had to be abandoned.

A resolution was passed on the 5th September following:

"That the Treasurer be directed to pay to Joseph Langton Esq the Secretary of the Coronation Ball Committee the sum of £135 15s. 0d. for the purpose of discharging the tradesmen's bills for expenses incurred by that Committee in making preparations for the Ball intended to have been held in the Town Hall on the 19th and 20th July in celebration of his Majesty's Coronation." {.marginnote}Payment of Expenses.

1821, July 19th. The Coronation day was celebrated by the most magnificent demonstration ever seen in Liverpool. A procession of the various trades paraded the streets with their insignia, banners, bands of music, &c. Their destination was the Prince's Dock, round which the procession {.marginnote}Coronation Day. Festivities.

deployed, whilst the ship May, a Liverpool West Indiaman, followed by other vessels, entered the dock.

Balance.

1821, Sept. 5th. A communication from the Coronation Committee of tradesmen mentioning the intended appropriation of a small balance of the sum of £600, voted by the Council on the day of his Majesty's coronation, and requesting that the Council would be pleased to accept the suit of brass armour worn by the Champion on the Coronation day, having been laid before the Council,

Brass Armour.

"Resolved, that the Council approve of the intended appropriation of the balance, and that the suit of armour be accepted with thanks.

Thanks to Committee.

"Resolved also, that the thanks of this Council be presented to the Coronation Committee of Tradesmen for the services rendered by them upon the recent celebration of his Majesty's Coronation."

"1827, Jany. 17. Thos. Littledale Mayor.

Death of Duke of York.

"Resolved that an address of condolence be presented to his Majesty on the occasion of the death of the Duke of York."

Canning's Monument.

1827, Aug. 27th. Pursuant to a requisition to the Mayor, a public meeting was called "for the purpose of taking into consideration and determining upon the propriety of showing some mark of respect to the memory of the Right Hon. George Canning, who died on the 8th August."

"It was Resolved, 'That a monument be erected to his memory, and that a subscription be entered into to defray the cost and contingent expenses of erecting such monument.'"

Subscription.

"1827, Sept. 5. Resolved, that the sum of £500 be subscribed towards the erection of the monument to the memory of the late Mr Canning."

The commission for a statue was given to Mr. Chantrey. It was completed in 1832.

1832, March 7th. Samuel Sandbach, Mayor.

Statue.

A letter was read from Mr. Littledale, chairman of the Monument Committee, requesting that the statue should be placed in the Town Hall, and recommending the first landing of the principal stairs as the most eligible site.

The request was granted, and on the 27th September following the statue was formally unveiled.

In 1828 the widow of Mr. Canning was created a viscountess. *Lady Canning.*

1828, March 5th. The Mayor announced to the Council that he had received a communication from Lady Canning, expressive of a wish that in the armorial bearings to be adopted by her Ladyship, some record should be introduced to denote the connection of Mr. Canning with the town of Liverpool; whereupon it was *Her request.*

"Resolved unanimously that the Council on the part of the town feel highly honoured by the sentiments expressed by Lady Canning, and that her request be complied with; any attendant expenses to be paid by the Corporation."

1828, Nov. Sir Robert (then Mr.) Peel paid a visit to the town. As a member of the Cabinet and leader of the House of Commons he was received with great respect, presented with the freedom of the borough and with an address, which referred especially to the improvements introduced into the Criminal Code and the administration of the law by his instrumentality. To this he gave a graceful and suitable reply. *Visit of Peel.*

1830, July 26. King George IV. departed this life, and William IV. succeeded. *Death of George IV.*

The usual address to the new monarch was voted by the Council. The Mayor, Mr. George Drinkwater, was deputed to present the address in person, accompanied by the Recorder and the Bailiffs. On the presentation the Mayor received the honour of knighthood. *Address.*

1830. On the occasion of the opening of the Liverpool and Manchester Railway, Sept. 15th, great preparations were made for the entertainment of the numerous distinguished visitors expected, especially the Duke of Wellington. *Opening of Railway.*

A Committee was appointed to carry out the arrangements, with unlimited powers of expenditure. The unfortunate accident by which Mr. Huskisson lost his life, put a stop to the proceedings, of which a report was presented to the Council on the 3rd November. It states that the arrangements had been made on the lines of the visit of the Prince of Wales in 1806; that it was their determination to exhibit a splendour in this entertainment worthy of the individual and the occasion; that they were confirmed in this by the very numerous list of nobility and distinguished strangers who were to be present at the opening of the Railway the day previous. A suitable service of plate was hired from Messrs. Gerrard, of London, at the cost of £250. A gold box for the presentation of the Freedom (which remained undisposed of) cost £157 10s. The contract with Mr. Lynn for the dinner was £235, from which he allowed a deduction of £40 in consequence of the dinner not taking place. The cost of fitting up the rooms was £168 4s. 9d. In the whole the sum expended on the abortive preparations amounted to £835 16s. 11d.

Huskisson's Death.

Preparations.

Freedom to Wellington.

Expenses.

The Duke in declining to join in the proposed festivities, expressed his deep regret at the melancholy circumstances, and his sense of the honour which the Corporation intended for him.

Duke's Regret.

Coronation of William IV.

1831. On the coronation of King William and Queen Adelaide in September, addresses to the King and Queen were presented by the Mayor, Mr. Thomas Brancker, in person, accompanied by the Bailiffs, " which," it is reported, " their Majesties were pleased to receive most graciously, and the Mayor also stated that upon this occasion his Majesty was pleased to confer the honour of knighthood upon him."

1832, July 4th. Samuel Sandbach, Mayor.

An address was forwarded for presentation to the King **Address.** expressive of the congratulations of the Council at his escape from the attack recently made on his person.

1834, July 2. John Wright, Mayor.

On the introduction of the Irish Appropriation Bill into **Irish Affairs.** Parliament, by which ten Irish Bishoprics were suppressed, King William had expressed himself very strongly to a deputation of Archbishops and Bishops in defence of the Church.

The Liverpool Town Council took up the subject very warmly, and

"Resolved unanimously, That a dutiful and loyal address be presented **Address.** to his Majesty the King from this Corporation, expressive of their unfeigned thanks for the recent declaration made by his Majesty to the Reverend the Archbishops and Bishops, in favour of the United Church of England and Ireland as by law established in these realms.

"That the Worshipful the Mayor (having to present a similar address from the inhabitants of the town) be respectfully requested to present this address in person to his Majesty."

The circumstances which prevented the Duke of Wellington from accepting the hospitality of the town in 1830 have been stated above. During the contest preceding the passing of the Municipal Reform Act, 1835, deputations from several of **Opposition to Municipal** the Corporate Bodies, including Liverpool, waited upon the **Reform Act.** Duke and other peers to endeavour to interest them in preventing the passing of the Bill.

"1835, Octr. 7. James Aspinall Mayor.

"Resolved, that the thanks of this Council be respectfully offered to **Thanks to** his Grace the Duke of Wellington, to the Most Honorable the Marquis of **Wellington.** Salisbury, to the Lord Wharncliffe and to Lord Skelmersdale for the kind attention afforded by them to the several deputations from this Council, and for the assistance rendered.

"Resolved that the Worshipful the Mayor be respectfully requested to communicate to his Grace the Duke of Wellington the sentiments of regret felt by this Council, that no seasonable opportunity has yet been afforded to this Council of enrolling his Grace as a Free Burgess of this **Freedom to** borough in accordance with the resolution of the special Council in July **Wellington.**

Gold Box.

1830; and that the Mayor be further requested to transmit for his Grace's acceptance the Gold Box then prepared for presentation; which has remained in the custody of the Mayor for the time being since that period."

The following reply was received from the Duke :—

"Walmer Castle, Octr. 10, 1835.

"To James Aspinall, Esq.,
"Mayor of Liverpool.

Wellington's Reply.

"I have had the honor of receiving your letter of the 8th instant, in which you have enclosed copies of the minutes of the Council of the Corporation of Liverpool of the 7th.

"I have always lamented the circumstances which prevented me in the year 1830 from receiving the honour which the Corporation of Liverpool intended to confer upon me, and I have regretted that I have since been prevented from waiting upon them.

"I beg to present to the Council my acknowledgements for their recollection of me at such a moment as this, and to assure them that however flattering this additional proof of their goodwill, it was not necessary to induce me at all times to feel the most anxious interest in the welfare and prosperity of their town; and to make every effort in my power to promote both.

"With many thanks for your polite communication, I have the honor to be,

"Sir, Your most obedient humble servant,

"WELLINGTON."

A usual mode of complimenting distinguished men consisted in presenting them with the freedom of the borough. Many names of eminence are thus recorded in addition to those already mentioned.

Freedoms Conferred.

In 1802. Dr. Currie, the editor of Burns.
  1807. Dr. Edward Jenner, the illustrious introducer of vaccination.
  1810. Admiral Sir Sydney Smith.
  1812. The Earl of Liverpool.
  1815. William Roscoe.
  1816. Lord Viscount Sidmouth.
  1820. Hon. E. G. Stanley (14th Earl of Derby).

In 1820. William George Brown, for his benefactions to the Blue Coat School, in which he was brought up.
    1822. The Duke of Athol.
    — Right Hon. George Canning.
    — Major-General Gascoyne.
    1823. Right Hon. William Huskisson.
    1833. George Stephenson.

MUNICIPAL AFFAIRS.

<small>Population.</small> The town had now entered upon its latest phase under the old exclusive Corporation. The population at the close of the 18th century had increased to 77,653, and including the suburbs and the seamen would probably amount to 90,000.

The litigation so often repeated during the 18th century, arising out of the usurped functions of the self-elected Council, had subsided, owing to the want of funds of the appellants, and the Council were left to administer the affairs of the Corporation in peace until the final break up.

<small>Toxteth Park.</small> The land in Toxteth Park, south of Parliament Street, belonged almost exclusively to the Earl of Sefton, who in 1775 obtained an Act of Parliament enabling him to grant building leases. By the end of the century a few houses had been erected, and a scheme was brought forward for creating <small>Harrington.</small> a new town to be called Harrington, after Isabella, the first Countess of Sefton, who was a daughter of the Earl of Harrington.

It is to this that the following entry refers:—

"1802, Octr. 6. Peter Whitfield Brancker Mayor.

"Resolved and Ordered, upon the motion of Mr. Earle, that it be an instruction to the Select Finance Committee in their intended application to Parliament, to obtain authority that the land purchased by the Corporation at the south end of the town from the Earl of Sefton and Messrs. Roe and Leigh, and which is now considered as a part of the Township of Toxteth Park in the Parish of Walton upon the Hill, may in future be <small>Extension of Borough.</small> considered and taken as part of the Township and Parish of Liverpool, entitled to equal benefits, and the same advantages in its rights, liberties, franchises, and immunities, as the present town and parish of Liverpool, and subject to the same and similar powers, jurisdiction and authority."

Nothing came of this scheme. The Act was never obtained. It was under the Reform Act of 1835 that a portion of Toxteth Park was incorporated with Liverpool.

In October 1803 Mr. Wm. Harper, Bailiff during the year then expiring, was elected Mayor. Doubts were expressed at Mayoralty. the time of the election, respecting the eligibility of the candidate, he being practically one of the Returning Officers.

In order to settle the question of the validity of the election, the Council made the following order:—

"1804, May 10. Jonas Bold, Mayor for the previous year, presiding.

"Whereas great doubts arose at the Court of Election held on the 18th day of October last respecting the eligibility of William Harper to the Harper office of Mayor, by reason of his being one of the Bailiffs at the time of elected. his election . . . the Council for the removal of all doubts and difficulties, and for the purpose of ascertaining the true construction of the Charters so far as they relate to the election of the Chief Officers of the said town, Ordered an information in the nature of a *Quo Warranto* to be Quo filed in the Court of King's Bench against the said Wm. Harper, and Warranto. James Gerard and Thomas Molyneux (Bailiffs), and such proceedings were thereupon had, that in the Easter term following, by the consideration and judgment of the same court, the said William Harper was then and there ousted from his said office of Mayor, and the said James Gerard Mayor and Thomas Molyneux were also ousted from their said office of Bailiffs ousted. of the said town, and a Writ of Mandamus was duly issued and awarded by the said court for the election of chief officers in their room and place."

1804, May 21st. John Bridge Aspinall was elected Mayor for the remainder of the Municipal year.

In October, 1804, Mr. Harper was again elected Mayor, Re-elected. and the following resolution was passed:—

"Ordered that the sum of £222 18s. 2d., being the amount of the costs of the present Mayor in his defence be paid by the Treasurer."

It had been the custom from time immemorial, for the outgoing Mayor to have the nomination of a friend to receive Mayor's the freedom of the borough. Mr. Thos. Staniforth, Mayor Freeman, in 1797, had neglected to exercise this privilege. After his decease in 1803, his widow applied to the Council that she might be allowed to take up the lapsed nomination, whereupon, it was

Inquiry.

"Resolved and Ordered, that the Town Clerk or his deputy examine the Council minutes for thirty years back, and make a report to the next Council of the names and trades or professions of the several persons who have been severally admitted Freemen of this borough upon the nomination of the Aldermen in right of their having served the office of Mayor during that period."

Request granted.

In March, 1806, the Council granted Mrs. Staniforth's request, but on reconsidering the matter, they came to the following resolution:—

"1806, April 2. Henry Clay Mayor.

"The present Common Council upon review of the order made at the last Council, giving to the widow of the late Alderman Staniforth Esquire the nomination of a Freeman of this borough, on reconsidering the same, find it not to be warranted under the Bye-law for the admission of a Mayor's Freeman; and do therefore now at this Council with the acquiescence of Mrs Staniforth, signified by her son Mr Samuel Staniforth, now present as a member of this Council, rescind the said order, but from motives of respect to the memory of the late Alderman Staniforth, this Council doth hereby nominate and appoint his friend Mr. Antony Littledale, merchant, a Freeman of this borough and Corporation."

Order rescinded.

Colonel John Bolton, an eminent merchant, who raised a regiment of Volunteers, and was the life-long friend of George Canning, was in 1807 elected a member of the Council, apparently without consulting his wishes, for he declined to serve; whereupon

Bolton elected.

"1807, Decr, 2. It was Resolved and Ordered,

"That the Town Clerk be directed to take measures for compelling John Bolton Esquire to take the oaths of a member of this Council and to attend in his place."

Compulsion.

This resolution brought forth a letter of remonstrance from Colonel Bolton, which led to the following resolution:—

"1808, Aug. 5. Henry Blundell Hollinshead Mayor.

"On reading a letter from John Bolton Esq[r] of the 5th January last to the Mayor, stating his reasons for wishing to decline the honor of becoming a Common Councilman, viz[t] that however anxious he should be to the

Reasons for declining.

utmost of his power to fill the duties of that situation, it would be impossible, both from the very uncertain state of his health and his almost constant absence from Liverpool to undertake the active duties of that office, and therefore hoping that he might be allowed to decline that honor; and upon considering the same,

"Resolved and Ordered that the vote for the said John Bolton to be a Common Councilman for this borough and Corporation, be and the same is hereby rescinded." *Election rescinded.*

There occur in the records few instances of Councillors being expelled. One such occurred in 1813.

"1813, Decr. 5. William Nicholson, Mayor.

"The opinions of Mr Holroyd and Mr Scarlett relative to the power of this Council to remove Mr Thos Jno Parke one of the members, for his gross misconduct when a partner in the late Banking house of Messrs Gregson and Co, and for his continued neglect of attendance at the Councils of this borough having been read, *Parke.*

"Resolved and Ordered, That the regular summons requiring the attendance of Mr Parke at the next Council be served upon him and repeated, as recommended in the Opinions, with a view to the expulsion of Mr. Parke as one of the members of this Council." *Proposed expulsion.*

"1814, April 6. Resolved, that the resignation of Mr Thomas John Parke as one of the members of this Council signified in his letter to the Mayor—now read—be, and the same is hereby accepted." *Res'gns.*

1814, April 6th. A letter from John Gladstone, Esq. (afterwards Sir John), as *Letter from Gladstone.*

"Chairman of the Sub-Committees of the associated bodies of merchants and Shipowners in this town, soliciting the support of this Council to the establishment of an office in London, to facilitate the despatch of Parliamentary business having been read,

"Resolved that the consideration of the said letter be referred to the Select Finance Committee."

This resulted in the establishment of the Liverpool Office in London, which has ever since been continued. *London office.*

"1814, July 6. William Nicholson, Mayor.

"A letter from William Roscoe Esqr Chairman of the Committee of the Liverpool Institution, requesting the grant by this Corporation of a piece of land for the purpose of erecting a building thereon having been read, *Letter from Roscoe.*

"Resolved, that the request contained in such letter be referred to the Select Finance Committee and that they be fully authorized to comply with the same upon such liberal and extended scale as to them may seem proper; this Council perfectly according in the sentiments expressed in the letter from Mr Roscoe as to the great utility of the institution and the benefits which will be derived by the town of Liverpool from its establishment therein. And that the Common Seal be affixed to such grant as may be deemed requisite by the Committee to be made out on the occasion."

<small>Royal Institution.</small>

This resolution is extremely creditable to the Council of that day, exhibiting a feeling of liberality, and an appreciation of culture hardly to have been expected. This was the origin of the Royal Institution, which has certainly not fulfilled the sanguine expectations of its founders.

The grant of land was not required, suitable premises for the purpose having been purchased in Colquitt Street.

An application for aid to an institution of a more popular kind was not so successful.

"1825, July 6. A resolution passed at a public meeting of the inhabitants convened at the Music Hall, requesting a contribution from the funds of the Corporation in support of the Mechanics' Institute, having been laid before this Council,

<small>Mechanics' Institution.</small>

"Resolved that this subject be postponed for further consideration until the next Council."

1825, August 3rd. At the next Council,

"The Council having resumed the consideration of the resolution, and Mr Alderman Case having moved that the sum of £500 be paid to the Committee of the Mechanics' Institute, and such motion having been seconded by Dr Gerard, the same was negatived."

<small>Grant refused.</small>

The matter however did not end here. The parties promoting the establishment of the Institute were earnest and determined. Their next move was to purchase a large plot of land on the south side of Mount Street, on contract from the Corporation. The payment for this was postponed from time to time until the accession of the reformed Council, when ultimately a free grant was made.

The Corporation of Liverpool were never backward in contributing to the relief of distress, whether at home or abroad.

<small>Relief Funds.</small>

" 1809, Feby. 5. Jas Gerard Mayor.
" Upon the report of the Bailiffs stating that in consequence of a Transport called the Maida having been driven into this port from Corunna by stress of weather, and having on board troops, they had thought proper to order the non-commissioned officers and privates a suitable dinner and refreshment in the kitchen of the Townhall and also each a flannel shirt, drawers and shoes &c. which they appeared to be greatly in want of, the expence of which amounted to the sum of £56. Maida Transport.

This was a detachment of the army under Sir John Moore, which, after the repulse of the French at Corunna in January, in which the General fell, was embarked for England. Corunna Detachment.

" 1811, December 10. John Bourne Mayor.
" The Mayor communicated to the Council that at the request of a deputation from the Society for bettering the condition of the poor, he wished to know the sense of the Council for his government in regard to the amount of the subscription they might wish to make on behalf of the Corporation. Poor Fund.

" Resolved and Ordered, That the Mayor be desired and authorized to subscribe the sum of 100 guineas towards carrying into effect the purposes of that charity." Subscription.

1814, April 20. A legacy for charitable purposes, of a somewhat doubtful character, had to be dealt with by the Council.

" Mr Alderman Crosbie produced the Probate of the Will of Joseph Hunt of which he was appointed Executor, by which the Testator gave the residue of his estate and effects to the Corporation ' on condition of their allowing interest for the same after the rate of Five pounds per centum per annum for ever for the purpose of providing dinner and ale for the Prisoners confined in the Borough Gaol upon every Christmas Day and New Year's Day.' Dinners for Prisoners.

" After due consideration, the Council resolved
" That it would not be advisable for the Corporation to accept of such legacy upon the condition expressed in the said Will," Bequest declined.

1817, Feby. Great distress and want of work prevailing in the town, a Committee was appointed at a public meeting, which requested the Council to appoint a deputation to meet them, to concert measures to be adopted for finding employ- Distress.

ment in some of the public works of the Corporation, for a great number of persons now out of employ.

A deputation was appointed to meet the Committee, with power to accept at interest upon security of the Corporation Bond, the sum of £10,000, to be applied to the purposes before mentioned, on the stipulation that the same remain at interest for not less than five years.

Contributions.

Loan to Docks.
"March 15. The Deputy Chairman of the Dock Committee stated that they had agreed to apply to the Lords of the Treasury for the loan of such a sum of money as would enable the Works at the Docks to be carried on to their fullest extent, by which great relief might be given to the labouring Poor, as well as the improvements of the Port to be completed with greater rapidity."

"1822, May 16. Richd Bullin Mayor.

Irish Distress. Subscription.
"Great distress prevailing in Ireland, a special meeting of the Council was called by the Mayor, when it was Resolved, That the sum of £300 be subscribed by this Corporation to the fund now raising for the relief of the distresses which exist in Ireland, and that the Mayor be thanked for calling the Council together for the purpose."

"1825, Decr. 7. Peter Bourne Mayor,

Fires, New Brunswick.
"Resolved that the sum of £500 be paid by the Treasurer in aid of the subscription entered into in this town, for the relief of the sufferers by the late dreadful fires in New Brunswick."

Distress.
"1826, May 5. Resolved that the sum of £500 be paid by the Treasurer to the Committee appointed at a public meeting on the 2nd inst in aid of the distressed manufacturers in this and the adjoining county of Chester."

"1830, Feby. 3. George Drinkwater Mayor.

Subscription.
"Resolved, that in consequence of the long continued frost and of the severe state of the weather, the Treasurer be authorized to pay the sum of £500 to be applied under the direction of a special Committee, in the providing of soup and coals and other necessaries for the poor."

Education and the Arts received occasional encouragement.

"1828, Aug. 13. Thos Colley Porter Mayor.

King's College. Donation.
"Resolved that the sum of £500 be subscribed towards the erection of the King's College, London."

Occasional mention is made of the Musical Festivals which were periodically held in the town, and which ultimately led to the erection of St. George's Hall.

"1830, Jany. 6. An application from the Committee for conducting the Liverpool Musical Festival, relative to the Oratorios being held in St. Luke's Church, and the erection of temporary galleries to be removable, having been laid before this Council, Resolved, that the same be referred to the Select Finance Committee." Festival.

"1828, Aug. 6. Thos Colley Porter Mayor.

"Resolved, that a premium of Twenty Guineas each be paid for the three best works of Painting, Drawing and Sculpture respectively, executed by artists resident in Liverpool or the immediate vicinity, which may be exhibited at the approaching Exhibition at the Royal Institution, in proof of the desire felt by the Corporation to encourage the productions of talent and genius in the town of Liverpool, and that the decision as to these premiums be made by the Council with the assistance of such three gentlemen as they may think fit to select." Art Exhibition. Premiums.

"1829, Jany. 7. A letter having been received from Mr John Smith suggesting the purchase by the Council, of a beautiful piece of Sculpture by the late Mr John Deare a native of this town, representing the marriage of Thetis and Peleus, to be placed in the Town Hall. Sculpture by Deare.

"Resolved that the Council feel obliged to Mr Smith for his communication on this subject, but regret that they cannot comply with his suggestion as to the purchase."

"1829, Feby. 4. Nicholas Robinson, Mayor.

"Resolved that a sum not exceeding 100 guineas be granted to artists resident in Liverpool or the immediate vicinity for the best productions in Painting, Sculpture or Drawing, to be exhibited at the Royal Institution Exhibition, such sum to be distributed in the proportions and under the regulations specified underneath— Art Exhibition.

"Prizes for Academicians. Prizes.

"No. 1. For the best Original Historical Picture in Oil colours 20 sovereigns.
— 2. For the best Landscape in Oil Colours 20 sovereigns.
— 3. For the best Water Colour Drawing 12 sovereigns.
— 4. For the best specimen of Wood Cutting in Alto or Bas-relief 12 sovereigns.

"Prizes for Students or Artists residing in Liverpool or the immediate vicinity.

"For the same subjects as above—
"No. 1. 9 sovereigns.
— 2. The picture to be not less than 30 in. by 20 in. 9 sovereigns.
— 3. 6 sovereigns.
— 4. 6 sovereigns.
— 5. For the best design in Architecture, consisting of one or more plans, an elevation and section, 9 sovereigns."

Then follow a number of stringent regulations.

Patronage. At this time of day one cannot but smile at the ideas of patronage then existing. The munificent offers of the Liverpool Corporation of that period would now be viewed with contempt.

This encouragement, such as it was, was continued for several years.

"1831, April 6. Resolved, that the Committee of the new Exhibition Room be authorized to award the several prizes at the next Exhibition of Works of living Artists."

"1833, July 3. A Memorial very numerously and respectably signed by the inhabitants of the town and neighbourhood anxious for the promotion of the Fine Arts, having been laid before this Council, setting forth the pecuniary embarassment of the Society of Artists, and their incapability of again opening the Exhibition Rooms without some effectual assistance.

Application for Aid.

Grant. "Resolved, that the occupation of the Exhibition Rooms in Church Street be guaranteed by this Council to the Society rent free for the present year, and that the Select Finance Committee be requested to report what in their opinion it may hereafter be desirable to do herein."

Lease of Rooms. The result was that a lease was granted of the rooms for a term of years, the Corporation paying the rent.

At the expiration of the lease, the reformed Council declined to renew it, and shortly afterwards the Exhibition was abandoned.

"1829, Aug. 5. Nicholas Robinson Mayor.

Alderman George Case. Portrait. "Resolved, That upon the present occasion of the opening of the new Council room, Mr Alderman George Case be requested to sit for his portrait, to be hung up in the Council room, in testimony of the sense entertained by the Council of Mr Case's highly valuable services for the long period of fifty-four years during which he has been a member of the body, and that Mr Case be requested to select his own artist for the painting."

Mr. Case entered the Council in the year 1775, and remained therein until the Municipal Reform Act of 1835, having been a member for more than sixty years. He was

Mayor in 1781, and for many years filled the office of Chairman of the Select Finance Committee.

Another venerable relic of antiquity finds a place in these records.

"1811, Decr. 4. Upon Mr Alderman Case's stating to the Council that Mrs Martha Linacre being now eighty-three years of age and upwards, wished to know the terms or rate per cent upon which the Corporation would grant her an annuity for her life on sinking the sum of £200 with them. Mrs. Martha Linacre.

"Resolved, that the said sum of £200 be received, and that thereupon a bond be passed under the Common Seal for securing to the said Martha Linacre an Annuity at and after the rate of Thirty guineas per cent for and during the term of her natural life." Annuity.

"1812, Jany. 4. Resolved and Ordered, that the Annuity of Sixty guineas now payable to Mrs Martha Linacre during her life as ordered by the Council on the 4th of December last be increased to the sum of Seventy guineas." Increase.

The bargain was not a profitable one for the Corporation. The old lady lived thirteen years longer, so that for her deposit of £200 in 1811 she received in all, the sum of £955 10s. 0d. Longevity.

She was born in 1728, and in 1745, at the age of seventeen, was present at a ball given on the occasion of the opening of the old Infirmary on the site of St. George's Hall.

In 1824, seventy-nine years afterwards, there was another ball at the opening of the new Infirmary in Brownlow Street, where Mrs. Linacre was again present at the age of 96. She died in 1825, having been born and lived in the same house in Oldhall Street for 97 years.

The entries illustrative of social manners and customs are not very numerous during this period. A few, however, may be noticed.

The wearing of gowns by the members of the Council had been gradually discontinued. The last entry on the subject is Gowns.

"1821, Feby, 7. Resolved, that the Mayor, Bailiffs and Town Clerk and other members of the Council be respectfully requested to continue to go in procession in their gowns to Church on Sundays as usual."

Liberties.

The ancient custom of riding the Liberties or bounds was continued, but was almost obsolete at the period of the Municipal Reform Act. Being an ordinary observance, it is not often noticed.

"1816, March 6. William Barton Mayor.

Expenses.

"Resolved that the Treasurer be authorized to reimburse to Mr Alderman Leyland the sum of £16 15s., the amount of certain expenses paid by him to Thomas Hamson for refreshments &c. on the 20th October last, the day on which the Liberties were rode."

"1815, Mar. 10. The expences occasioned to the Corporation by the several dinners given by the Mayor to the Court, and to the Grand and Traverse Juries at the several Quarter Sessions having been the subject of discussion at this Council

Dinners discontinued.

"Resolved that such dinners in future be discontinued."

"1820, Aug. 2. Sir John Tobin Mayor.

Golightly Presentation.

"Resolved that a Piece of Plate of the value of one hundred guineas be presented to Thomas Golightly Esq, late Treasurer to this Corporation in testimony of the approbation of this Council of the faithful discharge by Mr Golightly of the duties of his office during the period of his long continuance in the same, and that the Mayor, Mr Aspinall and Mr Staniforth be authorized to select the piece of Plate."

The Council have always been very choice in their selection of the beverage consumed at their festivities.

"1828, Nov. 5. Nicholas Robinson Mayor.

Wines purchased.

"Resolved that in future all the wines used at the Mayor's table, be provided at the expence of the Corporation, and that the supply of the cellar be left to the Select Finance Committee with the assistance of the Mayor, Bailiffs and Treasurer."

The question of licensing public-houses came under review.

"1826, April 5. Peter Bourne Mayor.

Licensing.

"The Mayor having laid before this Council a Bill now before Parliament for regulating the licensing of Alehouses in England by which the authority of the Justices of the Peace in this Borough to grant licences according to the invariable usage and practice is wholly taken away,

"Resolved that a Petition be presented under the Common Seal, for obtaining an alteration of the Bill with a view to the preservation of the rights and privileges of the Magistrates."

The Bill was withdrawn, but again brought on in the succeeding session.

"1827, May 2. Thomas Littledale Mayor.

"The Mayor and Magistrates having reported to this Council several very objectionable provisions in the licensing Bill now before Parliament,

"Resolved that a petition be presented against the Bill and that the Earl of Derby and the Members for the borough be requested to give their support to the petition."

The substance of the petition is as follows:—

"That ever since the Legislature deemed proper to enact regulations for the licensing of Alehouses, the authority of the Justices of the Peace to grant such licenses has been expressly sanctioned and preserved, and the Justices of the Borough of Liverpool have invariably granted licenses and had the superintendence and regulation of all Alehouses within the said Borough.

"That by some of the provisions of the intended Bill the jurisdiction of nearly all the Justices of the Peace of the Borough of Liverpool in regard to licences will be taken away, and other provisions will have the effect of interfering in a very material degree with the Police regulations of the said Borough, and may afford great facilities to the disposal and concealment of stolen property, and productive of riot and disorder in public houses at very early periods of the day, and particularly on the Sabbath day.

"Your petitioners therefore pray that the Justices of the said Borough may not be deprived of their authorities and privileges and that the said Bill may not be permitted to pass into a law in its present form."

The Police were paid by the Council and under their control, but the numbers were miserably insufficient.

"1811, May 10. James Drinkwater Mayor.

"The Mayor moved and was seconded by Mr. Alderman Aspinall, that the town being now divided into seven districts instead of five, there be one Head Constable and two assistant constables in each district, and that the Head Constables be paid twenty five shillings per week, and the assistants twenty one shillings."

There was need of Police protection, when we read as follows:—

Prosecution. "1811, Aug. 11. Resolved, that the sum of £500 on account of the expences of the several prosecutions against the rioters at the Theatre Royal Liverpool, be paid to the Town Clerk by the Treasurer."

"1813, April 7. Sam¹ Staniforth Mayor.

Footpads. "Resolved and Ordered, that the expences incurred by the Mayor and Magistrates in the apprehension of the desperate gang of footpads who have lately infested this town, and amounting in the whole to the sum of £209 14s. od. be paid by the Treasurer."

"1824, July 7. Charles Lawrence Mayor.

"The Council having adverted to the recent footpad robberies committed in the neighbourhood of this town by two men of the names of James Gallagher and Hugh O'Neill, and to the conduct of Mr Thomas Tinley, one of the parties robbed, and by whose exertions the offenders were discovered,

Prosecutions. "Resolved, That the reward of £50 offered by Mr Tinley be defrayed by the Corporation, and that the extra expences of the prosecutions for the said robberies be also defrayed out of the Corporate funds."

1832. The visitation of the Cholera in this year is noticed in the records.

"Feby. 1. The Mayor having brought under the consideration of the Council an application from the Board of Health respecting the erection of temporary Hospitals for the accommodation of patients who may be *Cholera.* unhappily attacked by the cholera,

"Resolved that the Select Finance Committee be authorized to appropriate such building, and land belonging to the Corporation as may be vacant, for the above purpose, which the Committee in conjunction with the Board of Health may deem desirable."

"1832, July 4. Resolved, that the vacant Wing in the Borough Gaol be granted for the use of the County Magistrates at a nominal rent of five *Precautions against Cholera.* shillings a month during the continuance of the cholera in Kirkdale House of Correction, provided the prisoners committed to the said wing be under the controul of the Governor of the Borough Gaol, and be kept at the expense of the County."

Assizes. The holding of the County Assizes at Lancaster, entailing an enormous expense and difficulty on Liverpool, Manchester and the southern districts of the County, had long been felt as a grievance. The movements towards a reform are recorded as follows:—

"1822, Jany. 2. Richard Bullin Mayor.

"This Council being of opinion that the County rate is most heavy and ought by every possible means to be reduced,

"Resolved, That with a view to effect the same, the Mayor and Magistrates be requested to take into consideration the propriety of applying to the proper quarter for an adjournment of the Assizes from Lancaster to Liverpool and Manchester, and if they deem necessary, to confer with the Magistrates of the County and the different Commercial Bodies of this town and Manchester on the subject." — Application.

"1823, Jany. 14. William Molyneux Mayor.

"A Memorial relative to an adjournment of the Assizes having been laid before this Council, — Memorial.

"Resolved, that the Common Seal be affixed thereto, and that the Mayor be requested to transmit the same to the Secretary of State for the Home Department, and also to the Earl of Derby, the members for the County, and for the several boroughs in the same, also to such other Members of Parliament connected with the County as he may think proper, requesting their consideration and assistance. — Resolutions.

"Resolved also, that the Mayor be requested to transmit a copy of the Memorial to the Boroughreeve of Manchester, soliciting the co-operation of the inhabitants of Manchester in the proposed measure."

No encouragement having been given to the effort, the subject remained in abeyance during six years, when it again came to the front.

"1829, Jany. 7. Nicholas Robinson Mayor.

"The Mayor having called the attention of the Council to the propriety of some endeavour being again made to obtain a removal or adjournment of the Assizes to this town, which would be of very great benefit and advantage both to the town and neighbourhood, — Adjournment of Assizes.

"Resolved that the consideration of this subject be referred to a Committee of the whole Council, the Mayor being chairman . . . but that a report be made to the Council previous to any final determination of the Committee." — Committee appointed.

"1829, Jany. 12. At a meeting of the Committee so appointed, after considerable discussion, the following resolution was recommended for adoption by the Council:

"The Council having reason to suppose from the general reports at present in circulation, that it is in contemplation to make an alteration in the circuits, and in the places for holding the assizes for the purpose of affording great relief and saving of expence to parties,

"Resolved, That it is the opinion of this Council that very great benefit would result to the inhabitants of this town and neighbourhood by an

Application.

adjournment of the Assizes for the trial of civil causes, to this town; and that the Mayor be requested to signify to the Law Commissioners, under whose consideration this question is understood to be, that ample accommodation can now be afforded for the conducting of the same in this town; and to solicit their earnest and early attention to this subject."

Peel.

"1829, Feby. 4. The resolution was adopted by the Council, with an addition, 'that the Mayor be requested to write to the Right Hon. Robert Peel, Secretary for the Home Department, soliciting his support.'"

Memorials to Commissioners.

"1829, May 6. The Mayor reported to the Council that he had presented two memorials on the subject, very numerously and respectably signed, to the Commissioners appointed by the Government, consisting of the Right Hon. Robert Peel, Sir James Scarlett, the Hon. Robert Henley Eden, and Thomas Starkie Esq; that accompanied by Mr Alderman Thomas Case and Mr William Wallace Currie he had solicited through

Huskisson.

Mr Huskisson the honor of an interview with Mr Peel which took place on April 30th, at which Mr Peel expressed himself extremely favorable to the principle of the proposed arrangement; that he thought there could be only one opinion as to the interests and convenience of so important a place as the town of Liverpool and the neighbourhood, being entitled to the fullest consideration; at the same time he felt it right to say, that the adoption of any general measure relative to a removal or adjournment of the Assizes, would, from the various parties and interests to be affected, require the most mature deliberation. But the Right Honorable gentleman, in conclusion gave the deputation to understand that the prayer of the memorial should receive his best attention; and further that he would go to the consideration of it without any previous pledge whatever as to the question; and that nothing should be determined without giving the memorialists an opportunity of rebutting any objections that might present themselves.

Report.

"In making the above reports, the Mayor and the other gentlemen of the deputation feel that they should be wanting in respect and courtesy to Mr Huskisson if they failed to apprize the Council of the great attention and civilities which they experienced from that Right Honorable gentleman upon the various occasions in which they found it necessary to solicit his assistance; and of the very important services which they derived from his personal attendances, and the able manner in which he introduced and explained the different subjects.

"It was therefore Resolved that the thanks of the Council be presented to Right Hon. Wm Huskisson for the able assistance afforded."

Four years more elapsed before anything further was done.

"1833, Sept. 4. Charles Horsfall Mayor.

"The Mayor having laid before this Council a letter from the Honorable George Lamb requesting to know for the information of Lord

Melbourne, his Majesty's Secretary of State, whether in the event of the Assizes for the western division of this County being holden in this town, the Corporation would be prepared at their own charge to provide convenient courts for holding such Assizes, and suitable lodgings and accommodation for the Judges of Assize, and also to defray any additional costs and charges to which the High Sheriff may be subjected in consequence of holding the said Assizes at Liverpool. Proposal.

"Resolved, that this Council is anxiously impressed with the great advantage to be derived by the inhabitants of this town from the removal of the Assizes to Liverpool, and is most ready to afford to his Majesty's Government all the assistance in its power, to carry this object into effect. Resolution.

"For this purpose the Council readily places the present courts in Liverpool at the service of the Judges and the Bar attending this circuit, and will have pleasure in providing suitable accommodation for the Judges; but owing to the litigation commenced regarding the right of the Corporation to receive Town dues, which Town dues comprize nearly one half of the annual income of the Corporate Estate, the Council regrets that it is thereby prevented from a sense of Justice to the Bond and other creditors, from undertaking any greater outlay at present." Courts.

At length, after a weary delay of twelve years from the time when the question was first mooted, the application was granted, as appears from the following minute:—

"1834, July 2. John Wright Mayor.

"At this Council the Mayor and Town Clerk reported with reference to the resolution of the Council in June last on the application of the Liverpool Law Society regarding the removal of the Assizes to this town, that the circuits for the ensuing Assizes have been some time fixed by the Judges, and that for this county they are to be holden in August next at Lancaster as heretofore; but that they have reason to believe from information afforded through Lord Sandon that his Majesty's Privy Council will determine the matter previous to the Assizes in March next, and also that there is every probability that the Assizes will then be held in this town. On this account the Mayor and Town Clerk submit to the Council the propriety of authorizing the Select Finance Committee to make such arrangements for the suitable accommodation of the Judges and the Sheriff and such alterations in the present Courts in the Sessions House as may be necessary for the accommodation of the Public Business. Application granted. Accommodation provided.

"Resolved that the foregoing report is approved, and that the Select Finance Committee is hereby fully authorized to adopt such proceedings as are recommended."

A very important episode in the history of the City is
the controversy respecting the town dues, which continued
during four years, from 1830 to 1834.

Town Dues Controversy.

The petty customs or town dues on the goods of non-freemen, had been levied from the foundation of the Port, and the right down to this period had not been questioned. The only dispute had been as to the exemption claimed by the citizens of London, which had been tried in 1799, as related above. The claim now made was to set the dues aside altogether, as an arbitrary and illegal exaction.

1830, May 5th. The following letter received by the Mayor, was laid before the Council.

" Liverpool, April 19th, 1830.
" To the Worshipful the Mayor of Liverpool,
 " Sir,

Letter to Mayor.

" You have already been informed verbally that a considerable number of the principal merchants in this place have come to the determination of ascertaining the legal right of the Corporation of Liverpool to Town dues on goods imported and exported, the property of non-freemen, and as you have stated that you could not receive any communication on that subject except in writing, I have now the honor to annex for the information of the Corporation a copy of a resolution which was passed at a general meeting of merchants held on the 3rd instant.

" In making this communication to you, I was particularly instructed by the merchants, to disavow all personal and unfriendly feelings, and to state that their only wish is, that the question may be so raised and tried as that the origin of the dues, the right of the Corporation to exact their payment and the proper application thereof may be ascertained, and set at rest by a judicial decision.

" I am further instructed to inform you that the merchants have appointed Mr Lowe their Attorney to conduct their case, and in the full expectation that the Corporation will meet the question with every fairness and candour,

 " I have the honor to be,
  " Sir, with respect, your most ob^t serv^t
   " Jos. HORNBY, Chairman."

The resolution ran as follows :—

Resolution.

" Resolved, That an opinion has long prevailed that the Town Dues collected at this Port, are an illegal exaction, and that the amount, being a severe tax upon trade, pressing very heavily upon salt and some other articles, while from the numerous exemptions from the payment, they operate unequally and unfairly; It is the opinion of this meeting, that no time should be lost in bringing the question of their legality to an issue."

To this communication the Mayor, Mr. Geo. Drinkwater, replied as under:—

"Townhall, Apl. 20th, 1830.

"Jos. Hornby, Esq.,
　"Sir,

"I have the honor to acknowledge the receipt of your letter of the 19th inst, inclosing the copy of a resolution relative to the legality of the Corporation to the Town Dues on goods imported and exported, and which I will not fail to lay before the Common Council at their next monthly meeting. _{Mayor's Reply.}

"As I observe your letter states the resolution to have been passed at a general meeting of the merchants, I shall consider myself obliged by your acquainting me for the information of the Council, with the mode in which such general meeting was called, and the names of the gentlemen who attended, not having myself seen any advertisement for such meeting, or heard of the same from any quarter.

"I am Sir
"Your m'. obed'. serv'.
"Geo. Drinkwater, Mayor."

On this correspondence being read it was

"Resolved, That the Council consider it to be their imperative duty to resist any proceeding calling in question the right of the Corporation to the Town's dues, whenever the same may be brought forward." _{Resolution to resist.}

A Committee was appointed — "for the purpose of affording assistance and giving such directions to the Town Clerk upon the subject of any proceedings which may be adopted relative to the Town's dues as they may deem advisable." _{Committee.}

The following reply was sent to the Mayor's letter:—

"Sir,　　　　　　　　　　　　"Liverpool, 23rd April, 1830.

"I have the honor to acknowledge the receipt of your letter dated the 20th inst, and to inform you in reply to the enquiries it contains that the Resolution enclosed in my letter to you of the 19th inst was not passed at a meeting of merchants convened by public Advertisement, but was adopted at an assemblage of many of the principal merchants of Liverpool coinciding in opinion 'that the origin of the Town dues, the right of the Corporation to exact their payment and the proper application thereof' were fit subjects for judicial investigation. I further beg to state _{Reply to Mayor.}

that I have no means of furnishing you with the names of the gentlemen who attended the above meeting, no minutes as I am informed having been taken of such names, and my recollection being confined to only a few of them.

"I have the honor to be, &c.,

"To the Worshipful
"The Mayor."

"Jos. HORNBY."

Committee's Report.

"1830, July 7. The Committee presented the following report to the Council:

Payment refused.

"The Committee have to report that on the 22nd June Messrs Bolton, Ogden & Co. refused to pay the Town's dues on several entries of merchandize both inwards and outwards, amounting to £38 3s. 9d., and on the 27th ult. they again refused payment of the Town's dues on several further entries amounting to £29 14s. 1½d., and on the 28th ult. they again refused payment on several further entries amounting to £18 13s. 2d.

"The Committee caused proper demands to be made by the Receiver, and the answer was a refusal to pay in order to try the legality of the right of the Corporation to the Town's dues. The Committee add that they are actively engaged in the prosecution of the matter, and have no doubt of bringing the question at issue to a successful termination."

Messrs. Bolton & Co. continued to refuse payment, and on June 30th the amount was £257 3s. 5½d.

The report proceeds:—

"That two or three other mercantile houses have attempted to pay the Town's dues under protest, but that by the advice of Counsel the sums so offered have been refused to be received, and the parties have therefore paid.

Investigation.

"The Committee feeling the vast importance of the trust committed to their charge, deemed it their first duty to direct the Town Clerk to institute an immediate and thorough investigation of the whole subject, not only with reference to the present dispute, but for the guidance and satisfaction of the Council at all future times, in order that such a body of evidence may be put into the possession of the Council as will enable them for ever hereafter to support their right to the Town dues. This investigation has been prosecuted by the Town Clerk, aided by the Clerk of the Committees, with a zeal and ability creditable to both of them, and the result of their labours fully justifies the Committee in the anticipation expressed in their former report that the right of the Corporation to the Town dues will be established in the most decided and unequivocal manner."

Right asserted.

They further report as to the proceedings instituted,

Proceedings.

"1831, Jany. 5. The Town dues Committee presented a report which stated that since the report of July 1830, Messrs Bolton Ogden & Co. had continued to refuse payment of the Town dues, the amount then due amounting to £751 5s. 2½d. for which regular demands had been made from time to time, but that no other merchant so far had refused payment. The necessary processes had been sued for raising the question, the different stages in the cause were proceeding, and the trial of the question approaching in the ordinary courses, when Messrs. Bolton and Co. thought proper to institute proceedings in the Court of Chancery against the Corporation, which had the effect not only of retarding the progress of the trial of the question, but if submitted to in the manner required would subject the Corporation to a disclosure of their title to these dues, and of all the grounds on which they intend to support that title in the approaching trial. Without going into particular detail of the whole of the objects sought for by this Bill of Discovery filed by the Defendants, they advise the Council to pause before they acquiesce in the inquisitorial requisitions the Bill contains. Among extraordinary objects one is to compel the Corporation to produce, ultimately for the inspection of Messrs Bolton & Co. even the cases confidentially stated by the Town Clerk for the opinion of Counsel on this very subject, in which are naturally exposed and submitted, not the facts and premises on which the Corporation might rely in a court of law for the establishment of their right alone, but some points which might serve to afford an opponent the means of some embarrassment in their proceedings. . . It is because the Committee feel it right to hesitate in acquiescing in such extraordinary demands, and to act under the deliberate and serious advice of their Counsel, that they cannot suggest to the Council a probable period when this contest may be brought to a termination, but they have elicited the most satisfactory and unanimous opinions as to the substantial merits of the case and the successful result of a trial at law, which is now only delayed by the proceedings in Chancery of their opponents." Stages in Cause. Bill of Discovery. Difficulties.

"1831, Jany. 5. Resolved that the Mayor and Bailiffs be authorized to proceed to London with the Common Seal, for the purpose of putting in the answer to the Bill in Chancery filed by Messrs Bolton and others relative to the Town dues." Answer to Bill.

"1831, Sept. 7. The Town dues Committee reported that the Vice-Chancellor had decided that the Demurrer filed by the Corporation could not be sustained. An appeal was therefore made to the Lord Chancellor. Demurrer. Appeal.

"The Committee further reported that since the previous report, forty seven mercantile houses had refused to pay the Town dues, against whom under the advice of Counsel actions had been commenced.

"Without having precise information of the motives for such extraordinary conduct on the part of the merchants, the Committee have reason to believe that this course has been adopted upon the allegation that the Corporation were merely seeking for delay in appealing against the Delays.

Vice-Chancellor's decision, but they beg to assure the Council that such allegation is altogether unfounded and that they are ready and most anxious to proceed; and that in resisting the extraordinary and inquisitorial requisitions of this Bill in Chancery to compel the Corporation to find Messrs Bolton & Co. materials for their defence, they are acting entirely under the advice and directions of Counsel."

The amount of dues for which payment was refused had now reached the sum of £6,310 13s. 3½d.

Expenses. "1831, Novr. 7. Resolved that the Treasurer be authorized to place at the disposal of the Town dues Committee the sum of £12,000.

Application to King's Bench. "The Committee further report that the answer to the Bill in Chancery would be filed in the course of the month, in which an application would be made to the Court of King's Bench to consolidate the many actions brought against the recusant parties. They state that they had fully and carefully completed their investigation, and although they do not think it right to detail all particulars, they cannot resist the gratification of submitting the concluding words of Sir James Scarlet's opinion after his final perusal of all the documents—' Upon the whole it appears to me that the Corporation of Liverpool have as strong a case as any that has fallen under my knowledge in support of their claim.'"

Trial fixed. The trial was fixed by Lord Tenterden, the Lord Chief Justice, for the 23rd May, 1832.

Death of Town Clerk. During these proceedings, the Town Clerk, Mr. William Statham died, and Mr. Thomas Foster (subsequently Town Clerk), was entrusted with the conduct of the case.

Verdict. The trial was again postponed to the middle of December, 1832, when a verdict was given in favour of the Corporation.

Writ of Error. "1834, Jany. 1. After considerable delay, the Committee report that a Writ of Error had been brought by the Defendants, by which the final determination of the question would be deferred for some months."

Death of Lowe. "1834, Feby. 5. The Committee further report that the death of Mr Jas Lowe the defendants' solicitor, had caused some delay in the preparation of a Bill of Exceptions, but in the succeeding Easter Term the cause would be taken."

Termination. "1834, June 2. The Committee report that communications had been made of the desire of the merchants resisting payment to terminate the protracted litigation. A letter was received from Mr Jos. Hornby, Chairman of the Committee of Merchants, stating that not wishing to throw any unnecessary obstacles in the way of a settlement, they consented to a verdict against Messrs Bolton & Co being recorded, each party paying their own

costs. Mr Hornby further stated in his letter, that in so doing the Com- *Negotiations.*
mittee of Merchants declared, that it was solely from a conviction that
the Legislature had in preparation a measure which would place Freemen
and Non-freemen on an equal footing in future ; and also in reliance that
the Corporation would act up to the spirit of the resolution of the Council
of the fourth of December last, arising from the evidence given before the
Municipal Commissioners.

"On the receipt of this Communication, the Committee considering that
it contained the fullest admission of the right of the Corporation to the *Admission.*
Town dues, recommended to the Council to accede to the proposition.

"Considering that the question at issue was of a public character the *Settlement.*
Committee also recommend that payment of taxed costs be not pressed
for."

These recommendations were adopted by the Council.

"1834, July 2. The final report of the Committee was presented recapitulating the proceedings, and stating that the sum of £44,182 10s 7d had been paid over by the Defendants to the credit of the Corporation. The account stood as follows—

Total amount received from 54 Defendants......	£40,620	9	1½	*Terms.*
Less Returns	676	8	2	
	£39,944	0	11½	
Total amount received from J. W. Gibsone......	1,605	7	10	
Total amount received from Bolton & Co.	2,751	7	2½	
Gross amount received...........................	£44,300	16	0	
Deduct Receiver's Commission 2½ ⅌ cent.	1,124	7	11	
Nett Town Dues	£43,176	8	1	
Interest on Exchequer Bills received	1,006	2	6	
	£44,182	10	7	

"Mem. The above is exclusive of Profit and further interest on the
Exchequer Bills when realized."

The political history of the Municipality during this *Politics.*
period is very significant, and was not without its influence
on the National and Municipal Reform Acts of 1832 and
1835.

The Parliamentary and Municipal Constituencies were *Constituencies.*
identical and exclusive, the freemen in the Parliamentary
representation shutting out the great bulk of the inhabitants,

and the self-elected Council, in turn, excluding the freemen from any share in the management of the estate, which by the charters belonged to them.

Elections.

The Parliamentary elections were usually corrupted by bribery and intemperance, which frequently led to riot and disorder. These elections are not ordinarily recorded in the Council proceedings, but matters arising out of them are very frequent.

"1817, Feby. 5. John Wright Mayor.

Rioting at Elections.

"Resolved that the sum of twenty pounds be paid to Enoch Broadley superintendent of the Dock Police, and ten pounds to John Hale, Dock watchman, for the apprehension and subsequent conviction at the Assizes of some of the rioters at the late election."

"1827, Novr. 7. Thos. Colley Porter Mayor.

"A memorial very numerously and respectably signed relative to the proceedings at the late election for Mayor, and suggesting the propriety of some measures being adopted to prevent their recurrence,

Measures adopted.

"Resolved, that the same be referred to the Select Finance Committee and that they be requested to make a report thereon to the Council."

Mayor's Election, 1827.

It may be stated in passing, that the election continued six days, that the votes of the freemen were openly bargained for, running up at the close of the contest to £30 or £40 a head, with treating and drunkenness, but no absolute rioting. The election was said to have cost Mr. Porter £10,000.

"1827, Decr. 5. The Mayor having laid before this Council certain resolutions accompanied by observations which had been transmitted to him from a public meeting of some of the inhabitants recently held, suggesting the propriety of an extension of the elective franchise, and an alteration of the present system adopted at Elections, with a view to facilitating the taking of the Poll—the prevention of abuses—and of the scenes of riot and disorder which so frequently prevail at those times; and also soliciting a conference upon these subjects with the Common Council:

Public Meeting.

Council Resolutions.

"Resolved, that in justice to those in whom the rights and privileges of Free Burgesses of this borough are at present vested, the Council cannot possibly entertain the principle of any extension of the elective franchise, and in the event of any application being made for that purpose to the

Legislature, they shall consider it a duty imperative upon them, to resist such application to the utmost.

"Resolved also, that the resolutions and observations as far as the same relate to all other points—except that of an extension of the elective franchise—be referred to the Select Finance Committee, with a request that they will make an early report to the Council. <small>Reference to Finance Committee.</small>

"Resolved also, That the Council decline any personal conference with the gentlemen with whom the resolutions originated; but that they be informed that the objection to such conference is not founded in the slightest degree of disrespect towards them; the Council being of opinion that it will be much more satisfactory that all proceedings should, upon this occasion, be conducted by means of written communications. <small>Conference declined.</small>

"A Memorial having been presented to the Council from several Free Burgesses stating their objections to any extension of the elective franchise; and also to the intended Bill for various purposes relative to Elections,

"Resolved, That the Council perfectly coincide in the opinions expressed by the Memorialists relative to the non-extension of the elective franchise; but that they consider that the intended Bill will prove extremely beneficial in many points of view, and in particular to the Free Burgesses themselves, as being the means of protecting their rights, and preventing the recurrence of the great frauds and impositions, which there is too much reason to believe have been practiced upon various occasions at Elections, by numerous individuals." <small>Opposition to Reform.</small>

"1828, Feby. 6. Resolved, That the intended Bill, relative to elections in this borough be read a first time in the House of Commons, and Prints of the Bill circulated generally for the information of the Burgesses; but that the Bill be not further proceeded with, till after the next Council in March; And that the Clauses against Bribery at elections of a Mayor and Bailiffs be introduced into the Bill, similar to those contained in the Act of the 2nd George the 3rd cap 24, relative to Elections of Members to serve in Parliament." <small>Bill.</small>

Nothing came of this movement.

"1828, Mar. 5. Resolved, that the Bill recently brought into Parliament relative to Elections within this Borough be not further proceeded with." <small>Bill withdrawn.</small>

The next item in the present record is the celebrated contest between Ewart and Denison, in November, 1830, which put the coping-stone on the monument of shameless profligacy, which the quondam electoral system had left behind. The story is told elsewhere. <small>Election, 1830.</small>

330   CHAP. IV, A.D. 1800—1835.

Petition.

A Petition was presented to Parliament against the return of Mr. Ewart. On March 28th he was unseated.

1831, April 6th. The Mayor having laid before the Council a letter from Rigby Wason, Esq., relative to a Bill intended to be introduced into Parliament for the disfranchisement of the Burgesses,

Council decline.

"Resolved, That inasmuch as the Bill alluded to in the letter has not yet been brought into the House of Commons, the Council do not feel themselves justified in adopting any measures respecting the same.

Petition against Ewart. Report.

"The Council having adverted to the Report of the Committee of the House of Commons upon the recent Petition against the return of William Ewart Esquire as one of the Representatives of this borough in Parliament, upon which other proceedings are, as it appears, intended to be adopted on the 18th inst, until which day the issuing of the Election Writ has been suspended,

Opposition.

"Resolved, that upon this important occasion the Mayor and Thomas Foster Esq' (with others) do proceed to London for the purpose of adopting such measures for the protection of the rights and interests of the Corporation as may be deemed most proper, and of preparing and presenting such a Petition to the House of Commons as they may consider advisable, and to which the Common Seal be affixed.

Deputation.

"Resolved also, that the Deputation be authorized to adopt such further measures as they may deem advisable for obtaining an alteration of such of the clauses in the general Reform Bill as appear to be incapable of being reduced into practice within this borough, or as inapplicable to the same."

"1831, April 28. Thomas Brancker Mayor.

"The Mayor on behalf of himself and the Bailiffs as returning Officers having brought under the particular notice of the Council the recent proceedings in the House of Commons relative to the bribery and corruption at the election for this borough in November last, and the Council having taken the same into consideration,

Bribery.

"Resolved Unanimously,

Measures against Bribery.

"That in the opinion of the Council every endeavour should be used to prevent a recurrence of this evil practice, and that in the event of any such misconduct being established, the party offending should not only be disfranchised, but otherwise proceeded with to the utmost rigour of the law.

"Resolved also that a public notification of the above resolution be immediately given to the Burgesses under the direction of the Mayor."

The following is a copy of the public Advertisement:—

"Notices to the Free Burgesses of the Borough of Liverpool — Notice to "Townhall 28th April 1831. Burgesses.

"The Common Council having taken into consideration at a special Council held this day, the evidence produced before a Committee of the House of Commons by which it appears that many of the Free Burgesses of this Borough had been guilty of Bribery and other corrupt practices, at the Election held in November last; and having also adverted to the subsequent Resolution of the House of Commons thereon, unanimously deem it their duty to caution the Free Burgesses against any repetition of the like offences at the ensuing Election; and do hereby give public notice of their determination to punish any Burgess who may be proved to have been guilty of the same, by disfranchisement, and the adoption of other proceedings to the utmost rigour of the law."

This virtuous indignation was no doubt stimulated by a motion brought forward seven days previously in the House of Commons by Mr. Benett, M.P. for Wiltshire, the Chairman of the Election Committee:—"That the system of bribery and treating, which prevails in the election of Burgesses to serve in Parliament for the Borough of Liverpool, demands the attention of the House." *Proceedings in Parliament.*

After the dissolution, which took place two days subsequently, Messrs. Ewart and Denison were returned. The latter gentleman preferred to sit for Nottinghamshire, to which he had been also elected. When the writ for a new election in Liverpool was moved, Mr. Benett again came forward, and proposed to bring in a Bill to disfranchise the bribees, and to alter the franchise in Liverpool. *Dissolution.*

"1831, Octr. 5. The Mayor having laid before the Council a Print of the Bill transmitted to him by Order of the House of Commons for disfranchising the Burgesses in consequence of alleged bribery and corruption at Elections, which Bill it appears, by the votes of the House is intended to be further proceeded with on the 12th inst., *Bill for Disfranchisement.*

"Resolved that the deputation appointed at the Council held on the 6th day of April last relative to a Bill then about to be introduced upon the same subject, be revived as a Committee with full authorities to oppose the Bill, and to adopt such measures as they may deem advisable for the protection of the franchise of the Borough." *Deputation.*

332   CHAP. IV, A.D. 1800—1835.

Writ Issued.

The Writ was ultimately issued on the 12th October, 1831.

"1831, Nov. 2. Sam¹ Sandbach Mayor.

Thanks to Vernon.

"Resolved unanimously, That the thanks of this Council be presented to the Hon. Granville Vernon, for his successfully moving in the House of Commons for the issuing of the Writ for the late Election of a Member to serve in Parliament for this Borough, whereby the Burgesses and the town at large obtained the full right and benefit of the Franchise."

Bill for Disfranchisement.

"1832, Feby. 1. The Mayor having laid before the Council a print of the Bill introduced in the House of Commons for disfranchising the Burgesses in consequence of alleged bribery,

"Resolved, that the Mayor, John Bourne Esq, Sir Thomas Brancker (with others) be appointed a Committee with full authority to oppose the Bill."

"1833, Feby. 25. Charles Horsfall Mayor.

Letter from Lord Sandon. Petition.

"The Mayor laid before the Council a letter from Viscount Sandon, by which it appears that a Petition from certain electors and inhabitants of this town had been presented on Thursday last, praying that the Burgesses may be disfranchised on the alleged ground of bribery and corruption at elections, as well of Mayor as of Members to serve in Parliament, and also that notice was given of an intended motion on Thursday next the 28th inst, for the appointment of a Select Committee of the House of Commons on the matters complained of in this petition,

Resolution.

"Resolved that the Worshipful the Mayor (with four others) do proceed to London for the purpose of making such representations and explanations on this subject to his Majesty's Ministers and other Members of Parliament as they may deem proper, and of preparing and presenting the necessary petition to the House of Commons, to which the Common Seal be affixed, and of adopting such other proceedings to protect the rights and franchises of the Corporation as they may deem expedient, and the expenses to be incurred be defrayed by the Treasurer."

Select Committee.

1833. On March 6th, a Select Committee was appointed by the House of Commons to inquire into the matters alleged.

"March 20. At a Special Council

Mayor's Report.

"The Mayor having reported that he with several of the Deputation had attended in London and had interviews with Lord Althorpe and other members of his Majesty's Government and with many Members of the House of Commons, on the subject of the charges alledged against the Burgesses of this Corporation, and that they had presented a petition praying to be heard by their Counsel and Agents, and to produce evidence before the Select Committee to whom the subject had been referred, and that it appeared advisable that instructions should be given by the Council as to the further proceedings to be adopted in relation thereto.

"Resolved, That the cordial thanks of the Council be presented to the Mayor and the deputation, and that a Committee be formed to adopt such further proceedings as they may from time to time deem expedient and proper, to protect the rights and franchises of this Corporation. *Resolution.*

"The Mayor also informed the Council that remonstrances signed by several hundreds of the Burgesses had been presented to him and the Bailiffs, denying the truth of the corruption imputed to the Burgesses, which he had left in London to be produced if required." *Remonstrances.*

1833, July 29. The final report of the Parliamentary Committee was presented. It stated that bribery and corruption had existed in the elections of Members of Parliament and Chief Magistrates for the Borough of Liverpool to an enormous extent. It recommended the introduction of a Bill to restrict the franchises, and to alter the whole system of elections in the borough. They added a rider, as follows:— *Report to Parliament.*

"Your Committee cannot conclude this report without directing the attention of your Honourable House to the conduct of freemen in a better class of life, and in good circumstances, who have shown fully as much readiness to take bribes as the poorest and most destitute of their fellow-burgesses."

A Bill for the disfranchisement of the Liverpool Freemen was introduced, and passed through its various stages, until it reached the second reading in the House of Lords, on May 1st, 1834. In July, further instructions were given to the Committee, but Parliament being soon after prorogued, nothing further was heard of the measure. *Bill for Disfranchisement.*

Having escaped this danger, the Corporation were very soon confronted with another, which terminated more fatally.

"1833, Nov. 1. John Wright Mayor.
"At a Special Council,
"The Mayor having acquainted the Council that Messrs. Wilkinson and Hogg, two of the Commissioners recently appointed to inquire into the existing state of the Municipal Corporations, intended to be at Liverpool for the purpose of inquiring into this Corporation, *Commissioners of Inquiry.*

"Resolved, that the Town Clerk and any officers of this Corporation who may be required, do attend and give all such information as may be called for by these Commissioners, except that the Town Clerk be directed *Resolution.*

to decline answering inquiries into the title of the Corporation to the Town dues, or to produce any deeds or documents relating thereto, on account of the litigation still impending respecting the right of the Corporation to their receipt ; or to produce any other deeds or documents relating to the estates and property of the Corporation, which in his opinion as the legal adviser of this Corporation may be prejudicial to its rights and interest."

Bills in Parliament.
" 1833, Nov. 6. Resolved, that the Select Finance Committee be authorized to watch the progress of any Bills brought into Parliament in the ensuing session which may be considered to affect the Corporation of Liverpool or the rights and interests of the town, and to affix the Seal to any petition or memorial which may be deemed necessary."

Investigation.
Termination.
" 1833, Decr. 4. The Mayor reported that Messrs. Wilkinson and Hogg the Commissioners appointed, had commenced their investigation on Nov 4th and continued it until Saturday Nov 30th when the inquiry terminated, and that during such investigation the Town Clerk together with other officers of the Corporation had attended and given their evidence, and all the information and copies of proceedings required, and that at the close of the investigation the Commissioners expressed themselves perfectly satisfied with the manner in which such evidence and information had been given.

Thanks to Town Clerk.
" Resolved unanimously, that the cordial thanks of this Council be given to Thomas Foster Esquire the Town Clerk, for the great zeal, ability and judgment displayed by him during the said inquiry and investigation before the Commissioners."

" 1834, Feby. 5. The Town Clerk having submitted several letters received from the Corporations of Norwich and Leicester, proposing that a meeting of deputations from Corporations should take place in London with a view to establish some common system of co-operation in reference to any measures to be proposed in Parliament, in consequence of the Reports of the Commissioners recently appointed to inquire into the existing state of Municipal Corporations in England and Wales.

Co-operation declined.
" Resolved, that the Town Clerk be instructed to state in reply to these communications that this Council declines being part of the proposed Association of Corporations."

" 1835, June 17. James Aspinall Mayor.

Municipal Corporation Bill.
" At a special Council the Mayor having stated that he had deemed it his duty to call this special Council, in consequence of his having received a copy of the Bill to provide for the regulation of Municipal Corporations which had been brought into the Commons, which he now submitted, and some of the provisions of which were now taken into consideration.

Resolution.
Opposition declined.
" Resolved that this Council, conscious of having always discharged the important duties devolved upon it as the Governing body of this Corporation with the utmost desire for the welfare and advantage of the town of Liverpool, does not feel itself called upon to offer any opposition to the

principle of the measure, so far as relates to the removal of the members of this Council and the substitution of another body by a different mode of election for the future management of the Corporate estate, but that the same should be left to such determination as Parliament may think fit to come to regarding it.

"Resolved, That inasmuch as this and former Common Councils have in the execution of public works contracted a debt now amounting to upwards of one Million, which is secured by Bonds under the Common Seal of this Corporation, representation should be made by petition to Parliament that the same may be recognised and confirmed . . . and that no material diminution of the Town or other dues payable to this Corporation should take place until provision had been made for the liquidation of this debt. *Provision for Debt.*

"Resolved, That the proposed enactment by the said Bill that no person shall acquire the rights and privileges of a burgess so far as regards the exemption from Town dues and other tolls who was not admitted and enrolled on the fifth of this present month of June, appears to this Council to deprive several hundred individuals who have completed their claim to such admission and enrolment, in addition to the just rights of several thousands, who as Apprentices and sons of Freemen have an inchoate right to such freedom, and therefore it is the duty of this Council to cause the same to be represented to Parliament." *Protection of Burgess Rights.*

Another Resolution relates to the Dock Trust, that due provision should be made for the appointment of a suitable Board of Management. *Dock Trust.*

A further Resolution sets forth,

"That the Corporation having the patronage of the Rectory and the appointment thereto, and of the Clergy of many of the Churches in the town, to whom salaries or stipends exceeding the endowments fixed by the several Acts of Parliament, and which are payable under resolutions of the Council made from time to time . . . the Council is of opinion that a representation of these circumstances should be made to Parliament and that provision should be made establishing these payments to the present, and suitable provision for the future incumbents, as also for the repairs and maintenance of the Churches. *Rectors and Clergy.* *Provision.*

It is added "that these resolutions are not passed with any object of offering opposition to the measure in its principle, but to protect those interests which have been confided to the Corporation for so long a series of years."

A Committee was appointed to prepare petitions, and a *Committee.*

deputation to proceed to London, to endeavour to carry these objects into effect.

"1835, July 10. The Mayor having stated that notice had been given in the House of Commons of a clause to be introduced, giving power to the new Council to dispute leases mortgages and sales, which may have been made subsequent to the 5th of June last, and it appearing that such clause would materially affect the routine as adopted by this Corporation in granting leases and sales of property,

Mortgages and Sales.

"Resolved, that the Town Clerk now in London be instructed to get the clause so modified as not to interfere with the ordinary business of the Corporation, and for this purpose a statement of leases granted and sales effected by the Corporation during the last twelve Months be prepared."

Modifications.

"1835, July 25. The Mayor communicated to the Council that the Municipal Corporation Bill had passed the Commons and had been read the first time in the Lords, and that the clauses still remained in it restricting the future granting of leases to a term of thirty-one years, and that the rights of freemen were only to be continued to those in being, their existing sons, and apprentices now serving, and not in perpetuity, and that in other respects the Bill had not been so amended as to remove all the objections against which the Council had petitioned the House of Commons.

Bill in Lords.

"Resolved, that a petition now approved be adopted, and that Lord Wharncliffe be requested to present it and support its prayer.

Petition.

"A deputation was also authorised to proceed to London to attend the Bill and to obtain the attendance of such evidence as might be required.

Deputation.

"The Petition set forth that the Corporation of Liverpool is an ancient Corporation by prescription, and possesses divers franchises and privileges both by charters and immemorial custom, . . . that the estate and property of the Corporation was not acquired by any Royal or other grant or donation except as to a very small portion, but that the Lordship and town, together with certain ancient Royal tolls and duties had been sold and transferred to different individuals, and ultimately became vested in the Corporation by purchase, That the revenues had been employed in the improvement of the town, and the charges and expences of the Municipal Government. That as the governing body, they have been solely influenced by an anxious desire to effect such objects as would most contribute to the welfare and comfort of the inhabitants at large, and they have the satisfaction to believe that for the most part their efforts have been successful and duly appreciated.

Statements.

Revenues: how employed.

"That your petitioners have the satisfaction to state, that upon the most searching examination before the Commissioners it was not attempted to be proved that any illegal or improper application of the funds had occurred, that the Commissioners had reported, that in the main the

Defence.

Corporation have evinced economy and good management in their affairs, and that as a governing body their conduct seems to be materially influenced by a desire to promote the public welfare."

They proceed to give at considerable length particulars of the position of their affairs, and conclude by praying to be exempted from the provisions of the Act, or, if that may not be, that protection may be afforded to the Burgesses and their descendants in the enjoyment of all their rights and privileges. Particulars.

"1835, Octr. 7. James Aspinall Mayor.

"The Mayor communicated to the Council that the Act for the regulation of Municipal Corporations had received the Royal Assent on the 7th September, that in pursuance of the power reserved, the Council had postponed the day of election of the new Council to the 26th December, upon the declaration of which election, the Mayor, Aldermen and Common Council men will go out of office and their whole powers and duties cease . . . that no election of Mayor and Bailiffs according to custom will take place on the next Charter day, Octr. 18th, but the present Mayor and Bailiffs will continue to hold their respective offices until the election of the new Council and Mayor." Act passed.
Elections.

CORPORATE ESTATE AND REVENUES.

Corporate Estate.
References have been made above to the management of the Corporate estate. There is considerable obscurity as to the disposal or alienation of lands at the north end of the town, which were certainly in possession in the early part of the 18th Century. The Great Heath and Mosslake Fields, comprising nearly all the lands north of Islington, remained in possession, and were from time to time leased for building. It has been already noticed, that in 1798, after an inquiry into the state of the Corporate affairs, it was determined to offer the reversions for sale.

Great Heath.

Sale of Reversions.
The following is an abstract of the accounts presented in August, 1801.

Balance Sheet.
"1801, Aug. 5. John Shaw Esq Mayor.
"*General Abstract of the Money Transactions &c of the Select Finance Committee from its commencement in May 1798 to the 1st of July 1801—*
"Amount of Bond Debt discharged by the Money arising from the Sales of Reversions £78,317 0 0
"Amount of Balance due to the Banks discharged by the Sales of Reversions 1,288 15 1
"Amount of Accounts discharged by the Sales of Reversions 5,705 2 5
"Amount of Bond Debt discharged by the Money received for Arrears of Town's Duties 7,830 0 0
"Amount of Bond Debt discharged by the Money taken up upon Bond 13,525 16 0

"£106,666 13 6

"By Amount of Money taken up upon Bond £21,988 7 6
"By Amount of Bonds given to discharge debts due from the Corporation 8,150 0 0

30,138 7 6

"Debt reduced............................ £76,528 6 0

CORPORATE ESTATE AND REVENUES. 339

"Amount of Reversions Sold and Accepted......... £74,691 18 0
"Amount of Fines for the renewal of lives in Premises Sold 8,493 8 0
"Amount of Sales of Ground Rents that produced to the Corporation £274 3s. 2d. ℔ an. 9,335 9 0

"£92,520 15 0

"N.B.—Returns have been made to applications for the purchase of Reversions amounting to £150,959 1 0

"Amount of the Sales of Premises &c. under the direction of the Select Committee since the reversionary interest began to be sold............ £39,438 15 0
"Of which remains unpaid 11,022 8 6

"£28,416 6 6

"The money arising from the Sales of these Premises &c has been applied to the payment of purchases made by the Committee, and for the discharge of Accounts, &c &c."

"1819, Octr. 6. Jonathan Blundell Hollinshead Mayor.
"Resolved, that the following Notice be issued—
"To Lessees under the Corporation.
"Notice is hereby given.

"That the Common Council having recently taken into consideration the charges made for the renewal of leases and the exchanging of lives thereon, have come to the determination in cases of renewal to alter the rate of calculation adopted of late years, and the principle of the renewal now fixed upon may be known upon application at the Town Clerk's office. <small>Terms of Leases.</small>

"It appearing from the reports of Mr Okill and Mr Mercer that up to the present period of their investigation into the registers, a considerable number of houses have been discovered by them to have fallen out of lease many years since; the aggregate amount of the rental of which exceeds £650 per annum, and the amount of arrears of rent due to the Corporation upwards of £3000, and that no less than 179 houses and buildings up to the period of such investigation have been found to be running on the terms of years only, and many of them nearly expiring, <small>Lapse of Leases.</small>

"Resolved, That such property be immediately leased out again upon fines in the usual way for three lives and twenty one years."

"1820, Jany. 5. John Tobin Mayor.
"The Council having adverted to the Reports recently made containing the result of the investigation of the state of the Corporate Property, by which it appears that in one part of the town only of a very small extent, no less than 548 houses and buildings are running upon the years in the <small>State of Leaseholds.</small>

Pool, by Sir John Tobin, Messrs. Laird, Askew and others, who, in 1828, made public a scheme for the construction of docks on the site.

"1828, Aug. 6. Thos Colley Porter Mayor.

"The Mayor having stated to this Council that a communication had been made to him that an application was intended to be made in the next Session of Parliament by the Proprietors of certain estates in the Hundred of Wirrall and others, for a Bill to authorize the construction of Docks in Wallasey Pool, and the making of a Ship Canal from thence to communicate with the river Dee near Helbree Island.

Bill for Docks in Cheshire.

"Resolved, that the Mayor be requested to apply to the gentlemen from whom the communication was received, to know whether they have any objection to favor the Common Council with a copy of the intended works and of the report of the Civil Engineers thereon."

"1828, Aug. 13. The Mayor laid before the Council the following letter—

"To the Worshipful the Mayor.

"Sir,

Letter from W. Laird.

"On my return from London I had the honour to receive your note dated 6th inst enclosing copy of the resolution passed at the meeting of Common Council of that day, requesting that they might be furnished with a copy of the plan of the proposed Docks &c in the Hundred of Wirrall, and the Report of the Civil Engineers thereon.

"The detailed plan is not now in my possession, but I send herewith a copy shewing the leading features of it, and also a copy of the Engineer's report for the inspection of the members of the Council.

"I have the honour to be, &c,

"Water Street,   "W. LAIRD.
"Aug. 9th, 1828."

On the receipt of this letter, prompt action was taken.

"Resolved, that as the Council are of opinion that this subject is one of great importance to the Corporation estate, the same be referred to the consideration of a Committee of the whole Council, with full powers to act in such way from time to time as to the Committee may seem most adviseable."

Committee.

"1828, Sept. 15. Committee of the whole Council.

"The Mayor stated that in consequence of the confirmation by the Council on the 3rd inst of the Agreement made by him for the purchase of the Bridge End estate on the south side of Wallasey Pool, and of the sentiments of the Council then expressed of the propriety of obtaining as much extent as possible of frontage in the Pool, he had deemed it right in conjunction with Mr George Case to ascertain with the utmost precision, <small>Negociations.</small> and at the same time with the utmost caution the situation of the various interests in the land; and the practicability of making purchases of the same upon such terms as might be advantageous not only to the Corporation Estate, but the Estate of the Trustees of the Docks and the town at large, and that with this idea, he, together with Mr Case, had through various private channels and agencies, been able to negociate and enter into agreements for the purchase of the whole of the frontage land on the <small>Agreements.</small> south side of the Pool, as appeared to them important to possess; and of such a portion of the frontage land on the north side of the Pool as will enable the Corporation to command any objects which may be desirable."

" Resolved, that the Agreements entered into by the Mayor and Mr Alderman Case for the land in question are hereby approved, and that the thanks of the Committee be presented to those gentlemen for the talents, exertions and zeal displayed by them in the making of the purchases in <small>Purchases.</small> question, which the Committee consider of the utmost importance to the Corporation estate, and to that of the Dock Trustees and of the town at large."

" 1828, Octr. 1. The Mayor having laid before the Council a letter from the Surveyor communicating an arrangement made by him with <small>Arrangements with</small> F R Price Esq for the purchase of a further quantity of land at the south <small>Price.</small> west end of Wallasey Pool, but to which arrangement was annexed a condition on the part of Mr Price that the Common Council would give a pledge that they would appropriate the Pool for a dock and other commercial purposes,

" Resolved, that the arrangement made by the Surveyor as far as regards the price and quantity of land is hereby approved and confirmed. That the Council decline giving any pledge to Mr Price as to the appropriation <small>Negociations.</small> of the Pool or land, but that Mr Price be informed that it is the present intention of the Common Council to appropriate the Pool to the purposes of trade connected with the interests of the port of Liverpool."

Some further correspondence took place, Mr. Price <small>Correspondence.</small> pressing for a definite undertaking as to the appropriation of the land, which the Corporation declined to give, referring back to their resolution as to their intention to appropriate the Pool to the purposes of trade.

" 1828, Octr. 15. Resolved that the Select Finance Committee make a report to the Council accompanied with plans, of the best uses to which <small>Report.</small> the land may be applied, due regard being had to the interests of the Dock Estate as well as of the Corporation."

Bill for Wallasey Pool.

"1828, Nov. 5. Nicholas Robinson Mayor.

"Resolved that notices be given for an Act of Parliament for the making and providing of commercial conveniences in Wallasey Pool, omitting therein the making of a dock or docks."

Estimates.

"1828, Decr. 3. Resolved that an estimate of the proposed Wharfage and Quay line in Wallasey Pool be laid before the Select Finance Committee and submitted by them to the next Council together with the heads of a Bill respecting the same for consideration."

The estimate was presented, by which it appeared that the expense of excavating a channel in Wallasey Pool and building and embanking the quay wall agreeable to plan, was, on an average of two schemes, about £100,000.

The Council resolved to postpone the subject, whereupon a letter of remonstrance was received from Mr. Francis Richard Price, in reply to which the following resolution was passed:—

Correspondence with Price.

"1829, Feby. 4. That the Mayor be requested to inform Mr Price that the Council are perfectly aware of their former resolutions upon the subject of Wallasey Pool, and that it is still their intention to appropriate the same to the purposes of trade connected with the Port of Liverpool, but inasmuch as the plans for the permanent appropriation of the Pool, particularly on the South side are not sufficiently matured, and as other plans of improvement have been very recently projected which appear well worthy of consideration; the Council are of opinion that a postponement of Parliamentary proceedings will be much more advantageous to the interests of the Corporation and of Mr Price himself."

Objections of Dock Board.

The Liverpool Dock Committee objected to the introduction of a Bill, considering that it would be injurious to the Dock Estate, and so the subject slumbered for fourteen years longer.

1829, October 7. Mr. Price again addressed the Council, urging them to proceed, when the following resolution was adopted:—

Bill withdrawn.

"That Mr Price be respectfully informed that it is not the intention of the Council to apply in the next Session of Parliament for a Bill respecting Wallasey Pool, but that it is still their intention to appropriate the land to the purposes of trade connected with the interests of the Port of Liverpool."

CORPORATE ESTATE AND REVENUES.

The subject was not again mooted during the existence of the old Council.

The proceedings of the Reformed Council in 1843, which opened the way to the construction of the Birkenhead Docks, do not come within the limits of the present Records. It may suffice to say that, had the Council of that time held their hands, and declined to part with the control of the land, the development of Birkenhead might have taken a different direction. Council Proceedings.

The large purchases of land in Birkenhead in 1828 caused some alarm as to the financial position of the Corporation. Finances of Corporation.

A Balance Sheet was therefore ordered to be prepared, a copy of which runs as follows:— Balance Sheet.

```
                "Balance Sheet
                 25th Sept 1829.

    "Income for Half year—
  18th Octr 1829 to Apl 18th 1830
                "Town Dues  ............  £22,000
                "Rents      ............   23,715
                                          ────────
                                          "£45,715

    "Expenditure—
         "Interest on Bond Debt ........  £16,445
                "Annuities ..............     420
                "Allowance to the Mayor .    1200
                                          ────────
                                          "£18,065

                "Surplus Income .........  £27,650
                "Amount of Bond Debt ....  791,145
                "Owing by the Trustees of the
                    Docks for Land ......  125,900

                "General Balance.
  "Total Debt £791,145.    Assets
                           "Due from Docks ........ £125,900
                           "Property in possession.  852,369
                                                   ─────────
                                                    "£978,269
```

"Area of Lands belonging to the Corporation 322¼ Statute Acres."

X X

"1829, Octr. 7. The particular attention of this Council having been called to the report contained in the proceedings of the Select Finance Committee relative to the situation of the Corporate funds and Estate, made in conformity with a resolution passed at the last Council,

Resolution.

"Resolved, that in the opinion of the Council, considering the great extent of the present expenditure which has been made in the purchase of property for public improvements, and with a view to the future benefit and advantage of the estate, such Report is extremely satisfactory, and tends most strongly to establish the perfect stability and the extensive resources of the Corporation Estate."

TRADE AND COMMERCE.

The trade of the port continued to extend in an ever increasing ratio. From the beginning of the century, down to 1835, the yearly tonnage had increased from 450,060 to 1,768,426, and the Dock Dues from £23,380 to nearly £200,000. *Increase of Trade.*

During the long period of the continental war, the commerce of Liverpool underwent various vicissitudes. The Slave Trade, which at one time formed so important a part of its commerce, was abolished in 1807. The Corporation, however hopeless, raised their voice energetically against the abolition. *Vicissitudes.*

1807, January 20th. Thomas Molyneux, Mayor.

A special Council was held

"To consider the propriety of petitioning Parliament and for adopting such other measures as may be deemed most expedient for obtaining compensation for and on behalf of the Trustees of the Liverpool Docks and of the Corporation, for the loss that will be sustained, if the Bill now pending in Parliament for abolishing the African Slave Trade be passed into a law." *Slave Trade.*

Petitions to the Lords were adopted from the Corporation and the Dock Trustees, setting forth:— *Petitions.*

"That large sums had been expended out of borrowed money, in public improvements, and on Docks, Lighthouses and other works, in full confidence that no innovation would be made in the established commerce of the Port of which the African trade has long formed a most important branch.

"That if the Slave trade were abolished, the petitioners would be greatly injured, and deprived of a considerable portion of those resources necessary for the improvement of the said town and port, which have been for some time in contemplation, besides the injury of a much more extensive nature *Injury.*

in the depreciated value of houses, warehouses and land. The petitioners therefore pray that the Bill be not passed, but if from considerations foreign to their interests it should be thought expedient that the Bill should pass, the petitioners pray that they may be heard by counsel, and by the examination of witnesses, and that such compensation may be made as to the wisdom and justice of the Right Honorable House shall seem fit."

<small>Compensation.</small>

On the 25th March, 1807, the Bill received the Royal assent, without any compensating clauses.

The immediate effect on the commerce of Liverpool was injurious.

<small>Tonnage.</small>

The tonnage, which had been unduly swelled in 1807 by a general rush to make the most of the little time left, fell in twelve months from 662,309 to 516,836, and the amount of the dues from £62,831 to £40,638.

In three years they had recovered themselves, and proceeded with their previous elasticity.

1808. Henry Blundell Hollinshead, Mayor.

<small>Distress.</small>

The price of grain was very high, and great distress prevailed. A movement was made, recommended by a Parliamentary Committee, to stop all distillation from grain for a time, which was met by petitions against the measure.

The Corporation of Liverpool adopted a petition as follows :—

<small>Prohibition of Distillation.</small>

"That your petitioners have seen with feelings of considerable regret, advertisements of meetings in several parts of the kingdom for the purpose of agreeing to petitions against the measure recommended by a committee of your honourable House, for a temporary suspension of the use of grain in the distilleries, as calculated to prove injurious to the agricultural interests of the country.

<small>Difficult Supplies.</small>

"That in the present state of our foreign relations, whilst so many of the ports of Europe are closed against us, and it is impossible to procure a supply of corn from the continent of Europe, whilst in addition to this, the embargo which has taken place in the United States of America precludes us from obtaining any importation from thence, and whilst it remains an undisputed fact that this country has for many years past been dependent upon foreign supply for a considerable part of the subsistence of her inhabitants, more particularly in this populous town and county,

"Your petitioners cannot but think it a measure of wise and prudent precaution to prevent the unnecessary consumption of the produce of our own soil, and by a well timed restriction to guard against an evil of so great magnitude as must result from the failure of the usual means of supply."

The restriction of trade with the East Indies, by the monopoly of the Company, was felt as a great grievance, and strenuous efforts were made to break through the restrictions. East India Trade.

1812, March 20th. The following petition to the House of Commons was adopted:—

"The Petition of the Mayor, Bailiffs and Burgesses most humbly sheweth, Petition.

"That your petitioners conceive that the subjects of these realms possess an inherent right to a free intercourse of trade with all other nations and countries in amity with this, subject only to such regulations as may be necessary for preserving a good understanding with those countries, and for securing to our own the revenues derivable from such intercourse.

"That the monopoly of the East India Company, however expedient at the period of their first charter, is in the present state of commerce no longer so, and it is moreover inconsistent with those principles which are universally admitted to be essential to the prosperity of commerce. That every other nation of Europe being by the signal success of his Majesty's arms deprived of all territory and influence in the East Indies, as well as of all means of annoyance to the navigation of those seas, an ample field is now open for the exertion of British skill and enterprise, and for the investment of that capital which is rendered in a great measure useless in those channels of trade where it has heretofore been employed. Monopoly. Extension of Trade.

"That your petitioners, as the guardians of the interests of the town of Liverpool, while they lament the distressing suspension of its commerce at this juncture, cannot but indulge a sanguine hope that the era is arrived which presents to the merchants and traders of Liverpool in common with those of every part of the British Empire, new and brighter prospects, in the participation of a traffic from which they have been hitherto excluded. Distressing Suspension.

"That your petitioners disclaim any wish to interfere with the rights of the East India Company, which they apprehend may be maintained East India Company.

inviolate without the continuation of a system that infringes the privileges of others."

Charter modified.
These efforts were partially successful. In 1813 the East India Company's charter was modified by the trade to India being thrown open, that with China being still reserved.

First Ship.
The first ship from Liverpool to Calcutta was the Kingsmill, 516 tons burden, belonging to Messrs. John Gladstone & Co., which sailed on May 27th, 1814.

Renewal of Agitation. Meeting.
The Company's Charter was granted for a period of 21 years. In 1829, in anticipation of its expiry, the agitation was renewed. A public meeting was held in the Town Hall, on January 28th, the Mayor (Mr. Nicholas Robinson) in the chair, supported by all the chiefs of the mercantile world in Liverpool.

The first resolution was moved by Mr. (afterwards Sir) John Gladstone, and seconded by Mr. Wm. Rathbone, and carried unanimously:

China Trade.
"That the opening of a free trade to China, and the removal of the restrictions which impede the Commerce between this country and India, would be productive of incalculable benefits, both to this Kingdom and to the British territories in the East Indies."

A string of other resolutions followed, a strong Committee was appointed, and a subscription opened.

1829, February 4th. A Memorial from the Committee appointed at the public meeting held on the 28th January, having been laid before the Council,

Memorial.
"Resolved, that the subject be referred to a special Committee consisting of the Mayor (with 14 others) with a request that they will take the subject into consideration, and make a full report thereon to the Council."

"1830, Mar. 3. George Drinkwater Mayor.

"A Resolution of the Merchants Committee on the East India and China trade of the 25th ul^{to} having been submitted to this Council;

Deputation.
"Resolved, that the Committee of the Common Council be authorized to appoint a deputation to London, should they deem it requisite; and that the Treasurer be authorized to advance £1000, in such sums as may

be from time to time required, to be applied in such way as the Committee may think proper."

These efforts were successful, and the trade to India and China has become a very important part of the commerce of Liverpool. Success.

There is much interesting matter in the Records connected with the conservancy of the estuary of the Mersey and its shores.

"1813, Aug. 12. Samuel Staniforth Mayor.

"A letter from Mr Wm Statham, agent to Robert Vyner Esq, relative to the encroachment of the sea over the Leasowe in the county of Chester, and the probability of its making a junction with Wallasey Pool, which might be extremely detrimental to the town and Port having been read, and Mr Statham having offered on the part of Mr Vyner to contribute the sum of fifty guineas towards the expences to be incurred in procuring the opinion of Mr Rennie upon this matter, Encroachment of Sea.

"Resolved, that Mr Rennie be requested to come over for the purpose of making the necessary survey and reporting thereupon." Rennie to report.

There is no copy of Mr. Rennie's report on the Records.

In 1822, a Commission of Engineers, consisting of Messrs. Whidbey, Chapman and Rennie, presented an elaborate report thereon.

They state,

"That after examination they report their opinion on the most advisable measures to be adopted for preserving the navigation, and preventing further encroachments on the tideway of this important estuary, which if continued in the same ratio as hitherto, must ultimately, and that period is not very distant, terminate in the great deterioration of this harbour, and in consequence thereof, of the prosperity of the town of Liverpool and the surrounding country depending upon it." Engineers' Report.

They proceed,

"That between Runcorn and Fidler's Ferry they found large tracts of Marsh land outside the line of the present backs, serving as important receptacles for back water, intersected by numerous jetties which were extended much further out than necessary, and operated as injurious impediments to the tideway; and by obstructing its course, diminish its velocity, and allow time for the alluvial matter to be deposited, and form banks and shoals highly injurious to the navigation. Obstructions.

CHAP. IV, A.D. 1800—1835.

River Weaver.

"On the river Weaver they found similar obstructions. At Ince they found in addition to the Ferry Quay, several very extensive jetties, followed by destructive consequences."

They state,

"That a number of harbours in this kingdom have been ruined for want of preserving back water. No time, they say, ought to be lost in obtaining sufficient powers to have the complete conservatorship or control of all the waters in the river Mersey and all its branches."

Further Report.

A further report was presented by the same parties on the lines of wharf walls, at the south and north ends of the Liverpool Docks, upon Pluckington's Bank, Wallasey Leasowe, Tranmere Pool, &c.

They recommend,

Wharf Wall.

"That a Wharf wall should be built from the south end of the then existing docks in a curve to Pottery Point, there to terminate. The flood and ebb tide flowing regularly along it, would produce an easy navigation, and prevent the difficulties which now exist."

They say,

Extension of Docks.

"We understand it is in contemplation to increase the number of docks at the North end, and that it is very desirable that a plan should be fixed upon to give shelter to the steam-packets; that being the case, we recommend that a Wharf wall should be built now, that will form the Northern boundary of the intended docks, where the Steam-packets can lie in safety and be protected from all winds. The erection of suspension piers which has been spoken of for the above purpose, we particularly object to as being extremely dangerous and unsafe for vessels to lie alongside in gales of wind from the Northward.

Pluckington Bank.

"With respect to Pluckington's Bank there is nothing new in such formations; that Bank we conceive is formed on the principle of every bar at the entrance of all Harbours in the world. Rivers bring down from the Country a quantity of alluvial matter, and when it is on the point of entering the sea, it falls on a body of water that is either still or taking another direction, so that the current of the river strikes another body of water at right angles, and as it has not the power to force such a body out of its

Currents and Eddies.

course, it must produce eddies, and cause the alluvial matter in the river water to fall to the bottom, by which the Bar is formed, and in this way Pluckington Bank has been formed. The great body of water that is at

Mud Deposit.

times let out of the docks and the large quantity of mud thrown into such streams and carried against the river tide, is by that tide stopped in its progress, and must deposit the contents, which have formed and made

Pluckington Bank, and we strongly recommend that the docks should never in future be cleared of the mud in the way above mentioned, but that it should be taken from the docks in barges and deposited in the river at the North end of the docks—on the ebb tide.

"We are of opinion that there is no immediate danger to be apprehended from the present state of the shore at Wallasey Leasowes, and we think it will be quite time enough to embank out the sea at that place when danger is more apparent, which may not be for many years to come, for although it has been stated to us that the sea is increasing upon the shores at that place, it may in time recede, and we cannot advise the Corporation to go to any expense on that account, but we strongly recommend that no gravel should be removed from this shore in future." Wallasey Leasowe.

" 1824, Feby. 4. Cha' Lawrence Mayor.

" Resolved, That notice be officially given by the Town Clerk to the Company of Proprietors of the Mersey and Irwell Navigation, that the Works now constructing by them near Runcorn, are not only expressly against the consent and approbation of the Common Council of this town, but that the Council now most strongly protest against the same, and resolve, that if hereafter such Works shall be found injurious to the navigation of the River Mersey, legal measures will be taken to remove the same and to abate the nuisance." Obstructions at Runcorn.

" 1826, June 7. Peter Bourne Mayor.

" The Council having adverted to the recent Resolutions, proceedings and recommendations of the Select Finance Committee relative to the encroachments and embankments in the River above Runcorn, in consequence of which there is great reason to apprehend that very serious injury will arise to the Port and the Navigation of the River, Encroachments above Runcorn.

" Resolved, That the Select Finance Committee be authorized to adopt such measures either legal or Parliamentary, as to them may seem most advisable for effectually preventing the injury."

" 1826, Decr. 6. The Town Clerk having laid before this Council the Report of the recent proceedings in the Court of Chancery against the Company of Proprietors of the Mersey and Irwell Navigation, Mersey and Irwell.

" Resolved, that in compliance with the strong recommendations expressed by the Lord Chancellor upon that occasion, the Select Finance Committee be authorized to adopt such measures as they may deem advisable for ascertaining by legal decision or otherwise, and with the least possible delay, the rights of the Crown, the rights of the Public, the rights of the Corporation, the rights of the Mersey and Irwell Company, and the precise extent of the powers and authorities of their Act of Parliament; and that a copy of this resolution be transmitted to the Chairman of the Committee of the Mersey and Irwell Company." Legal Proceedings.

1828, March 5th. An elaborate survey and report was

submitted by Messrs. Stevenson and Nimmo, Civil Engineers, on the state of the Wallasey Leasowe, and the inroads making by the sea.

"The Council having taken into consideration the Report as above, and being of opinion that the subject is one of very considerable importance, to a certain extent to the interest of the Corporation and the Trustees of the Docks,

<small>Leasowe Embankment.</small>

"Resolved, That the Select Finance Committee be authorized to co-operate with the Dock Committee in the immediate adoption of some temporary embankment for the prevention of any further irruption which may possibly occur from the very high tides in the present month, and that the Committee be also authorized, in conjunction with the Dock Committee, to adopt such other measures of a permanent nature as may be deemed advisable, upon a communication with the owners of lands under the level, and to whom a copy of the above resolution be transmitted, accompanied by a copy of the report of Mr Stevenson and Mr Nimmo."

<small>Act of Parliament.</small>

This led to an Act of Parliament, by which the Dock and Harbour Board, and the owners of the low-lying lands, are assessed towards the repairs and maintenance of the embankment.

"1825, Apl. 6. Jonathan Blundell Hollinshead Mayor.

<small>Leeds Canal.</small>

"Resolved, That in the event of the Company of the Leeds and Liverpool Canal being disposed to solicit the introduction of a clause in the Dock Bill for altering the situation of the junction of the Canal with the

<small>Junction with River.</small>

River Mersey as specified in the Canal Acts, and for allowing of such junction to the Northward of the Prince's Dock, the same be acquiesced in, the plan being previously submitted to and approved by the Trustees of the Docks and the Common Council."

"1829, Mar. 4, Nicholas Robinson Mayor.

<small>River Weaver Act.</small>

"A print of a Bill for improving the River Weaver Navigation having been laid before the Council, which appears to contain powers of a most extensive and undefined nature, which may possibly materially affect the River Mersey and the Port of Liverpool,

"Resolved, that the Bill be referred to the early consideration of the Select Finance Committee, with full authority to adopt measures for preventing the extension of powers which may interfere with the navigation of the river Mersey, or affect the rights and interests of this Corporation."

<small>Conservancy of River.</small>

"1829, April 1. Resolved, that the Council are more strongly impressed than ever, with the necessity of the Conservatorship of the River being vested in some fixed body of persons, and the rights, duties, and interests of all parties defined; and that the Mayor be requested to transmit to his

Majesty's Commissioners of Woods and Forests, copies of the resolutions which have been recently passed on the subject of the conservancy of the River, and to request that they will be pleased to give this subject their early consideration, and favor the Mayor with a communication thereon, for the information of the Council."

"1829, May 6. The Mayor reported to the Council that he with a deputation had had an interview with the first Commissioner of Woods and Forests, and with the Chancellor of the Duchy of Lancaster on the subject of the general conservancy of the River, to which the attention of the two Boards had been previously drawn by the resolutions recently passed by the Council. The result of this interview had been extremely satisfactory. The subject of the conservancy had been for some time under consideration, and it was their intention to advise his Majesty to grant a Commission of Conservancy, and that every practical dispatch would be given to the issuing of the same." Commission.

"1830, July 7. George Drinkwater Mayor.

"At this Council a letter was read from Mr Huskisson relative to the Conservancy, stating that he had communicated with Lord Lowther the Chief Commissioner, and found that the case was still in the hands of the Attorney General, who represented it to be encumbered with many difficulties; indeed, he doubts the power of the Crown, as the law now stands, to issue any such Commission of Conservancy in the present case, and is decidedly of opinion that without an Act of Parliament the Corporation of Liverpool or any part of it, could not be invested with the powers of such a commission." Letter from Huskisson.
Question of the Law.

"1830, Dec. 7. Thomas Brancker Mayor.

"At this Council a letter was read from the Secretary to the Lords of the Treasury relating to the encroachments on the River Mersey, stating that from the documents transmitted my Lords are of opinion that a Bill ought to be brought into Parliament, to provide for the conservation of the River Mersey and the Port of Liverpool, full notice being given to all the parties concerned." Conservancy Act.

"1832, April 4. Sam¹ Sandbach Mayor.

"Resolved that the Select Finance Committee be requested to take into their early consideration the necessity of the gradual inclosing of the strand from the northern extremity of the Dock Works to Beacon's Gutter, in the line laid down on the plan submitted to Parliament in 1825." Enclosures of Strand.

These inquiries led to a claim on the part of the Crown to certain portions of the foreshore.

"1828, Mar. 5. Thomas Colley Porter Mayor.

"The Mayor stated to the Council, that he had been served with a notice of a claim by the Duchy of Lancaster to the shore in Toxteth Park Claims of Crown.

lying between high and low watermark, which had been purchased by the Corporation from the Earl of Sefton ; that the Town Clerk had had interviews with the Solicitor to the Duchy, in the course of which it was stated to be the intention to extend the claim of his Majesty to the shore of the River between high and low watermark within the Borough of Liverpool."

Legal opinions.

"1828, Apl. 2. The Town Clerk laid before the Council the opinions of Mr Richmond and Mr Brodie relative to the title of the Corporation to the shore of the River in Liverpool, which opinions are expressed in the strongest language in favour of the title of the Corporation to the same."

Payment to Okill.

"1828, July 2. Resolved, That the sum of £150 be paid to Mr Charles Okill as a remuneration to him for the preparation of the valuable plans and documents denoting in the most satisfactory way, the right and title of the Corporation to the shore of the river within the manor and lordship of Liverpool, upon the recent claim of the King in regard of his Duchy of Lancaster thereto."

"1804, Aug. 10. Jno Bridge Aspinall Mayor.

Ferry.

"On Mr Joseph White's application as proprietor of the Rock Ferry in Cheshire, stating that he had purchased a house from the Earl of Sefton in Toxteth Park nearly opposite to the Rock Ferry, which he intended to convert into another Ferry House, and to build a commodious quay or wharf, extending to low water, for the accommodation of the Public, and that he intended to apply to Parliament for an Act to enable him to demand a reasonable toll, and wishing to have the assistance and countenance of the Common Council to enable him to carry his scheme into effect ;

Toxteth Park.

White's application.

"Resolved and Ordered, that the subject matter of the said application be referred to the Select Committee to consider and report ; it being expected however that Mr White acquiesce in any reasonable proposal on the part of the Corporation, in the appointment of Commissioners for the better regulation of the Ferries and Fisheries."

"1805, May 6. Wm Harper Mayor.

"A special Council was held to consider the Bill promoted by Mr Joseph White, when it was

Petition against Bill.

"Resolved, that a petition be presented against the said Bill, on the ground that it contains provisions for erecting Piers, Slips, or Quays on each side the River Mersey of an unlimited extent, which may prove injurious to the navigation of the said river.

"That it also contains clauses which if passed into a law, would greatly affect the interests of the Public in general, and the town of Liverpool in particular. And that the said Bill also contains several clauses and provisions highly injurious to the rights and interests of your petitioners as Owners of the Port and Harbour of Liverpool."

Withdrawn.   This Bill was withdrawn, and nothing came of the scheme.

The introduction of steam navigation on the Mersey is thus noticed. — Steam Navigation.

"1817, Feby. 10. A petition from William Batman on behalf of himself and others, proprietors of a Steam Boat intended to ply between Liverpool and Cheshire, for the accommodation of steps and landing places having been read;

"Resolved, that such petition be referred to the consideration of the Select Finance Committee, with full powers to the Committee to act thereon as to them may seem proper."

"1829, April 1. A memorial from Messrs J S Walker and George Shaw, requesting some recompense for constructing two models of proposed landing places, applicable to the Liverpool Piers on the eastern shores of the Mersey, having been laid before this Council, — Landing Places.

"Resolved, that the Treasurer be authorized to give the memorialists the sum of £10 10s."

Several of the modern commercial improvements are foreshadowed many years before their accomplishment.

"1802, March 23. Peter Whitfield Brancker Mayor.

"Upon an application made by and on behalf of the supporters of the Bill now depending in Parliament for the forming a junction between the Isle of Anglesea and the main land, by means of an iron bridge over the Straits of Menai, and also of another bridge over the River Conway, according to the plans produced, and upon considering also the objections urged against this plan by the agents of the inhabitants of Carnarvon. — Bridge over Menai.

"Resolved and Ordered, that the subject matter of these several applications appears of too much consequence under all the circumstances for the Council at present, from what has hitherto been laid before them, to form any precise or proper judgment; and therefore that the same be referred to the Dock Committee to consider, and to countenance or oppose as to them shall seem most advisable upon further investigation, and that the Mayor and Bailiffs be authorized to affix the Common Seal to such petitions for or against either of the said schemes as they shall think most expedient." — Referred to Dock Committee.

The project failed for the time.

In 1810 the scheme was revived, whereupon the Council passed the following resolution :—

"1810, Mar. 7. It having been stated to this Council that the supporters of the scheme for forming a junction between the Isle of Anglesea and the main land by means of a bridge and of another bridge over the river Conway are now renewing their application to Parliament; — Revival of Scheme.

358   CHAP. IV, A.D. 1800—1835.

"Resolved, that the Dock Committee be desired to reconsider the question, and to take such measures as they may deem expedient for opposing or supporting the same as may be advisable."

"1817, Feby. 10. Jno Wright Mayor.

"The Mayor having produced to this Council the copy of a resolution passed at a Meeting of the Committee for carrying into effect the proposed bridge at Runcorn, requesting that the Common Council would give their countenance and support to the undertaking,

Bridge at Runcorn.

"Resolved, that the Town Clerk do write to Mr Fitchett, the Secretary of the meeting, acknowledging the receipt of the copy of the resolution, and stating that in the present stage of the proceedings, and without further information, the Council decline taking the subject into consideration."

"1818, Decr. 9. Jonathan Blundell Hollinshead Mayor.

"Resolved, that the Select Finance Committee be authorized to watch the progress of two Bills intended to be brought into Parliament the next Session, the one relative to the erecting of a bridge at Runcorn, and the other relative to the establishment of a Fishery Company on the River Mersey, and to take such measures as they may deem expedient."

Fishery Company.

The measure was not carried, and the matter remained over until the erection of the Railway bridge, which has only partially remedied the inconvenience.

After the inception of the Liverpool and Manchester Railway, many schemes were proposed for uniting the two shores of the Mersey.

"1827, May 2. Thos Littledale Mayor.

"A letter having been laid before this Council from James Lowe Esq, relative to the formation of a Company to carry into execution a projected Tunnel under the Mersey from Liverpool to Cheshire,

Tunnel under River.

"Resolved, that this Council cannot give any opinion on this subject, without plans and other documents fully explanatory of the measure being submitted; but that when the same are presented, the Council will give the subject due consideration."

"1830, Jany. 6. A letter from Mr Forsyth and Mr Lawton inclosing the copy of a resolution passed at a meeting of land proprietors at Birkenhead, and a plan and reports of Mr Vignoles and Mr Stephenson, and a letter from Mr Giles, relative to the formation of a Tunnel under the River between Liverpool and Woodside, and soliciting the Corporation to sanction and encourage the measure, having been laid before this Council,

Vignoles and Stephenson.

"Resolved, that the Mayor be requested to inform the parties, that the subject is one of such magnitude that the Council are not prepared to give any reply to the application."

"1830, Feby. 3. A Resolution passed at a meeting of Proprietors of
land in Birkenhead relative to the constructing of a tunnel under the river Tunnel.
having been laid before this Council,
 "Resolved, That the same be referred to the Select Finance Committee
to report."

Another project of a more daring character contemplated a bridge across the estuary.

"1828, July 2. A Report accompanied by Plans from Messrs Twyford
and Wilson of Manchester relative to a Bridge being placed across the Bridge over
River Mersey opposite Birkenhead having been laid before this Council, Mersey.
 "Resolved, That the subject is one of too great importance with reference to the navigation of the river, for this Council to give any reply to the same, without the further opinions and report of some of the most eminent Civil Engineers of the day, being obtained by the promoters of the measure."

Whether these reports were favourable does not appear, but nothing further was done.

The most important work connected with the commerce of Liverpool during this period was the construction of the Liverpool and Manchester Railway, to which there are many Manchester
references in the Records. Railway.

"1824, June 2. Charles Lawrence Mayor.
 "A memorial of the subscribers to a projected Railroad between Liver- Memorial.
pool and Manchester, soliciting the support of the Common Council having been read,
 "Resolved, That the Mayor be requested to communicate to Mr Moss, the Chairman by whom the Memorial was signed, that when the measures are more matured, the Council will be disposed to receive the plans, and to give the same and the general subject of the memorial, due consideration."

"1825, Jany. 5. Another memorial from the subscribers was laid before Further
the Council, soliciting assent to the Railroad passing through the Corpora- Memorial.
tion Property and the support of the Corporation to the undertaking by Petition to both Houses of Parliament.
 "Resolved, that the memorial and the plan therein alluded to, be referred to the Select Finance Committee, and that they make a report thereon to the Council."

"1825, March 2. The Bill for the making of a Railway from this town Bill.
to Manchester, having been laid before this Council,
 "Resolved, That the same be referred to the Select Finance Committee, for the purpose of their taking into consideration how far the same may in

their opinion affect the general rights and interests of the Corporation and
<small>Petition.</small> the town, with authority to present any Petition they may think proper against the same, it being expressly understood that the Bill be opposed unless a clause is introduced therein against the admission of any steam engine, stationary or locomotive, into the town."

<small>Amendments.</small> "1825, April 6. Resolved, that the several alterations and amendments in the Liverpool and Manchester Railway Bill as now submitted to this Council be acquiesced in; but that the Bill be opposed unless the clause requiring the Railway to be carried under the Liverpool and Preston Turnpike Road be introduced."

<small>North entrance.</small> It is evident from this entry that the Railway was intended at first to enter Liverpool from the north, nearly in the same line as that subsequently adopted by the Lancashire and Yorkshire Railway.

<small>Plans submitted.</small> "1825, Decr. 7. A Memorial from the Committee of the Liverpool and Manchester Railway, accompanied by a plan of the line of the intended tunnel within the town having been laid before this Council,

"Resolved, that the Surveyor be directed forthwith to send a competent draftsman to Preston to take an accurate copy of the plan of the Railway lodged with the Clerk of the Peace there."

<small>Tunnel assented to.</small> "1826, Jany. 4. Resolved, that the Town Clerk be authorized to give the assent of the Corporation to the carrying of the Rail Road in a tunnel through Liverpool as described in the plan deposited, provided the Committee of the Rail Road Company undertake to introduce a clause in their Bill, binding themselves to construct the said tunnel to the entire satisfaction of the Surveyor of the Corporation, the general provisions of the said Bill being still subject to the consideration of the Council."

"1826, March 4. A Print of the Liverpool and Manchester Railway Bill having been laid before the Council, with the several alterations recommended by the Select Finance Committee, and also copies of the
<small>Clauses settled.</small> several clauses recommended by the Committee to be inserted in the Bill together with an additional clause submitted by the Town Clerk and the same having been read, it was

"Resolved, That the same are approved and confirmed, with the exception of the clause relative to the property of the tunnel, which in the event of the same being abandoned, provided that it shall revert to the Corporation, but as to which it is

"Resolved, That it shall only extend to that part of the said tunnel carried under the property of the Corporation, and that the Town Clerk be directed to take the requisite measures to have these several clauses and alterations introduced into the Bill now before Parliament."

"1826, Octr. 7. Resolved, that in the confirmation of the Resolutions

TRADE AND COMMERCE.

and Recommendations of the Select Finance Committee relative to the applications of the Company of Proprietors of the Liverpool and Manchester Railway, such confirmation is not to be considered as affecting any question in respect of compensation or purchase of property as between the Corporation and the Railway Company." Compensation.

"1830, July 31. Sir George Drinkwater Mayor.

"The Mayor having communicated to the Council that it had been announced to him by Charles Lawrence and John Moss Esqrs the Chairman and Deputy Chairman of the Liverpool and Manchester Railway Company that it was the intention of his Grace the Duke of Wellington to honor this town with a visit on the 15th September next, the day of the opening of the Railway, Duke of Wellington.

"Resolved unanimously, that all possible respect be paid to his Grace upon this occasion; that a suitable Address be prepared and that the Freedom of the Borough (already voted by the Council upon the ever memorable Battle of Waterloo) be presented to his Grace in a suitable gold box." Address.

"1830, Decr. 1. Thomas Brancker Mayor.

"The Town Clerk having reported that the plans of the projected Railroads between Liverpool and Birmingham, and Liverpool and Leeds, and of the Branch Railroad from the Liverpool and Manchester Railroad from Huyton to the North end of the town, had been deposited with him and the assent of the Corporation requested thereto, Birmingham Railway.

"Resolved, that the several plans be referred to the Select Finance Committee to report thereon to the Council."

"1831, Jany. 5. A letter from the Surveyor upon the subject of retaining some Civil Engineers, whose assistance may be wanted in Parliament in the course of the progress of the projected Bills for Railroads, with reference to the construction of bridges across the river, having been laid before this Council, Reference to Engineers.

"Resolved, that the same be referred to the Select Finance Committee."

"1831, March 2. A communication having been received from John Moss Esqr, chairman of a Deputation from the Liverpool and Birmingham Railway Company in London, upon the subject of the line of Railway within the town,

"Resolved, that the same be referred to the Select Finance Committee."

"1831, April 6. The Council having adverted to the Resolution of the Select Finance Committee of the 5th instant relative to the proposed line of the Liverpool and Chorlton Railway through Frederick Street and to the scite of the present Custom House, Chorlton Railway.

"Resolved, That as far as regards the line of the Railway in the town, the Council approve of the same in lieu of the line described in the Parliamentary Plan now deposited, the introduction of any clauses which may appear requisite on the part of the Corporation being expressly understood to be reservéd for consideration when the Bill is brought in."

Lime Street Tunnel.
"1831, Sept. 7. A letter from John Moss Esq, Deputy Chairman of the Committee of the Liverpool and Manchester Railway Company relative to the construction of a tunnel from a point in the line of Railway between Edge Hill and Wavertree Lane to the side of the Cattle Market in Lime Street, having been laid before the Council,

"Resolved, that the Council entertain a favourable opinion of the principle of a tunnel, provided the same be appropriated to Passengers only; and that the subject be referred to the Select Finance Committee to report thereon."

"1835, Feby. 4th. Jas Aspinall Mayor.

Façade.
"A letter from Charles Lawrence Esq, Chairman of the Directors of the Railway Company on the subject of the proposed ornamental Façade to the Company's Station in Lime Street, accompanied by a design, having been laid before the Council,

"Resolved, that this letter and the said Design be referred to the Select Finance Committee, with full powers to carry the same into execution."

Removed.
This façade, after an existence of forty years, was swept away to make room for the erection of the North-Western Hotel.

STREETS AND BUILDINGS.

Down to the latter part of the 18th century, Liverpool might have vied with any town in the kingdom for narrow, tortuous, ill-paved streets. The first Improvement Act was Act of 1785. passed in 1785.[1] Under the power thus given, Castle Street was laid out as at present, Brunswick Street was formed, and Dale Street widened as far as Moorfields.

In 1801, provision was made for extending the town eastward.

"1801, June 3. John Shaw Mayor.

"Resolved and Ordered, That the entire completing of the Plan of the Moss Lake fields, now submitted to the Council by Alderman Naylor, Mosslake Deputy Chairman of the Select Committee of Improvements, together Fields. with the Agreement of the several proprietors, and the award of the Arbitrators touching the same, be entirely referred and submitted to that Committee to carry into full effect, and that the Mayor and Bailiffs be authorized to affix the common seal to the said Agreement."

"1802, Jany. 6. Resolved and Ordered, that it be an instruction to the Select Committee to consult the physicians to the Infirmary and Dispensary, in respect of any proposed alteration in the extension of the Improvement Act that may in any degree contribute to the health and comfort of Health of the inhabitants." Town.

"1802, Decr. 10. Resolved and Ordered, That it be referred to the Select Finance Committee with full powers, to solicit an Act in the present Session of Parliament for authority to turn or direct a common highway intended to have been made on the east strand or shore of the River Mersey from Bath Street to Beacon's Gutter, and instead thereof to open and make two new roads to the eastward of, and nearly parallel with the Roads said originally intended road, and for other the purposes in the recom- northward. mendation of the Select Finance Committee particularly mentioned, and that the Mayor and Bailiffs be authorized to affix the Common Seal to the requisite petitions."

"1810, Feby. 8. Alderman Leyland having stated to this Council that he understood an application was intended to be made in the now present

[1] *Vide supra*, p. 259.

Preston Road.	Session of Parliament for an Act for more effectually repairing, widening, improving and amending the road from Liverpool to Preston,

"Resolved, that it be referred to the Select Finance Committee to watch the progress of the said intended Bill through both Houses of Parliament."

Dale Street.	"1818, Novr. 4. The present extremely narrow, and consequently dangerous state of a considerable part of Dale Street having become the subject of discussion at this Council,

"Resolved, that the Surveyor do furnish the Mayor for production at the next Council with a plan, specifying the property therein now belonging to the Corporation and other individuals, and also denoting the frontage which would be required to widen and improve that street, so as to make it not only a handsome entrance to the town, but to render it safe and commodious for the Public. And to be accompanied with an estimate of the value of the different Properties."

"1819, Jany. 10. Report and Plan presented to the Council.

"The Plan produced to the Council having been laid before the Committee, inspected, and examined;

Widening Dale Street.	"Resolved, that it is the opinion of the Committee that the widening of Dale Street by taking down and receding of the houses and buildings on the north side as far as Johnson Street will be of the most essential service to the Public; and that the widening of any part of the street on that side, although the whole cannot be accomplished, is extremely desirable.

Bull and Punch Bowl.	"Resolved that the Mayor be requested to send a note to Mr James Hargreaves, the owner of the Inn called the Bull and Punch Bowl, desiring an interview upon the subject of the sale of his premises, respecting which a long correspondence had taken place with Mr Foster some time back. And that the following note be sent to the owners of the several other properties on the north side of Dale Street; and that the Mayor be requested to summon the Committee again when requisite.

"'Sir,

"'The Common Council being desirous of ascertaining the practicability of the widening of Dale Street, as Chairman of the Committee to whom this subject has been referred, I shall be much obliged by your favouring me with the terms upon which you are disposed to sell so much of your property as may be required for the purpose. I shall be happy to give any further explanation in my power which you may deem necessary.

"'I am &c

"'J Blundell Hollinshead

"'Mayor.'"

"1819, March 3. The Report of the Dale Street Committee having been read,

Purchase of Property.	"Resolved, that the said Committee be invested with full powers to make the purchases necessary for the widening of the street and effecting

STREETS AND BUILDINGS. 365

the intended communication [1] in the same manner and upon the same terms as the Committee were originally invested with, viz, Authority to make the purchases on the North side of Dale Street for the purpose of widening the same."

"1819, Octr. 6. The plans of the unproductive properties belonging to the Corporation situate in Water Street, Juggler Street and Pemberton's Alley having been produced at this Council, Water Street, &c.

"Resolved, that the materials of the buildings formerly occupied as the Old Gaol [2] be immediately disposed of by public auction in order that they may be removed, and part of the land laid to the street, in the intended line of improvement. And that the remainder of the land be leased out in the usual way for three lives and twenty one years, under the directions of the Select Finance Committee." Materials of Tower.

"1821, June 6. Thos Leyland Mayor.

"The Mayor having stated to this Council that much Idleness prevailed on a Sunday evening at St. James's Walk—Resolved, that with a view of preventing the same, a lodge be built at each end of the Walk, to be inhabited by the gardener." St. James' Walk.

"1824, Jany. 7. Resolved, that the street across the Old Dock from Pool Lane to Mersey Street be made according to the Act of Parliament of the 51st of the late King as soon as practicable after the completion of George's Dock." Street across Old Dock.

"1824, Feby. 4. Resolved, that the Improvement Committee be authorized to carry into effect the widening of Tithebarn Street alluded to in the proceedings of the Committee of the 2nd inst. Tithebarn Street.

"A Memorial having been presented to this Council very numerously and respectably signed, relative to the widening of Derby Square and the North end of James Street so as to effect a better approach to the intended Baths and the various slips on the west side of George's Dock, Derby Square.

"Resolved, that such memorial be referred to the consideration of the Improvement Committee."

1825, Nov. 2nd. Forty years had elapsed since the date of the first Improvement Act of 1785. The time had now arrived when the subject again pressed itself on the notice of the Council.

"Resolved, That it is the opinion of this Council that application should be made in the next Session of Parliament for an Act for opening and widening Lord Street, Castle Ditch, New John Street, Marshall Street, Love Lane, Trafford's Lane, Pool Lane, Lancelot's Hey, and also for Improvement Act.

---

[1] This refers to the opening of Manchester Street, through land occupied at that time by timber yards.
[2] The Tower, the ancient seat of the Stanleys, Earls of Derby.

Widening Streets.

opening and widening James Street, or converting the same into a road for foot passengers only, and making in lieu thereof a new Street from Preeson's Row to Strand Street; and also for widening Leece's Street and the top of Bold Street and improving the cemetery of St. Luke's Church; and also for widening and improving the entrances into the town from London Road down Shaw's Brow, and St. John's Lane; and also the entrance from Lancaster along Scotland Road, and also for widening and improving the communication between Byrom Street and Dale Street.

General Improvements.

"Resolved, also, That the Improvement Committee be requested to take such measures as they may deem expedient, to carry the above resolution into effect, together with such other general improvements of streets within the town and the prevention of nuisances and annoyances therein from which public benefit would be derived, and that they be authorized to direct the requisite notices to be given for an Act of Parliament in the ensuing Session, and including in such notice the establishment of a Fire Police."

Lord Street.

This Improvement Act, the most extensive ever carried out in Liverpool, was passed in the following Session. The new buildings in Lord Street and the Crescent were required to be built to prescribed architectural designs. The only other instance of the kind was the rebuilding of the west side of Castle Street under the Act of 1785.

New Buildings.

"1826, July 5. The Surveyor having submitted the plans and elevations of the new buildings on the south side of Lord Street and the intended new Crescent opposite St. Georges' Church,

"Resolved, that the same be approved."

Boulevard proposed.

"1816, April 5. A memorial from several of the Burgesses and other inhabitants of the town, relative to establishing on the Corporation Boundary a spacious handsome public road, with wide footpaths planted on both sides with rows of trees; of appropriating some open pieces of land in the outskirts to amusements for the working classes, and of stationing opposite to the centre of the town a Public Floating Bath.

"Resolved, that such memorial cannot be entertained."

Engraved Plan.

"1807, July 5. On the Mayor's notification to the Council of his having received from Mr William Lawson a valuable copper plate plan of the town of Liverpool as it appeared in 1725, with some remarks as to its Liberties and Boundaries, and also a letter wishing the same to be received by him for the purpose of being lodged amongst the records of the Corporation;

"Resolved and Ordered, upon the motion of the Mayor, seconded by Mr Alderman Case, that the said Plan, being considered as an authentick

STREETS AND BUILDINGS.

and valuable relick, be accordingly preserved amongst other similar documents belonging to the Corporation, and that the Mayor be desired to signify the same to Mr Lawson with the thanks of the Council."

"1828, Nov. 5. A letter from Mr Michael Alexander Gage relative to a Plan of the Town and Port of Liverpool, and its environs, accompanied with specimens of the engraving of the same, and expressive of his intention of presenting a copy of the Plan upon a large scale to the Common Council having been read; *Gage's Map.*

"Resolved, that the thanks of the Council be presented to Mr Gage for his intended present; and that the Select Committee be authorized to order such a number of the Plans as they may think proper."

The numbering of the houses in the line of the streets has frequently been a source of perplexity. *Numbering Houses.*

"1807, April 5. It being intimated that Mr Gore purposed to make a new Directory of the inhabitants of the town of Liverpool and its neighbourhood, and that he had employed Mr Robert Phillips to call at each individual house to take the number and the name of the occupier, but that he had found the numbers very irregular and incorrect, and had therefore requested the authority of this Council to number each house in regular order, *Gore's Directory.*

"Resolved and Ordered, that the said Robert Phillips be hereby authorized to cause the Number on each house in this town to be painted on the door, and also the names of the streets to be painted at the ends of each of them, under the direction of the Select Committee." *Numbering ordered.*

Thirteen years afterwards the same order had to be repeated.

"1820, Decr. 6. Resolved, that the names of the several streets throughout the town be painted therein, and the number of the houses be also painted on the doors of the same, under the directions of the Surveyor agreeable to the clause in the Act of Parliament of the 26th of the late King." *Names of Streets.*

The insecure mode of building began to attract attention.

"1823, Feby. 5. The copy of a Presentment of the Grand Jury at the late Quarter Sessions, relative to the dreadful effects of the late storm on the 5th of December last, in consequence of the modern insecure mode of building, and suggesting the adoption of some legislative enactment to prevent the recurrence of accidents, having been laid before the Council, *Insecure Building.*

"Resolved, that the same be referred to the Select Finance Committee, and that they be requested to make a report thereon."

"1824, Michaelmas Sessions.—'The Grand Jury cannot separate without *Grand Jury.*

again calling the attention of the Magistrates to the Presentment made at the Quarter Sessions of January 1823 respecting the slight and dangerous mode of erecting Dwelling houses now practised in this town and neigh-
Presentment. bourhood. This presentment prayed that steps might be immediately taken to procure a Legislative enactment, which might empower a proper Officer carefully to survey every building hereafter to be erected, and in case of insecurity to cause the danger to be removed. The Grand Jury earnestly request the attention of the Magistrates to this most important Presentment, the necessity of which they dread will be again speedily shewn as that period approaches at which during three years past most awful calamities have occurred.'

"This Presentment having been laid before the Council,
Resolution. "Resolved, That the Council perfectly coincide in opinion with the Grand Jury relative to the insecure mode of the erection of buildings and the necessity of obtaining some legislative enactment for the prevention of the same, and that the Select Finance Committee be authorized to take this subject into consideration, and to direct the preparation of a Bill to be submitted to the Council for approval, and that the requisite Parliamentary notices be given."

Building Act. The notices were given and the Act passed, which has been the basis of all subsequent legislation on the subject in Liverpool.

Public Buildings. In taking a review of the buildings of a public nature erected during this period, the Town Hall claims the first notice. Its original designation was the Exchange, the ground floor having been devoted to this purpose, and so continued until the erection of the New Exchange Buildings, completed in 1809.

The fire at the Exchange has been noticed in the last chapter. On the reconstruction, considerable alterations were made.

"1801, Feby. 4. Resolved and Ordered, That the Plan produced at the last Council for making the alterations in the public offices within the
Exchange. Exchange, signed by the Chairman of the Select Committee, be approved, and directed to be carried into execution."

"1802, Jany. 6. Resolved and Ordered, that the Surveyor be autho-
Completion. rized to proceed immediately in completing the present building called the Exchange, agreeable to the plans now produced, and certified by the Mayor and also by Alderman John Gregson the Chairman, under the

direction of the said Committee *i.e.*, the Select Committee of Improvements."

" 1816, July 10. Sir Wm Barton Knt Mayor.

" Resolved, that the expenses of lighting the Town hall at a Ball given by the late Mayor amounting to the sum of Fifty three Pounds be defrayed by the Treasurer." — Lighting.

" 1817, Decr. 5. Resolved, that the large room in the Town hall be finished as a Ball Room without delay." — Ball Room.

" 1820, Mar. 1. Resolved, that the large Ball Room in the Town hall be furnished under the direction of the Select Finance Committee, so that the same may be opened on the 12th August next (the King's Birthday)." — Furnishing.

" 1828, Feby. 6. The Mayor having stated to the Council that the new Sessions Room would in all probability be completed in a short time, — Sessions House.

" Resolved, that the Surveyor be directed to prepare a plan to be submitted to the Council, of an alteration of the present Court Room in the Town hall into a Council Room with an Ante-room and of an arrangement for a repository, and an Office for the Clerk of Committees." — Council Chamber.

The lower storey of the Exchange used by the merchants was never satisfactory, and at the close of the eighteenth century efforts were made towards the erection of a more commodious building.

" 1801, Mar. 4. John Shaw Mayor.

" The Council proceeded to take into consideration the application from a Society of Merchants for assistance to enable them to erect a public, extensive, and ornamental building for the general accommodation of the merchants, traders, and other inhabitants of the town, as now explained by those members of the Council who have attended several meetings of the merchants on this subject. — New Exchange.

" Unanimously Resolved, That this Council does highly approve of the intentions of the Merchants as before mentioned, and that the Select Finance Committee be desired to confer with them thereon, and be fully authorized to make such purchases for account of this Council as they in their judgment and discretion may find necessary, with a view to resell such parts of the same to the Merchants, and eventually to adopt such plans as may be required to obtain the situation now recommended to carry this great undertaking into effect." — Resolution. Purchases.

" 1802, Feby. 3. Resolved and Ordered, upon the application of the Society of Merchants and subscribers to the scheme for erecting the intended building to the northwards of the Exchange for the general accommodation of the Merchants, traders and other inhabitants of this town, agreeable to the resolution entered into at the Special Council held on the 21st March last,

A A A

"That the Mayor and Bailiffs, the Treasurer and Town Clerk be authorized to affix the Common Seal to such Petitions to Parliament in favour of the said scheme or undertaking as may be recommended by the said Chairman and Committee, and may be deemed reasonable for the encouragement and support of the said undertaking, and giving assistance to have the same properly carried into effect."

Act of Parliament.

This project was taken up warmly and attended with complete success.

"1827, Nov. 7. Thomas Colley Porter Mayor.

"A Memorial very numerously and respectably signed by the inhabitants of this town relative to the erection of a large Hall, to be appropriated to the use of the Musical Festivals and other purposes having been laid before this Council,

Hall for Festivals.

"Resolved, that it is the unanimous opinion of the Council, that the erection of such a building would not only be a great ornament to the town, but that much better accommodation would be thereby afforded to the public at Musical Festivals; and that it would consequently be the means of increasing the funds distributable amongst the Public Charities, and thereby prove highly beneficial to the same; and that the building might be rendered otherwise useful upon various occasions.

Resolution.

"Resolved therefore, that this subject be referred to the Select Finance Committee, and that they be requested to make a full report thereon to the Council accompanied with Plans and Estimates."

"1827, Decr. 5. The Mayor having laid before this Council a letter from the Surveyor together with Plans and Estimates for a large Hall for Public Festivals &c,

Plans for Hall.

"Resolved, that the same be referred to the Select Finance Committee, with a request that they will make a full report to the next Council."

From some cause not apparent the scheme was dropped, but revived in 1837 by the Reformed Council, which led to the erection of St. George's Hall. It is worthy of record that, although the holding of Musical Festivals was the ostensible cause of the original scheme, no such use has ever been made of the building.

St. George's Hall.

The Tower in Water Street, the fortified mansion of the Stanley family, had passed into the hands of the Corporation, and was occupied as the Gaol.

Tower.

It seems to have been very insecure and unsuitable for the purpose.

"1806, April 2. It having been represented to this Council that the present Borough Gaol was in so decayed and ruinous a state as to render it very insecure, and unfit for the safe custody of prisoners; and that in consequence of the increased number of prisoners, great irregularities were committed; and that from the want of space and accommodation it was found impracticable to separate the different descriptions of prisoners; and it having been represented that the present House of Correction [1] was very defective in its construction, and inadequate to the purposes intended, and that the Parish Officers were desirous of removing it, and for treating for so much of the intended new Gaol as would form a complete House of Correction; *Ruinous State.*

"Resolved, that it is the opinion of this Council that it is highly necessary that the buildings erected for the purpose of a new gaol in this town, should be finished with all convenient expedition, in lieu of the present Borough Gaol. *New Gaol.*

"Resolved also, that it is the opinion of this Council that it is expedient to appropriate a part of the new buildings intended for a Gaol to the purpose of a House of Correction agreeable to the original intention, provided an adequate compensation can be obtained from the Parish for the same." *House of Correction.*

"1806, April 2. On reading the petition of Mr Edward Frodsham, the keeper of the Borough Gaol, stating that he had been obliged to pay the sum of £46 6s. 6d. the debts due from several persons who had escaped out of the Gaol, together with ten guineas as a reward for apprehending those who were retaken; and upon the Mayor and Mr Alderman Harper and Mr Staniforth stating that they had seen the place through which it was alledged these persons had so made their escape, and that in their opinion and judgment the same had happened from the insufficiency of the Gaol itself, and not from the carelessness or inattention of the Gaoler; *Escape of Prisoners.*

"Ordered, that the Corporation Treasurer do pay to the said Edward Frodsham the sums above mentioned amounting to £56 16s. 6d." *Payments.*

"1806, July 2. The Committee appointed on the 2nd April last to consider the measures to be taken for compleating the new Borough Gaol, having reported that they had taken into consideration the best mode of complying with the wishes of the Council for finishing the prison upon the most improved system, and that they were desirous of obtaining information from places where the plan of reformed prisons had been carried into practice, recommend that the Surveyor should be authorized to visit such prisons for the purpose. *New Prison.*

"Resolved, that the Surveyor be empowered accordingly."

"1807, April 10. Upon reading the petition of Edward Frodsham, Sergeant at Mace and keeper of the Borough Gaol, stating that seventeen *Escape of Debtors.*

---

[1] This was situated in Brownlow Hill, within the precincts of the Workhouse.

debtors had made their escape out of the Gaol by breaking through the roof, whose debts together amounted to £234 19s. 8d., which he was called upon to pay, and threatened with actions if he did not, and therefore prayed the Council to take the same into their consideration, and grant him such relief as might be deemed proper.

Inquiry.

"Resolved and Ordered, That it be referred to the Mayor and Magistrates to make inquiry into the conduct of the Gaoler in respect of the escape, and into the sufficiency of the Gaol at the time, and to report accordingly."

Gaol unoccupied.

After the erection of the new Gaol, in Great Howard Street, the old building remained unoccupied.

Dispute about Gaol.

"1809, Resolved and Ordered, that the Treasurer do repay to the Mayor the sum of £193, advanced to the Town Clerk to pay Counsel's fees and consultations on the two questions now in dispute, viz' the one between the Magistrates and the Parish of Liverpool relative to the hiring of the two wings of the new Gaol for a House of Correction, and the other between the Magistrates of the County and the Borough of Liverpool as to the right of the Borough Magistrates to send the prisoners convicted at their Sessions to the County House of Correction."

Finishing of New Gaol.

"1810, Mar. 13. Resolved and Ordered, that the new Gaol Committee have full power forthwith to give directions for the finishing, compleating and occupying such a portion of the building situate in Great Howard Street intended for a Gaol or Prison as may be sufficient for the accommodation of prisoners heretofore and now confined in the present Borough Gaol, in such manner as the said Committee shall be advised, bearing in mind the intended combination of the Borough Gaol and House of Correction within the same boundary wall, but not permitting that consideration to interfere with the completion and occupation of such portion as may be required for a Borough Gaol."

Gaol as Barracks.

"1812, Nov. 2. At a Special Meeting of the Select Finance Committee the Mayor having laid before the Committee a letter he had received from Major Gen. Dirom, Commanding Officer in this district, requesting to know if the Council would accommodate Government for the term of six months, with the Old Gaol—now unoccupied,—for the purpose of a temporary Barrack for the accommodation of his Majesty's Troops intended to be stationed here;

Rent.

"Resolved Unanimously, That it is the opinion of this Committee that it is expedient and proper to comply with the wishes of Government, by granting them the use of the Old Prison, now vacant, upon their consenting to pay the sum of One Hundred Pounds for the term of six months, and in that proportion for any longer time; and upon entering into an engagement to quit the premises at any time after the expiration of six months, upon giving three months' notice, and also upon agreeing that the entrance or communication with the building shall be on the West and East Sides only."

"1819, Octr. 6. Resolved, that the materials of the buildings formerly occupied as the Old Gaol be immediately disposed of by public auction in order that they may be removed and part of the land laid to the street in the intended line of improvement." Materials of Gaol.

So passed away the old fortress, after an existence of more than four hundred years.

The Old Dock, the cradle as it may be termed of the commerce of Liverpool, was opened in 1715. A century had not elapsed before measures were taken to fill it up and appropriate the site. Old Dock.

"1808, Aug. 3. Henry Blundell Hollinshead Mayor.

"This Council having taken into consideration the Report of the Select Finance Committee of the 27th May last relative to the obtaining an eligible site for a new Custom House and other Public Offices, and for a Market Place, Site for Custom House.

"Resolved and Ordered, that it be referred to the Select Finance Committee to take such measures as they may deem most expedient for obtaining an Act of Parliament to carry these Plans into effect.

"Also, Resolved and Ordered, that it be referred to the Dock Committee to obtain Parliamentary authority to appropriate the scite of the Old Dock to the purpose of a new Custom House, and other Public Offices, and for a Market Place, upon such terms and conditions as they shall consider equitable." Public Offices. Market.

"1809, Feby. 10. James Gerard MD Mayor.

"The Chairman of the Select Finance and Dock Committees having reported to this Council that the Heads of the intended Act of Parliament had been read and approved, but that some doubts and difficulties had arisen with respect to the propriety of pursuing the plan at present, Act of Parliament.

"Resolved and Ordered, that the further consideration of this subject be referred to the Select Finance and Dock Committees in consultation, with full powers to adopt and pursue the plan and to proceed, or postpone their endeavours as they shall deem most advisable and expedient."

"1809, Sept. 14. Resolved and Ordered, that the Select Finance Committee be authorized and empowered to take measures for obtaining an Act of Parliament for filling up the Old Dock and appropriating a part of the scite for the purpose of a new Custom House &c and the remainder to the scite of a Public Market Place; and for opening a street of communication Southward. New Street Southward.

munication from Pool Lane to Mersey Street, so as to connect in a more convenient and direct manner the Northern and Southern parts of the town."

Act obtained. The Act was obtained in 1811 (50th Geo. III., c. 143), but no action was taken upon it for some years.

"1823, Nov. 5. Charles Lawrence Mayor.

"Resolved, that the Select Finance Committee be requested as early as possible to take the sense of the associated Mercantile Bodies, as to the propriety of carrying into execution the powers of the Act relative to the filling up of the Old Dock and the appropriation of the same upon any plan which may be considered most conducive to the trading interests of the town."

Filling up Old Dock.

"1824, Jany. 7. Resolved, that the street across the Old Dock from Pool Lane to Mersey Street, be made according to the Act of Parliament, as soon as practicable after the completion of (the repairs of) George's Dock."

Proceedings. "1825, Nov. 2. Resolved, that the Dock Committee be requested to inform the Council at what early period it will be convenient to relinquish the Old Dock, in order that the eastern part of the same may be filled up, and the communication made between Pool Lane and Mersey Street in conformity with the provisions of the recent Dock Act."

"1826, April 5. The Dock Committee having by resolution expressed their opinion that the site of the Old Dock cannot be appropriated to any use more conducive to the comfort and convenience of the merchants and other inhabitants of the town, than for the erection of a Custom House, Excise and other Public Offices agreeably to the plan then produced,

Custom House.

"Resolved, that this Council fully coincides in the opinion expressed by the Dock Committee, and refers the subject to the consideration of the Select Finance Committee with a request that they will report their opinion upon the most advantageous and practicable means of carrying the same into effect."

Opposition. "1826, June 7. A Resolution from the Liverpool Shipowners Association, wishing the filling up of the Old Dock to be deferred until some additional accommodation for shipping could be provided,

"Resolved, that the request of the Association cannot be complied with."

"1826, Decr. 6. Thomas Littledale Mayor.

Custom House Plans. "This Council having inspected the plans and elevations of the Custom House, Excise Offices and other Public Offices prepared by Mr John Foster Jun' the Architect and Surveyor to the Corporation; proposed to be erected on the scite of the Old Dock, and having attentively considered his Report accompanying the same;

Approved. "Resolved, that such Plans and Elevations are approved, and that so much of the scite of the Old Dock as belongs to the Corporation be granted without charge, provided the Government will undertake to erect the building and afford the requisite accommodation therein, for the establishment of the Office of the Receiver of the Town's Dues free of any Rent.

"Resolved also, that the Mayor be requested to transmit to the Right Honorable William Huskisson a copy of the above resolution, and also of the resolution of the Dock Committee (copied underneath) and that the Surveyor proceed to London to lay the plans before Mr Huskisson and to receive his instructions. *Reference to Huskisson.*

"Copy of Resolution of Dock Committee.

"'Resolved, that the plans and elevations be approved, and that this Committee will grant the site without charge, upon the condition that the Government erect the building and grant the accommodation provided for the Dock Committee free of expence.'" *Dock Committee Resolution.*

"1827, May 2. Resolved, that a deputation consisting of the Mayor, Messrs Thos Case and Drinkwater be requested to proceed to London upon the subject of the intended public buildings on the scite of the Old Dock, and to make a Report to a Committee of the whole Council to be called from time to time by the Deputy Mayor, before any final arrangements are concluded with Government." *Deputation.*

"1827, July 3. A Minute of the Lords Commissioners of the Treasury of the 26th June having been read, together with a letter from Mr. Huskisson to the Mayor; *Lords Commissioners.*

"Resolved unanimously, that the proposal contained in their Lordships' Minute be accepted and that the deputation be authorized to conclude the arrangement, subject to such modifications as the deputation may deem adviseable.

"Abstract of a Treasury Minute.

"Read Report of the Commissioners of Customs of the 6th April 1826 upon a proposition from the members of the Common Council and Trustees of the Docks at Liverpool in regard to the erection of a Custom House upon a scite offered for that purpose by the said Corporation. *Report.*

"Mr Canning states to the Board that he has had a conference with a deputation from the Corporation of Liverpool upon this subject, in which it has been proposed that the Building should contain accommodation not only for the Customs, but also for the Excise Office, Post Office and Stamp Office, together with an Office for the Trustees of the Docks, and for other purposes connected with the public business of the Town and Port of Liverpool. *Mr. Canning.*

"For a building of sufficient extent for these various purposes the Corporation and Dock Trustees have offered the scite of the Old Dock in Liverpool, and the Corporation have proposed to undertake the erection of it, to which their Lordships are ready to accede, on the following terms, vizt—

Building.	"That the building shall be commenced so soon as the scite shall be legally conveyed to Trustees to be named by this Board, and as soon as the Plans &c shall be approved by the proper officer.
	"That the Corporation shall undertake to complete all the buildings in five years, shall further undertake to expend in the erection and completion a sum not less than the amount of the Architect's estimate
Cost.	£175,000.
Payment.	"That in consideration of this undertaking, the Board shall engage to pay to the Corporation the sum of £150,000 by instalments at a rate not exceeding £30,000 in any one year, and that the difference between this amount and the whole estimate shall be borne by the Corporation in consideration of the estimate including the erection of an office for the Dock Trustees and other objects.
Inspector.	"The Board to have power to appoint an Inspector both of the buildings and of the Accounts, and to certify before payment of the several instalments.
	"The Corporation to keep the whole of the buildings in good and substantial repair for the first twenty years after the completion."

Letter from Huskisson.

This Minute was accompanied by a letter from Mr. Huskisson to the Mayor, expressing his hope that there was nothing in the conditions which ought to be an obstacle to the Council undertaking a work which would be attended with so much accommodation to the commercial interests of the Port, and would add in a very great degree to the embellishment and general improvement of the town.

The Mayor, writing from London, in transmitting these documents to the Council, observes:—

Letter from Mayor.

"That in this negociation, we have had to encounter considerable difficulty from the pressure of the times, and the pledges of rigid economy made by Ministers to the country. We are informed that Ministers consider the claims of Liverpool as urged by the deputation so strong that they have conceded much more than was expected by Mr. Huskisson.

Mr. Canning.

"I further beg to acquaint you that we adhered firmly to the original proposition of the Council, but to this Mr. Canning replied that he should meet us with a counter proposal, principally on the ground of a portion of the buildings being required for the purposes of public revenue.

"The Deputation strongly recommend the confirmation of this arrangement."

"1827, July 23. The Mayor having reported to the Committee the result of the proceedings of the Deputation,

STREETS AND BUILDINGS.

"Resolved, that the arrangement concluded with the Treasury is highly approved of and that the Mayor and the other gentlemen of the Deputation be authorized to proceed with as little delay as possible in carrying the same into execution." <small>Arrangement.</small>

A further arrangement was made by which the Corporation undertook to provide offices in the new building for the various departments of the Dock Trust, receiving from the Trustees a conveyance of such portion of the site of the Old Dock as belonged to the Trustees under the Act of 6th Geo. III., the Corporation undertaking "to fill up, level, and keep open and in repair such part of the same to the westward as may not be required to be conveyed to the Government for the erection of the Public Buildings." <small>Offices for Departments.</small>

The first stone of the new buildings was laid by the Mayor, Mr. Thos. Colley Porter, on the King's Birthday, Aug. 12th, 1828, after a grand public demonstration and a procession of the Trades and Schools, including a champion in brazen armour, with pyrotechnics in the evening, and a banquet at the Town Hall. <small>Laying of first Stone.</small>

"1832, May 2. Sam¹ Sandbach Mayor.

"Resolved, that the space at present known under the name of the Old Dock, be altered, and that it be hereafter called "Canning Place," out of respect to the memory of the late Right Honorable George Canning, to whose exertions the Council are so mainly indebted in the assistance afforded them in carrying into effect the plan for erecting a new Custom House and other Revenue Buildings on the above-named site." <small>Canning Place.</small>

A portion of the area of the Old Dock was set apart in the original scheme of 1808, and subsequently, for a public Market. On the erection of St. John's Market in 1822, this scheme was dropped.

The public Markets for vegetables and provisions have, in late years, in our large cities occupied a less important position than formerly. The system of wholesale consignments and supplies, distributed amongst the retail dealers, <small>Markets.</small>

has rendered obsolete, and to a great extent unnecessary, the former contact between the producer and the consumer. The markets in Liverpool have always been considered a very important part of the Corporate Estate. In 1322 the market tolls produced nearly one third of the entire income of the Corporation, and down to a recent period they were considered very valuable.

<small>Tolls.</small>

<small>High Cross. White Cross.</small>
Originally held at the High Cross and the White Cross, on the destruction of the Castle about 1725, the market was removed to the site which then took the name of Derby Square. As the town increased, inconvenience was felt for want of accommodation, and many expedients were propounded from time to time.

"1810, Feby. 10. John Clarke Mayor.

"Resolved and Ordered, that the Select Finance Committee with the assistance of the Mayor and Magistrates be empowered to adopt such measures as they think expedient for the improvement of the Markets and establishing rules and regulations; and also for procuring a scite for a Market Place at the north end of the town in lieu of the late ancient White Cross Market. And likewise to take measures for establishing a Market upon Shaw's Brow, opposite the Infirmary."

<small>Sites and Rules.</small>

<small>Memorial.</small>
"1819, Octr. 6. A Memorial from the Occupiers of Shops in Castle Street relative to the great inconvenience and loss of trade experienced by them in consequence of the market being held in such street, having been laid before this Council,

"Resolved, that such Memorial be referred to the Select Finance Committee with a request that they will take into consideration the practicability of curtailing the extent of the market standings in the street.

"Resolved also, that with a view to remedy as speedily as possible the evil complained of by the Occupiers of Shops in Castle Street, the Select Finance Committee be requested to treat with Messrs Shaw and Roe for such part of their unbuilt land in Great Charlotte Street as in the opinion of the Committee will be sufficient for a Public Market for Provisions—that situation being in every respect eligible for the purpose."

<small>Land, Great Charlotte Street.</small>

<small>Plans and Specifications.</small>
"1820, Feby 2. Resolved, that Specifications agreeable to the Plans now produced to this Council be prepared; to be seen at the Surveyor's Office, relative to the Market in Great Charlotte Street, and that sealed tenders be sent in and contracts entered into for the same."

<small>Annuity to Robinson.</small>
"Resolved, that an Annuity of £20 be paid to Mary Robinson, the late

Collector of Ingates and Outgates at the end of Scotland Road, during her life; the collection of which was discontinued in the month of June last, under the Act of Parliament relative to the Markets."

"1820, July 5. Advertisements to be inserted in the Liverpool news- *Advertise-*
papers for the work connected with the intended Market in Great Char- *ments.*
lotte Street."

"1821, Feby. 7. Thos Leyland Mayor.

"Resolved, that the Cattle Market heretofore held in Church Lane, be *Cattle*
removed into Lime Street, and the Tolls authorized by the Act of Parlia- *Market.*
ment, 59th Geo. 3rd for the exposure to sale of Cattle in the said Market be taken, and that sixpence per night for each cart put under the shed erected in that market be also taken."

"1822, Feby. 6. Richard Bullin Mayor.

"Resolved, that from and after the 7th day of March next, the new market lately erected in Great Charlotte Street be a Public Market for *Market*
the sale of all sorts of provisions therein, and that an advertizement *completed.*
respecting the same be inserted in the Liverpool newspapers.

"'Market in Great Charlotte Street.

"'Notice is hereby given, that from and after the 7th day of March next, *Notices.*
the several streets within the town called Castle Street, Lower Castle Street, Preeson's Row, Redcross Street and Pool Lane, heretofore used and occupied as public Market Places will be discontinued to be used and occupied as such, and that the present Fish Market on the north side of James Street and the south side of Moor Street, and the Market held in the building opposite to the same, will also be discontinued. And that in lieu thereof from and after the 7th day of March next the building lately erected on the west side of Great Charlotte Street, north side of Elliot Street, and south side of Roe Street will be a public Market Place for the sale of all sorts of Provisions therein.'

"It is Ordered that the choice of the Shops, Stalls &c shall be deter- *Letting of*
mined by lot." *Shops.*

"1822, Feby. 23. Resolved, that the Order of Council on the 6th day of February instant relative to the Markets be confirmed, but that the Select Finance Committee be authorized to give directions for the erection of such a number of Fish Stones in Derby Square or on the South side of *Fish Stones.*
St. George's Church as they may think proper for the accommodation of the neighbourhood.

"Resolved, That the Fish Stones be covered."

"1822, June 5. The proceedings of the Select Finance Committee having been read,

"Resolved that the same be confirmed with the exception of the recommendation of the 28th May last relative to the sale of goods, wares and merchandize in Islington Market, which subject the Committee are *Islington*
requested to reconsider." *Market.*

Fish Market.

"1826, Decr. 6. Resolved, that the Select Finance Committee be requested to take into consideration and to report a plan for the establishment of a Fish Market, with a view to the prevention of the monopoly which at present exists in this town with regard to the sale of fish, and which has the effect of so much enhancing the price of that article."

Petition for Market, Cook Street.

"1828, June 4. A petition from several inhabitants of Castle Street and the neighbourhood praying that a Market may be erected on the vacant land at the bottom of Cook Street; and a similar Petition from the inhabitants of Richmond Row, praying that Richmond Fair may be converted into a Market Place, having been laid before this Council,.

"Resolved, that the prayer of the Petitioners be declined."

Botanic Garden.

The Old Botanic Garden, situated at the top of Oxford Street, is now built over and almost forgotten. The following references are found:—

"1801, June 3. Ordered, that the Petition of the proprietors of the proposed Botanical Garden for a Lease or Grant of a field late belonging to Mr John Howard, situate between Crabtree Lane and Brownlow Hill Lane, intended to be appropriated to the purpose of a Botanical Garden, be postponed."

Garden, Moss Lake Fields.

"1802, April 14. Upon the application of the Committee of the Botanic Garden, stating that they had now inclosed the land in the Moss Lake Fields appropriated to the Garden, with a stone wall, and had erected and nearly completed the buildings necessary for their present purpose, and had also begun to plant the Garden, which was expected to be open for the use of the subscribers in the course of the ensuing summer, and requesting that the Council would think the institution deserving of their patronage, and would honour it by a grant of a permanent nature;

Grant of Reversion.

"Resolved and Ordered,—In consideration of the very favourable opinion which this Council entertains of the general public utility likely to arise from the institution of the Botanic Garden, and its becoming an ornament to the town, that a Grant of the reversionary interest of the land appropriated to that purpose and of the buildings now or hereafter to be erected for the use of the Institution (but exclusively of the land belonging to the said proprietors which now is or shall hereafter be appropriated to other uses) be made and passed under the Common Seal to the Trustees and their successors so long as the said Botanic Garden and its appendages shall be and continue to be used and appropriated for the purpose of such Garden according to the original institution."

Request for Aid.

"1828, Feby. 6. A letter from John Moss Esq, President of the Committee of the Botanic Garden, accompanied by a Resolution, requesting some support from the Corporation in aid of that Institution having been laid before this Council;

"Resolved, that the sum of 500 guineas be presented and the annual sum of 30 guineas paid to the Institution." Donation.

After an existence of thirty years, the advance of building rendered the locality unsuitable.

"1831, March 2. A letter from C S Parker Esq, Chairman of the Committee of the Proprietors of the Botanic Gardens, submitting for the approval of the Council certain land between the Wavertree Road and Edge Lane, contemplated as the scite of the new Garden; Proposal for Removal.

"Resolved, that the same be referred to the Select Finance Committee, with full powers to act thereon as they may think proper."

"1834, June 4. A Memorial from the Committee and Proprietors of the new Botanic Gardens, requesting the Council to release the reversionary interest of the Corporation in the Garden on account of the Proprietors not having been able to raise the requisite funds for the undertaking on Mortgage or Security of the property on account of such reversionary interest, having been laid before this Council, Memorial for Reversion.

"Resolved, that the same be referred to the Select Finance Committee, and that they be requested to report their opinion and recommendations thereon."

After the Reformed Council came into office in 1836 an arrangement was made by which the Gardens were taken over, and dedicated to the use of the Public. Gardens taken over.

About the beginning of the 19th century there was a great demand for Newsrooms. The Athenæum, in Church Street, was founded in 1798, and not long afterwards the Lyceum, in Bold Street, was established. Newsrooms. Athenæum. Lyceum.

"1801, Mar. 4. Upon the application of William David Evans Esquire President, on behalf of the Proprietors of the proposed News Room and Library on the North East side of Bold Street for a grant of the reversion and inheritance of the land on which the same is, and are, intended to be erected, upon such terms as the Council may think proper,

"Resolved and Ordered, that the consideration thereof be postponed until the building shall be completed."

"1804, Octr. 3. In consequence of a renewal of the petition of the proprietors of the News Room and Library at the North East corner of Bold Street now called the Lyceum for the reversion and inheritance of the land and building to be granted to them on similar terms to those granted to the proprietors of the Athenæum, Petition for Reversion.

"Resolved and Ordered, upon the motion of Mr Ald^n Hollinshead,

Grant.

seconded by Mr Aldⁿ Bold, that the reversion and inheritance of the said land and building be accordingly granted to the proprietors or trustees for their use; extending as far towards Church Street as they have a right to under the original lease, and the assignment from the late Thomas Staniforth Esq, so long as the said building shall continue to be used and enjoyed for the uses and purposes of its institution only; and no other; agreeable to the original articles of its establishment."

Union Newsroom.

The Union Newsroom, Duke Street, was founded about the same time.

"1802. Resolved and Ordered that a grant of the reversion and inheritance of the News Room and proposed Library in Duke Street, with the land and other appurtenances thereunto belonging, in consideration of its general public utility, be made and passed under the Common Seal without fine, to the Trustees and their successors for the benefit of the proprietors at large, so long as the same shall continue to be used and enjoyed for the purposes of the original institution only, but no longer."

Theatre Royal.

The Theatre Royal, Williamson Square, was erected in 1772. In 1802 it was proposed to enlarge it and bring forward the front as it now stands.

Enlargement.

"1802, Jany. 6. The Proprietors of the Liverpool Theatre Royal having signified their intention of enlarging and altering the same agreeable to the Plans, Sections &c now produced, whereby it appears to be necessary to permit them to extend their building somewhat further into Williamson Square than the present colonnade, but in no part to project more than four yards beyond the same,

"Unanimously Resolved, That in the opinion of this Council such alteration will be of public convenience and ornament and that the proprietors be allowed, as far as any authority from this Council may be necessary, to proceed upon such alterations without further loss of time."

Brunelagh.
Moss Lake.

The following entry indicates the condition of the original *Brunelagh*, or Brown-Law, the rocky eminence adjoining the Moss Lake, which served for ages as the Stone Quarry, and is now the site of the University College and the Workhouse. This is shown in Eyes's Map of 1785.

Stone Quarry, Brownlow Hill.

"1801, Aug. 5. Ordered, that the consideration of the Application made by Mr Edwd Blackstock the Vestry Clerk, on behalf of the Parish Committee to know upon what terms the Corporation would grant the reversion of the Delf on the south side of Brownlow Hill and of the field near the House of Correction, originally leased to the late Mr Brooks, but now the property of the Parish and intended to be appropriated for the scite of a Fever Ward, be referred to the Select Finance Committee."

The following record will be found of interest in connection with an illustrious name.

"1805, May 1. William Harper Mayor.

"Resolved and Ordered that Mr John (Sir John) Gladstone on behalf of himself or purchasers have leave to change the three lives now in being in his dwelling house and ground on the west side of Rodney Street, of 80 yards front and 50 yards deep, on paying a fine of Three Pounds three shillings, and one shilling per yard per annum ground rent to Rodney Street, and also upon paying seventy two Pounds for his proportion of levelling and paving the back street; and subject to satisfactory proof being produced that the life stated to be in the East Indies was in good health on the sixth of February last, or subsequent to that date." *Gladstone's House, Rodney Street.*

In this house, four years subsequently, first saw the light William Ewart Gladstone, a name which will ever be distinguished in the history of our country, and of which Liverpool may well feel proud. *W. E. Gladstone.*

"1806, April 2. Upon reading the Report of the Select Finance Committee on the subject of the intended Corn Exchange, proposed to be established in this town, stating that the proceedings of an open commercial Corn Exchange in the town of Liverpool will meet with their entire approbation and co-operation under proper and suitable rules and regulations." *Corn Exchange.*

The Infirmary at the summit of Shaw's Brow, erected in 1745, after an existence of seventy-five years, had become antiquated and its removal was determined on. *Old Infirmary.*

"1820, Decr. 6. Thomas Leyland Mayor.

"A letter from Mr Robert Benson, the Chairman of the Committee for building the new Infirmary requesting the Common Council would be pleased to grant to the Trustees of the new Infirmary the materials composing the present Lunatic Asylum, having been read, *New Infirmary.*

"Resolved, that the consideration of this subject be postponed until the next Council."

1821, June 6th. The matter was again brought before the Council and postponed for a report.

"1825, Decr. 7. On bringing up the proceedings of the Select Finance Committee, it was

"Resolved, that they be confirmed with the exception of the recommendation relative to the appropriation of the present Lunatic Asylum to the purpose of a Barrack."

Lunatic Asylum.

It was, however, so appropriated, and continued so for several years.

Subscription.

"1829, Feby. 4. An application from a Sub-committee of the Liverpool Infirmary soliciting a subscription towards enabling them to complete the present buildings, and also the Building of the new Lunatic Asylum having been laid before the Council,

"Resolved, that the Treasurer be authorized to subscribe the sum of £500."

The Quarter Sessions for the borough were formerly held in the Old Exchange, now the Town Hall, but in 1824 it was proposed to remove them.

Sessions House.

"1824, July 7. A Plan for the erection of a Police Office and a Sessions House on the land opposite the Bridewell, and also a Plan for the erection of a Police Office on the land opposite the Bridewell and for a Sessions House on the land on the South side of the Gaol in Great Howard Street having been laid before this Council, accompanied with estimates of the expence,

Police Office.

"Resolved, that the Plan for the erection of a Police Office and Sessions House on the land opposite the Bridewell be adopted, and that the same be erected by Public contract under the directions of the Select Finance Committee."

Assizes.

It was in this building that the Assizes were first held in Liverpool in 1834. In 1873 the building was removed and the site absorbed into the New Exchange Buildings.

Battery. Lighthouse.

"1824, July 7. Resolved, that the Select Finance Committee be requested to obtain as early as practicable, a reply to the Memorial recently transmitted to the Board of Ordnance, relative to the erection of a Battery, conjointly with a Lighthouse at the Rock Perch, and to transmit another Memorial upon this subject to the Ordnance Board, should the Committee deem it requisite."

Alms Houses.

At the time of the erection of the Infirmary at the top of Shaw's Brow, a row of Alms Houses in connection with

STREETS AND BUILDINGS.

the Seamen's Hospital were built. When the Infirmary was removed it became necessary to remove the Alms Houses also.

<small>Seamen's Hospital.</small>

"1825, Sept. 7. An application from the Trustees of the Seamen's Hospital for a grant of land or of money for the purpose of enabling them to erect new Alms Houses in the room of those at the top of Shaw's Brow, recently purchased by the Corporation having been laid before this Council,

"Resolved, that the same be referred to the Select Finance Committee to report upon."

<small>Landing Stage.</small>

The construction of the present great Landing Stage does not fall within the limits of the present compilation. Much consideration and many attempts had been previously made towards a solution of the problem, of which the following entry is a specimen:—

<small>Brunel's Landing Stages.</small>

"1826, Decr. 6. Resolved, that the consideration of the Model and Plan executed by Mr Brunel and referred to the Council by the Select Finance Committee for the Landing Places at George's Dock Pierhead be for the present postponed in consequence of other Models and Plans being in a state of forwardness to be submitted to the Council at the next meeting."

ECCLESIASTICAL AFFAIRS.

<small>Connection of Church.</small>
The close connection of the Corporation with the Church remained until the passing of the Municipal Reform Act. The Council were the patrons of the Rectories, and had the appointment of the incumbents, and of their successors, to the other churches, a large portion of the stipends being paid out of the Corporate funds. Many points of contact therefore presented themselves which are duly recorded in the archives.

"1802, Decr. 12. Jonas Bold Mayor.

<small>Rector's Fees questioned.</small>
"A Petition having been presented by the Revd Philip Kitchen, Minister of St. Thomas's Church, and the Rev^{ds} Henry Barton and George Monk, Ministers of St. Paul's, setting forth that they had received from the Rectors a Table of Dues to be taken by such Rectors, in which there were not only many new but additional claims, unauthorized by ancient and established custom; and praying the serious attention of this Council (in which is vested the whole and entire patronage of this borough) to that very important business, and the direction of this Council in what manner the said Ministers are to conduct themselves. Now this Council upon full and mature deliberation, conceive clearly, that neither by the Common Law nor by the Act of the 11th William 3rd, first erecting the township of Liverpool into a Parish, nor by any of the subsequent Acts constituting Chapels of Ease within the said Parish, have the Rectors of this Parish a <small>Right denied.</small> colour of right to increase any of their antient Dues or Fees, or to create any new ones; and they do therefore recommend to such Rectors to take good legal advice herein. And do further recommend them to desist in the mean time from demanding any other than such their antient Dues and Fees."

"1811, Aug. 4. Jas Drinkwater Mayor.

<small>Stipends of Clergy.</small>
"Resolved, that the consideration of the stipends now paid by the Corporation to the Clergy of Liverpool be referred to the Select Finance Committee, with a request that they will as soon as convenient, report to the Council their opinion on this important subject."

The matter lay over for four years, when it was again taken up.

ECCLESIASTICAL AFFAIRS.

"1815, Decr. 10. Considerable discussion having taken place at this Council, relative to the increase in the salaries of the several clergymen holding appointments under the Corporation; — Increase.

"Resolved, that a Special Committee of seven be appointed for the purpose of taking into consideration the present situation of the Clergy with reference to an increase in their respective salaries, and the probability or practicability of obtaining the benefit of Queen Anne's Bounty, and that the Committee be requested to make a report to the next Council upon the matters referred to them." — Committee appointed.

Consequent on this Resolution, a material increase was made.

The non-residence within the town of some of the Clergy had been a subject of complaint, and in 1794 a resolution was passed by the Council, requiring a bond from every clergyman elected to any of the ecclesiastical benefices in the gift of the Council, for residence within the town or within ten miles thereof. This being reconsidered, the following resolution was passed:— — Non-Residence of Clergy. Requisition.

"1812, March 10. That such requisition being considered illegal and improper, the same is hereby rescinded, and declared null and void." — Illegal.

In 1820 a serious collision took place between the Council and the Clergy, which led to a long and somewhat angry correspondence with the Bishop of Chester. The occasion will be seen from the following documents:— — Collision with Clergy.

"1820, Decr. 6. Thomas Leyland Mayor.

"The non-performance of the duty in person by several of the Clergy at the churches under the patronage of the Corporation having been from time to time the subject of discussion, the following resolutions were at this Council proposed and adopted viz, — Resolutions.

"That the practice alluded to is inconsistent with the implied understanding both of the Council and the Clergy at the time of their original appointment, and at variance with all ancient and established usage.

"That presuming the same, strictly speaking, to come under the sanction of the law, this Council cannot as the Patrons, refrain any longer from recording their disapprobation of conduct which is unsupported by precedent, and not to be justified on principle. — Disapprobation.

"That as the increase of the salaries of the clergy which took place in the year 1816, and which was only to continue during the pleasure of the — Salaries during pleasure.

Council, has failed in operating as an additional inducement to a personal performance of the duty, and has only been converted by some into the means of obtaining a sinecure emolument, this Council feels itself fully justified in withholding and does withhold, from henceforth that increase from such of the clergy as neglect to perform the service in person at the respective churches to which they have been appointed.

Withheld.

"That this Council entirely disclaims the right of exercising any controul over the clergy themselves, leaving to their own honorable feelings, and to their correcter judgment to decide as to the line of conduct they ought to pursue.

Control disclaimed.

"That the Council equally disclaims any right of interference with the province of the Diocesan, but cannot refrain from calling the attention of his Lordship—with the greatest possible submission and respect—to the impropriety of the non-residence of the clergy in question, and the consequent non-performance of the duty in person, bearing in mind the circumstances and nature of their appointments, and as respects some of them, the other church preferments of which they have become possessed.

"That, as it appears to this Council according to legal decision, that a patron has the right upon presentation, to require from an incumbent the personal performance of the duty, and which as expressed in such decision, the Incumbent is bound in morality, religion, and law to perform.

Patron's Rights.

"Resolved, that in future any clergyman who shall be appointed to any of the churches under the patronage of the Corporation, shall before presentation thereto, give bond to the Corporation in the penal sum of £2,000 for the personal performance at the church of the several duties appertaining thereto.

Presentees to give Bond.

"Resolved also, that the Mayor be requested to transmit copies of the above resolutions to the Lord Bishop of the Diocese, and to furnish his Lordship with any further information on the subject he may require. And that the Mayor be also requested to transmit copies of the resolutions to the

Letter to Bishop.

"Revd Dr Hodson, the Chaplain of St George's
"Revd Richd Loxham, the Minister of St John's
"Revd Henry Barton,   Do   of St Paul's
"Rev^d P Kitchen,   Do   of St Thomas's
"Revd Thos Moss, the Lecturer of St John's,"

These were the non-resident Incumbents.

This brought the following letter from the Bishop (Law):—

"Mr Mayor.

Reply from Bishop.

"I must own that I have received with some degree of surprise and concern, the communication which you have transmitted to me from the Corporate body of your town. I should have been glad and indeed should have expected, that you would have apprized me of your wishes and intentions previously to their final adoption. I could then more satisfactorily than now, have stated to you the reasons which might have probably had their due weight in inducing you to reconsider the resolution which has been formed. If, in the several cases which you have stated to me, there be one in which I have any jurisdiction or power; if there be one in which the Incumbent absents himself without a valid and legal ground of exemption, I am ready to go hand in hand with you, and to call the said Incumbent into residence. No one can possibly be more anxious Anxiety. than I am to promote the residence of my clergy. But anxious as I am, I cannot transgress the law. Pluralities are allowed, and neither the Bishop nor the Corporation of Liverpool can set themselves against the laws of the land. We may, in some cases regret their operation, we may The Law. think that we could legislate better, but while the law continues as it is, we must obey it. But even now, the remedy is in your own hands, and Remedy. the adoption of it might be less exceptionable than the measure now contemplated. If the circumstances remain the same as they were when you augmented the salaries of the absentees, it does not appear to me fair or Unfairness. just, without any fresh reason to withdraw them. It is casting a stigma where it is not deserved, and I think that your honorable body will pause before they carry the measure into effect. I have only further to observe, but it is an important observation, that Patrons can make no provisional Patrons stipulations or agreements with the clerks they nominate to their vacant cannot benefices. It is the duty of the Patron to look out for the best Incumbent Stipulate. he can, and then to present him to the Bishop, but with that act all his powers terminate, all interference should cease. Such a bond as you describe would be simoniacal, and could not be signed by the Incumbent, nor permitted by the Diocesan.

"I hope that in giving you my opinion, as it becomes me, it may give No desire to no offence to any one. I see the necessity of having a resident clergy in offend. Liverpool. I am as desirous of furthering the measure, much less I trust will you attribute my disapproval of what you have done to any want of regard collectively or individually. Far from it, on the contrary it has been my wish and endeavour ever since my accession to the see of Chester to promote by every means in my power not only the credit and interests of the Clergy, but those also of the Corporate body of the Town of Liverpool.

"I have the honor to be
"Mr Mayor

"Hardcott House,   "Your faithful H S
   Sarum Decr 10ᵗʰ 1820.'   "GEO H. CHESTER.

"1821, Jany. 3. A letter from the Bishop of Chester in reply to the Resolutions of the last Council, having been read,

"Resolved, that it is with feelings of considerable surprise and regret Resolution.

that the Council have received his Lordship's letter, conscious as they are that in the adoption of the Resolutions in question, they were solely guided in their capacity of Patrons, by a consideration for the interests of the established Church,

<small>Grounds of Exemption.</small>
"That the Council were aware, as expressed in the Resolutions, of the legal grounds of exemption, of which some of the Clergy might probably have the power of availing themselves; and it was only with reference to established usage and precedent, to the honour of the parties themselves, and the principle of the measure, that the Council ventured, with the greatest possible submission and respect, to call his Lordship's attention to the subject, in the confident expectation that through his Lordship's interference, the personal performance of the duty, which has heretofore subsisted, but which has only of late been infringed upon, might be restored.

<small>A Bond valid, not Simoniacal.</small>
"That, as it appears from the legal decision alluded to in the Resolutions, and from the opinions of eminent legal characters since obtained, that a bond for the personal performance of the duty is good and valid in the law, and not simoniacal, the Council still venture, with the greatest possible deference to the judgment of the Diocesan, to adhere to their former Resolutions, that in future such a bond be required from the clergy upon presentation; a measure they regret the conduct of the clergy in question should have rendered necessary to be resorted to. In adverting to one part of his Lordship's letter relative to the remedy being in the hands of the Council, and the adoption of it less exceptionable than that

<small>Query as to Remedy.</small>
contemplated, the Council beg to assure his Lordship that such remedy has not occurred to them, but they shall be most happy to take the same into consideration, if his Lordship will be pleased to point it out.

<small>Withdrawing increase.</small>
"With respect to the propriety or justice of withdrawing the increase of the salary; the Council, in vindication of their conduct upon that point, beg to apprize his Lordship that the total dereliction of the personal performance of the duty on the part of the clergy in question, did not take place until after the period of that increase having been voted, a circumstance deemed by the Council not immaterial in itself in the consideration of the subject matter of the Resolutions.

<small>Amount of Stipends.</small>
"That it appears upon reference to the various Acts of Parliament relative to the churches in this town, that the total amount of the stipends of the clergy payable under such Acts by the Common Council, does not exceed the sum of One Hundred Pounds, but that the yearly stipends already paid amount to no less a sum than upwards of two thousand guineas, and as it also appears that the clergy in question now stand upon their legal rights, and upon those alone, the Council, acting upon the same principle, under the sanction of eminent legal advice, and in strict justice to the trust reposed in them for a due distribution of the funds of the Corporate Estate, feel themselves imperiously called upon at once to

maintain their rights by withholding the whole of the voluntary donations <small>Rights to be maintained..</small> from such of the clergy in question as are in the receipt of the same, with the exception of the Reverend Philip Kitchen, whose situation as now represented by himself appears to require further consideration.

"That with respect to Mr Kitchen, by whose letter now produced to <small>Mr. Kitchen.</small> the Council it appears that he is prevented from performing in person the <small>Incapable.</small> service of the church, in consequence of age and infirmities, and that he is not possessed of any other church preferment—It is

"Resolved, that the salary of One Hundred and thirty five pounds here- <small>Salary</small> tofore payable to Mr Kitchen be continued during his life; but the Council <small>continued.</small> in the adoption of this Resolution cannot avoid regretting that they were not apprized by Mr Kitchen of his retirement from the town at the period he thought proper to do so; confident as they feel that no instance can be found upon record in which a due consideration has not been had by the Council for services performed.

"The Council trust that upon mature reflection on the part of the <small>Confidence in</small> clergy themselves, the measures now contemplated may be prevented <small>Clergy.</small> from being carried into effect; should the contrary be the case, at the same time that the Council feel that such measures may materially affect the interests of the established church in this town, they feel also that their adoption must alone be attributed to the conduct of those by whose personal exertions the interests of that church ought to be more immediately promoted.

"That the Mayor be requested to transmit copies of the above Resolu- <small>Mayor to</small> tions to the Bishop of Chester, and to the several Clergymen alluded to. <small>write.</small> And that the further consideration of this question, if requisite, be resumed at the next Council."

To these Resolutions the Bishop returned the following rejoinder:—

"Mr Mayor

"I must own that I have received your second communication <small>Bishop's</small> with greater surprise and concern than I did the first. I had flattered <small>Rejoinder.</small> myself and hoped that mature consideration would have led to a very different result. Connected as I am with the town of Liverpool, and aloof from every feeling but a wish to do my duty, I deem myself called upon to state the reasons why I disapprove of your resolutions, and I will do so <small>Reasons.</small> with all unreservedness, but I hope with all due civility. In the first place, I think it would have been no more than a proper attention, had your Corporate Body consulted the Bishop of the Diocese before they <small>Bishop not</small> passed Resolutions so materially affecting the credit and interests of many <small>consulted.</small> of the clergy. If there were any grounds for believing that I should have turned a deaf ear to your remonstrances; had I shown myself on any one occasion indifferent to the religious interests of your town, you might then indeed with propriety have acted as you have done. But the reverse I hope, has always been the fact. In the next place, I have always been taught to look with suspicion or abhorrence upon *ex post facto* laws. Now, I must affirm that all the circumstances are in effect precisely the same at present as they were when you augmented the salaries of the clergy. To increase therefore their stipend, and then capriciously to withdraw it, appears to me a mode of conduct which I should not have expected from the Corporation of Liverpool, and which I am unwilling to designate by its proper appellation. The penal bond, also, whatever may have been the decision of an inferior Court, I still continue to disapprove of, and indeed so much so, that unless the law calls upon me to license a clergyman who has signed it, I shall certainly not accept the nomination. A bond compelling a clergyman to fulfil his duty is valid and proper, but a bond in contravention of the law and preventing him from doing that which the law allows him to do, appears in my judgment to fall under the opposite description. How can the Bishop administer or the clergyman take the oath that he has done nothing directly or indirectly for or concerning the obtaining the Benefice, if he would not have been nominated to it but upon the condition of signing a penal bond. Having thus stated the principal grounds of my objection to your proceedings, let me point out that line of conduct which in my judgment at least it would have been more to your credit to have adopted. You might then with perfect propriety have informed the clergy when you nominated them to your Benefices, that you wished for, and expected residence from them. You might have fairly added that you gave your augmentation conditionally, that if they failed in the personal performance of their duty, you on your part, would immediately withdraw their stipend. The very same object would then have been gained, but in a manner totally unexceptionable; and as the clergy are gentlemen by birth, as they are men of liberal education and of liberal habits, believe me you would not have been often obliged to have recourse to the compulsory measure,

"With respect to myself, let not my own official conduct be misunderstood or misrepresented. If a clergyman holds two livings, he may reside on whichever he chuses. The Bishop calls upon him annually to notify the grounds of his exemption from residence on the other. Now all the clergy complained of, with the exception of Mr Kitchen, did possess this ground of exemption, and surely the calling back the old man into residence with his inefficiency and infirmities would not have advanced the cause of religion among his parishioners. Dr Hodson, as I suppose you know, is exempt by a specific Act of Parliament. I have always understood that he offered to resign St. George's on his being elected Principal of Brazenose, as I am sure from my knowledge of his honorable character that he would not have continued to hold his curacy, if you had properly signified any wish on the subject, or if the filial tie which can now alone bind him to your town were dissolved by death. I would merely further observe, that as a nomination to chapels of ease is vested by law in the Rector of the Mother Church, the Corporate Body may perhaps no longer be able to claim the right of patronage than whilst they perform those conditions on the implied expectation of which, such patronage was originally made over to them by the Bishops and Rectors. If the request be in no degree irregular or objectionable, I should be glad to be favored with the names of those persons who signed or voted for the Resolutions. _{*Nominations vested in Rectors.*}

"Still anxious to promote the real credit and interests of your Corporate Body,

                      "I am Mr Mayor
"Langham Place,   "Your faithful H S^t
    "Jany 20th 1821."   "GEO. H. CHESTER."

"1821, Feby. 7. The above letter having been read, it was

"Resolved, that as the further discussion of the question relative to the Clergy seems to have the effect of disturbing that good understanding which has heretofore subsisted between the Lord Bishop of the Diocese and this Council, and as the circumstances of each particular case do not seem to have been sufficiently explained, the operations of the several resolutions regarding the Clergy be suspended and that the further consideration of the same be referred to the Select Finance Committee, and that they be requested to report on the salaries, stipends and allowances to the several Clergymen under the patronage of this Council, and how far the duties of their respective pastoral offices have been discharged, and any other matter or thing that may have a tendency to promote harmony between this Council and the Clergy, and the more especially to give time for a conference with the Diocesan on the subject." _{*Resolutions. Suspended. Report on Stipends.*}

So ends this somewhat memorable correspondence. There is no record of any further action having been taken. As to which side had the advantage in logic or temper, each reader will judge for himself. _{*No further action.*}

The provision of dwellings for the two Rectors had been a source of dispute from the formation of the Parish in 1699. The following entry finally disposed of the matter:— _{*Houses for Rectors.*}

"1828, Decr. 3. Resolved that the providing of houses for the Rectors is not at present acquiesced in; but that an additional sum of £150 per annum be paid to each of the present Rectors in lieu of House rent during the pleasure of the Council."

Free Grammar School.

The history of the Free Grammar School, with which the clergy were closely connected, has been traced in the preceding chapters. The subject continued to attract attention somewhat spasmodically.

"1801, June 3. John Shaw Mayor.

Report. "Resolved and Ordered, That the Select Finance Committee be desired to take into their consideration the state and situation of the present Free School in this town, and the propriety of adopting some scheme for the establishment of a new Free School in a different situation upon a much more enlarged and extensive Plan in all respects than the present."

"1802, Feby. 3. Peter Whitfield Brancker Mayor.

Assistant Masters. "Agreeable to the Order of Council of the 3rd June last respecting the Free School, and also in consequence of the Report of the Master of the said School, stating his want of a Writing Master and Usher (vacancies in those offices having lately happened) and likewise stating that he was not able to procure any persons competent to fill those situations in a proper manner at the salaries heretofore paid viz £26 5s. and £40,

Restrictions to Admissions. "Resolved and Ordered, That in future none others but the sons of freemen be admitted into the School agreeable to the original institution; and those by recommendations from the members of the Common Council, but that the present scholars be permitted to remain at the School, also,

Boarders. "Resolved and Ordered, That the Head Master be permitted to take not more than fifteen scholars not inhabitants of this town as Boarders, **Salaries.** and to educate them in the School, and that the salaries of the Writing Master and Usher be increased to such sums of money as may hereafter be found necessary in the judgment of the said Committee, and the Council shall approve on their Report.

Blue Coat School. "And it having been represented that the Trustees of the Blue Coat Hospital were extremely anxious to have the possession of the present Free School now rented from them, it is further

Plans for New School. "Resolved and Ordered, that the Surveyor be directed to prepare a plan of a School upon an extended scale with a view that a part of it may be immediately erected upon the ground purchased for that purpose in Brownlow Street, and that he be also directed to erect a boundary wall round the land purchased for the scite of the Free School, with the waste stone now raising out of the Quarry near the Workhouse.

Assistant Masters' Salaries. "And further on a report from Mr John Baines, the Master of the School, that he was not able to provide two proper assistants as Writing Master and Usher for less than fifty guineas per annum each,

Resolutions. "Resolved and Ordered, That fifty guineas per annum each be allowed, and that Stafford Wilson be appointed Writing Master and John Turner, Usher, during the pleasure of the Council."

These arrangements were all set aside on the decease of Mr. John Baines, the Head Master, which took place in 1805. The appointment was not filled up, and the School virtually ceased to exist. Decease of Head Master.

"1815, Octr. 6. A letter from the Bishop of Chester to the Mayor relative to the re-establishment of a Free Grammar School in the place of the one formerly existing within the town having been read, and the several Resolutions of the Council and its Committees upon the subject in the years 1801, 1802, having been referred to, Letter from Bishop.
Resolutions.

"Resolved, that copies of such Resolutions be made, and that the Mayor be requested to transmit the same to the Bishop."

After the lapse of another eleven years, a tardy movement was made to supply the deficiency. Two Schools were erected, one in Park Lane for the South, and another in Bevington Bush for the North. North and South Schools.

"1826, Octr. 7. Resolved that the establishment of the Free School in Park Lane recently completed be referred to the Sub-Committee appointed upon the subject of the Free Schools." Park Lane.

"1826, Decr. 6. The Sub-Committee having recommended the appointment of Mr William Barrett as Master and Miss Elizabeth Jones as Mistress, Teachers.

Resolved that such appointments be confirmed subject to Rules and Regulations to be submitted to the Council."

These buildings were subsequently made over to the School Board at a nominal rent. Transference.

"1801, Feby. 4. Sunday Schools.
"Ordered that the Treasurer be authorized to accept the sum of One hundred pounds, being a legacy left in trust to them by the late John Sparling Esquire for the benefit of the Sunday Schools in this town, and that the Common Seal be affixed to a Bond for securing the same with interest at five Pounds ⅌ cent ⅌ annum." Sunday Schools.

There is no record as to how this money has been applied, or what has become of it.

The churches built during this period all came more or less into connection with the Corporation, either as promoters or patrons. Churches.

St. Luke's.

St. Luke's.

Revd. Sanderson.

"1801, June 3. Upon reading a letter from Mr Bardswell on behalf of the inhabitants in and near Bold Street, who are subscribers to the building a Church in that neighbourhood for the Reverend Mr Sanderson as the first Incumbent, being a Clergyman of the present established Church of England, and stating that he had had an interview with the Rectors, who were willing to give their consent,

"Resolved and Ordered, That the consideration thereof be referred to the Select Committee to enquire and report to the Council."

Proposal to build.

"1802, Feby. 6. Upon reading the proposals of several respectable persons, who offer to erect and build a church with stone in a firm and substantial manner, according to the Plan drawn by Mr Foster and now produced, upon ground situate on the south east side of Berry Street, which the Corporation had some time ago considered as a proper situation for a church, or according to any other design that may be more agreeable to the Council, and engaging to appropriate a sufficient space for the accommodation of the Poor, and to conform to such other particulars as the Common Council or any Committee appointed by them may think reasonable. And also, upon reading a letter from the Rectors of the

Acquiescence of Rectors.

Parish, expressive of their acquiescence in the erection of such church for the purpose of religious worship according to the rites, ceremonies and usage of the Church of England, and also of their approbation of the Reverend John Sanderson B A to be the first incumbent,

Approval.

"Resolved and Ordered—For the reasons and from the motives stated and set forth in the said petition and letter, and with a view to give all reasonable encouragement to so laudable an undertaking, that the Select Committee be authorized and empowered to treat and finally agree with the Proprietors of the said intended church upon the terms as to the right of presentation and other requisites to be stated and stipulated in the Bill to be brought into Parliament in confirmation of the agreement, and that the Mayor and Bailiffs affix the Common Seal to such petitions as may be necessary to testify the consent and approbation of the Council."

Proceedings.

"1802, Decr. 13. Resolved and Ordered, that it be referred to the Select Committee to take immediate measures for carrying into effect the Order of Council made the 2nd day of January 1793 for erecting one church upon a piece of land purchased for that purpose situate on the south east side of Berry Street, opposite the south end of Renshaw Street and Bold Street, and that the Churchwardens and Overseers of the Poor be applied to by the said Committee to carry into effect the order of Vestry made the 8th of January 1793, for erecting another church at the expense of the Parish conformable to the agreement then entered into for building two churches, one by the Parish and another by the Council.

Plans.

"And the Select Committee are requested to cause Plans of the said church intended to be built by the Council to be prepared for the inspection and determination of the Council." [1]

It would appear from this that the Council had taken the matter into their own hands, and had parted company from Mr. Sanderson.

The subject was then dropped for some years, but revived in 1810. *Scheme postponed.*

"1810, Feby. 10. John Clarke Mayor.
"Resolved and Ordered, that the Select Finance Committee be authorized and requested to give immediate directions for the erecting and completing with all convenient expedition the church in Berry Street opposite the south end of Bold Street, conformable to the Orders of Council of the 2nd January 1793, the 1st of December 1802, and the 2nd March 1803." *Building resumed.*

The church was commenced and carried out to a certain extent.

"1819, Aug. 4. On bringing up the proceedings of the Select Finance Committee it was
"Resolved, that the same be approved and confirmed with the exception of the recommendations relative to the erection of the church in Berry Street, and that all further proceedings relative to the said church be postponed until a statement of the expenses already incurred, and an Estimate of the further expenses to be incurred in the erection and completion of the church be laid before the Council." *Proceedings postponed.*

Another two years' delay intervened. *Delay.*

"1821, June 6. Resolved, that the erection of St. Luke's church be carried into effect with all convenient speed under the directions of the Select Finance Committee." *Resumption.*

"1822, Jany. 2. Richard Bullin Mayor.
"Resolved, that the Select Finance Committee be authorized to give directions for the addition of a Chancel to St. Luke's Church, according to the plan now produced." *Chancel added.*

"1827, Nov. 7. A letter from the Surveyor, suggesting an alteration in the plans of the interior and exterior of Saint Luke's Church and for laying out the ground surrounding the same, having been read, *Alterations.*
"Resolved, that the subject be referred to the Select Finance Committee."

Vide supra, p. 281.

Completion.	The church was finally completed in 1831, having occu-
Cost.	pied nearly thirty years in building, at a cost of £53,418. A peal of eight bells was hung in the tower.

"1829, Octr. 7. A Memorial from the inhabitants and proprietors of houses in Rodney Street and Bold Street, and in the vicinity of St. Luke's Church, relative to the serious annoyance occasioned to them by the bells at that church, having been laid before this Council,

"Resolved, that the subject be postponed, and the Surveyor to make a report as to the practicability of placing the bells in Saint Martin's Church steeple.

"A letter having been laid before this Council from Mr Dobson of Downham suggesting some experiments which might vary the sound of St. Luke's bells,

"Resolved, that these experiments be tried under the directions of the Surveyor; but that the Surveyor do make a report in conformity with the resolution of the last Council."

"1829, Decr. 5. At this Council the Surveyor made a report relative to the bells at Saint Luke's Church which was read."

No proceedings were taken thereon, and the bells were never disturbed.

"1830, Jany. 6. An application from the Committee for conducting the Liverpool Musical Festival relative to the Oratorios being held in St. Luke's Church, and the erection of temporary galleries to be removable, having been laid before this Council,

"Referred to the Select Finance Committee."

"1830, July 7. Resolved, that the Select Finance Committee do make a report to the Council relative to the expense of a Stained Glass or painted Window for the Chancel of St. Luke's Church, accompanied with a design of the same."

St. George's.

Reference has been made in the previous records to the building of this church and the subsidence of the steeple.

"1809, May 10. It having been represented to this Council that the steeple of St. George's Church had been for some time past considered by the public to be in a dangerous state; and the Mayor having laid before this Council separate reports from the following Architects viz[t] William Porden and Jeffrey Wyatt Esq[rs] of London, and Mr Foster the Corporation Surveyor, stating that they had carefully examined the said steeple, that they had found it was upwards of three feet out of perpendicular

ECCLESIASTICAL AFFAIRS. 399

position, and that the principal defects—which had occasioned the frac- Fractures. tures and insecurity of the structure—were to be attributed to the want of solidity in the foundation, and to the perishable quality of the stone. That they concurred in opinion that there was no immediate danger of its falling, but that it was in a progressive state of decay, and the danger was consequently increasing. They were of opinion that any further repair would not afford any additional security, and that they were not competent to suggest any plan for amending or supporting the said steeple, that warranted them on stating it would give permanent security to it, and that considering its situation, together with the expence and hazard attending any experiment of repairing and supporting the said steeple, Steeple they were of opinion that it was expedient to take it down and rebuild it condemned. upon a secure foundation, with proper stone; and submitted the same to the consideration of the Council.

"Resolved Unanimously, that it is the opinion of this Council that it is Resolution. necessary and most expedient to take down the said steeple of St. George's Church.

"Ordered, that Mr Foster, the Corporation Surveyor, be directed to cause the said steeple to be taken down with all convenient speed, under the immediate orders and directions of the Select Finance Committee."

The steeple was taken down, and no further action taken Steeple taken during nine years. down.

"1818, Octr. 7. Resolved, that the Select Finance Committee be empowered to give directions for the erection of Saint George's Church Re-erection. Steeple, according to the Plan No 2 now produced to this Council, the estimated expence of which is stated to be ten thousand one hundred Pounds (£10,100)."

"1825, July 6. Resolved, that the Select Finance Committee be author- ized to hire an Organ for Saint George's Church until the Church shall Organ. be considered in a suitable state for the reception of the new Organ."

The rental at this period was very productive, as appears Rental. from the following return:—

"Rents of seats in St. George's Church—
"In the Nave, Nos 1 to 77, total £475 13
" „ Gallery, Nos 78 to 137, total ... 272 18
"£748 11"

"1815, Mar. 10. A Report from the Surveyor, stating the ruinous and delapidated condition of many of the covers to the graves in the vaults of Vaults and Saint George's Church, which not only rendered it dangerous for any one Graves. to walk over the same, but exposed the bodies interred to great insecurity, and this Council having adverted to the recent practice of prohibiting burying under any church for which Acts of Parliament have lately been obtained,

Filling up.
"Resolved, that the several graves for which no owner or claimant can be discovered, be filled up with earth, and annihilated as burying places in future, under the direction of the Surveyor at the expence of the Corporation.

"Resolved, that from henceforth no new or additional graves or vaults be sold or opened under the said church.

Covering.
"Resolved, that the Bailiffs for the time being do take such measures as they may deem most expedient for causing all the graves or vaults to be covered—at the expence of the owners thereof—with stone or cast iron and that the same be laid level with the general surface of the ground.

"Resolved, that the Bailiffs for the time being give directions for the filling up with earth at the expence of the Corporation, all those graves or vaults, the owners whereof do not, after three months notice, cover the same in the manner before described, or the claimants to which may not within that time be discovered."

St. Mark's.

St. Mark's.

"1802, Octr. 6. Upon reading a letter from Mr James Brandreth on behalf of himself and the other proprietors of the building lately erected on the north side of Duke Street by the Reverend Mr Jones and others as a place of religious worship according to the Establishment of the Church of England, requesting that the Council would take the same under their patronage, for the reasons therein particularly stated,

Application for Reversion.

"Resolved and Ordered, that the subject matter of the said letter be referred to the Select Committee to examine into and report."

"1803, Mar. 2. Resolved and Ordered, that the Petition of the proprietors of the building at the upper end of Duke Street proposed to be used and appropriated as a place of religious worship, for a grant of the reversionary interest in the same be rejected for the reasons set forth in the proceedings.

Rejected.

"This Council being informed that the Right Reverend Father in God Henry William (Majendie) Lord Bishop of Chester has, at the instance of James Brooke and others, granted his Faculty or License for the performance of Divine Worship in a certain edifice or building situate at the upper end of Duke Street in Liverpool until the same may be duly consecrated; and conceiving that his Lordship has granted such Faculty or License upon suggestion that all circumstances necessary by law for the establishing the same edifice as a Chapel of Ease, would shortly take place—this Council think it necessary to take the earliest opportunity in the most respectful manner to apprise his Lordship that so far as depends upon them they cannot either as patrons of the Mother Church or as

Notice of Refusal to Bishop.

Owners of the reversionary interest of the said edifice or building, give their assent to such measures as alone could or can constitute the same a chapel of ease according to law.

"Also Resolved, that the Mayor be requested to transmit official copies of the above Order of Council to the Lord Bishop and to Mr James Brooke, one of the principal proprietors, as an immediate notification of the sentiments and resolutions of the Council upon the subject."

St. Catharine's, Temple Court. _{St. Catharine's.}

Reference has been made to this church in a previous chapter.

"1802, Decr. 1. Upon reading a letter of the 30th November from the Revd Thomas Hassell minister, and Edward Cearns and John Phillips members of a congregation of Baptists in this town to Mr Foster, desiring him to lay before the Council their request to become purchasers of Saint Catharine's Church or Chapel in this town as a place of Divine worship for a congregation of persons of their persuasion, _{Application to purchase.}

"Resolved and Ordered, that it is not the intention of this Council to sell or dispose of the said Church or Chapel to any sectarists or dissenting congregation whatever." _{Refusal.}

"1811, May 15. Upon the motion of Mr Alderman Dawson,

"Ordered, that it be recommended to the Select Finance Committee to take the most speedy and effectual measures for obtaining an Act of Parliament for the consecration of that church, and for the settlement of the salaries with the fees and other emoluments of the ministers and inferior officers." _{Act of Parliament.}

"1819, Aug. 4. Resolved, that the Select Finance Committee be authorized to direct the taking down of Saint Catharine's Church and to dispose of the materials and of the land there belonging to the Corporation, and to make such communication between Temple Court and Temple Place as they may think proper." _{Removal of Church.}

St. Catharine's, Abercromby Square. _{St. Catharine's.}

"1829, Feby. 4. A letter from Robert Gladstone Esq on behalf of several gentlemen who had set on foot a subscription for the purpose of building a Church on the East Side of Abercromby Square, having been laid before this Council, soliciting a grant of the reversion of the land, and the right of presentation of the Minister for the term of forty years, _{Application for Reversion.}

"Resolved, that this request be complied with, under the direction of the Select Finance Committee, and that the Mayor and Bailiffs be authorized to affix the Common Seal to the requisite conveyance." _{Granted.}

E E E

St. Michael's, Pitt Street.

St. Michael's.

This church was commenced by the Parish of Liverpool, but completed by the Corporation.

Application of Parish.
"1811, July 3. Resolved, that the Petition of Mr Edward Blackstock the Vestry Clerk for the grant to the Parish of Liverpool of the Reversion of a Piece of Land in Kent Street &c for the purpose of a scite of an intended Church and Church Yard, be referred to the consideration of the Select Finance Committee."

"1823, Jany. 14. Parish of Liverpool.

"At a meeting of the Commissioners for building St. Michael's Church this 26th Dec. 1822,

Money spent.
"The Commissioners having expended the whole of the money (£34,500) which by the Act they were empowered to raise, without having completed the Church, and it being reported by their Architect that it will require a

Sum required.
further expenditure of £10,000 or thereabouts to finish the same, with which the inhabitants are not likely to burden themselves,

Appeal to the Council.
"It was Resolved, that the Commissioners most respectfully take leave to request the Worshipful the Mayor and Common Council of the Borough of Liverpool to undertake the completion of the said Church, with the ample funds at their command, which the Commissioners are led to believe will be an agreeable appropriation of the Corporate property to a large proportion if not to all the Burgesses; the Commissioners securing the repayment of any advance the Common Council may come under by giving them (till repaid from the church) the entire controul over the said church and the land thereto attached, as amply as if the same were their own Property, but not to extend to vest in that body the power of diminishing the extent of the Church Yard as now walled in."

"1823, Feb. 5. This Resolution and proposal having been fully discussed in the Council it was

Consent of Council.
"Resolved, That the Council acquiesce in the church being completed out of the Corporate Estate, the Parish agreeing to relinquish the church and church yard to the Corporation as their own property, but the repairs of the church being provided for as in the present Act and the Corporation

Conditions.
having the power of disposing of the Burial Ground towards reimbursing of the money to be advanced by them, and the Parish being at the expence of the Act of Parliament."

St. Paul's.

St. Paul's Church, St. Paul's Square.

"1812, Octr. 10. Ordered, that the Petition of the Churchwardens, Owners and Occupiers of Seats in St. Paul's Church for a contribution

Organ.
towards the erection of an organ and a gallery in the Church for the reception of the same and the payment of the Salary for the Organist be referred to the Select Finance Committee with full powers therein."

St. Andrew's, Renshaw Street.

St. Andrew's.

"1815, Aug. 2. A letter from John Gladstone Esquire (Sir John) soliciting the consent of this Corporation to an Act of Parliament for the consecration of the church now building by him in Renshaw Street, having been read,

Application from Gladstone.

"Resolved, That such letter be referred to the consideration of the Select Finance Committee."

St. Philip's, Hardman Street.

St. Philip's.

"1816, July 5. Resolved, that the Petition from several inhabitants in the neighbourhood of Hardman and Rodney Streets for a grant of the reversion of a building intended to be called Saint Philip's Church, and the application of Mr John Cragg the Proprietor or Builder thereof relative to the terms and conditions upon which the Common Council as Patrons may be willing to accede to the consecration of the said church, be referred to the Select Finance Committee with full powers."

Application for Reversion.

The Church was built and consecrated. In 1884 an Act was passed for its secularization, and shops were built on a portion of the site.

Secularized.

St. Thomas's, Park Lane.

St. Thomas's.

"1822, May 1. Resolved, that the following Report of the Surveyor relative to the cause of the late dangerous state of St. Thomas's Church Steeple be entered in the Council book.

Steeple dangerous.

"'In obedience to the Order of Council of the 3rd April 1822, directing the Surveyor to report the cause of the late dangerous state of St. Thomas's Church Steeple he begs respectfully to state that it appears to have been caused by the iron shaft or spindle 21 ft long which was originally placed in the top part of the spire when it was built, having by continual vibration failed in one of its joints.

Report.

"'The Surveyor has taken leave to place this shaft in the Entrance Hall of the Town Hall for the inspection of such gentlemen as choose to view it as a matter of curiosity.'"

The spire was taken down, and so remained for twelve years.

Spire taken down.

"1834, Feby. 5. Resolved, that the plan for the erection of the spire of St. Thomas's Church adopted by the Resolution of the last Council be completed so far as regards the repair and restoration of the tower, but that the rebuilding of the spire be postponed until the settlement of the Town Dues question."

Plan for Spire.

Postponed.

The spire has never been rebuilt.

St. John the Baptist, Park Road.

"1828, Apl. 2. A letter from the Rev⁴ W Hesketh, Minister of St. Michael's Church Toxteth Park soliciting a contribution towards the erection of an intended church in Harrington, having been laid before this Council,

"Resolved, that the sum of £500 be given for this purpose."

St. Martin's-in-the-Fields.

"1828, July 2. The Proceedings of the Select Finance Committee having been read,

"Resolved, that the same be confirmed except as to the Resolution to make the recommendation to the Rectors, of a stipendiary curate to the New Church in Oxford Street north, in the month of August next; which subject is to be considered as postponed until the result of a further communication with the Lord Bishop of the Diocese and of an interview between the Mayor, the Chairman of the Committee and the Rectors, relative to the presentation is made known to the Council."

"1828, Decr. 3. A letter read from Geo. Jenner Esq communicating the acquiescence of the Board of Commissioners, in the heads of the Bill transmitted relative to the new church in Oxford Street North, and requesting the draft when prepared to be transmitted."

Church for the Blind.

"1829, Feby. 4. The proposed Bill relative to the Church for the indigent Blind was this day laid before the Council, and the same appearing to be prepared as far as regards the rights and interests of the Corporation in conformity with the proceedings confirmed by the Council on the 4ᵗʰ Jan⁷ last,

"Resolved, that the Common Seal be affixed to the Bill in testimony of the assent of the Corporation to the same and should any further consideration of the Bill be requisite the same to be referred to the Select Finance Committee."

St. Saviour's, Huskisson Street.

"1829, May 6. An application from Ambrose Lace Esq relative to a proposal for the erection of a new Church upon part of the land held by him at the north west corner of Huskisson and Catharine Streets, and for a grant of the reversion of the land and the usual patronage having been laid before this Council,

"Resolved, that the same be referred to the Select Finance Committee to report."

St. James's Cemetery.

Cemetery.

"1825, Sept. 7. A letter from the Revd Jonathan Brooks relative to the sale of the old Quarry at the top of Duke Street for the purpose of a Cemetery in connexion with the Church of England having been laid before the Council,

Sale of Old Quarry.

"Resolved that the same be referred to the Select Finance Committee to make a report, accompanied with plans and a prospectus of the general regulations intended."

"1826, Feby. 1. Resolved, that the Select Finance Committee be authorized to co-operate on the part of the Council in carrying into effect the plans and prospectus of the intended Cemetery in connection with the Established Church,

"Resolved also, that the Select Finance Committee be authorized to advance upon loan such sum of money as the Committee may think proper towards the intended Cemetery not exceeding £500."

Loan advanced.

The closing period of the Ancient Corporation possesses considerable interest, and is intimately connected with ecclesiastical affairs.

Closing period.

Reference has been made above to the visit of the Commissioners of Inquiry in 1833. In 1835 the Municipal Reform Bill was introduced in the House of Commons.

Commission of Inquiry.

"1835, June 17. James Aspinall Mayor.

"At a Special Council held in the Council chamber within the Town Hall for the purpose of taking into consideration the provisions of a Bill brought into the House of Commons, intituled a Bill to provide for the regulation of Municipal Corporations in England and Wales, and adopting such Resolutions and measures respecting the same as may be deemed proper,

Municipal Reform Bill.

"Present James Aspinall Esq Mayor and 26 others.

"The Mayor stated that he had deemed it his duty to call this Special Council in consequence of having received a copy of the Bill, which he now submitted, and some of the provisions of which were now taken into consideration.

Provisions of Bill.

"Resolved, that this Council, conscious of having always discharged the important duties devolved upon it as the governing body of this Corporation, with the utmost desire for the welfare and advantage of the Town of Liverpool, does not feel itself called upon to offer any opposition to the principle of the measure, so far as relates to the removal of the members of this Council, and the substitution of another body, by a different mode of election, for the future management of the Corporate

Resolution.

No opposition.

Estate; but that the same should be left to such determination as Parliament may think fit to come to regarding it.

Provision for Debt.
"Resolved, that inasmuch as this and former Councils have in the execution of public works and improvements contracted a debt amounting to upwards of a million, provision should be made for its redemption, and that no material diminution of the town or other dues should take place until provision is made for its liquidation.

"That as this Council has in the execution of the improvements entered into extensive contracts and obligations, these should be recognized and confirmed.

Rights of Burgesses.
"That as the proposed enactment deprives of the exemption from town dues, all burgesses not enrolled at the present time, thus depriving hundreds of individuals who have completed their claim to admission, in addition to the just rights of many thousands who have an inchoate right, it is the duty of this Council to represent the same to Parliament.

Dock Trust.
"That the management of the Dock Trust heretofore vested in the Council, will be interfered with by the proposed Bill, they therefore feel it their duty to apply to Parliament to make due provision to remedy any inconvenience which may arise from the Bill in its present form.

"Resolved also,

Clerical Patronage.
"That as the patronage of the Rectory of Liverpool is vested in the Corporation and the Council has the appointment thereto, and of the clergy of many of the churches erected in the said town, and in pursuance of such authority have appointed the ministers now officiating therein, with salaries or stipends exceeding the endowments fixed by the several Acts of Parliament, and which are payable under Resolutions of this Council made from time to time, and that as such stipends do not exceed a moderate and reasonable provison for the said ministers, the Council is of opinion that a representation of these circumstances should be made to *Provision for Stipends.* Parliament, and that provision should be solicited for recognizing and confirming these Resolutions, and establishing these payments to the present, and suitable provision for the future incumbents, as also for *Maintenance of Churches.* the future repairs and maintenance of such churches and for the other expences usually attendant on the performance of Divine Service therein.

Protection of Interests.
"The foregoing resolutions are not proposed with the object of offering opposition to the measure in its principle, but to protect those interests which have been confided to this Corporation for so long a series of years; and as the rights and interests of this Corporation are essentially involved in the proposed measure."

Committee.
A committee was appointed, petitions drawn up, and a deputation despatched to London to act on behalf of the Corporation.

ECCLESIASTICAL AFFAIRS.

"1835, July 10. The Mayor having stated that Notice had been given to introduce a clause into the Municipal Reform Bill which would give power to the new Council to dispute leases, mortgages and sales made subsequent to the 5th of June last, which would materially affect the routine adopted by this Council in granting leases and sales, the Town Clerk was instructed to endeavour to get the above clause modified." Leases, Mortgages.

"1835, July 25. The Mayor having communicated to the Council that the Municipal Corporations Bill had passed the Commons and been read a first time in the Lords, with the obnoxious clauses unaltered, it was resolved to forward a petition to the House of Lords, with a request to Lord Wharncliffe to present it."

The Town Clerk was also directed to obtain the attendance of such evidence as might be requisite to support the petition, and to retain counsel. Evidence.

The petition enters very fully into the history of the Corporation and the progress of the town and port, and concludes thus:— Petition to Lords.

"'Your Petitioners submit to your Lordships' deliberate consideration the expediency and advantage of separating the concerns and government of this Corporation from a measure intended for the general government of all the Corporations of England and Wales, with scarce any of which this Corporation can be justly compared, either in reference to the extent and variety of the interests committed to its charge, or to the amount and importance of its estate and revenues; and that you would exempt this Corporation from the provisions of the said Act, and provide for the future government of the same, by a separate and specific Act of the legislature for that purpose.'" Proposed Exemption.

It is needless to say that this prayer met with no response, but the clauses in the Bill materially interfering with the ordinary course of leasing and dealing with the estate were considerably modified. Clauses modified.

"1835, Octr. 7. James Aspinall Mayor.
"The Mayor communicated to the Council that the Act for the regulation of Municipal Corporations in England and Wales had received the Royal Assent on the 9th September, and that in pursuance of power given by the Act the day of election of the new Council had been fixed for the 26th December; upon the declaration of which election, the Mayor, Aldermen and Common Councilmen and all other Members of this Common Council by whatever name or style they may be known, will then go out Act passed. New Election.

of office, and their whole powers and duties then cease, and that by a further provision no election of Mayor and Bailiffs will take place on the next Charter day vizt the 18th day of October instant, but that the present Mayor and Bailiffs will continue to hold their respective offices until the next election of the new Council and Mayor."

Provision for Clergy.

The provision for the clergy next occupied the serious attention of the expiring Council. They had acted on many occasions in a very firm and decided manner in keeping the clergy to their duty, notably in the passage of arms with Bishop Law in 1821, relative to the non-residence of the incumbents, but their feeling towards the church was very loyal and devoted. The stipends secured to the ministers of the churches by the respective Acts of Parliament were for the most part sadly too small, and had been eked out by grants from the Corporate funds. The Council *Proposal for Provision.* now desired before their retirement to convert these voluntary grants into a permanent provision, in fear lest the incoming Council might cut down the stipends to the legal amount.

"The Council having adverted to the proceedings adopted in the House of Commons with reference to the future provision for the Rectors of the Parish, and the situation of several of the Clergy officiating at churches in the patronage of this Corporation whose stipends are not permanently fixed,

Resolution. "Resolved, that it is expedient to take into consideration the propriety of securing a permanent income or provision for the Rectors of the Parish and such of the Clergy of the several churches in the patronage of the Corporation as are at present without any adequate endowment. That a *Committee.* Committee be appointed to carry this resolution into effect, to report to a future Special Council."

1835, Octr. 12. The Council met to reconsider the subject. They confirmed the previous resolution as to the endowment, *Deputation.* and deputed the Town Clerk to proceed to London to take the advice and opinions of the most eminent counsel as to the best mode of carrying this resolution into effect.

1835, Octr. 28. The Town Clerk reported that he had

had a consultation with Sir Frederick Pollock, Mr. Cresswell and Mr. Jacob, when the proposal had been very fully discussed and the opinion stated below had been given by those counsel. _{Counsels' advice.}

"'Copy—Opinion.

"'It is impossible to point out any mode by which the Corporation can effect the object of permanently continuing the present provision for the Clergy of Liverpool so as to be entirely secure from being impeached hereafter. And it is only by the exercise of the discretionary power vested in the King in Council by the latter part of the 97th Section of the Stat. 5th & 6th Will 4. ch 76, that any such arrangement can be rendered available. _{Opinion.}

"'We consider upon the whole that the plan most adviseable would be, for the Corporation to raise by Mortgage of part of their Real Estates a sum sufficient to produce the annual stipends proposed to be secured. And we should recommend that the money so raised should be invested in the names of Trustees upon trust to pay those stipends to the Ministers, unless the Mortgage should be successfully impeached and in that case to restore the money to the persons advancing it. And we should think it best that the Mortgage and the declaration of Trusts of the Money should be included in the same deeds or so connected as to form one transaction. _{Plan. Mortgage. Investment.}

"'Fred. Pollock
"'Cress. Cresswell
"'Temple 19th October 1835.'   "'Edward Jacob

"The Committee having taken into consideration the foregoing Opinion, directed the Treasurer to make inquiries and submit a list of parties willing to make the advance and in conjunction with the Surveyor and Clerk of Committees, to report what portion of the Corporate Estate it would be most convenient to mortgage. _{Inquiries.}

"The Council then proceeded to consider the several annual sums which they recommend to be secured by the proposed endowments and _{Annual payments.}

"Resolved,

"That the present Rectors and their four Curates, and the several present officiating Ministers at St George's, St Thomas's, St Paul's, St John's, St Anne's, and St David's Churches now receiving annual stipends from the Corporation, do continue to receive the amounts of such annual stipends for their respective lives, and that the future Rectors be endowed in perpetuity with the sum of £710 per annum to each Rector for his own use, and also with the further sum of £360 per annum to each Rector for two Curates. _{Stipends provided. Rectors.}

"That the future Chaplains of St George's be endowed in perpetuity with the sum of £250 per annum, in addition to the sum of £50 ⅌ an. _{St. George's.}

payable by the Act of Parliament·; and that there be also paid a Lecturer or second Minister of that Church at the sum of £200 ℔ an.

St. Thomas's. "That the future senior Minister of St Thomas's be endowed with the sum of £220 ℔ an. in addition to the sum of £80 ℔ an. now payable by Act of Parliament and that there be also paid to a Lecturer or second Minister the sum of £165 ℔ an.

St. Paul's. "That after the death, resignation or removal of the present evening lecturer at St Paul's there be only two Ministers appointed to the same. That the future senior Minister be endowed with £170 ℔ an. in addition to £50 ℔ an. payable under the Act of Parliament, and that there be also a lecturer or second Minister at £100 ℔ an.

St. John's. "That there be a lecturer or second Minister of St John's at £180 ℔ an.
St. Anne's. "That the future Minister of St Anne's be endowed with £140 ℔ an. and the future Minister of St David's with £100 ℔ an.

Mortgages. "Resolved, that the Town Clerk be directed to prepare such deeds as may be necessary to carry the foregoing resolutions into effect, and for the necessary mortgage security for such a sum of money as may require to be raised for that purpose."

Letter from Bolton. "1835, Nov. 4. A letter was read from Mr Thos Bolton protesting against the proposed endowments out of the Corporate Funds."

Investment. "1835, Nov. 11. The Town Clerk reported that in pursuance of the Resolution of the last Meeting he had communicated with John Moss Esq, Chairman of the Grand Junction Railway Company, and that at a Meeting of the Directors they had agreed to receive a sum of about £100,000 upon security of their land, Works and Capital at 4 ℔ cent ℔ an. interest, and with the understanding that the principal money might be called in at a short notice.

Resolution. "Resolved, that it be recommended to the Council to invest the money to be raised for the proposed endowment of the Clergy, with the Grand Junction Railway upon the security before mentioned.

Amount. "Resolved, that the sum of £105,000 appears to this Committee sufficient to be raised and invested for this purpose, and that a Trust Deed declaring the purposes to which the interest is to be applied be prepared, and that the following gentlemen be named as the Trustees—

"THE RIGHT REV^D. THE LORD BISHOP OF CHESTER

"MESSRS JOHN BOURNE   "MESSRS RICHARD HOUGHTON
"JOHN WRIGHT   "JAMES COCKSHOTT
"CHARLES LAWRENCE   "ROBERTSON GLADSTONE
"JAMES ASPINALL   "JAMES POWNALL
"THOMAS SHAW   "SIR THOMAS BRANCKER."

"1835, Nov. 13. Jas Aspinall Mayor.
"Special Council.

Protest. "At this Council, a Protest signed by one hundred and twenty five Burgesses of the existing Borough of Liverpool, and persons qualified to be Burgesses under the Municipal Reform Act, against the endowment of certain Churches and the payment of the Parochial and other Clergy, and against the intended loan and mortgage and all the proceedings of this Council in relation thereto was read.

"Resolved, that the proceedings, resolutions and recommendations of the Committee of the whole Council be hereby adopted, approved, ratified and confirmed by this Council, and that the same be fully carried into effect under the directions of the Select Finance Committee." Confirmation.

"1835, Novr. 18. Special Council.

"The Mayor having laid before this Council the copy of minutes of an Order of Injunction made on the 14th of November instant by his Honor the Master of the Rolls, on the information of the Attorney General at the relation of Thomas Bolton and Timothy Jevons, restraining this Corporation from carrying into effect the proposed endowment of the Clergy, Injunction.

"And a letter from the Town Clerk stating that he had proceeded to London there to await the directions of the Council having been read,

"Resolved, that the Town Clerk do immediately advise with Counsel as to the course to be pursued by the Corporation, and that he take such steps as he may be recommended to adopt." Counsel's advice.

"1835, Decr. 2. The Town Clerk having acquainted the Council that he had conferred with counsel as to the validity of the Bonds proposed to be given to secure the repayment of the money to be borrowed, and that counsel had under the circumstances recommended that a mortgage of some portion of the Corporation Estate should be given to the parties as an additional security, Bonds.

"Resolved, that the Select Finance Committee be authorized to cause such mortgage security as they may think expedient to be granted on some part of the Corporate Estate, and that the necessary deeds be executed under the Common Seal. Mortgages.

"The Town Clerk reported that he had attended in London and had prepared and filed an affidavit fully detailing the existing provisions made for the Clergy, and also the entire proceedings of the Council and its Committees in relation to the proposed endowment in respect to which the injunction had been granted by the Master of the Rolls, that a motion had been made to dissolve the injunction, which had been fully argued by counsel on both sides, and that the judgment of the Court was to be given yesterday. Injunction disputed.

"Resolved, that the above proceedings of the Town Clerk be approved, ratified and confirmed, and that he be directed to cause a copy of the shorthand writer's notes of the argument and determination of the Court to be printed and published at the expense of the Corporation."- Notes of the argument.

"1835, Decr. 22. The following Resolutions of a meeting of the Clergy of this town, held on the 17th inst were read and ordered to be entered on the proceedings.

412   CHAP. IV, A.D. 1800—1835.

<small>Meeting of Clergy.</small>

"At a meeting of the Clergy of Liverpool held in the Blue Coat Hospital on Thursday the 17th Decr 1835

"It was Resolved unanimously,

<small>Resolution.</small>

"That the Clergy, deeply sensible of the important services rendered by the Common Council of Liverpool to the maintenance of true religion, by the building of Schools and Churches and providing for the moral and religious education of the people in the principles of the Established Church, are unwilling to permit the Members of the present Council

<small>Expression of gratitude.</small>

to render up their trust into other hands, without expressing a grateful sense of the favour and protection which the Church has experienced from them; more particularly by their last act in securing as far as lay in their power the independence of the Clergy by a sufficient permanent provision for those Churches which before were inadequately endowed.

"Resolved, that the two Rectors be appointed to wait on the Mayor, and request him to communicate this Resolution to the Council."

<small>Old Municipality.</small>

Here terminate the Records of the old Regime of the Municipality of Liverpool, which had existed for more than six hundred years. Like most, if not all its sister Corporations, it had become an anachronism, unsuited to the circumstances of the times. The antique bonds of exclusiveness of the middle ages could no longer restrain the expansive movements of modern society, and had to be burst asunder.

<small>Allowances.</small>

In passing judgment on the Old Corporation, we must not be too exacting. We must make allowance for the spirit of the age, for the traditional influences which had

<small>Mistaken Principles.</small>

operated during a long series of years, for the mistaken principles of commerce and political economy which prevailed to a late period, and for the natural desire to maintain privileges which had once been enjoyed.

<small>Exclusiveness.</small>

It must be acknowledged that the old Municipality was exclusive in a double sense, first in the monopoly of the Burgesses and Freemen, with its exclusions and restrictions, driving away trade and preventing competition; and, secondly, in the self-election of the governing body, the

<small>Illegality.</small>

Common Council, which illegally, contrary to the tenor of

the charters, and in spite of repeated adverse decisions of the courts, persisted in retaining the management of Corporate affairs to the exclusion of the Burgesses.

Admitting all this, there is much to be said on the other side. Any one who reads the Records impartially, will be struck with the vigour, tenacity, courage and pluck manifested during the whole of their history by the Burgesses and Council of the town. From the year 1573, when it is related that "Mr. Mayor and all the town made ready upon the Heath, every man with their best weapons, eager as lions," they have always been ready to defend themselves, from whatever quarter the attack might come. Allowing for the prejudices of the age, there is much good sense in many of their proceedings. *Vigour, Tenacity, Courage. Readiness. Good Sense.*

Coming down to a later period, when the property and income of the Corporation became important and valuable, there is no evidence of the venality and corruption which unfortunately disgraced some Municipalities. Nepotism undoubtedly existed in the promotion of their own families to places of trust and emolument, but on the whole the town was honestly served. The Corporate property was well husbanded, and the improvements of 1786 and 1825 were carried out on a large scale without the slightest tax upon the inhabitants. In this respect the reformed Corporation does not compare advantageously with its predecessor. *Honesty. Improvements.*

Our local institutions have been popularized and the powers of self-government ostensibly diffused throughout the community. This is right in principle, and in accordance with the spirit of the age, but there are a few dangers which should be borne in mind—one, and that the most obvious, is the control of the Central Government. The Ancient Corporation by virtue of its Charter, was an independent body, holding its own courts, appointing its own Recorder, its Judge of the Court of Passage, and other officials. These offices are now in the gift of the Ministry of the day. This tendency to centralization manifests itself in a variety of ways, and is fostered and encouraged by the permanent officials of the Government. Vigilance on the part of the Municipalities is required to guard against this bureaucracy, which would infringe upon and eventually destroy the self-governing principle which is the great characteristic of the Anglo-Saxon race.

<small>Anticipations.</small>
If five hundred years hence the Municipality of the coming age can present a Record as full of interest and progress, of difficulties overcome, and of bright anticipations of the future, the task of its historian will be as pleasing as the one now brought to a close.

INDEX.

A

Abercromby square, 401.
Adams, ——, 128.
Addresses to the Crown, 105, 113, 114, 116, 119, 175, 178, 180, 188, 189, 286, 290, 291, 292, 294, 295, 296, 297, 301, 302, 303.
Aldersey, Richard, 94, 98.
Alehouses, 202.
Alexander, Peter, 83.
Allegiance, oath of, 195.
Almshouses, 45, 63, 155, 156, 262, 385.
Amherst, John, 108.
Anderton, George, 53.
—— Thomas, 83.
Ansdell, James, 173.
Apprentices, 54.
Aqueduct at Runcorn, 244.
Arcades to warehouses, 232.
Archery, 84.
Armitage, Robert, 142, 143, 154.
Armour (coronation), 300.
Armoury, ——, 36, 41.
Arms, record of, 105, 128.
Arms of Liverpool, 191.
Art exhibitions, 313, 314.
Ashcroft, Abraham, 173.
Askew, John, 342.
Ashton, William, 83.
Aspinall, James, 303, 304, 334, 337, 362, 405, 410.
—— John Bridge, 307, 317, 356.
Assemblies, 130, 131.
Assizes, removal of, 318, 321.
Athenæum, 381.
Atherton, James, 55.
—— John, 166.
—— Peter, 58.
—— Rev. Robert, 66.
—— street, 58, 62.
Athol, Duke of, 104, 305.

B

Back o' th' Castle, 58.
Baines, John, 173, 283, 284, 395.
Baldwin, Rev. Thomas, 69, 128, 172.
Bank hall, 262.
Banks, Mr., 154.
Banks, run upon the, 249.
Bardesley, Rev. ——, 173.
Bardswell, Charles, 396.
Barnes, John, 217, 218.
Barracks, 290.
Barrett, William, 395.
Barton, Rev. Henry, 386, 388.
—— Sir William, 296, 316, 369.
Bateman, Samuel, 53.
Bath street, 184, 249, 263.
Batman, William, 357.
Batteries, 118, 150, 181, 182, 183, 294, 384.
Beacon's gutter, 363.
Beauclerk, Lord Sidney, 105.
Beaumaris, 52.
Bedford, Duke of, 112.
Bell, Rev. Thomas, 69.
Bells, complaints about, 398.
Bellingham, John, 294.
Bendish, Major, 108, 111.
Benett, ——, M.P., 331.
Benn, James, 6, 57, 58, 73.
Benson, Major-General, 287.
—— Robert, 383.
Bent, Theophilus, 121.
Bernard, M., 53.
Berry, Henry, 273.
—— street, 396.
Bevington bush, 395.
Bibby, William, 47.
Bidston lighthouse, 242.
Billinge, John, 249.
Birch, Thomas, 211, 239.

INDEX.

Birchall, Daniel, 54.
Bird, Joseph, 107, 114, 122, 129, 143, 158.
Birkenhead docks, 341, 342, 345.
Blackburn, John, 175, 201, 231, 240, 241, 257, 276.
—— Jonathan, 42.
Blackburne, Robert, 242.
—— Architect, 260.
Blackstock, Edward, 282, 382, 402.
Bladwell, William, 108.
Blair, Captain, 185.
—— Sir John, 11.
Blevin, James and Ann, 80.
Bluecoat hospital, 75, 284.
Blues, Liverpool, 184.
Blundell, Bryan, 20, 29, 64, 74, 75, 86, 89, 90, 96, 124, 143.
—— Hollinshead, Henry, 185, 197, 204, 206, 217, 280, 308, 348, 373, 381.
—— —— Jonathan, 297, 339, 354, 358, 364.
Bold, Jonas, 262, 286, 289, 307, 386.
—— Street, 262, 366, 381, 396, 398.
Bolton, John, 202, 250, 308.
—— Thomas, 410.
—— Ogden & Co., 324, 325, 326.
Booth, Langham, 15.
Bootle, Thomas, 5, 12, 15, 16, 61, 70, 79, 86, 87, 91.
—— Springs, 24, 25, 209, 210.
Botanic garden, 380, 381.
Boundary boulevard, 366.
—— stones, 137.
Bounties to seamen, 180, 181.
Bourne, John, 294, 311, 410.
Bowling-green house, 139, 255.
Bowen, Owen, 209.
Braddock, William, 50, 52, 58.
Bradshaw, Ellen, 82.
Braithwaite, secretary, 11.
Branagan, Owin, 22.
Brancker, Peter, 217, 219.
—— Peter Whitfield, 218, 306, 357.
—— Sir Thomas, 302, 330, 355, 361, 410.
Brandreth, James, 400.
Brereton, Owen Salusbury, 190.
—— Thomas, 92, 93, 94, 98, 142, 149.
Brees, Christopher, 59.

Brett, ——, 167.
Bribery, notice against, 331.
Bricks, making of, 32.
Bridge, John, 255.
—— proposed to Birkenhead, 359.
Bridgwater, Duke of, 244, 247.
Brindley, James, 243, 245.
Bristol, 22, 149.
Britannia, statue of, 267.
British prisoners, relief to, 294.
Broadneux, Col. Robert, 84.
Bromfield, James, 109, 110, 112, 121, 139, 143, 153.
Brooks, James, 45.
—— John, 93, 105, 107, 157, 158, 160, 165, 169.
—— Rev. Jonathan, 405.
—— Roger, 136.
Brooke, James, 401.
Brookes, Joseph, 200, 227, 234, 250, 254, 285.
Brown, Henry, 212, 227.
—— William George, 305.
Brownell, ——, 226.
Brown Low, The, 32, 382.
Brownlow hill, 129, 156, 157, 227, 228.
—— street, 139.
Brunel, J. K., 385.
Brunelagh, 156.
Brunswick street, 363.
Bryer, Thomas, 209, 210.
Buckingham, Marquis of, 189.
Building Act, 367.
Bull-baiting, 83.
Bull and Punchbowl tavern, 364.
Bullin, Richard, 312, 319, 379, 397.
Burgage rents, 227.
Burial ground, new, 138.
Butchers, 43, 136.
Butler, Henry, 195.
Byrom, George, 273.
—— street, 60, 273, 366.

C

Cable street, 47, 136, 261.
Cairnes, Sir Alexander, 23.
Caldwell, Charles, 204, 206.

INDEX.

Caldwell, Smyth & Co., 249.
Callender, John, 255.
Campbell, George, 128, 200.
Canals, Bridgewater, 243.
—— Derbyshire and Mersey, 243.
—— to Docks, 246.
—— Hull to Liverpool, 244.
—— Leeds and Liverpool, 221, 222, 245, 246, 354.
—— Weaver and Trent, 243.
Canning, George, 300, 301, 305, 375, 376.
—— Lady, 301.
Canning place, 377.
Cannon, Patrick, 82.
Carr, William, 124, 136.
Carter, Robert, 57.
Case, George, 204, 206, 218, 220, 250, 258.
—— Thomas, 296, 320, 375.
Castle, 33, 36, 37, 39, 41, 60, 61, 69, 70, 71, 135.
—— ditch, 61, 365.
—— hey, 58, 154.
—— hill, 35.
—— street, 58, 229, 258, 259, 274, 363, 366, 378, 379.
—— —— Lower, 379.
Cattle market, 379.
Cearns, Edward, 401.
Certiorari, writ of, 67.
Chadwick, James, 64.
Chaffers, 192.
Chanting, 167.
Chantrey rents, 227.
Chantrey, F., 300.
Chapel yard, 58.
—— street, 43, 58, 135, 232.
Charitable funds, 45.
Charlotte, Princess, 296.
Charters, 3, 4, 21, 101, 104.
Cheesemongers, 48.
Cherbourg, 117.
Cheshire lands, 341.
—— Mrs., 166.
Chester, Bishop of, 144, 387-393, 395, 400.
Cheyné, John, 187.
China trade, 350.
Cholera, 318.
Chorley, John, 195.

Church building, 276, 281.
Clarence, Duke of, 217, 220, 291.
Clarke, John, 292, 378, 397.
—— Mary, 285.
—— William, 285.
Clay, Henry, 290, 308.
Clayton, John, 73.
—— Richard, 133, 134.
—— Sir Richard, 226.
—— William, 37, 62, 75.
Clegg, Joseph, 101, 102, 103, 104, 110, 112, 113, 123, 124, 130, 158, 159, 169, 177.
Clemens, James, 180, 192, 199, 246, 264.
Cleveland, John, 4, 15, 37, 38, 75.
—— square, 233.
Clergy, non-residence, 387.
—— provision for, 335, 408.
—— salaries, 387.
Clitherall, Joseph, 63.
Clothes for officers, 127.
Coals, 63.
—— boring for, 31.
Cockshott, James, 410.
Cockshutte, John, 38.
Colquitt, John, 154.
—— Scrope, 124.
Commerce, committee of, 237, 238.
Commercial loans, 250.
Commission to raise forces, 107.
Common hall, 96, 97, 203, 204, 207.
—— shore, 157, 260.
Coney, Charles, 198.
Conscience, court of, 129.
Conservancy of navigation, 143, 240, 351, 355.
Constable of castle, 33.
Conway bridge, 357.
—— General, 193.
Cook street, 58, 330.
Cooper, Joseph, 73.
Cooper's row, 261.
Coore, Thomas, 38, 55, 64, 68, 78, 166.
Coppuck, ——, 167.
Coronation, George III., 177.
—— George IV., 298.
—— William IV., 302.

G G G

Coroner, dispute with, 82.
Corn Exchange, 383.
Correction, house of, 227.
Council, 3, 19, 20, 23, 29, 36, 89, 90, 95, 97, 99, 105.
—— room, 369.
Court of Bequests, 180.
—— room, 369.
Courtney, John, 127.
Covent garden, 58.
Cowdock, Robert, 81.
Crabtree lane, 380.
Cragg, John, 403.
—— William, 53.
Crescent, 366.
Cresswell, Mr. Justice, 409.
Crompton, Alice, 82.
Crosbie, James, 128, 144, 170.
—— John, 201, 236, 243.
—— William, 181, 199, 200, 255, 260, 261, 311.
Cross-hall, 137.
Cross, Thomas, 137.
Crosse, John, 283.
Crosses, 155, 378.
Crown street, 30.
Culcheth's yate, 59.
Cumberland, William, Duke of, 110, 112, 113.
Cunliffe, Sir Ellis, 116, 117, 118, 119, 176.
—— Sir Foster, 27, 31, 50, 79, 90, 96, 97, 135, 162.
—— Robert, 118, 137, 143, 150.
Curfew bell, 83.
Currie, Dr. James, 304.
—— William Wallace, 320.
Cust, Sir John, 120.
Custom house, 63, 373, 374, 377.

D

Dale street, 58, 63, 81, 137, 152, 156, 161, 259, 262, 363, 364, 366.
Dalzell, Archibald, 215.
Dandy, Daniel, 98.
Dansey, James, 134.
Dartmouth, Earl of, 236.
Davies, Frances, 122.
—— Joseph, 114, 122, 143, 147, 154, 158.
Dawnay, Bryan, 45.

Dawson (engineer), 254.
—— Major, 182.
—— Pudsey, 229, 233, 274, 282, 401.
Deare, John, 313.
Dedimus, writ of, 10.
Dee, river, 92.
Defences of the town, 117, 181, 183, 184, 185, 186, 187, 254, 287, 289, 290.
Denison street, 184.
Derby, Edward, 12th Earl, 195, 249, 260, 291, 319.
—— James, 10th Earl, 9, 28, 41, 59, 78, 96, 98, 195.
—— square, 11, 24, 55, 60, 61, 135, 163, 232, 233, 365, 378.
Derrick, Samuel, 130.
Despard, Col., 286.
Dinners, 125, 126, 199, 200, 316.
Directory, 367.
Dirom, Major-Gen., 294, 372.
Disfranchisement threatened, 331, 333.
Distillation, restrictions on, 348.
Distress, 124, 149, 192, 249, 311, 348.
Dixon, Robert, 92.
Dobb, Thomas, 233, 234.
Dobson, of Downham, 398.
Dock trust, 335.
Docks, 46, 47, 48, 50, 51, 62, 133, 141, 142, 347, 348, 365, 373, 374.
—— rating of, 249.
Doghouse lane, 154.
Dog kennels, 261.
Dove, Samuel, 64.
Drinkwater, Sir George, 301, 312, 323, 350, 355, 361, 375.
—— James, 294, 317, 386.
Dry dock, 143.
Ducking stool, 81.
Duke street, 137, 262, 382.
Dunbar, Sir George, 185, 199, 209, 250.
Duncan, Lord Viscount, 189.

E

Earle, John, 27, 28, 46, 48, 49, 60, 75, 133.
—— Thomas, 206, 214, 227, 234, 250, 262.
—— William, 251, 306.
—— Willis, 204, 206, 207.

East India Co.'s charter, 249, 349.
Eden, Henley, 320.
—— John, 149.
Edge, Richard, 42.
—— lane, 381.
Edmund street, 154.
Edmunds, Simon, 25.
Elections, 4, 93, 328, 329.
Elliot street, 379.
Ellison, Robert, 241.
Entwistle, John, 14, 136.
Estate of Corporation, 30, 132, 338.
—— —— reports on, 222, 345.
Euston, Dorothy, 53.
Evans, W. David, 381.
Ewart and Denison election, 329, 331.
—— —— petition against return, 330.
Exchange, 81, 90, 149, 154, 157, 158, 160, 258, 264, 265, 266, 269, 368.
—— —— new, 369.
Excise bill, 148.
Executions, 79.
Exhibitions of pictures, 313, 314.
Expulsion of councillors, 309.
Eyes, John, 144, 146, 221, 260, 263.
—— —— map, 382.
Eyre, Mr. Justice, 79.

F

Fabius, Daniel, 60.
Falkner, Edward, 250.
Fall well, 273.
Farrington, William, 36, 39.
Fauster, Elizabeth, 82.
Fawcett, Thomas, 53,
Fawkener, Everard, 113.
Fazakerley, John, 122, 158.
—— street, 58.
Fearon, ——, 146.
Fenwick street, 259.
Ferguson, ——, 249.
Ferries, 227, 241, 356.
Festivals, musical, 312, 398.
Festival hall, 370.
Fillingham, Thomas, 28, 46, 51, 64.

Fire at Exchange, 269.
Fire police, 366.
Fish dock, 261.
—— market, 135, 379, 380.
—— supply, 146, 241.
—— yards, 144, 240, 241.
Fitchett, ——, 358.
Flashes, The, 81, 257, 262.
Fogg, Thurstan, 53.
Footpads, 318.
Forbes, ——, 114, 130, 143, 147, 158.
Foreshore, claim of Crown to, 355.
Formby, ——, 50.
—— channel, 51.
—— Rev. Richard, 279.
Forsyth and Lawton, 358.
Fortifications, 33, 78, 79, 106, 107, 254, 290.
Forts (see batteries).
Foster, John, 226, 235, 257, 262, 265, 266, 271, 272, 278, 280, 364, 374, 396, 399, 401.
—— Thomas, 326, 330, 334.
Frederick William, Prince, 289, 290.
Free Grammar School, 171, 283, 395.
Freemen, 54, 90, 91, 94, 99, 194, 307.
Freemen's fines, 30.
French, landing of the, 185.
—— prisoners, 183, 186, 234, 257.
Frodsham, Edward, 371.
Frog lane, 260.

G

Gage, M. A., 367.
Gallagher, James, 318.
Galley, ——, 101.
Galloway, Randle, 72.
Gallows field, 62.
—— mills, 62, 262.
Gaol, 133, 234, 256, 311, 371, 372.
Gascoyne, Bamber, 183, 239.
—— General, Isaac, 185, 210, 219, 286, 305.
George I., proclaimed, 78.
—— II., do. 79.
George's dock, 263.
Georgia, emigration to, 92.
Gerard, ——, 242.

INDEX.

Gerard, James, M.D., 292, 307, 373.
Gibson, William, 273.
Gildart, James, 114, 147, 201, 254, 264.
—— Richard, 17, 31, 43, 55, 64, 69, 91, 98, 99, 108, 120, 123, 129, 134, 142, 145, 156, 160, 163, 164, 166, 255.
Gildoes, Nehemias, 60.
Giles, —, 358.
Gladstone, Sir John, 230, 249, 250, 309, 350, 383, 403.
—— Robert, 401.
—— Robertson, 410.
—— Right Hon. William Ewart, 230, 383.
Glasshouses, 55.
Gloucester, Duke of, 290.
Golightly, Thomas, 181, 199, 207, 316.
Goodrick, Francis, 49.
Goodwin, John, 19, 54, 61, 70.
—— William, 117, 133, 151.
Goore, Charles, 114, 126, 128, 130, 144, 146, 158, 167, 169, 200, 244, 263, 277.
Gordon, Lieut.-Col., 108, 111, 182, 183.
Gore, John, 249.
Goree, 259, 263, 264.
Gorge, Lieut.-Gen., 42.
Gowns, 78, 79, 197, 315.
Grace, Widow, 55.
Graham, General, 108, 111.
Grant Peter & Co., 280.
Grason, David, 55.
Gray, Sir Charles, 189.
Great Charlotte street, 378.
—— George street, 282.
Green, —, 72.
—— Edward, 165, 166.
—— Isaac, 51.
—— Samuel, 217, 218.
—— Tuttle & Barry, 24, 25, 26.
Greenhalgh, Mary, 82.
—— Ann, 82.
Gregson, William, 178, 254.
Grimbleston, William, 68, 75.
Gryffith, George, 57.
Gwyllim, Robert, 242.

H

Hackin's hey, 58, 60, 154.
Halberdiers, 19, 126.
Hall, Peter, 18, 36.
Halsall, James, 3, 65.
Hamilton, Arthur, 92, 157.
Hamlett, —, 138.
Hamson, Thomas, 316.
Hanover street, 50, 157, 262, 273.
Hargreaves, James, 364.
Harper, William, 250, 307, 356, 371, 383.
Harrington town, 306.
—— street, 35.
Harris, Rev. Raymond, 215, 216.
Harvey and Waln, 279.
Hassell, Rev. Thomas, 401.
Hatton garden, 263.
Hawkesbury, Lord, 191.
Haymarket, 261.
Heath, The, 30, 58, 132, 137, 338.
Henderson, Rev. John, 277.
Herbert, —, Hon., 144.
Herford, Jonathan, 53.
Hertford, Earl of, 273
Heskain, —, Rev., 168.
Hesketh, Rev. W., 404.
—— William, 197.
Heywood, Captain Nathaniel, 118.
—— Richard, 195.
High cross, 42, 64, 155.
High street, 43, 136, 158.
Highways, 64, 152.
Hilbree Island, 45, 342.
Hodges, C. —, 77.
Hodgson, Rev. George, 284.
Hodson, Rev. Dr., 388.
Hogarth, Rev. James, 277.
Hog's hey nook, 151, 181, 186.
Holden, Rev. George, 242.
Holding, Christopher, 278.
Holland, Ralph, 167.
Hollis, Marquis of Newcastle, 108.
Holroyd (Q.C.), 309.
Holt, Henry, 53.

Hood, Lord, 189.
Hope, John, 256, 263, 264, 280.
—— street, 140.
Hopkins, John, 54.
—— Thomas, 149.
Hornby, Joseph, 322, 324, 326.
—— William, 153.
Horse races, 83.
Horsfall, Charles, 320.
Horwood, R., 275.
Hotel, Corporation, 274.
Hough, Charles, 146.
Houghton, John, 283.
—— Richard, 410.
Hounds, Corporation, 129, 262.
Howard, John, 380.
Hoyle lake, 92, 143, 146, 242.
Hughes, John, 17, 19, 32, 86, 89, 90, 91, 98, 99, 100, 163.
—— Richard, 122, 124, 131, 145, 244.
—— Thomas, 82.
Hunt, Joseph, 311.
Hurst street, 231.
—— Thomas, 50.
—— William, 36, 59, 75.
Huskisson, Right Hon. William, 302, 305, 320, 355, 375, 376.
Huss, Henry, 47.
Hutchinson, Captain William, 146, 147, 148.

I

Illuminations, 293, 295.
Improvement Acts, 363, 365, 366.
Infirmary, 139, 161, 262, 378, 383.
Ingates and Outgates, 126, 136, 379.
Inmates, 80, 81.
Inquiry Commissioners, 334.
Ireland, union with opposed, 211, 239.
—— export of arms to, 239.
Islington market, 379.

J

Jackson, ——, 256.
Jacob, Edward, 409.
James street, 60, 61, 135, 136, 150, 365, 366, 379.

Jeffry, Captain, 118.
Jenner, Dr. Edward, 304.
—— George, 404.
Jervis, Sir John, 189.
John street, 365.
Johnson, Alice and Margaret, 139.
—— Thomas, senr., 57, 59.
—— Sir Thomas, 4, 5, 12, 13, 15, 24, 37, 42, 47, 48, 51, 53, 57, 75, 139.
—— Thomas, (Lord street), 197, 254, 264.
—— street, 364.
Jones, Ellis, 270.
—— Elizabeth, 395.
—— James, 209.
—— Rev. Thomas, 283, 400.
—— Paul, 182, 183.
—— Roger, 59.
Jordan, John, 208, 209.
Jubilee of George III., 292.
Juggler street, 57, 58, 365.
Justice, Jane and Margaret, 81.

K

Kaye, Mrs., 166.
Kelsall Richard, 6, 27, 55, 63, 69, 71, 79, 96, 97, 98, 142.
Kemp, James, 59.
Kendrick, ——, 6.
Kennish, Robert, 138.
Kent street, 402.
Kenyon, James, 61.
—— Lord, 229.
Key street chapel, 59.
King street, 51.
Kingsmill (ship), 350.
Kisshaw, Richard, 59.
Kitchen, Rev. Philip, 386, 388.
Knight, John, 203.
Knives and forks, 125.

L

Ladies' walk, 155, 245, 256.
Laird, William, 342.
Lamb, Hon. George, 320.
Lancaster, Earl of, 30, 132.

INDEX

Lancaster, John, 82.
Landing places, 385.
Landmarks, 50, 146.
Langdale, Henry, 83.
Langhorn, John, 202.
Langton, Joseph, 299.
Lathom, Earl of, 15, 17.
Lawrence, Charles, 318, 341, 359, 361, 362, 374, 410.
—— Sir Thomas, 298.
Lawson, Thomas, 112.
—— William, 366.
Lead ore, 31.
Leasing, 89, 339.
Leather hall, 55, 108.
Leece street, 366.
Legh of Lyme, 11.
Leverton, ——, 265.
Leyland, Thomas, 210, 234, 274, 295, 298, 316, 363, 365, 379, 383, 387.
Libels, 67, 90, 102.
Liberties, riding the, 126, 316.
Licensing alehouses, 316.
Lighthouses, 242, 384.
Lighting streets, 64, 83, 154.
Lightoller, 242.
Lime street, 379.
Linacre, Anna, 82.
Linaker, Martha, 130, 315.
—— Robert, 134.
Litherland, Edward, 32, 71, 156, 163.
Littledale, Thomas, 300, 317, 358, 374.
Liverpool Arms Hotel, 291.
—— Blues Regiment, 108, 109, 111.
Liverpool, Earl of, 190, 304.
—— office, 309.
Livesey, John, 156.
Lloyd, Edward, 10.
Lobsey, John, 91.
Local courts, 28.
Loggerheads Tavern, 154, 279.
London City, disputes with, 21, 212, 213.
—— Lord Mayor of, 21.
—— road, 366.
Longworth, Nicholas, 44.

Lord street, 55, 58, 61, 71, 154, 227, 261, 365.
Louisbourg, capture of, 117.
Love lane, 365.
Lowe, James, 326.
—— Robert, 20.
Lowther, Lord, 355.
Loxham, Rev. Richard, 388.
Lukenars, ——, 81.
Lunatic Asylum, 383, 384.
Lyceum, the, 381.
Lyon, widow, 72.
Lyons, Edward, 55.

M

McGee, John, 82.
McHoy, James, 127.
McKenzie, ——, 240.
Macclesfield, Earl of, 39.
Maddock, Rev. ——, 165, 168.
Maddocks, Agnes, 272.
Magazines, 254.
Magistrates (county), 212.
Maida transport, 311.
Maiden's green, 255.
Malpas, Viscount, 91.
Mandamus (writ), 90, 95, 96, 102, 104, 177, 307.
Manesty, ——, 124, 128.
—— John, 254.
Mansfield, Lord, 102.
Maps, 64.
Market tolls, 30.
Markets, 42, 60, 61, 135, 232, 263, 373, 377, 378, 379, 380.
Markland, 154.
Marsden, William, 63, 68, 70.
Marshall street, 365.
Martin, Rev., ——, 172.
—— William, 267.
Martindale, John, 17, 132, 157.
Martindale's house, 140.
Mason and Bourne, 262.
Matthews, John, 215.
Maudit, Jasper, 5, 6, 20, 36, 75.
May (ship), 300.
Mayor's allowance, 8, 88, 95, 125, 199.

INDEX. 423

Mechanics' Institute, 310.
Melbourne, Viscount, 321.
Menai bridge, 212, 357.
Meoles, 146.
Mercer, —, 339.
—— Richard, 134, 135.
Meredith, Sir William, 176.
Mersey Street, 152, 365, 374.
—— and Irwell navigation, 353.
Meyetye, Jane, 81.
Mile house, 162.
—— —— lane, 255.
Miles, Richard, 217.
Mollinex, of Mossborough, 50.
Molyneux, Lord, 30, 35, 36, 37, 38, 39, 41, 58, 60, 132, 168, 226.
—— Sir Richard, 34.
—— Thomas, 307, 347.
—— William, 319.
Monk, Rev. George, 386.
Montague, Baron, 79.
Moorcroft, Sylvester, 6, 10, 11, 12, 13, 17, 18, 26, 38, 53, 54, 62, 98.
Moor street, 58, 136, 263, 379.
Moore, Sir Cleave, 25, 27, 28, 57, 208.
—— Sir John, 311.
Moorfields, 58, 363.
More, Captain, 150.
Moss, John, 361, 362, 380.
—— Robert, 204, 206, 258.
—— Thomas, 43.
—— Rev. Thomas, 388.
Moss Lake, 28, 30, 58, 132, 156, 363, 382.
Mostyn, Sir Roger, 92.
Mount pleasant, 140.
—— Sion, 32, 255.
Municipal Reform Act, 336, 405 to 412.

N

Naming streets, 367.
Navigation, conservancy of, 143, 240.
Naylor, Thos., 190, 193, 218, 227, 253.
Nelson, Lord, 189, 290.
—— monument, 296.
New Quay, 231, 249.

Newsrooms, 381, 382.
Nicholls, John, 165.
Nicholson, William, 309.
Norman, Robert, 129.
Norris, Rev. John, 105.
—— Richard, 5, 6, 10, 11, 12, 38, 42, 47, 48, 75, 83.
—— Robert, 215, 217, 218.
North, —, Hon., 199.
—— Lord, 183.
Northey, Sir Edward, 10, 40.
Norton, George, 125, 133, 141.
Notes issued by Corporation, 252.
Numbering houses, 367.

O

O'Neill, Hugh, 318.
Oath of abjuration, 78, 196.
—— mayor, 7.
Octagon, The, 279.
Okill, Charles, 356.
—— John, 136, 137, 169, 339.
Old Buffs Regiment, 119.
—— Church alley, 138.
—— —— yard, 138.
Oldhall street, 42, 58, 63, 152, 161, 232, 255.
Onslow, Sir Richard, 189.
Orange street, 284.
Organs, 73, 278.
Orme, —, Rev. 68.
Oxford street, 380.
Oyl Mill Field, 139, 161.
Oysters, 54, 143.

P

Palatines, 22, 23, 24.
Palmer, John, 189.
Paradise street, 47, 58, 62, 260, 261, 282.
Parish, disputes with, 227.
Park lane, 395.
Parke, Thomas John, 309.
Parker, C. S., 381.
—— Edmund, 152.
—— Sir Thomas, 10.
Parkgate, 92.
Parlour hey, 57.

Parr, John, 198, 236, 245, 258, 264.
Patrick's cross, 257, 259.
Paving streets, 152, 273, 274.
Pearse, Thomas, 129.
Peel, Sir Robert, 301, 320.
Pellew, Sir Edward, 189.
Penmon, 52.
Penny, James, 215, 217, 218.
Perceval, Spencer, 294.
Perrin, Geddes & Co., 292.
Peters, Francis, 10.
—— Ralph, 11, 14, 36, 38, 39, 40, 42, 49, 53, 200, 209, 238, 285.
Phenwick alley, 58.
—— street, 58.
Phillips, John, 401.
—— Robert, 367.
Pickance, William, 264.
Pier in river, 143.
Pinfold lane, 154.
Pipe making, 55.
Pitt, Right Hon. William (Lord Chatham), 119.
—— street, 402.
Plague, 45.
Plate, 73, 198.
Pluckington, —, 59.
—— bank, 231, 352.
Plumbe, Mrs., 279.
—— Thomas, 186.
Point of Air lighthouse, 242.
Pole, Charles, 91, 116, 177, 259.
—— William, 93, 94, 95, 96, 99, 107, 112, 119, 124, 126, 130, 137, 146, 153, 164, 167, 170, 204.
Police, 201, 317.
Pollock, Sir Frederic, 409.
Pool, The, 152.
—— bridge, 60.
—— lane, 51, 58, 60, 61, 135, 136, 154, 232, 263, 365, 374, 379.
—— stream, 30, 62.
Poole, David, 155.
—— Josia, 44, 50, 63, 65, 72, 91, 92.
Poole's almshouses, 155, 156.
Population, 306.
Porden, William, 398.

Porter, Green & Lucas, 38, 39, 40.
—— Thomas Colley, 312, 313, 328, 342, 355, 370, 377.
—— William, 59.
Portland, Duke of, 186.
Portmoot, 29.
Pottwork, 55.
Powder magazines, 129.
Pownall, James, 410.
Precedence, 72.
Preeson, William, 57, 58, 60.
Preeson's row, 58, 61, 154, 366, 379.
Prescot, 128.
Press warrants, 180.
Preston road, 364.
Price, F. R., 343, 344.
—— Richard Parry, 241.
Prince's dock, 248, 298.
Prince of Palestine, 193.
Pritchard, Owen, 93, 94, 105, 106, 111, 167.
Privateers, 184, 213.
Prizage of wines, 8, 88, 95.
Public walks, 137, 155.

Q

Quakers, 195.
—— meeting, 60.
Quarries, 156.
Quarry hill, 58, 137, 169, 254, 255.
Quo warranto writs, 94, 307.

R

Railed road, 235.
Railways, 301, 359, 360, 361, 362.
Rainford, Peter, 59, 134, 137.
Ratchdale, Edward, 31.
Ratcliffe, John, 99.
Rathbone, William, 230, 247, 251, 350.
Rating of dues, 229.
Rawlinson, —, 195.
—— Sir Thomas, 21.
Read, Sir William, 11.
Rebellion (1715), 33, 78.
—— (1745), 105, 109, 110.
Rectors' dues, 386.

INDEX.

Rectors, grants to, 36, 279, 393.
Redcross street, 58, 141, 379.
Reed, Sarah, 82.
Regalia, 198.
Regiments raised, 108, 184.
Rennie, —, 351.
Renshaw street, 396.
Restrictions on trade, 120, 122.
Reversions, sale of, 226.
Rhodes, James, 121.
Richmond & Brodie, 356.
—— fair, 234, 380.
—— Rev. Henry, 4, 6, 45, 66, 67, 68, 69.
—— row, 155, 233, 261.
Rigby, Edmund, 206.
—— Peter, 208, 227, 238, 283.
Riots, 149, 200, 318.
Roads, 257, 262.
Robinson, Captain, 111.
—— Mary, 378.
—— Nicholas, 313, 314, 316, 319, 344, 350, 354.
—— Peter, 265.
—— Thomas, 3.
Rock perch and battery, 384.
—— ferry, 356.
Rockingham, Marquis of, 236.
Rodney street, 383, 398.
Roe & Leigh, 306.
—— street, 273, 379.
Roscoe, William, 139, 140, 215, 230, 304, 309.
Rosemary lane, 58.
Royal Institution, 309, 310.
Rudd, Thomas, 72.
Runcorn aqueduct, 244.
—— bridge, 358.
Ryder, Sir Dudley, 102.

S

Sadler, John, 102.
St. Andrew's church, 403.
—— Anne's church, 234, 279.
—— Catharine's church, Abercromby square, 401.
—— Catharine's church, Temple court, 279, 282, 401.
—— George's church, 69, 70, 86, 157, 163, 164, 166, 167, 168, 278, 398.

St. John the Baptist church, 404.
—— Luke's church, 313, 366, 396, 397, 398.
—— Mark's church, 283, 400.
—— Martin's church, 398, 404.
—— Mary's church (for blind), 404.
—— Matthew's church, 59, 282.
—— Michael's church, 282, 402.
—— Nicholas's church, 71, 278.
—— Paul's church, 170, 277, 402.
—— Peter's church, 66, 69, 75, 152, 157, 168, 278.
—— Philip's church, 403.
—— Saviour's church, 404.
—— Stephen's church, 60, 280.
—— Thomas's church, 157, 169, 170, 386, 403.
St. George's hall, 370.
St. James's cemetery, 405.
—— street, 58, 282.
—— walk, 254, 365.
St. John's lane, 366.
—— street, 58.
St. Patrick's cross, 155.
St. Vincent, Earl, 289, 290.
Salisbury, Marquis of, 303.
Salt trade, 53.
—— works, 231.
Sandbach, Samuel, 300, 302, 332, 355, 377.
Sanderson, Rev. John, 396.
Sandiford, John, 13, 14.
Sankey navigation, 144.
Sawrey, William, 21.
Scarborough, Earl of, 120.
Scarisbrick, James, 45, 63.
—— John, 42, 52.
—— almshouses, 156.
Scarlett, Sir James, Q.C., 309, 320, 326.
Scavenging, 64, 153.
Schofield, John, 59.
School, free, 395.
—— free grammar, 73, 283, 284.
—— house, 63, 74.
—— lane, 74, 75, 284.
Scire facias (writ), 5, 6.
Scotland road, 366, 379.
Seacome, John, 14, 23, 25, 27, 37, 38, 41, 42, 47, 60, 61, 132, 133, 221.

INDEX.

Seamen, impressment and bounties, 114, 115, 118.
Seamen's hospital, 385.
Seed, Ellen, 82.
Seel, Thomas, 262.
Sefton, Countess of, 306.
—— Earl of, 227, 256, 306.
Senegal, capture of, 117.
Sephton, 70.
Sermons, loyal, 108.
Serres, J. T., 273.
Sessions house, 384.
Sewage, 260, 261, 274.
Sewell, Rev. Cuthbert, 164.
Sharples, Cuthbert, 37, 38.
Shaw, James, 61, 70, 123, 163.
—— John, 192, 220, 253, 269, 272, 338, 363, 369.
—— Thomas, 158, 161, 167, 169, 410.
—— Samuel, 276.
—— William, 62.
—— and Roe, 378.
Shaw's brow, 59, 366, 378, 383.
Shipbuilding, 52, 136, 137.
Shooting butts, 84.
Shoreditch, 63.
Sickman's lane, 45, 262.
Sidmouth, Viscount, 304.
Silk mill, 149.
Sims, Richard, 68, 69, 73.
Sir Thomas's buildings, 13, 24.
Skelmersdale, Lord, 17, 303.
Slave trade, 191, 213, 220, 347.
Smith, John, 313.
—— Sir Sydney, 294, 304.
Smyth, Thomas, 204, 246, 262.
Sorocold, ——, 47.
Sparling, John, 204, 206, 207, 237, 255, 257, 277, 279, 395.
Spencer, Lawrence, 119, 128, 129, 150, 170.
Squire, William, 51, 91.
Stage coaches, 153.
Stalls in markets, 232.
Staniforth, Samuel, 318, 351.
—— Thomas, 187, 199, 204, 210, 212, 218, 222, 307, 371.
Stanley, Elizabeth, 82.

Stanley, Hon. E. G., 304.
—— Hon. and Rev., 168.
Starkie, Thomas, 320.
Statham, Richard, 227, 241, 250, 259, 260.
—— William, 326, 351.
Statues, 267, 292, 300.
Steam navigation, 357.
Steers, Thomas, 27, 49, 50, 52, 61, 70, 71, 106, 121, 123, 124, 141, 143, 145, 146, 155, 157, 158, 169.
Steers, Spencer, 115, 122, 126, 147.
Stephenson, George, 305, 358.
—— William, 159.
Stevenson & Nimmo, 354.
Stone quarries, 32.
Strand, 138.
—— street, 366.
Street, Samuel, 107, 111.
—— improvements, 258, 262.
Strong, Matthew, 108, 244, 272.
Styth, Rev. Robert, 45, 66, 68, 73, 75.
Subscriptions, 107, 180, 184, 192, 193, 295, 296, 298, 300, 311, 312.
Suffolk street, 262.
Sunday schools, 193, 284, 395.
Survey of the town, 58.
Sweeting, Thomas, 36, 57, 72.

T

Tanners, 55.
Tarleton, Captain, 43, 45.
—— Clayton, 195, 204, 206, 217, 250, 272, 281, 284.
—— Edward, 62, 72, 78, 81.
—— Lieut.-General, 286.
—— John, 202, 215, 243, 244, 264, 276, 278.
Tax on trade opposed, 236.
Taylor, Henry, 19, 49, 64.
Temple court, 401.
—— place, 401.
Tenterden, Lord, 229.
Theatre Royal, 272, 382.
Thompson, Baron, 208.
—— John, 126.
Thurot, Mons., 120.
Tillinghurst, ——, 232.
Tinley, Thomas, 318.

Tobacco trade, 148.
Tobin, Eleanor, 127.
—— Sir John, 297, 316, 339, 342.
Tower, The, 130, 133, 134, 138, 226, 365, 370, 372, 373.
Town dues, 30, 45, 136, 212, 229, 322-327.
—— field, 132, 221.
—— hall, 136, 157, 264, 369.
—— wall, 62.
Townsend, James, 53, 66.
—— mill, 59.
Toxteth park, 306.
Trafford, Edward, 143, 153.
—— Henry, 18, 91, 100, 121, 131, 137, 142, 143, 157.
—— lane, 365.
Travers, William, 57.
Trinity church, 279, 280.
Trowbridge, Sir Thomas, 290.
True Love (ship), 82.
Tunnel under the Mersey, 358.
Turbary, grant of, 30.
Turner, Thomas, 53.
Tyrer, George, 6, 17, 20, 51, 53, 61, 86, 87, 91, 96, 97, 98, 99.
—— Thomas, 37, 62.
Tythebarn street, 42, 58, 149, 154, 232, 259, 262, 365.

U

Underhill, Samuel, 129.
Union newsroom, 382.
—— street, 58.
—— with Ireland, petition against, 211, 239.
Usury laws, 83.

V

Vernon, Hon. Granville, 332.
—— Thomas, 90.
Vexon, Jane, 82.
Vignoles, —, 358.
Virginia, labourers for, 82.
Volunteers, 183, 185, 288.
Vyner, Robert, 242, 351.

W

Wagner, Benedict Paul, 262.
Wainwright, —, bailiff, 42.
—— Thomas, 170.
Waits, 84, 131, 202.
Wales, Prince of, 290.
Walker, Richard, 204, 206.
—— and Shaw, 357.
Wallasey leasowe, 144, 353.
—— pool, 341, 342, 344.
Walpole, Sir Robert, 11, 148.
Walsingham, Lord, 189.
Walton, 46.
War of the succession, 77.
Warburton, Sir George, 11.
Wards, division into, 29, 127.
Waring, —, 249.
Warren, Sir John Borlase, 189.
Warrington, 42, 55.
Wason, Rigby, 330.
Watch and ward companies, 108.
Watching, 127.
Water bailiff, 50, 52, 55.
—— street, 43, 58, 138, 158, 263, 365.
—— side, 58.
—— supply, 24, 25, 26, 28, 123, 208, 210.
Waterford, claims of, 22.
Waterworks companies, 210.
Waterworth, —, 256.
Watson, Hugh, 100.
Watts, Thomas, 72.
Wavertree road, 381.
Weaver, river, 51, 145.
Weavers, 53.
Webb, Nicholas, 52.
Webster, William, 38, 45, 82.
Wedgwood, Josiah, 243.
Wellington, Duke of, 295, 301, 303, 304, 361.
West Indies, free ports, 236.
Westmacott, Richard, 266, 267.
Westmorland, Earl of, 189.
Wexford, claims of, 22.
Wharncliffe, Lord, 303, 336.
Whetton, —, 265, 266.

INDEX.

Whidbey, Chapman and Rennie, 351.
White cross, 42, 64, 155, 232.
White, Joseph, 356.
Whitechapel, 58, 62, 137, 260, 261.
Whitfield, Peter, 54, 91, 123, 124.
—— Robert, 17, 95, 96, 97.
—— widow, 61.
Whyte, Lieut.-General, 185, 187.
Wilbraham, Richard, 17.
Wilkinson & Hogg, commissioners, 333, 334.
William Brown street, 62.
Williamson, John, 178.
—— Ralph, 221.
—— square, 272, 382.
Willis, Thomas, 75.
Willoughby of Parham, Lord, 92.
Wills, General, 78.
Wilson, Robert, 163.
—— Thomas, 202, 231.

Wimsley, Joshua, 53.
Winstanley, Henry, 130, 134, 135, 158, 159.
—— Mary, 82.
—— Mrs., 166.
Wirrall, hundred of, 342.
Wolstenholme, Rev. Henry, 164, 165, 167, 278.
Wood, John, 158.
—— —— junr., 159.
Woolpack (tavern), 43.
Workhouse, 160, 227, 228.
Worthington, Richard, 10.
Wright, John, 303, 321, 328, 333, 358, 410.
Wyatt, James, 265, 266, 267, 268, 272.
—— Jeffrey, 398.

Y

Yeoman, Elizabeth, 82.
York, Duke of, 300.

LIST OF SUBSCRIBERS.

Abraham, A. C.
Abraham, T. Fell.
Adelphi Bank Limited.
Aldam, William.
Arkle, Benjamin.
Armstrong, Joseph.
Ashcroft, J.
Ashlin, W. C.
Atkinson, George James.
Atkinson, Jonathan.
Band, William.
Banner, Edward.
Barrett, W. S.
Barrow, James.
Bartlett, William.
Baylis, T. Henry, Q.C.
Beardwood, W. H.
Beaven, Rev. A. B.
Beckett, Richard.
Benas, B. L.
Bennett, Richard.
Bennett, Thomas.
Bennett, William.
Berey, John.
Birch, Alfred J.
Birkenhead Free Library.
Blundell, Col. H. B. H.
Blundell, James.
Bolton Subscription Library.
Boult, C. R.
Bradbury, G.
Bramley-Moore, J.
Brancker, John.
Bremner, H. Hodgson.

Broadbridge, Frederick.
Brocklehurst, Septimus.
Bromilow, David.
Bromley, James.
Brooke, Thomas, F.S.A.
Brown, Joseph.
Brunner, Henry.
Brushfield, T. N., M.D.
Bushby, John.
Bushell, Christopher.
Caine, Mrs.
Cambridge Free Public Library.
Cameron, John, M.D.
Carson, William.
Cates, Arthur.
Chambres, William.
Chate, A. C. W.
Chester Free Public Library.
Chetham's Library, Manchester.
Chorlton, John.
Chorlton, Thomas.
Clarkson, William.
Colman, J. J., M.P.
Connell, Thomas R.
Cooban, Adrian.
Cook, Henry J.
Cooper, William.
Cowell, P.
Cox, George R.
Crewe, W. Outram.
Crooks, J. Kirke.
Crosfield, John D.
Crosfield, William.
Cross, The Right Hon. Viscount.

LIST OF SUBSCRIBERS.

Cross, William, M.D.
Crosse, Col. T. R.
Davies, Mrs. L. S.
Deakin, Thomas S.
Derby, The Right Hon. the Earl of.
Dixon, Isaac.
Dixon, William.
Donaldson, James.
Doulton, Henry.
Doyle, J. F.
Dransfield, William.
Dwerryhouse, William.
Dyall, Charles.
Earle, Arthur.
Earwaker, J. P., M.A., F.S.A.
Edmonds, William.
Edwards, E. E.
Ellacott, J. H.
Elliot, John.
Ellison, Thomas.
Evans, Edward.
Evans, Edward, Jun.
Evans, James.
Evans, Joseph.
Fazakerley, John.
Ferguson, William, F.L.S., F.G.S., &c.
Fingland, William.
Ffoulkes, W. Wynne.
Forwood, Sir W. B.
Foulkes, Isaac.
Gair, Henry W.
Gamble, Col. David.
Garnett, P. F.
Gaskell, John Rooth.
Gittins, Edward.
Gladstone, A. R.
Gladstone, Robert.
Glover, G. T.

Goffey, Thomas.
Graham, Edward.
Gratrix, Samuel.
Green, Rev. C. V.
Grindley, Edward.
Guest, W. H.
Guthrie, M.
Habershon, E.
Hall, Charlton R.
Hanson, Sir Reginald.
Harrison, Robert.
Hassan, Rev. Edward.
Hawley, H. C.
Haworth, Abraham.
Healey, E.
Heblethwaite, J. W.
Henderson, John.
Henderson, W. G.
Higgin, Thomas.
Hocken, Joshua.
Hodgkinson, W. C.
Holden, Adam.
Holden, Thomas.
Holder, Thomas.
Holme, George.
Holt, Alfred.
Holt, George.
Holt, R. D.
Holt, W. D.
Hope, Thomas Arthur.
Hornby, H. B.
Hornby, T. D.
Horsfall, Charles E.
Howell, Howell.
Hughes, John.
Hughes, Lewis.
Humberston, Col. Philip S.
Hutchinson, Edward.

LIST OF SUBSCRIBERS. 431

Isherwood, Thomas Henry.
Jensen, Christian.
Jevons, Henry.
Johnston, A.
Johnston, John.
Johnson, J. H.
Jump, Henry.
Keates, William.
Kelk, John William.
Kirk, William.
Kurtz, Charles G.
Lambert, Major George, F.S.A.
Lancashire Independent College, Manchester.
Langton, Miss.
Laurence, Thomas D.
Lawrence, Edward.
Leeds Free Public Library.
Leicester, Samuel B.
Lester, Rev. Canon T. Major.
Lingard-Monk, R. B. M.
Little, William.
Liverpool, Bishop of,
   Right Rev. B. O'Reilly, D.D.
Liverpool Free Public Library.
Liverpool Free Lending Libraries.
Liverpool Library.
Logan, James Pender.
London, Library of the Corporation of the City of.
Lonsdale, John R.
Lunt, W. J.
Maddock, F. T.
Main, Thomas.
Manchester Free Public Library.
Marrow, W. J.
Marsh, John A.
Martin, Studley.

Mawdsley, James P.
McArdle, Charles.
McCarte, Matthew.
McDowell, C. A.
McWean, Thomas.
Meade-King, H. W.
Meade-King, R. R.
Milne-Readhead, R.
Molineux, G.
Montgomery, James.
Moubert, A. B.
Moulding, J.
Muspratt, Edmund K.
Musson, G. G.
Naylor, James.
Nevins, J. Birkbeck, M.D.
Newell, John.
Newton, John D.
Nicholson, Walter C.
Oakshott, T. W.
Ormerod, Henry M.
Oulton, William.
Owen, Owen.
Owen, Peter.
Pain, Miss M. Charlotte.
Parker, Edward.
Paton, Andrew B.
Pearson, John.
Pelling, T. L.
Perkins, Hugh.
Philip, T. D.
Picton, F. H.
Picton, W. H.
Pierce, William.
Pilkington, Lieut.-Col. John.
Pinnington, William.
Pooley, Henry.
Portsmouth Free Public Library.

Poulsom, W.
Prickard, Watson.
Priest, John.
Queen's College Library, Oxford.
Quilliam, Alfred.
Radcliffe, Sir David.
Radcliffe, William.
Rathbone, P. H.
Reid, Francis Nevile.
Rhind, P. S.
Rigby, T.
Rigmaiden, A. H.
Riley, John.
Ripley, W.
Roberts, Isaac.
Roberts, William.
Rochdale Free Public Library.
Rogerson, G. R., F.R.S.L., &c.
Russell, Edward R., M.P.
Rutherford, R. H.
Ryley, Thomas C.
Salford Royal Free Library.
Scholfield, George.
Sephton, Rev. J.
Shaw, J. S.
Sherlock, Cornelius.
Sing, Joshua.
Sinnott, Richard Francis.
Sion College Library, London.
Smith, Charles W.
Smith, Edward.
Smith, Egerton & Co.
Smith, James.
Smith, J. Barkeley.
Smith, Samuel.
Squarey, A. T.

Stead, J. C.
Stead, T. W.
Steele, R. T.
Stevenson, John.
Stewart, Rev. Canon Alexander.
Stuart, D. Gordon.
Tate, A. Norman.
Taylor, Henry.
Thornely, James.
Tolhurst, John.
Tomlinson, Ralph.
Tonge, Rev. Canon Richard.
Turner, Alfred.
Turner, Col. George.
Unwin, William.
Wainwright, Henry.
Waite, John.
Wakefield, Arthur.
Waldron, James, junr.
Walker, Sir Andrew Barclay, Bart.
Walmsley, Thomas.
Ward, Thomas.
Waterhouse, N.
Webster, Daniel.
Weightman, W. H.
Westmorland, John.
Whinnerah, Henry.
Whinnerah, William.
Wigan Free Public Library.
Wood, J. W.
Woodhouse, Samuel.
Wren, Abraham.
Wright, Albert T.
Yates, John.
Young, Henry.
Young, Reginald.

www.ingramcontent.com/pod-product-compliance
Lightning Source LLC
Chambersburg PA
CBHW032130010526
44111CB00034B/574